JAPAN
IN TRADITIONAL AND
POSTMODERN PERSPECTIVES

JAPAN
IN TRADITIONAL AND
POSTMODERN PERSPECTIVES

EDITED
BY

Charles Wei-hsun Fu
and
Steven Heine

STATE UNIVERSITY OF NEW YORK PRESS

Published by
State University of New York Press, Albany

© 1995 State University of New York

All rights reserved

Printed in the United States of America

For information, address State University of New York
Press, State University Plaza, Albany, N.Y., 12246

Production by Diane Ganeles
Marketing by Nancy Farrell

Library of Congress Cataloging-in-Publication Data
Japan in traditional and postmodern perspectives / co-edited by Charles Wei-hsun Fu
    and Steven Heine.
        p.   cm.
    Includes index.
    ISBN 0-7914-2469-3 (alk. paper).—ISBN 0-7914-2470-7 (pbk.:alk. paper)
    1. Japan–Civilization.   I. Fu, Charles Wei-hsun, 1933-   II. Heine, Steven,
1950–   .
    DS821. J33855   1995
    952—dc20   94-28445
                                                                    CIP

10 9 8 7 6 5 4 3 2

Contents

Introduction:
From "The Beautiful" to "The Dubious": Japanese Traditionalism, Modernism, Postmodernism

STEVEN HEINE AND *CHARLES WEI-HSUN FU*

> When some Orientals oppose racial discrimination
> while others practice it, you say "they're all Orien-
> tals at bottom" and class interest, political circum-
> stances, economic factors are totally irrelevant . . .
> History, politics, and economics do not matter . . .
> the Orient is the Orient, and please take all your
> ideas about a left and a right wing, revolutions, and
> change back to Disneyland.
>
> Edward Said, *Orientalism*[1]

On the Dubiousness of the Dubious

In 1968, Kawabata Yasunari gave a lecture on the occasion of accepting the first Nobel Prize in literature awarded to a Japanese entitled "Japan, the Beautiful, and Myself" (*Utsukushii Nihon no
Watakushi*). In that lecture, Kawabata, known for his eloquent portrayals of traditional Japanese lyricism and romanticism in a contemporary context filled with angst and despair, celebrates Japan's
medieval Buddhist poet-priests, including Saigyō, Dōgen, Myôe and
Ikkyū. He is especially fond of their vivid appreciation of nature,
which inspired his writings, that is conveyed through "elements of
the mysterious, the suggestive, the evocative and inferential."[2]
Kawabata concludes by explaining that his own works, often perceived by critics as expressions of nihilism, actually reflect "the
emptiness (*kyomu*), the nothingness (*mu*), of Japan and of the

Orient . . . [which] is not the nothingness or the emptiness of the West. It is rather the reverse, a universe of the spirit in which everything communicates freely with everything, transcending bounds, limitless."[3] Thus, Kawabata associates the outlook of his modern literary efforts with an essential, premodern Japanese spirit and a transcendental Oriental mysticism deeply embedded in traditional literary arts and religious sentiment that remain incomprehensible to the "Orientalist" gaze of the modern Western observer who projects categories that bifurcate being and nothingness, and presence and absence.

A generation later, in 1993, another world-famous novelist, Kenzaburō Ōe, who in 1994 became the second Japanese recipient of the Nobel Prize, criticized Kawabata and other modern Japanese authors. Known for his postwar critique of Japanese society, Ōe delivered a lecture in New York (published here for the first time, parts of which are similar to Ōe's Nobel speech, "Japan, the Ambiguous, and Myself") entitled "Japan, the Dubious, and Myself," which comments critically on Kawabata's speech that is "bedecked with such beautiful ambiguity." Ōe calls into question, and to a large extent seeks to undermine and reorient, the understanding of Japanese tradition Kawabata presents. On one level, Kawabata's address seems to be quite direct and straightforward in its allusions to the classical period. But, according to Ōe, by emphasizing things ineffable and inscrutable to the West, Kawabata was being purposefully ambiguous. He attempted to cloak himself in the aura of an idealized, antiquated Japan—"a time-encrusted Japanese aestheticism"—so as to avoid communicating with his international audience or even with the Japanese people. Ōe maintains that while evoking "the beautiful" conveyed in medieval songs,

> Ironically, though, Kawabata himself knew that such a Japan did not exist; and, in any case, he knew that he himself was not part of that Japan. He was talking only to the fruit of his imagination, his apparition of beauty. And by so doing, he shut out the real world; he severed all ties with all living souls.

For Ōe, Kawabata's nihilistic tone lies precisely in his unwillingness to confront contemporary reality at the same time that he is claiming that he will not let Western nihilism "weasel its way into [his apparition, the imaginary] bond that united his very being to what he called "Japan, the Beautiful, and Myself."

Therefore, Ōe contends that Kawabata—and by extension, Japanese tradition—is fundamentally "dubious," or, in Japanese, *aimai-na.* Ōe notes the multiple implications of the term *aimai,* including "shady" or duplicitous, which do not apply in this case as they refer to a deliberate, willful concealing of intentions, and also "vague," "ambiguous," and "obscure," which are evident here despite the otherwise penetrating clarity in Kawabata's fiction and in some passages of his Nobel lecture. The second set of meanings suggests an uncertainty or unsettledness reflecting an unconscious ambivalence or a culturally conditioned failure to come to terms with the real world. The target of Ōe's deconstructivist critique of the deficiency in contemporary Japanese discourse about the meaning of the traditional is not so much directed at Kawabata, but rather at a syndrome that infects a wide range of modern authors and thinkers as well as the Japanese people as a whole, who have let themselves be lulled into and deceived by the ambiguity the intellectuals have created. Writers including Natsume Sōseki, Mishima Yukio, and Abe Kōbō, who are widely read throughout the world, have never wholeheartedly tried to communicate the significance of Japan or of Japanese experience to outsiders but are content to stay within the reinforcing cocoon of Japanese self-interest, or to be hidden by a veil of vagueness and obfuscation. Among the main consequences of this dubiousness in the postwar period are a numbing sense of complacency about the need to compensate other Asians for acts committed by Japan during the Asian-Pacific war and the continual quieting of the voices of marginalized and dispossessed individuals and communities who tend to be excluded from membership in the mainstream of the tradition.

Another implication in Ōe's remarks, especially when they are seen in juxtaposition with Kawabata's speech, is that the dubious quality reflects a two-sidedness or a twofoldness harbored within the discourse by and about Japan, which, in turn, functions on at least two levels. One level of the twofoldness is that there seems to be a breach or a setting off in separate directions between two factions: those twentieth-century writers and intellectuals like Kawabata, Mishima, Tanizaki Jun'ichirō, Watsuji Tetsurō, Yanagita Kunio, and Umehara Takeshi, among others, who assert the priority of traditionalism in interpreting the basis of Japanese culture; and those who in increasing numbers are—from what can be referred to as a postmodern perspective—highly skeptical of traditionalist claims as being little more than an apparition, a collective fantasy generated to a large extent by a nationalist/nativist sociopolitical agenda.

The second level of dubiousness, which is inherent in the first level, is that there is a double sense of critique and affirmation, or refutation and valorization, in the interaction between the traditional and postmodern perspectives in discourse on Japan. That is, the dubious quality of the relation between the traditional and the postmodern must itself be considered dubious, so that there is a dubiousness, or twofoldness, of the dubious. Ōe criticizes the obscurantist rhetoric of Kawabata, who would likely respond by viewing the critique as part of a modern misrepresentation of the tradition. But while these parties may refute one another, it is also often the case that the reverse is true in that there is a mutual support and legitimation of the seemingly contradictory positions. For example, one aspect of the traditionalist argument is that the integrity of Japanese traditionalism has been able to offset and "overcome modernity" (*kindai no chōkoku*) and thereby establish itself at the forefront of an antimodernist movement. For some interpreters, antimodernism is associated with postmodernism, while for others these terms represent polarized viewpoints that should not be conflated.

Another aspect of the traditionalist standpoint suggests an additional way of viewing the link between the traditional and the postmodern. According to this view, the traditional Japanese way, which emphasizes pluralism, discontinuity, dispersion and differentiation without substratum, has always had a profound fundamental affinity with the perspective that has emerged today as postmodernism. Traditional Japan was thus able to dispense with or circumvent the need to work through a modern period—at least in the Western sense of that term—characterized by structure, systematization, rationality and linear progression. Instead, it has anticipated and smoothly entered into the postmodern era. Postmodernist commentators in the West, including Roland Barthes and Jacques Derrida, tend to confirm this aspect of the traditional view by seeing Japan as a decentric or non-logocentric society in which Oriental nothingness represents the absence of a privileged Signified standing above and beyond (or behind or beneath) what Barthes calls the "empire of signs." Japanese poststructuralists, such as Karatani Kōjin, who points to the absence in Japan of modernity in the Western sense, tend to agree with some of these arguments. But others, like Ōe, take a much more skeptical view of what they consider naive assertions that recreate the apparition of traditionalism in a new setting. In a harsh critique of traditionalism disguised by its antimodernist rhetoric as postmodernism, Asada Akira refutes the duplicitous agenda which betrays itself by endorsing a compliance or false sense of harmony (*wa*) with the nationalist-imperialist status quo. As some critics argue, "when the post-modern 'scene' in Japan is seen as merely another way to express Japan's cultural uniqueness in order to explain its superiority to the West, the discourse on the postmodern can never hope to be anything more than an inexpertly concealed attempt to cover up the aporias that dogged the earlier modernist discourse, even as it seeks to fulfill the role of a simulacrum."[4] The situation can become even more complicated than this because the imperial sense of postmodernism has already smuggled and in so doing distorted Western categories, wittingly or not, into its mode of discourse. "In short, postmodern Japan theory has transformed the agenda of Western postmodernism—which originally was concerned with artistic, literary, and hermeneutical problems—*into a set of highly competitive, nationalistic self-images.*"[5]

In discussing the connection between traditionalism and postmodernism, the question of modernism, and in particular its origins in the Tokugawa "early modern" (*kinsei*) period, must be confronted. To some extent, the traditional, as the premodern, and the postmodern, as a development subsequent to the modern, stand in sequential relation to modernity that necessarily defines the boundaries of their advency and withdrawal. Yet, another aspect of the dubious quality is that the traditional and the postmodern do not only or even primarily refer to historical stages. Rather, as in the case of the argument that Japanese tradition represents an incipient postmodernism, these terms designate modes of discourse or rhetorical devices disconnected to sequence or chronology. In the generation since Kawabata's lecture, the contours of the debate have been reoriented from a consideration of the question of what lies at the base of the success of Japanese culture as a modern entity to the question of Japan's success as a postmodern phenomenon in a way that casts doubt on the consequences of modernization.

For example, in his 1957 work, *Tokugawa Religion: The Cultural Roots of Modern Japan*, Robert Bellah, influenced by sociologist Talcott Parsons, was concerned with analyzing "the role of Japan's premodern culture in its modernization process,"[6] especially the impact of Tokugawa merchant ideology on its rapidly successful economic growth in the postwar period. In his introduction to the 1985 reissue of the book, however, Bellah questions whether the results of that rapid growth—the breakdown of social relations, the lack of loyalty to a *furusato* (home village) or to a genuine sense of community—"undermine the very conditions that made that growth possible . . . [and] whether the newly prosperous life [the

Japanese salaryman] enjoys does not threaten his hold over tradition."[7] It is also important to note that Bellah ultimately attributes
any weakness in his book not to anything lacking in his description
of Japan, but to "a weakness in the modernization theory I was
using." Bellah's comment seems to suggest, somewhat ironically for
a sociological approach, that description is theory, or that so-called
fact cannot be separated from the rhetorical structure in which its
expression is encased. While Bellah challenges modernity in terms
of a new appreciation for the traditional, and Karatani argues that
Japan has passed directly from the traditional to the postmodern
without ever having had to undergo the intermediary stage of the
modern, Ōe suggests that the whole notion of tradition is a convenient modern invention, a nostalgic rhetorical flourish. Furthermore, Asada argues that Japan, rather than having skipped over let
alone surpassed the modern, is an example of "infantile capitalism,"
especially when contrasted with European societies, that is just now
entering into a modern period.

Aims and Themes

The central, underlying theme of this collection is to explore the
implications of dubiousness by considering the question of the
uniqueness and creativity of Japan as seen in terms of the interplay
of traditional and postmodern perspectives. These perspectives are
at times conflicting and competing with one another while in other
circumstances, as the issues and orientation are shifted, they become overlapping and complementary standpoints. Japan is distinctive both in its role as a non-Western country that has become
highly modernized and mo   productive economically than the
West and as a modern natio   ustained by and continuing to promote its traditions. As Ōe's comments vis-à-vis Kawabata suggest,
one of the fascinating things about Japanese culture is that, on the
one hand, it seems to have held onto its native, localized traditional
foundations with a greater sense of determination and celebration
than most societies and, on the other hand, it appears to have
attained a position as an international leader of postmodernist developments.

    Which of these directions is the more pertinent and applicable
one? Reflecting the dubious quality, there are several approaches to
this issue. One school of thought emphasizes the distinctive features of Japanese traditionality, including (according to Nakamura

Hajime's categories) formalism, communalism, naturalism and intuitionism, as the essential cultural tendencies providing the key to understanding classical and current intellectual and artistic formations. Another approach, which seems to be opposite and yet also in some ways reinforces the first approach, is influenced by Western poststructuralist commentators who see Japan's focus, from earlier times to the present, on empty spaces or nothingness as representative of a postmodern discourse or "text" consisting of an open-ended universe of decentric, deconstructive signs and signifiers devoid of substantive essence or teleology. Yet a third possibility, in some ways a variation of the second, or postmodern, option and in other ways a refutation of this, is to argue against the cultural exceptionalist thesis known as *nihonjinron* ("Japanism" or "Nihonism") by suggesting that the notion of Japanese uniqueness is itself a myth generated by nationalistic and particularistic trends operative at least since the Tokugawa era.

It seems clear that the discursive gap on the first level of dubiousness—the breach between traditionalism and postmodernism— has widened considerably in the several decades since Kawabata's lecture. There has been a remarkable variety of developments both within and outside of Japan and Japanese discourse, many of which are critically discussed in Steve Odin's article, contributing to the influence of postmodern perspectives. Perhaps the first major turning point was the appearance of Roland Barthes' *The Empire of Signs* in 1970 followed by the application of various aspects of postmodern methodology (poststructuralism, deconstructivism, semiotics, narratology, intertextuality) in the works of a range of scholars from the late 1970s on. These works, which are quite diverse in approach and in no way constitute a school of thought, include among others Noel Burch's semiotic approach to modern cinema, Robert Magliola's Derridean view of traditional philosophical issues, H. D. Harootunian's Foucauldian examination of Tokugawa era nativist thought, Bernard Faure's literary critical studies of Kamakura-era Zen, and Peter Dale's deconstructivist approach to contemporary intellectual history involving the *nihonjinron* theory. Some of the important contributions to postmodernism in Japan in the 1980s include: Karatani's semiotic study of the origins of modern Japanese literature, *Nihon kindai bungaku no kigen (Origins of Modern Japanese Literature)*;[8] Asada's work *Kōzō to chikara* (Structure and Power), which, in introducing French poststructuralist theory from a Marxist viewpoint, became an instant media sensation (referred to as the "AA phenomenon"); the wildly popular novel *Nantonaku kurisutaru* (Somehow, Crystal), a deceptively simple work using descriptive language in very innovative and sophisticated ways; the devastating social critique in the films of Itami Juzo, including *The Funeral, Tampopo* and *Taxing Woman;* the semiotic theories concerning Japanese culture of Yoshihiko Ikegami[9] and the hermeneutic philosophy of Sakabe Megumi;[10] and the art of Masami Teraoka, which reworks traditional "floating world" style and imagery to make a scathing commentary on the foibles of modern life, as in "31 Flavors Invading Japan/French Vanilla" and "Condom Trade Wars."[11]

It must also be noted that another major development in 1980s' Japanological discourse was a recorded conversation between then Prime Minister Nakasone and Umehara, leading representative of the so-called New Kyoto school, which reraised much of the prewar nativist and nationalist rhetoric. However, due to the impact of the postmodernist developments, traditionalism can no longer be considered the only or even the dominant view, and it has become complemented or perhaps even surpassed by the postmodern perspective in interpretive studies of Japan. Odin maintains that "against the background of the differential logic of acentric Zen Buddhism, the art, literature, cinema and other sign systems in the Japanese text have been analyzed as a fractured semiotic field with no fixed center." Yet postmodernism as applied to Japanology is a multiperspectival view. Steven Heine's article suggests that another aspect of dubiousness is that postmodernism is not a uniform position, but has taken on two distinct, contradictory yet overlapping perspectives (which are evident in this volume's essays): a valorization of the tradition as an incipient postmodernism, and a critique of the illusory, triumphal claims of traditionalists often smuggled into some form of postmodern rhetoric. According to Heine's analysis of various discourses concerning "sacred familism" (*ie*), it is necessary to develop a methodological approach that encompasses, without being bound by any particular model, the full range of discursive possibilities as well as their counterparts and critiques situated in continuing, decentric hermeneutic interaction.

A major vehicle for displaying the new postmodernist thinking and research was the 1989 collection, *Postmodernism and Japan,* edited by Masao Miyoshi and H. D. Harootunian and featuring articles by Karatani, Asada and Ōe in addition to numerous prominent Western scholars.[12] While some of our planning is indebted to the topics treated in that book, the main difference between volumes is suggested by the respective titles. *Postmodernism and*

Japan focuses on the postmodern "scene" today, that is, the relation between modernism and postmodernism. As the editors point out, "Nearly all of the papers consider the spectacle of the modern and how the Japanese have tried to extract the guarantee of stable meaning from a ceaselessly changing landscape and wrenching social transformations in daily life."[13]

Our volume deals primarily with the traditional element in Japanese culture as seen either in light of or in contrast with postmodernism, that is, the dubious relation between the traditional and the postmodern. Each of the articles, which, after the first two articles that introduce the central themes, are presented more or less in chronological sequence in terms of the historical material under consideration, offers an in-depth analysis of the origins and development of an important aspect of Japanese culture. These aspects include religion (Zen and Pure Land Buddhism, Shinto and folk religions, Confucianism and Tokugawa-era ideology), philosophy (classical Buddhism and the contemporary Kyoto school), literature and the arts (medieval poetry and drama, modern novels and films), and social behavior (family life, suicide, feminism, and sexuality as well as nationalism, militarism, and economic productivity). Some papers deal specifically with key examples of traditional religious thought and literature, such as Shinto ritualism and aesthetics, the literary theory of *waka* poetry, Noh theater, and *yūgen* aesthetics, and the view of truth expressed in the classics including the *Manyōshū* poetry collection. For example, Richard Pilgrim examines the pre-Buddhist "religio-aesthetic paradigm" of *ma*, a sense of betweenness or empty spaces that refers to spatial and temporal gaps, fissures, crevices or intervals in light of postmodern notions of difference and discontinuity. The notion of *ma* is rooted in folk religiosity yet has a strong impact on the literate/intellectual traditions including Noh drama and various applications of the Buddhist doctrine of *mu* (nothingness) in meditation and art. Several articles analyze how traditional culture is appropriated by and reflected in modern arts, including fiction and films. For example, Sandra Wawrytko shows how prominent examples of postwar cinema become a "murky mirror," recalling a primordial Shinto symbol, at once critically reflecting and liberating—despite also displaying the biases of male directors—traditional views of women as self-sacrificing and repressed. Wawrytko focuses on the role of sexuality, the most sensitive and psycho-socially revealing of topics, often in relation to the films' view of the repressive and egalitarian aspects of Buddhist thought and institutions. In addition, Dale Wright discusses the significance of Nishitani Keiji's Zen-based philosophy of religion. Wright deals with tradition as a realm of discourse, which he argues is independent of and thus should resist contemporary Western categorizations of the antimodern and the postmodern, which themselves may inevitably be undermined, as the basic Buddhist philosophy of existence suggests, by the pervasiveness of the impermanence of all aspects of existence.

In addition to the developments in the field of Japanology, another important influence over the past two decades in calling for a rethinking of Japanese tradition in light of the postmodern has been Edward Said's attempted overcoming of the phenomenon of "Orientalism." Said analyzes the cultural stereotyping of the Orient by centuries of ethnocentric Western commentators who disguise their insensitivity to the challenge of cultural relativism. Although Said is mainly concerned with the effects of Orientalism on Islam and the Near East, his analysis of the structures and restructures of such thinking also applies in many respects to the way Japan and the Far East has been perceived and represented. According to Said, the Orient is never objectively described because it is always seen through a filter of cultural misperceptions or wishful thinking and fantasy about the indecipherable, mysterious Other, so that the Orient is not a geopolitical place but a rhetorical device, an arena of ambiguity reflecting views often unknown or unrecognized by their holder: "In the system of knowledge about the Orient, the Orient is less a place than a *topos*, a set of references, a congeries of characteristics, that seems to have its origin in a quotation, or a fragment of a text, or a citation from someone's work on the Orient, or some bit of previous imagining, or an amalgam of all these . . . [T]he Orient is a re-presentation of canonical material guided by an aesthetic and executive will capable of producing interest in the reader."[14]

An intriguing recent literary attempt to identify and weed out the roots of Orientalism concerning Japan (and China) is the award-winning play (and film) *M. Butterfly*, which author David Henry Hwang refers to as a "deconstructive *Madame Butterfly*."[15] Written over eighty years after the original opera by Puccini, in which a dominant American male mistreats a submissive, unprotesting Japanese woman, Hwang's play tries to turn the tables on Orientalist myth-making. The play is based on a true story demonstrating how cultural misperceptions of the Orient have contributed to the decline of the West, as symbolized by a French diplomat who is unable due to distorted assumptions about Oriental demureness to recognize the sexual identity of his Chinese spy/lover after their twenty-year relationship and who, in the play, commits suicide after donning the transsexual garb of his ironic heroine, Madame Butterfly.

One of the main implications of the deconstructivist approach to Orientalism is the recognition that postmodernism often contributes to the causes, rather than to the demise, of the problematics of mystification and obfuscation, or of dubiousness in the negative sense of ambiguity and vagueness. As Said points out, "One aspect of the electronic, postmodern world is that there has been a reinforcement of the stereotypes by which the Orient is viewed . . . [so that] standardization and cultural stereotyping have intensified the hold of the nineteenth-century academic and imaginative demonology of 'the mysterious Orient.' "[16] Yet, it is an interesting and important irony, which Said himself does not dwell on, that in the case of Japan, at least, much of the myth of inscrutability and uniqueness is generated by and for the sake of the Orient over and against the West, so that the position embraced by Kawabata and representatives of the Kyoto school is accused by Bernard Faure of creating a "reverse Orientalism" (or "Occidentalism"). Another twist involved in this context is that Hwang reports that he first considered calling his play "Monsieur Butterfly" as a counterpoint to Puccini but abandoned the idea because he felt that *M. Butterfly*, "far more mysterious and ambiguous," would more effectively eradicate the effects of Orientalism. At the same time, it is often the case that the professional Orientalists, who are subject to Said's critique, are the ones striving to de-mystify and de-Orientalize the deficient standpoint in which traditionalism and postmodernism are conflated by virtue of their shared ulterior—nationalist/nativist—motives. But, it can also be asked, are the de-Orientalizing Orientalists liberated from their own biases for or against the dubiousness they observe and interpret?

This situation frequently leads to a dizzying, rhetorically dazzling and sociopolitically disturbing Disney-ish realm in which Orientialists seeking to defuse the effects of Orientalism accuse Orientals of reverse Orientialism, and are in turn subject to being accused by traditionalists of perpetuating the problematics of Western categories they seek to overcome. As Jean Beaudrillard notes, a consequence of the postmodern era is that "all the hypotheses of manipulation are reversible in an endless whirligig. For manipulation is a floating causality where positivity and negativity engender and overlap with one another, where there is no longer any active or passive."[17] Or, to paraphrase Heidegger's comment on the dubiousness inherent in the relation between Being and beings in Western metaphysics, "The question has become ever more questionable." Heidegger, who, like many of the Japanese traditionalists he personally and philosophically influenced, is often accused of crafting a neo-conservative romantic philosophy to conceal his support for fascism, responds to the ever more questionable question by developing a ludic notion of "purposeless play." Heideggerian play, based on pre-Socratic and Germanic mystical sources, has been hailed by Western philosophers as a forerunner of postmodern thought and by Japanese intellectuals thinkers for its correspondences to traditional Buddhist conceptions of nonsubstantive reality. But as Faure cautions in his essay on the Kyoto school, the stakes involved in coming to terms with the dubiousness of Japan cannot be underestimated, and we must vigilantly watch for and be willing to step out of the snare of responses that are deliberately rhetorically couched in ambivalent metaphor. "Obviously," Faure writes, "we have to face the problem of our participation in *nihonjinron* discourse—even when we believe that we can remain critical. Thus, even a project like the present book—admittedly a hybrid collection of scholars—raises questions: for it is not clear whether the outcome will be a genuine critique or another attempt at containment." For Said, the overriding problem is how to free interpreters from their implicit, unconscious involvement in Orientalist discourse, but it is equally imperative for Japanologists to be liberated from their participation in the discourse of Nihonism created in the Orient.

The contributors to this volume suggest innovative ways of achieving a constructive compromise between critique and containment, participation and liberation, through the application of critical/self-critical methodological approaches. For example, Charles Fu shows that an analysis of the complexity of the tradition, which is by no means monolithic, yields surprising, illuminating results. Fu is critical of conventional interpretions of the "economic miracle" in Japan and other East Asian countries which stress the role of Confucianism in a simplistic, uniform manner. Fu emphasizes the need to carefully examine the differences in the Confucian traditions in the respective countries (especially between China and Japan), to assess the development of Confucian influence between the Tokugawa and the modern era, and to take more fully into account other aspects of Japanese society and religiosity. Fu concludes by highlighting the "multilayered structure" (*jūsōteki kōzō*) of the Japanese tradition as a key to understanding the possibilities for an ideological revitalization of Confucianism.

While several authors, including Odin and Wawrytko, cite affinities with Nietzschean multiperspectivism, other authors employ the postmodern literary critical category of "intertextuality," which breaks down conventional barriers between text and context, author and reader, subjectivity and objectivity, as an effective tool both to reflect and to assess the tradition. For example, Haruo Shirane sheds new light on the technique of "allusive variation" (honkadori) in Shunzei's waka poetry from an intertextual standpoint. According to the conventional view largely based on modern (nineteenth-century romantic) Western interpretive models, the 5-line, 31–syllable waka is seen as a discrete poetic entity which, in mimetically depicting nature, often evokes earlier poems to express the author's individual invention. According to Shirane's view influenced by Barthes, Harold Bloom and Julia Kristeva, the "waka was also a genre that functions within an elaborate fabric of rules, conventions, and literary associations, within a highly codified, intertextual context . . . in which the primary stress was not on individual invention but on . . . subtle, imitative variation of pre-texts and traditional literary associations." Yumiko Hulvey, who provides translations and plot summaries of some of Enchi Fumiko's writings for the first time in English, discusses Enchi's modern intertextual allusions to traditional literary sources and to references to female shamans (miko) that are radically reoriented from the perspective of a contemporary feminist narrative strategy. Enchi's feminism employs the older symbols and images in ways that emphasize empowerment rather than submissiveness in order to subvert the authority of social and religious patriarchy. John Maraldo shows that tradition, including the Japanese philosophical tradition, is not a static entity passed down over time. Instead, the emergence of tradition is a dynamic process of intertextual creativity that takes places retrospectively as well as progressively (into the past and the future), or is "created and re-created, formed and re-formed by, among other things, the translation of texts—a translation as much into the past as of it." The articles by Wawrytko and Hulvey disclose various perspectives of Buddhism and Shinto from a feminist perspective, and the articles by Faure, Wright and Maraldo provide alternative views of the philosophical and political implications of the Kyoto school.

From a broader view, the intertextuality involved in the relation between various aspects of the Japanese tradition can be also seen as a matter of "intra-textuality," especially when the tradition is placed in an encounter with and relativized by its otherness.

Masao Abe stresses that for the traditionalist perspective to remain viable in the postmodern world it must be open and responsive to the differences and criticisms generated by the Other. Despite very different orientations concerning the fundamental debate, for both Abe and Ōe this openness includes hearing the marginalized, alternative, subversive voices within the culture (a dialogical intratextuality) as well as engaging in a throughgoing, genuinely openended dialogue with international traditions, especially Western science, literature and religion (a dialogical intertextuality)—all of which is essential for mutual and for self-understanding.

Finally, please note that Japanese names are presented in the traditional order, with surname first, except when cited for English-language writings, such as our contributors Masao Abe and Kenzaburō Ōe.

Notes

1. Edward Said, *Orientalism* (New York: Vintage, 1978), 107. Said here makes an ironic comment on remarks by Gibb, which Said feels suggest that any attempt to break open the lock of cultural stereotyping that comprises the structures of Orientalist discourse is a fantasy, a wandering into "Disneyland." For Said, however, it is Orientalism that is characterized by the Disney-ish quality.

2. Kawabata Yasunari, *Japan, the Beautiful, and Myself*, tr. E. G. Seidensticker (Tokyo: Kodansha, 1969), 44–45. For an examination of Kawabata's discussion of classical Japanese poetry, especially Dōgen, see Steven Heine, *A Blade of Grass: Japanese Poetry and Aesthetics in Dōgen Zen* (New York: Peter Lang, 1989).

3. Kawabata, *Japan, the Beautiful, and Myself*, 41, 36 (slightly altered).

4. Masao Miyoshi and H. D. Harootunian, eds., *Postmodernism and Japan* (Durham: Duke University Press, 1989), xvi–xvii.

5. Winston Davis, *Japanese Religion and Society: Paradigms of Structure and Change* (Albany: SUNY Press, 1992), 256.

6. Robert N. Bellah, *Tokugawa Religion: The Cultural Roots of Modern Japan* (New York: Free Press, 1985), xi. This is a reprint of Bellah's 1957 work which carried a different subtitle, "The Values of Pre-Industrial Japan."

7. Ibid., xvi.

8. Another influential work by Karatani is *Hihyō to posuto-modan* (Criticism and Postmodernity) (Tokyo: Fukumu shoten, 1985).

9. Yoshihiko Ikegami, ed., *The Empire of Signs: Semiotic Essays on Japanese Culture* (Amsterdam and Philadelphia: John Benjamins Co., 1991).

10. Sakabe Megumi, *Kamen no kaishakugaku* (Hermeneutics of Masks) (Tokyo: Tokyo Daigaku shuppankai, 1976).

11. Howard Link, *Waves and Plagues: The Art of Masami Teraoka* (San Francisco: Chronicle Books, 1988).

12. Many of the articles in *Postmodernism and Japan* also appeared in a 1988 issue of *South Atlantic Quarterly*. Miyoshi and Harootunian have published a subsequent volume, *Japan in the World* (Durham: Duke University Press, 1993), which develops similar issues and themes.

13. *Postmodernism and Japan*, xvii.

14. Said, *Orientalism*, 177. Note that Said uses the term *topos* in this context in contrast to "place," while in the philosophy of Kyoto school thinker Nishida Kitarō, based on Platonic sources, *topos* is understood as the place (*basho*) or concrete manifestation of absolute nothingness. Yet Asada Akira from a Marxist standpoint accuses Nishida's notion of a so-called empty place of having a "fairy tale" quality harboring imperialist implications; see "Infantile Capitalism and Japan's Postmodernism: A Fairy Tale," in *Postmodernism and Japan*, 273–78.

15. David Henry Hwang, *M. Butterfly* (New York: Plume, 1986), 95.

16. Said, *Orientalism*, 26.

17. Jean Beaudrillard, *Simulations*, tr. Paul Foss, Paul Patton and Philip Beitchman (New York: Semiotext(e), 1983), 30.

Acknowledgments

This volume consists of newly written papers in addition to revised versions of previously published papers. We thank the editors of the following journals for granting us the rights for reprinting articles with revisions: the *Journal of Chinese Philosophy*, for Steve Odin, "Derrida and the Decentered Universe of Ch'an/Zen Buddhism," 17 (1990); the *History of Religions*, for Richard Pilgrim, "Intervals (*Ma*) in Space and Time: Foundations for a Religio-Aesthetic Paradigm in Japan," 25/3 (1986) (© 1986 by the University of Chicago Press); the *Harvard Journal of Asiatic Studies*, for Haruo Shirane, "Lyricism and Intertextuality: An Approach to Shunzei's Poetics," 50/1 (1990). Also, Kenzaburō Ōe's paper was originally presented at the New York Public Library in May 1993. In addition, several of the papers in this volume were first presented at a panel on "Japan and Postmodernism" at the national meeting of the American Academy of Religion held in San Francisco, November 1992, and we thank everyone who participated in this event.

We are also grateful for funding from the College of Liberal Arts, Pennsylvania State University, which helped support the editorial work necessary to complete the volume. Finally, we express our greatest appreciation to William Eastman, Director of SUNY Press, for his guidance during the planning and execution of this project.

Chapter One

Derrida and the Decentered Universe of Ch'an/Zen Buddhism

STEVE ODIN

Derrida's Strategy of Critical Decentering

Jacques Derrida, the foremost philosopher of contemporary poststructuralism, has developed a style of critical thinking which has come to be called "deconstruction." In a word, Derrida has endeavored to deconstruct all notions of "self-presence" or "self-identity" which have arisen as correlates to the dominant category in the *episteme* of Western culture: namely, "being." The basic strategy by which Derrida carries out his project of critical deconstruction is to undermine all notions of self-identity through the logic of *différance*. That is to say, Derrida endeavors to demonstrate how any category of presence, being or identity can be deconstructed into a "play of differences," or in Nietzchean terms, an irreducible "play of forces." As Derrida writes in his book entitled *Positions*: "*Différance* is the systematic play of differences, of the traces of differences, of the spacing by means of which elements are related to each other."[1]

The key in terms of Derrida's ever-shifting lexicon of technical terms, *différance*, is a combination of two French verbs: "to differ" and "to defer." On the one side, *différance* indicates "to differ" (*différer*), in the sense that no sign can be simply identical with itself, but instead disseminates into a chain of differences. Derrida's differential logic has here been especially influenced by the semiology of Ferdinand de Saussure's *Course on General Linguistics*, which asserts: "in language there are only differences without positive terms."[2] On the other side, *différance* indicates "to defer" (*différer*), in the sense that the meaning of a sign is always deferred by intervals of spacing and temporalizing so as to be put off indefi-

nitely. The idea of *différance* as "difference/deferral" thus functions
to prevent conceptual closure—or reduction to an ultimate meaning. In other words, *différance* is a critical deconstruction of the
"transcendental signified"; each "signified" is revealed as an irreducible play of floating signifiers so that any given sign empties out
into the whole network of differential relations.

The project of critical deconstruction is itself expressed in
terms of what Derrida calls the language of "decentering." In this
context a "center" is any sign which has been absolutized as having
self-identity. His polemic here is that any sign thought to be an
absolute "center" with self-identity can itself be fractured into
différance, a chain of differences/deferrals. In a key statement,
Derrida describes his theme of decentering as "the stated abandonment of all reference to a center, to a subject, to a privileged reference, to an origin, or to an absolute archia."[3] He further asserts that
his project of decentering emerged as the development of a major
"rupture" in the history of structure, which took place in the late
nineteenth and early twentieth centuries, heralded especially by
Nietzsche's destruction of all axiological-ontological systems as
well as Heidegger's destruction of traditional metaphysics and onto-
theology. Hence, Derrida writes: "the entire history of the concept
of structure, before the rupture of which we are speaking, must be
thought of as a series of substitutions of center for center, as a linked
chain of determinations of the center."[4] He adds that although the
history of metaphysical structure has run through a long series of
"centers" like substance, essence, subject, energy, ego, consciousness, God or man, "it was necessary to begin thinking that there
was no center."[5] Consequently, Derrida endeavors to deconstruct
the various "centrisms" which have afflicted philosophical and
theological discourse such as ethnocentrism, anthropocentrism,
phallocentrism, egocentrism, theocentrism, and logocentrism.
Derrida commences his deconstruction of the Western metaphysics
of presence with an effort to critically decenter onto-theological
discourse. In the Western metaphysics of presence, God has been
comprehended as Absolute Being, Presence or Identity. In other
words, God is the absolute Center. In this context Derrida speaks of
a "negative atheology" which endeavors to deconstruct the transcendent God of theocentrism, thought of as the Transcendental
Signified. He writes: "Just as there is a negative theology, there is a
negative atheology. An accomplice of the former, it still pronounces
the absence of a center."[6]

Yet Derrida is not propounding nihilism since all absolute centers deconstructed through *différance* are said to reappear as "trace," understood as an interplay of presence and absence or identity and difference. As differential trace all fixed metaphysical centers including the transcendent God of theocentrism and the individual self of egocentrism or anthropocentrism are placed "under erasure" (*sous rature*), that is, written with a cross mark ×, thereby to signify a presence which is at the same time absent and an absence which is at the same time present.[7]

The Decentered Universe of Zen Buddhism

The postmodern deconstructionist boom in America and on the Continent has arrived in Japan. This can be especially seen in the writings of Karatani Kōjin and Asada Akira, foremost among postmodernist critics in Japan. One need only mention the sudden and unprecedented popularity of a book about poststructuralism by Asada Akira, entitled *Kōzō to chikara* (Structure and Power, 1983).[8] In several weeks this work sold nearly eighty thousand copies, and its author became a sensation in the weekly magazines and newspapers. Read by office workers, university students, artists, and musicians, the media announced the advent of a "new academism." Indeed, this event soon came to be known in Japan as the *AA genshō* ("Asada Akira phenomenon").[9] Karatani Kōjin's deconstructionist texts such as *Nihon kindai bungaku no kigen* (*The Origins of Modern Japanese Literature*, 1980) have also become controversial bestsellers in Japan. This Japanese postmodern boom has been intensified by the advent of Jacques Derrida's visit to Japan in 1984, at which time he met with Asada Akira and Karatani Kōjin. The *Asahi Journal* (May 1984) published part of the transcript of this discussion as "The Ultra-Consumer Society and the Role of the Intellectual" ("Chōsōhi shakai to chishikijin no yakuwari").[10]

According to Karatani Kōjin, postmodernism in Japan is a movement which seeks the "deconstruction of modernism or, more fundamentally, of the framework of Western metaphysics."[11] It involves the "disappearance of the subject, the decentering (or 'multicentering') of the [putative] center."[12] In his conversation with Derrida and Asada Akira, Karatani Kōjin argues that since Japan has no fixed structures, deconstruction as such is not possible. By this view, deconstruction has already taken place in Japan, insofar as

Japan has already arrived at a radically decentered or multicentered reality in which God, the ego, and all other fixed metaphysical centers have been displaced through a differential logic.[13] However, in response to Karatani Kōjin, Derrida suggests that the "Asada Akira phenomenon" is not simply a repetition of deconstructive elements already present in Zen Buddhist modes of thought, and that there are structures in Japan which still require critical decentering. In Derrida's words:

> I wonder if deconstruction is truly so easy in Japan. I have my doubts about whether we can say that deconstruction is a direct element in Japanese-type thought. Certainly, Japanese often say that Buddhist thought or the Zen of Dōgen was already a kind of deconstruction, but I wonder if that is so. If that were really so, then why, for example, had Asada's book received such tremendous attention? If that phenomenon of Asada were nothing more that a repetition of deconstructive elements already found within Japanese thought, then it shouldn't have called down such an enormous response in contemporary Japan.[14]

As pointed out by Derrida, it is held by many scholars that deconstruction is already a basic element in Japanese thought, especially Zen Buddhism. Indeed, some scholars have argued that the nonsubstantialist and uncentered worldview of Mahayana Buddhism in general and radically acentric Zen Buddhism in particular can best be interpreted through Derrida's postmodern vision of a dislocated reality devoid of all fixed centers. For instance, the thesis of Robert Magliola's *Derrida on the Mend* is that the Buddhist logic of *śūnyatā* (Chinese: *kung*; Japanese: *kū*) a is in fact a "differential logic" which is itself structurally isomorphic with Derrida's logic of *différance*. Magliola writes: "I shall argue that Nagarjuna's *śūnyatā* ("devoidness") is Derrida's *différance*, and is the absolute negation which absolutely deconstitutes but which constitutes directional trace."[15] According to Magliola, the *différance* of Derrida, like the *śūnyatā* of Buddhism, represents a critical deconstruction of the principle of "self-identity," that is, what in Buddhist discourse takes the form of deconstituting all substantialist modes of "own-being" or "self-existence" (*svabhāva*). Through deconstructive analysis all metaphysical centers understood as a mode of absolute self-identity are disseminated into a network of differential relationships in which there are no positive entities. Magliola goes on to assert that the differential Buddhism of Nagarjuna with its radical deconstruction of all fixed metaphysical centers reaches its culmination in the tradition of East Asian Zen (Chinese: Ch'an) Buddhism. In this context, he criticizes all forms of "centric Zen" wherein "the Buddha-nature thus understood becomes an infinite Center,"[16] arguing that "differential Zen like Nagarjuna's Mādhyamika, disclaims 'centered' experience of any kind."[17]

However, the absolute negation of *différance* also signals the emergence of nonsubstantial "trace" which is simultaneously absent yet present, present yet absent. In this context, Magliola argues that *différance* as the interplay of identity and difference or presence and absence is equivalent to Nagarjuna's Buddhist notion of *śūnyatā*, since it constitutes a Middle Way between the "it is" of eternalism and "it is not" of nihilism.[18] He further asserts that this Middle Way between eternalism and nihilism is best seen in the aestheticism of Japanese Zen, whose various art forms have the status of Derrida's differential trace as the interplay between presence and absence:

> Buddhists in the Nagarjunist tradition can function as productive, often outstanding members of society. . . . They can savor and create the exquisitely esthetic (think of Zen painting, ceramics, gardens, poetry); yet, I argue, they are doing all this as trace, as indeed, Derridian trace![19]

As I have argued elsewhere, in contemporary Japanese philosophy the differential logic of acentric Zen Buddhism and its deconstructive strategy of critical decentering has itself been fully appropriated by Nishida Kitarō (1870–1945) and the Kyoto school.[20] In the postscript to his translation of Nishida Kitarō's essay, "The Logic of the Place of Nothingness and the Religious Worldview," David A. Dilworth provides a detailed explanation of "Nishida's Logic of the East." Dilworth persuasively argues that Nishida's paradoxical logic of *soku/hi* or "is and yet is not" is structurally isomorphic with Derrida's deconstructive logic of *différance*, which is described as operating through the adversative edge of presence and absence in the play of textual significations.[21] By this view, both Derrida's logic of *différance* and Nishida's logic of *soku/hi* are cross-cultural variants of the paradoxical or agnostic paradigm of articulation. According to Nishida's paradoxical logic of *soku/hi*, God, the self and all things "are" and "are not," just as for Derrida's logic of *différance* they have the status of differential "trace" which is simultaneously both absent and present, both present and absent. Hence, Nishida's "logic of the East" (*tōyōteki ronri*), which assumes the form of a "self-identity of absolute contradictions" (*zettai mujunteki jiko dōitsu*), can be said to have a deep structural proximity to Derrida's logic of *différance* wherein all self-identity is constituted by a play of irreducible differences. In the case of Derrida's logic of *différance*, each fixed metaphysical center erroneously thought of as having self-identity is shown to involve an aporia (a contradiction or irreconcilable paradox in the form of is/is not)[22] which subverts its own grounds and disperses its seeming meanings into indeterminancy, thereby disseminating into a chain of differential traces and floating signifiers without end.

Nishitani Keiji's *Shūkyō to wa nanika* (What is Religion?), translated into English under the title *Religion and Nothingness*,[23] fully incorporates the Zen Buddhist paradoxical *soku/hi* or "is and yet is not" mode of discourse along with Nishida Kitarō's differential logic of "the self-identity of absolute contradictions." The major problematic raised by Nishitani in this work is the overcoming of modern nihilism as described by Nietzsche. According to Nishitani, nihility (*kyomu*) or relative nothingness (*sōtaiteki mu*) can only be overcome by converting to true emptiness (*kū*) or absolute nothingness (*zettai mu*) as described by Zen Buddhism. Hence, all substantial things in the realm of "being" (*yū*) which have been nullified in the abyss of nihility are now affirmed just as they are in their positive suchness at the standpoint of emptiness or absolute nothingness. In this way, Nishitani follows Nagarjuna's differential logic, which itself establishes a Middle Path between substantial being and nihilistic nothingness so as to avoid the philosophical extremes of "eternalism" on the one side and "annihilationism" on the other.

According to Nishitani, the locus of absolute nothingness is to be comprehended as an infinite openness devoid of all fixed metaphysical centers. In this context, Nishitani describes the kenotic self-emptying of both the "theocentric" (*kami-chūshinteki*) and the "anthropocentric" (*ningen-chūshinteki*) standpoints in the ultimate standpoint of *śūnyatā* or emptiness. He writes:

> Thus it can be said that the theocentric standpoint, as represented by Christianity, and the anthropocentric standpoint of secularism both find themselves currently at the brink of mutual elimination. . . . Nietzsche's philosophy could not have come to birth without such a brink.[24]

As is indicated in the passage above, Nishitani's use of postmodernist language of "decentering" in order to express the standpoint of emptiness or absolute nothingness has been influenced not only by the deconstructive element of Zen thought in the East but also by the deconstructionism inherent in Nietzsche's positive nihilism in the West. In this context Nishitani emphasizes the total shattering of all "man-centered" (ningen-chūshinteki) and "God-centered" (kami-chūshinteki) orientations by Nietzsche's sledgehammer of Eternal Recurrence. He writes:

> Not only the man-centered but also the God-centered mode of being has to be smashed, Nietzsche would claim, by the sledgehammer of the idea of Eternal Recurrence. Only when every sort of optical illusion has been demolished through this "transnihilism" does the standpoint of the Great Affirmation of the Great Life come to light.[25]

According to Nishitani, then, the smashing of all metaphysical centers with Nietzsche's sledgehammer of Eternal Recurrence culminates in the negation of both the transcendent God of theocentrism and the individual self of egocentrism. However, the negation of both God-centered and man-centered standpoints does not result in the nihilism of relative nothingness since all things are affirmed exactly as they are in their positive suchness on the field of absolute nothingness. Hence, following the direction of Nietzsche's positive nihilism or trans-nihilism, Nishitani deconstructs all substantial metaphysical centers in order to arrive at a standpoint of complete affirmation. Indeed, using Nietzschean terms Nishitani calls emptiness or absolute nothingness the "field of Great Affirmation" (kōtei no ba) where we can say Yes to all things.[26] For this reason Nishitani regards the negation of all transcendent and interior centers as well as the total affirmation of life in the Innocence of Becoming depicted by Nietzsche's vision of Eternal Recurrence as achieving a close structural proximity to the Mahayana Buddhist philosophy of śūnyatā or emptiness. Speaking of Nietzsche's philosophy, he thus writes: "It might also be interpreted as one of the currents of Western thought to come closest to the Buddhist standpoint of śūnyatā."[27]

Furthermore, it should by emphasized that for Nishitani, as for Nishida, the deconstruction of all fixed metaphysical centers having self-identity is in fact tantamount to a *multicentering* of the reality continuum wherein each and every event is now affirmed in its positive suchness as a unique center. That is to say, since the infinite openness of śūnyatā or emptiness is devoid of all absolute centers, including both the God-centered standpoint of

theocentrism and the human-centered standpoint of anthropocentrism, now all phenomena are affirmed as individual centers in
the locus of absolute nothingness. For this reason, he writes: "The
field of *śūnyatā* is a field whose center is everywhere."

Abe Masao also argues that the true *śūnyatā* or emptiness is
a boundless openness devoid of any metaphysical centers. Every
metaphysical center, including the transcendent center represented
by anthropocentrism or egocentrism, must be dissolved and emptied out in the standpoint of *śūnyatā*. In his essay "Kenotic God and
Dynamic Śūnyatā" Abe writes that the "locus of śūnyatā . . . is completely free from any centrism and is boundlessly open."[28] Again, he
asserts:

> Śūnyatā indicates boundless openness without any particular fixed
> center. Śūnyatā is free not only from egocentrism but also from
> anthropocentrism, cosmocentrism and theocentrism. It is not ori-
> ented by any kind of centrism. Only in this way, is "emptiness"
> possible.[29]

Moreover, just as Nagarjuna propounds that "emptiness must itself
be emptied," Abe emphasizes that *śūnyatā* cannot be reified,
absolutized, or substantialized in any way whatsoever but is that
which can never be objectified as some independently existing
thing. For this reason, he states that "following Martin Heidegger,
who put a cross mark × on the term *Sein*, rendering it instead as
S̶e̶i̶n̶, in order to show the unobjectifiability of Being, we should also
put a cross mark × on the term *Śūnyatā*, and render it S̶ū̶n̶y̶a̶t̶ā̶."[30]
He adds:

> Śūnyatā is fundamentally non-Śūnyatā with a cross mark, that is.
> That is the true and ultimate Śūnyatā. This means that true
> Śūnyatā empties not only everything else, but also empties itself.
> Through its self-emptying it makes everything to exist as it is and
> to work as it does. Śūnyatā should not be understood in its noun
> form but in its verbal form because it is a pure and dynamic
> function of all-emptying.[31]

Abe puts a cross mark on Emptiness or Nothingness just as
Heidegger put a cross mark on *Sein* to affect the cancellation of
Being. In such a manner he employs the fundamental postmodernist
strategy for avoiding every kind of ontological reification, which
Derrida refers to as placing all signification "under erasure" (*sous
rature*). By placing *śūnyatā* under erasure so as to render it non-

śūnyatā with a cross mark ×, it thereby takes on the ontological status of differential trace, understood as a dynamic interplay of presence and absence or identity and difference in the locus of absolute nothingness.

Japan as a Decentered Text

Poststructuralist criticism has pointed to certain artistic/literary paradigms of the decentered Text. For instance, in her book *The Decentered Universe of Finnegans Wake* Margot Norris suggests that the "chaosmos" of James Joyce's *Finnegans Wake* is the exemplar of a multicentered Text devoid of any absolutes or ultimate reference points which might anchor the play of textual significa- tion.[32] However, it was *Empire of Signs* (*L'Empire des signes*, 1970) by the literary critic Roland Barthes which first made famous the idea that traditional Japanese culture was itself a dislocated semiotic field illustrating the decentered or multicentered text de- scribed by poststructuralist discourse. Since then an ever-growing body of deconstructionist literature has emerged which attempts to read the Japanese text in light of postmodern semiotic theories abandoning all the "centrisms" of Western thought, including such works as *To the Distant Observer* by Noel Burch,[33] *The Fracture of Meaning* by David Pollack,[34] and *Things Seen* and *Unseen* by H. D. Harootunian.[35] This movement has recently been brought into sharper focus by a special issue of *The South Atlantic Quarterly* (87/ 3, Summer 1988) on "Postmodernism and Japan" (subsequently published as a volume).

Barthes clarifies his own poststructuralist concept of textuality in his famous essay, "From the Work to the Text." Whereas a Work is a closed system with a fixed center of meaning, a Text is an open system with no fixed center. The Text is therefore a decentered or multicentered play of differential traces and floating signifiers with no positive entities which functions to generate an irreducible plu- rality of meanings. Moreover while a Work is simply "lisible" (read- able), a decentered Text is "scriptable" (writable), that is, it induces multiple interpretations. In Barthes' words:

> In this way the Text is restored to language: like language, it is structured but decentered without closure.... The Text is plural. This does mean just that it has several meanings, but rather that it achieves plurality of meaning, an irreducible plurality.[36]

In his book entitled *Empire of Signs* Barthes proceeds to argue
that Japanese Zen Buddhist thought and culture is a kind of mirror
which reflects semiotic theories of the text formulated by contemporary postmodernism. According to the postmodernist theory of
semiotics tracing back to the ideas of Saussure, language is a differential, or relational, system in which there are no positive entities.
Each sign is a play of signifiers which empties out into the entire
web of differential relationships. Moreover, as defined by Saussure,
semiology is "a science that studies the life of signs within society."[37] Taking this approach, Barthes argues that Japan is an "empire
of signs." Through this poststructuralist analysis of the Japanese
"text" Barthes thereby endeavors to demonstrate how Japan is a
wholly decentered semiotic field wherein the signs are all empty.
The food, clothing, customs, rituals, games, sports, painting, poetry,
drama, landscaping, interior decorating, city planning, and other
"sign systems" of the Japanese text are all analyzed as differential
networks of floating signifiers in which there is a complete absence
of a fixed "center."

In his discussion of Japanese aesthetics, Barthes argues that
haiku poetry reveals a Zen Buddhist worldview of *mu* or nothingness which is itself free of all absolute metaphysical centers, including both the transcendent God of theocentrism and the individual
subject of egocentrism:

> The haiku . . . articulated around a metaphysics without subject
> and without God, corresponds to the Buddhist *Mu*, to the Zen
> *satori*, which is not at all the illuminative descent of God, but
> "awakening to the fact," apprehension of the thing as event and
> not as substance. . . . [A]ccording to an image proposed by the Hua-
> yen doctrine, one might say that the collective body of all haikus is
> a network of jewels in which each jewel reflects all the others and
> so on, to infinity, without there ever being a center to grasp, a
> primary core of irradiation.[38]

In his analysis of Japanese cuisine, he argues that the arrangement of food is completely decentered—no dish has a "center" as in
Western meals since everything is fragmented and dispersed so as to
serve as the ornament of another ornament. Barthes thus writes:
"No Japanese dish is endowed with a center (the alimentary center
implied in the West by the rite which consists of arranging the meal,
or surrounding or covering the article of food)."[39] Then in his discussion of city planning he opposes the "concentric" structure of Western cities whereby "in accord with the very movement of Western

metaphysics, for which every center is the site of truth, the center of our cities is always full."[40] He contrasts this to the "acentric" structure of Tokyo, the capital of Japan, which instead has an "empty center" or "sacred nothing"—a vacant palace surrounded by moats and walls, inhabited by an emperor who is never seen: "The city I am talking about (Tokyo) offers this precious paradox: it does possess a center, but this center is empty."[41] Barthes proceeds to demonstrate the manner in which the interior decorating of a traditional Japanese room also reflects a completely decentered worldview:

> In the Shikidai gallery, as in the ideal Japanese house, stripped of furniture . . . the center is rejected (painful frustration for Western man, everywhere "furnished" with his armchair, his bed, proprietor of a domestic location). Uncentered space is also reversible . . . there is nothing to grasp.[42]

In such a manner Barthes employs his poststructuralist theory of semiotics in order to demonstrate how the free play of signifiers in the various sign systems of Japanese culture are to be comprehended as a radically dislocated and open-ended text devoid of any fixed center. Japan is thus an empire of "empty" signs. Or in Barthes' own words: "Empire of signs? Yes, if it is understood that the signs are empty and that the ritual is without a god."[43]

In a study entitled *To the Distant Observer*, Noel Burch has applied the semiotic theories of Saussure, Derrida and especially Barthes to the analysis of Japanese film aesthetics. Burch asserts that *Empire of Signs* by Barthes "is the first attempt by any Western writer to read the Japanese "text" in the light of contemporary semiotics, a reading informed by a rejection of ethnocentrism—and indeed all of the "centrisms" which have anchored ideology in the West."[44] Burch goes on to assert that his own book is an effort to understand Japanese cinema as a decentered semiotic field in the manner suggested by Barthes' reading/writing of the Japanese text. He especially applies Barthes' analysis of Japanese Bunraku puppet theater to Japanese film, arguing that both are decentered into multiple texts or codes. Barthes has stated that Bunraku puppet theater fractures into at least three independent subtexts. He writes: "Bunraku thus practices three separate writings, which it offers to be read simultaneously in three sites of the spectacle: the puppet, the manipulator, the vociferant."[45] In this context, Burch asserts that the "golden age" of Japanese cinema as exemplified by the silent films of Mizoguchi and Ozu was also radically decentered insofar as it operated through independent but simultaneous texts, including the visual film presentation, the separate musical accompaniment, and the spontaneous narration/interpretation of the *benshi* or "narrator." Moreover, Burch argues that there is a decentering of Japanese cinema into multiple interpretations which results from the interpretative response of the *benshi* or live narrator to the silent film presentation, similar to the role of the *gidayu bushi* in Bunraku, Noh and Kabuki theater.[46] That is to say, both Japanese silent film and Japanese classical theater are to be understood, not as closed works with a fixed center of meaning, but as open and decentered texts which induce a plurality of meanings through the cooperation of artist and interpreter.

In his important paper (included in this volume) on "*Ma*: A Cultural Paradigm," Richard Pilgrim has shown the extent to which the art, literature and other sign systems in the decentered text of Japanese culture are totally fractured or displaced in terms of the aesthetic principle of *ma*, a rich, multi-nuanced term indicating "space, spacing, interval, gap, blank, room, pause, rest, time, timing, or opening."[47] The religio-aesthetic principle of *ma* refers to the opening of a space-time interval whereby each object has a relatedness or betweenness with its surrounding context. For instance, the spacing and timing of *ma* is seen in the intervals of non-action in the Noh drama, the empty spaces in *haiku* poetry, and the silent pauses in the films of Ozu, as well as the blank or negative spaces in Japanese inkwash painting, architecture, and sand gardening. In the artistic and literary forms of the *ma* aesthetic, "the intervals or gaps serve as an empty space within which the forms of the art function."[48] Pilgrim contends that "a *ma* aesthetic or *ma* paradigm . . . simultaneously locates and dislocates the world of form and order."[49] *Ma* is an "open-ended aesthetic" which underscores "the unfixed, dislocated sense of space or place" without being anchored in any kind of "fixed center."[50] In the uncentered sign systems of Japanese discourse, the "negative, imaginative, open moments of space-time are as important as what is objectively there."[51] He moreover states that "*Ma* resides in that between-ness which is continually breaking open the literal, descriptive world and inviting direct experience of the inarticulate, deconstructed, 'empty' reality of immediate experience."[52] The characteristic voids of the *ma* aesthetic thereby "function to dislocate that world of meaning and action, emptying yet opening it to another level of experience and reality."[53]

This traditional Japanese *ma* paradigm of artistic/literary discourse at once bears a deep structural proximity to Derrida's notion of *différance*, which the latter has explicitly defined throughout *Positions* in such terms as "spacing," "temporalizing," "opening," as well as "blank," "void," and "nothing." To repeat Derrida's definition of *différance* cited above: "*Différance* is the systematic play of differences . . . of the spacing by means of which elements are related to each other." Derrida's concept of *différance*, the interval of spacing and temporalizing by means of which elements are interrelated in the differential web of textual significations, is thus profoundly brought to light through the radically dislocated *ma* aesthetic operative in the non-centered "empire of signs" constituting the Japanese cultural text.

The Decentered Image in Japanese Aesthetics

In his essay on "Decentering the Image," Joseph Riddel has argued that the Imagist movement of Ezra Pound develops a radically decentered concept of the poetic image based on the seminal text of Ernest Fenollosa, entitled *The Chinese Written Character as a Medium for Poetry* (compiled and edited by Ezra Pound). In this context Riddel cites a significant passage from Derrida's *Of Grammatology*, wherein the latter makes direct reference to the work of Pound and Fenollosa.[54] According to Derrida, the work of Pound and Fenollosa based on the Chinese and Japanese writing system functioned to effect a critical decentering of the Western metaphysics of presence, that is, what Derrida calls the tradition of logocentrism. Concerning the Chinese and Japanese ideogrammic writing system, Derrida remarks: "But we have known for a long time that largely nonphonetic scripts like Chinese or Japanese . . . remained structurally of a powerful movement of civilization developing outside of all logocentrism."[55] Derrida then cites Pound and Fenollosa because of their "irreducibly graphic poetics [which] was with that of Mallarmé, the first break in the most entrenched Western tradition. The fascination that the Chinese ideogram exercised on Pound's writing may thus be given all its historical significance."[56] Like Nietzsche, he adds, Pound and Fenollosa "at first destroyed and caused to vacillate the transcendental authority and dominant category of the episteme: being."[57] In his analysis of Derrida's discussion of Fenollosa and Pound, Riddel states: "If the 'graphic symbol' is Fenollosa's 'centre,' then it is a noncentered noncentering center, irreducibly multiple. And nature is not an agent, but already a play of forces, a constellated and constellating field."[58]

The means by which Pound arrived at his notion of a decentered Image on the basis of the Chinese and Japanese ideogrammic writing system is clarified by Riddel with a reference to Fenollosa's concluding example of the triumph of ideographic precision in the graph for the English sentence, "The sun rises in the east."[59] Fenollosa explains it as follows: "The [ideograph of the] sun, on one side, on the other the sign of the east, which is the sun entangled in the branches of a tree."[60] Hence, in the Chinese and Japanese writing system, the character for "east" (東), is itself a complex ideogram composed of a two simpler pictographs, that of "sun" (日), and "tree(s)" (木), which when juxtaposed together show the sun rising in the east behind the trees. The written character of the Chinese/Japanese script is thereby wholly displaced and decentered into a free play of images, a complex ideogram which disseminates into a play of pictographs.

 As Riddel shows in his essay, Pound's idea of the Image based on the Chinese and Japanese ideogram is itself fully dislocated into a play of forces. He cites Pound's famous definition of the Image as "an intellectual and emotional complex in an instant of time."[61] He adds: "In Pound's definitions, the Image (that is, the whole Poem) is always a 'node' or 'cluster' of figures, a constellation of radical differences . . . that Image, is a 'field'—in short, 'originally' a Text."[62] As a "cluster," a "complex," a "vortex," or a "field," the self-identity of the Image is thereby wholly decentered into an irreducible play of differences/deferrals. As Riddel states: "The visual is reinscribed as a play of differences (that is in writing), which decenters any imagistic representation."[63] Riddel concludes that the project of the Imagist-Vorticism movement in America was to develop "a poetry of uprootedness, of radical innocence, of the radical origin, of the radical as origin—the 'decentered' Image."[64]

The concept of the "decentered Image" as outlined above provides the theoretical foundations for a wholly postmodern interpretation of Japanese aesthetics which articulates the dislocated structure of art, literature and cinema in Japan. The literary and artistic tradition of Japan is commonly analyzed by scholars of Oriental aesthetics in terms of Images which have come to be standardized in the Japanese canons of beauty: for instance, Images of *aware* (pathos), Images of *yūgen* (profound mystery) and Images of *sabi/wabi* (rustic poverty). Against the radically dislocated worldview of acentric Zen Buddhism it can be demonstrated that the aesthetic Images of traditional Japanese art and literature are completely decentered or multicentered in structure. For purposes of analysis I will especially focus on *yūgen* as a paradigm of the decentered Image in Japanese aesthetics.

As an illustration of a dislocated Japanese art form expressed through the decentered Image one can point to the celebrated film entitled *Rashomon* (1950) directed by Kurosawa Akira. This film presents the successive testimonials of witnesses to what is thought by police to be a rape and murder case. However, each testimonial is so divergent from the others that what gradually emerges is a total displacement of the event into a bewildering multiplicity of perspectival interpretations, an irreducible plurality of meanings. The nature of the film brings into question the possibility of absolute truth and suggests the relativity of all knowledge. Perhaps this poststructuralist view has been given its most famous expression by Nietzsche's "Perspectivism" as expounded in *The Will to Power*:

> Against positivism, which halts at phenomena—"There are only facts"—I would say: No, facts is precisely what there is not, only interpretations. . . . In so far as the word "knowledge" has any meaning, the world is knowable; but it is interpretable otherwise, it has no meaning behind it, but countless meanings— "Perspectivism."[65]

In the case of *Rashomon* the event described is presented, not as a closed work with a fixed center of meaning, but an open text which is completely multicentered in structure so as to generate an irreducible plurality of interpretations and meanings.

The film *Rashomon* is itself based on two short stories by Akutagawa Ryūnosuke entitled "Rashomon" ("Rashomon") and "In a Grove" ("Yabu no naka").[66] Rashomon—an ancient gate in Kyoto destroyed by fires and earthquakes—evokes the dark and mysterious twilight world of *yūgen* and provides the atmosphere in which the murder plot of "In a Grove" unfolds. In this case, the "ambiguity" or "mystery and depth" of this story is not conveyed simply by its atmosphere of darkness and shadows, but also by the radically decentered nature of the *yūgen*-Image as its plot and characters are displaced into a multiplicity of interpretations and meanings.

In an aphorism entitled "Interpretation" ("Kaishaku"), Akutagawa presents the literary theory underlying his approach to literature, a theory which at once calls to mind the poststructuralist criticism of Roland Barthes developed several decades later:

> Any interpretation of a work of art presupposes a degree of coopera-
> tion between artist and interpreter. In a sense, the interpreter is an
> artist who, using another artist's work for his theme, creates his
> own work of art. Hence, every famous work of art that has with-
> stood the test of time is characterized by its capacity to induce
> multiple interpretations. But, as Anatole France has pointed out,
> the fact that a literary work has the capacity to induce multiple
> interpretations does not make it ambiguous in the sense that the
> reader can easily give it any interpretation he likes. Rather it
> means that a good work is like Mount Lu; it is many-sided and
> therefore encourages viewing from many angles.[67]

As emphasized by Akutagawa in this remarkable passage, a great
work of art functions "to induce multiple interpretations." He relates this idea to Anatole France's book *The Garden of Epicurus*,
wherein it is stated that the words in a book are magic fingers that
play on the harp strings of the reader's brain, and that the sounds
thus evoked depend on the quality of the strings within each individual reader. Akutagawa further illustrates this idea with reference
to Mount Lu, a famous mountain located near the Yangtze River in
China. Because of its scenic beauty and its close association with
Buddhism, it has provided fitting material for poetry and the arts
through the centuries. In particular, he argues that great art, like
Mount Lu, is many-sided and therefore generates a plurality of
meanings. For this reason, it is often emphasized that *sumie* mono-
chrome inkwash landscape paintings in the *yūgen* style which de-
pict mountains fading out into the unfathomable mystery and
darkness of the surrounding void are characterized by their many-
sidedness or their capacity to induce multiple interpretations.

As Makato Ueda has pointed out, in Akutagawa's short story
entitled "The Painting of an Autumn Mountain," multiplicity of
interpretation is itself the main theme. In this story the famed
Chinese inkwash landscape painting called "Autumn Mountain"
gives such different impressions at different times that the onlook-
ers are not sure if they have viewed the same painting.[68] The dark
spaces and black voids of the *sumie* picture conveyed through a
decentered Image of *yūgen* functions to dislocate reality into multiple perspectives. The inkwash landscape painting in Akutagawa's
story is thus not a "lisible" (readable) work with a single meaning
but a "scriptible" (writable) text which generates a plurality of
meanings through the cooperation between artist and interpreter.

D. Andrew's discussion of the film "Miss Oyu" directed by
Mizoguchi Kenji further clarifies the structure and dynamics of the

decentered Image in Japanese aesthetics. Mizoguchi's film "Miss Oyu" is itself based on a novella by Tanizaki Jun'ichirō entitled *Ashikari*. As Tanizaki explains in his essay on literary aesthetics entitled *In Praise of Shadows*, he regards the function of literature as preserving the dark and mysterious twilight world of *yūgen* which is rapidly disappearing through modernization. Yet in Tanizaki's novella *Ashikari*, as in Mizoguchi's film "Miss Oyu," the Image of *yūgen* is wholly decentered. In this story, a tourist encounters a traveller on the evening of the traditional moon-viewing ceremony by the River Yoda. The depiction of a full moon half-veiled by mist and clouds in the darkness of night is itself a classic Image of *yūgen* in Japanese literature. On this misty moonlit eve the tourist is told a story which the traveller heard from his father about the tragic romance of Miss Oyu. However, throughout this story we never gaze upon Miss Oyu directly; we instead observe her from afar through a multiplicity of perspectives such that she appears to be a completely decentered self with no fixed core. The mystery of Miss Oyu conjured through the shadowy darkness of *yūgen* imagery is further enhanced by this dislocation of self into multiple interpretations. As Andrews writes:

> And so we approach the tableau of the revered figure, Miss Oyu, through Tanizaki, through the tourist, through the traveler he meets, and that traveler's memory of his father's tale. Oyu is indeed a hazy moon of a lady casting her glow coolly and from afar.[69]

This decentering effect of *yūgen* imagery in traditional Japanese aesthetics can also be seen in Natsume Sōseki's novel *Kusamakura* (Grass Pillow, 1906),[70] which has appeared in English translation as *The Three-Cornered World*.[71] In this novel an unnamed painter and poet from Tokyo ventures on a poetic journey into the depths of nature in order to realize enlightenment through the detached contemplation of beauty. Through the exercise of aesthetic distance he endeavors to transform every natural event into a scene from a sumie inkwash landscape painting, a Noh drama or a *haiku* poem—art forms characterized by the Image of *yūgen*. As the subject for his work the artist-hero sets out to paint a woman called Nami, as well as to capture her through a series of *haiku* poems.

However, the decentered or multicentered structure of *yūgen* imagery as it functions in Sōseki's novel becomes evident through the montage construction of his text. Throughout the novel the unity of Nami's self-image is shattered into a multiplicity of view-points. The artist-hero views Nami from a plurality of perspectives so that she becomes as many-sided as a sumie inkwash painting. In his autocommentary entitled *Yo ga kusamakura* (My Grass Pillow, 1906) Sōseki describes the basic idea of his novel as follows:

> In *Kusamakura* there is a painter who observes things in a peculiar way. He meets a beautiful woman by chance and observes her, and she becomes the heroine of the work. She is always standing in the same place and does not move at all. The painter observes her from the front or from the back or from the left or from the right. He observes her from various directions—only that.[72]

Through this multiperspectival depiction of Nami the painter builds up a complex montage—a sequence of juxtaposed images derived by means of observing her from many angles as well as from gossip, a rumor, a legend, a story, a painting, a poem, and a drama. Masao Miyoshi summarizes this decentering of Nami's self-image into multiple perspectives in his book *Accomplices of Silence: The Modern Japanese Novel*:

> Here is, then, the ever expanding (living) series of images—some gossip, a *haiku* image, an oil painting, a *Man'yōshū* poem; each one is taken up at a different angle and from a different context, a different tradition. . . . But there is even further amplification. Wakeful into the night, he keeps seeing a shadowy figure flitting about in the moonlit garden, and he tries again to arrest the vision in a series of *haiku*. . . . As the artist comes to know her better, Nami continues to appear from all sorts of unexpected angles: as a dancer-performer, a sharp wit, an eccentric. Her montage, too, becomes more complex: besides the Shakespearean Ophelia, the Pre-Raphaelite Ophelia, and the legendary maiden, we now have her own ancestor who drowned herself, and the generations of crazy women in her family. As each adds her own peculiarities to the composite, Nami takes on more and more aspects of a general-ized woman figure.[73]

Hence, again it can be observed how the dark voids and black spaces of the *yūgen*-Image functions to dislocate the subject into a plural-ity of viewpoints devoid of any fixed center or core. The unity of the fictive self disintegrates; it is multiple. Like "Miss Oyu" in Mizoguchi's film by that name, Nami is a misty moonlit woman, whose elusive, ambiguous, and mysterious nature results from the acentric structure of the *yūgen*-Image. In such a manner, Sōseki's novel employs the decentered Image to deconstruct and disseminate the self-identity of Nami into an irreducible chain of differences/deferrals, which in contemporary poststructuralist discourse is named: the play of *différance*.

Conclusions

Throughout this essay it has been emphasized that Derrida's project of deconstructionism involves a critical strategy of *decentering*, that is, what he describes as "the stated abandonment of all reference to a center, to a subject, to a privileged reference, to an origin, or to an absolute archia." As shown by Magliola, the theoretical basis for the convergence of Western deconstructionism and Japanese Zen can be seen in the structural proximity between Buddhist *śūnyatā* and Derrida's *différance*—both of which function to place "under erasure" (*sous rature*) and thereby to disseminate all fixed metaphysical centers having "self-identity" or "self-presence" into a chain of differential relationships with no positive entities. Moreover, it has been seen that the dislocated worldview of acentric Zen Buddhism as well as the differential logic of Western deconstructive thought have both been appropriated into the contemporary Japanese philosophy of Nishida, Nishitani and Abe of the Kyoto school. According to the Kyoto school, emptiness or absolute nothingness is a boundless openness devoid of all fixed metaphysical centers, including the God-centered standpoint of theocentrism and the human-centered standpoint of anthropocentrism or egocentrism.

After Barthes' *Empire of Signs* Japan has come to be read in light of a postmodern semiotics as a radically dislocated and uncentered text constituted by "empty" signs wherein the meaning of the signified is always infinitely deferred through a freeplay of signifiers. Against the background of the differential logic of acentric Zen Buddhism, the art, literature, cinema and other sign systems in the Japanese text have been analyzed as a fractured semiotic field with no fixed center. In Japanese aesthetics, this radically disruptive freeplay of textual signifiers is depicted through the gaps and fissures of the decentered Image, which displaces all self-identity into multiple perspectives and accomplishes the irreducible plurality of meaning. It is in this way that we have arrived at a fully postmodern vision of Japan as a decentered text wherein each sign is emptied into a chain of differential traces and floating signifier—without closure, without origin, and without a privileged center.

Notes

1. Jacques Derrida, *Positions*, tr. Alan Bass (Chicago: University of Chicago Press, 1981), 27.

2. Derrida, *"Différance"* in *Margins of Philosophy*, tr. Alan Bass (Chicago: Chicago University Press, 1982), 10–11. Also, see Ferdinand de Saussure, *Course in General Linguistics*, tr. Wade Baskin (New York: McGraw-Hill, 1959), 120.

3. Derrida, *Writing and Difference*, tr. Alan Bass (Chicago: University Press, 1978), 286.

4. Ibid., 279.

5. Ibid., 280.

6. Ibid., 297. Derrida's suggestive notion concerning a deconstructive atheology devoid of an absolute Center has been systematically developed by Mark C. Taylor in his book *Erring: A Postmodern A/theology* (Chicago: The University of Chicago Press, 1984). Taylor uses Derrida's principle of *différance* to formulate a postmodern atheology based on the Christian idea of *kenosis* (self-emptying) wherein all fixed metaphysical centers including the transcendent God of theocentrism and the independent self of egocentrism are completely emptied out into a network of differential relationships.

7. Derrida, *On Grammatology*, tr. G. C. Spivak (Baltimore: John Hopkins University Press, 1974), 60–61.

8. Asada Akira, *Kōzō to chikara: kigoron o koete* (Structure and Power: Beyond Semiotics) (Tokyo: Keisō shobō, 1983).

9. See Marilyn Ivy, "Critical Texts, Mass Artifacts: The Consumption of Knowledge in Postmodern Japan" in *South Atlantic Quarterly* 87/3 (Summer 1988; special issue on "Postmodernism and Japan"), 424. This issue of *South Atlantic Quarterly* was reprinted with some changes as Masao Miyoshi and H. D. Harootunian, eds., *Postmodernism and Japan* (Durham: Duke University Press, 1989).

10. Transcribed discussion of Asada Akira, Jacques Derrida, Karatani Kōjin, "Chōshōhi shakai to chishikijin no yakuwari" ("The Ultra-Consumer Society and the Role of the Intellectual"), *Asahi jaanaru* (Asahi Journal) (25 May 1984). Also see Marilyn Ivy, "Critical Texts, Mass Artifacts," 438.

11. Karatani Kōjin, "Ri no hihan: shisho ni okeru puremodan to posuto-modan" ("The Critique of Confucian Principle: Premodern and Postmodern in Philosophy") in *Gendaishi techo* (May 1985), 40. Cited by J. Victor Koschmann, "Maruyama Masao and the Incomplete Project of Modernity" in *South Atlantic Quarterly* 87/3 (Summer 1988), 506.

12. Ibid.

13. Marilyn Ivy, "Critical Texts, Mass Artifacts," 438.

14. Transcribed discussion of Asada Akira, Jacques Derrida, Karatani Kōjin, "Chōshōhi shakai to chishikijin no yakuwari," 8–9. Cited by Marilyn Ivy, "Critical Texts, Mass Artifacts," 439.

15. Robert Magliola, *Derrida on the Mend* (Indiana: Purdue University Press, 1984), 89. While arguing for the analogy between Buddhist *śūnyatā* and Derrida's *différance*, Magliola argues for not only a "Buddhist differentialism" but also for what he calls a "Christian differentialism" based on trinitarian notions of God. He relates "Christian differentialism" to *kenosis* (self-emptying) theology based on Philippians 2:5–11. In the Kyoto school of Japanese philosophy, Nishida Kitarō, Nishitani Keiji, and Masao Abe have also developed a Christian/Buddhist differentialism based on the *kenosis/śūnyatā* motif. See also my article on *"Kenosis* as a Foundation for Buddhist-Christian Dialogue" in *The Eastern Buddhist* 20/1 (Spring 1987).

16. Magliola, *Derrida on the Mend*, 103.

17. Ibid., 104.

18. Ibid., 88.

19. Ibid., 89.

20. Odin, *"Kenosis* as a Foundation for Christian-Buddhist Dialogue." See especially 51–54, wherein I articulate the *kenosis/śūnyatā* motif in relation to postmodern strategies of "decentering" as developed by Nishida, Nishitani and Abe of the Kyoto school.

21. Nishida Kitarō, *Last Writings: Nothingness and the Religious Worldview*, tr. David A. Dilworth (Honolulu: University of Hawaii Press, 1987). See translator's Postscript on "Nishida's Logic of the East," 137.

22. Derrida, *On Grammatology*. See G. C. Spivak's Translator's Preface, which discusses Derrida's idea of *aporia* (a contradiction, an irreconcilable paradox) as having the logic form of "both is and yet is not."

23. Nishitani Keiji, *Shūkyō to wa nanika* (What is Religion?) (Tokyo: Sobunsha, 1961; 2nd edition 1984). The English edition is *Religion and Nothingness*, tr. Jan Van Bragt (Berkeley: University of California Press, 1982).

24. Ibid., E.228/J.250.

25. Ibid., E.233/J.256.

26. Ibid., E.124/J.140.

27. Ibid., E.215/J.236.

28. Abe, "Kenotic God and Dynamic Śūnyatā" (delivered at the Second Conference on East-West Religious Encounter, "Paradigm Shifts in Buddhism and Christianity" held in Honolulu, Hawaii, 3–11 January 1984; expanded and revised version), 45; published in John Cobb and Christopher Ives, eds., *The Emptying God: A Buddhist-Jewish-Christian Conversation* (Maryknoll, NY: Orbis, 1990), 3–65.

29. Ibid., 45.

30. Ibid., 41.

31. Ibid., 50.

32. Margot Norris, *The Decentered Universe of Finnegans Wake* (Baltimore: John Hopkins University Press, 1974).

33. Noel Burch, *To the Distant Observer: Form and Meaning in the Japanese Cinema* (Berkeley: University of California Press, 1979).

34. David Pollack, *The Fracture of Meaning: Japan's Synthesis of China from the Eighth through the Eighteenth Centuries* (Princeton: Princeton University Press, 1986). Pollack argues that the *différance* or "fracture of meaning" in the dislocated Japanese text is located in the unique *wakan* or "Japanese/Chinese" dialect between the antithesis of alien form and native content.

35. Harootunian, *Things Seen and Unseen: Discourse and Ideology in Tokugawa Nativism* (Chicago: University of Chicago Press, 1988). This work analyzes Tokugawa "nativism" (*kokugaku*) as a form of discourse from the standpoint of postmodern semiotic theories of textuality.

36. Roland Barthes, "From the Work to the Text," in J. H. Harari, ed., *Textual Strategies* (Ithaca, New York: Cornell University Press, 1979), 75–76.

37. de Saussure, *Course in General Linguistics*, 16.

38. Roland Barthes, *Empire of Signs*, tr. Richard Howard (New York: Hill and Wang, 1982), 78.

39. Ibid., 22.

40. Ibid.

41. Ibid., 30.

42. Ibid., 109.

43. Ibid., 108.

44. Burch, *To the Distant Observer*, 13.

45. Barthes, *Empire of Signs*, 49.

46. Burch, *To the Distant Observer*, 72.

47. Richard B. Pilgrim, "*Ma*: A Cultural Paradigm," in *Chanoyu Quarterly: Tea and the Arts of Japan* 45 (1986), 32; also published in *History of Religions* 25/3 (1986).

48. Ibid., 39.

49. Ibid., 47.

50. Ibid., 45.

51. Ibid., 48.

52. Ibid., 44.

53. Ibid., 43.

54. Joseph Riddel, "Decentering the Image," in *Textual Strategies*, 332.

55. Derrida, *On Grammatology*, 90.

56. Ibid., 92.

57. Ibid.

58. Riddel, "Decentering the Image," 339.

59. Ibid.

60. Ibid.

61. Ibid., 341.

62. Ibid.

63. Ibid., 344.

64. Ibid., 358.

65. Friedrich Nietzsche, *The Will to Power*, tr. W. Kaufman and R. J. Hollingdale (New York: Vintage Books, 1968), 267.

66. Ryunosuke Akūtagawa, *Rashomon and Other Stories*, tr. Takashi Kojima (Tokyo: Charles E. Tuttle, 1952). See "In a Grove," 13–25; and "Rashomon," 26–34.

67. Cited by Makoto Ueda, *Modern Japanese Writers* (Stanford: Stanford University Press, 1976), 129.

68. Ibid., 130. Also, see Akutagawa Ryūnosuke, "Autumn Mountain," tr. Ivan Morris in Ivan Morris, ed., *Modern Japanese Stories: An Anthology* (Tokyo: Charles E. Tuttle, 1962), 173–84.

69. Dudley Andrew, *Film in the Aura of Art* (Princeton: Princeton University Press, 1984). See chapter 10 on "The Passion of Identification in the Late Films of Kenji Mizoguchi," 186–87.

24 Steve Odin

70. Sōseki Natsume, *Kusamakura* (Grass Pillow, 1906) in *Sōseki zenshū* (Tokyo: Iwanami shoten, 1925), vol. 2. For a recent paperback edition see *Kusamakura* (Tokyo: Kodansha, 1972).

71. Natsume Sōseki, *The Three-Cornered World*, tr. Alan Turney (Tokyo: Tuttle, 1984).

72. Sōseki Natsume, *Yo ga Kusamakura* (My Grass Pillow) in *Sōseki zenshū: Besatsu* (Tokyo: Iwanami shoten, 1925), vol. 14, 565–68, esp. 567. Sōseki's essay first appeared in *Bunsho sekai*, November 1906.

73. Miyoshi, *Accomplices of Silence: The Modern Japanese Novel* (Berkeley: University of California Press, 1974).

8/1997

consider examining "power and authority in a decentered universe"; multiple perspectives and the irreducibility of plural meanings (p 19)

useful in discussions of Rashomon, Ozu and Soseki; defining interplay between author/audience and notion of image

Power and Authority Contemporary Japan

Chapter Two

Ie-Ism ("Sacred Familism") and the Discourse of Postmodernism in Relation to Nativism/Nationalism/Nihonism

STEVEN HEINE

Problematic: Decentrism versus Centrism

Postwar period discussions concerning the essential nature or character of Japan often revolve around the role of the family or household (*ie* 家), which is considered to have a sacred quality based on Confucian as well as Shinto and Buddhist influences that serves as a support for many other aspects of social behavior. Indeed, some argue that "translating the *ie* as 'family' or 'household' is inaccurate, for the *ie* incorporates far more than the ordinary connotations of either [English term] . . . providing an ongoing dynamic in which human beings located *in* space/time mutually interact with social order continuing *over* time."[1] The *ie* structure is quite complex and can be broken down into its internal or background (*uchi, ura*) and external or foreground (*soto, omote*) components.

A number of competing and at times conflicting or overlapping viewpoints have emerged in recent investigations. One viewpoint argues that the family system, which contributes to a group or communal mentality, is a singularly important factor in Japan's modern success as a highly advanced industrial and economically powerful Asian nation; that is, there is a direct structural link between the local family unit governed by a main household and the centralized, vertically oriented partriachal authority (*iemoto*, literally, family head) of large corporations and of family capitalism constituting "Japan, Inc."[2] Another argument is that the Japanese family unit has been a precursor and is currently a leader of the flexible, amorphous structure of the postmodern "network" society because of the decentric, horizontal lines of authority inherent in

25

the system. In one sense, these two arguments are opposite, with the first emphasizing centrism as a key to modernity and the second emphasizing decentrism as a key to postmodernity. Yet, in accord with what Kenzaburō Ōe refers to in his essay in this volume as a fundamentally dubious quality (*aimai-na*) that characterizes discourses about Japan, in another sense both arguments can be subsumed under a common discourse which valorizes the family system that is prized both for its integrity, consistency and continuity and for its adaptability in a contemporary context. These values are largely attributable to a Confucian sense of hierarchical loyalty, a Buddhist emphasis on patriarchal lineage in the transmission of tradition, and a Shinto view of the veneration of ancestry.

At the same time, other voices have taken a more critical view of the family system in the twentieth century. One of the critical views begins by lavishly praising the family ideal in Japanese tradition, but goes on to criticize the way the family institution tends to operate in a modern setting. This viewpoint makes a call for a renewal of traditional family life according to the antiquated village pattern prior to its corruption due to urbanization and the compartmentalization of functions in modern society. A very different critical view has been expressed in a number of sources, including several examples of contemporary art such as popular films in the 1980s, *Family Game* (*Kazoku Geimu*, 1984) and *The Funeral* (*O-Sōshiki*, 1987). According to these films, the family unit is a fragile, thin veneer concealing all sorts of internal turmoil and strife. When disturbed by some interruption in the normal routine like a funeral or the arrival of a tutor, the family irrupts in behavior that betrays underlying problems of manipulation, hypocrisy, greed, excessive drinking, openly committed adultery and other forms of abnormal or perverse behavior. The artistic portrayal of the problematics inherent in the dynamics of family life is supported by intellectual arguments that call into question and at times aggressively repudiate the "Japan is Number One" syndrome and the "myth of Japanese uniqueness." Furthermore, some critics point to an insidious, fundamentally scandalous agenda of support by the family structure for imperial Japan conceived as the "great family system" (*dai kazoku seido*).[3]

The first form of criticism, despite opposing the emphasis on the value of contemporary life, shares with the modern and postmodern standpoints a valorization of the family. Indeed, it may appear that the traditionalist view provides the ideological basis for some of the claims made by the other two standpoints which accept the fundamental valorization and extend its applications chronologically from past to present and future. The second form of criticism, however, signals the need to recognize the flaws in the system which must be overhauled by a genuine, thoroughgoing liberation from the romanticized illusions of traditionalist conceptions. From this standpoint, the nostalgic notion of the family in the traditional as well as in the modern and postmodern viewpoints is a mirage or an invention designed to legitimate either a particular sociopolitical agenda or to reflect an idealization of the Japanese nation. While all of the above views express an attitude or judgment, pro or con, about familism, another perspective based on a social scientific model has attempted an impartial, objective observation and analysis of the family in terms of ethnographic and statistical studies as well as the textual examination of relevant documents, such as the corporate codes of Tokugawa-era merchant families and the Meiji Civil Code. Yet the question can be asked whether pure neutrality or objectivity is at all possible in the context of the heated ideological debates generated by the other arguments.

Four Discourses

Do these perspectives enhance or simply contradict one another? How is it possible to make sense out of the multiple interpretations of the same phenomenon? My aim in this paper is to reflect on the implications involved in the conceptual notions or the discourses about *ie* particularly in terms of recent discussions of Japan and postmodernism. I will consider the question of whether, as some interpreters have claimed, Japan fulfills postmodernist ideals of decentric textuality and the ongoing function of floating signifiers devoid of a transcendental signified; that is, whether Japan is uncentered at its root and in its multiple cultural manifestations. In doing so, I will begin with two disclaimers. First, I am not so much concerned with the actual institution of the family in a sociological sense as with the discourses on familism, that is, with the rhetorical structure and impact of the utterances and arguments concerning the family found in a variety of sources, including folklore and social scientific studies in addition to the works of artists, literary and social critics as well as nationalist and nativist thinkers East and West. In other words, my concern is with the ways that the hermeneutic issues of how to interpret source materials are intimately related to and tend to supersede the so-called substantive questions of how to observe and describe phenomena free of interpretation. At the same time, however, I want to emphasize that rhetoric needs to be grounded in concrete observation so long as the limits of the observability are clearly defined.

The second disclaimer acknowledges that at first glance linking familism with postmodernism appears to be an odd or even self-contradictory goal since discussions of *ie* tend to emerge from a very different type of discourse, one located at the opposite end of the ideological spectrum from postmodernism. This is a discourse generated by traditionalist claims stemming from Tokugawa nativist (*kokugaku*) doctrines and also associated with prewar nationalist (*kokutai*) rhetoric concerning the uniqueness and integrity of Japanese traditions that goes under the rubric today of *nihonjinron* theory, or "Nihonism" (or "Japanism").[4] Nihonist discourse stresses the flexible yet cohesive role of *ie* in Japanese society precisely because of its strict and consistent adherence to hierarchical structure revolving around the centralizing authority of the *iemoto*, or patriarch, and these values seem to be the inverse of the non-hierarchical, non-logocentric postmodernist view. But it is just this apparent polarity, which is somewhat deceptive and elusive, that needs to be encountered in order to test the strengths and limits of the postmodernist position by highlighting several similarities underlying the two perspectives. For example, as indicated above, the traditionalist view could be seen as the base or foundation, often concealed, out of which the postmodernist (and modernist) arguments are formed.

One way of coming to terms with the apparent polarity between centrism and decentrism is to consider these perspectives in light of a third area of discourse, which is another form of postmodernism that exposes and deconstructs the apparent myths in the first two perspectives by uncovering the underlying, suppressed connections between them. The second form of postmodernism based on deconstructivism shares a methodological orientation with the first type of postmodernism based on decentrism in that both seek to overcome logocentric tendencies in Western onto-theological and sociopolitical ideologies. Yet these two forms of postmodernism are also polarized in that they take opposite attitudes toward the Japanese tradition and its view of familism, with one favoring the tradition as an incipient anti-logocentrism and the other criticizing the tradition as a heightened though disguised form of logocentrism. Furthermore, these three highly charged perspectives—Nihonism, decentric postmodernism and deconstuctive postmodernism—must be seen in light of a fourth area of inquiry that is based on objective textual critical and social scientific evidence originating from the Tokugawa era concerning the nature and status of *ie-shakai* (household society). In contrast to the first three discourses, the fourth type seeks, though by no means with unvarying success, a neutral attitude devoid of judgment.

Therefore, in examining the question of postmodernism and familism, it will be necessary to analyze the relation between four forms of discourse that coexist in shifting alliances and polarities: traditionalism, social scientific/textual studies, and two types of postmodernism. My main argument is that the key to understanding the connection between these four discourses is the enigmatic role of hiddenness (*hiden*) or concealment lying at the heart of the *ie/iemoto* structure and giving rise to a foundational con-centrism in Japanese society, which must be interpreted in terms of interacting, hierarchical horizontal and vertical levels that generate both centric and decentric discourses. The strengths and limitations in the Nihonist and postmodernist discourses can be evaluated in terms of their respective ability and failure to come to terms with the significance of hiddenness. In order to clarify the reasons why the hidden (rather than empty) center is often misrepresented and idealized as exemplifying decentrism, I will discuss the relation between the hermeneutic issue of interpretation and the substantive issue of description by stressing the ongoing dynamic interplay between multiple forms of discourse.

First, to highlight the basic polarity between the two discourses of decentric postmodernism and centrist Nihonism/traditionalism, let us consider the following two hypothetical propositions:

First Proposition (Decentrism): Japan is the paradigmatic postmodern country (assuming the alliteration is not oxymoronic) because it is constituted by an "empire of signs" which create a conjunction of simultaneously discontinuous, open and dissymmetrical semiotic fields.

Second Proposition (Centrism): Japan is the traditionalist country par excellence because in the face of the inevitable changes wrought by the combined forces of modernization, industrialization, Westernization and secularization it has determinedly maintained its allegiance to the tradition of the "family system" (*kazoku seido*) which is the key to its success in an ever competitive world.

First Discourse: Decentric Postmodernism

The first proposition, initially expressed by Roland Barthes in his
1970 work, *Empire of Signs*, written as a philosophical reflection
and commentary on his recent lecture tour of Japan, seeks to read
Japan as an uninterrupted text that is perpetually fluid and lacking
solidity. Japan, according to Barthes, is "tapestried with opening,
framed with emptiness and framing nothing, decorated,"[5] yet
uncentered such that the free play of signs takes priority over the
content or substance supposedly lying behind them. The nation's
people and culture are in every instance characterized by division,
dissymmetry, discontinuity and difference, qualities seen not as
problematic in the sense of creating disorder but as the resolution of
human problems by fostering an alternative or decentric orderliness.
Barthes points out numerous examples of decentric floating
signifiers in Japanese culture ranging from the sublime to the ridiculous. These include: cuisine (serving sushi and sukiyaki); everyday
customs (bowing and gift-wrapping, stationery and stations); social
geography (maps and addresses); the literary (calligraphy and poetry),
performing (Bunraku and Noh), and structural arts (architecture and
city planning); and the religio-philosophical traditions (Zen Buddhist notions of *satori* and *haiku*-composition). He also uses several
intriguing visual images to illustrate his semiotic reading of Japan,
such as a photograph of Shikidai gallery in Nijo castle in Kyoto,
which does not appear altered when turned upside down, and a
birds-eye view map of Tokyo (figure 1),[6] which appears to lack any
center, or has an empty center representing the location of public
park grounds surrounding the moat-encircled imperial palace gardens that are generally forbidden and inaccessible to the public.
    Barthes contrasts the fullness at the center of the typical West-
ern city, symbolized by a cluster of cathedrals, government and/or
financial buildings, with the evaporated notion of center in the
Japanese capital that is a continually expanding ideogram revolving
around a sacred "nothing."[7] His comments on the fullness of the
center of the Western city recall Joseph Campbell's discussion in
The Power of Myth about the historical transition in the focal point
of European and American cities from late medieval cathedrals
(reflecting the authority of the church) to early modern princely
capitol buildings (the state) to modern financial high-rise structures
(corporate capitalism).[8] Furthermore, Barthes' remarks about the
decentric ideogram of the Japanese capital are supported by architect
Ashihara Yoshinobu's view of Tokyo as an "amoeba city" with ill-

Fig. 1. Tokyo (from Barthes, *The Empire of Signs*, 81).

defined boundaries sprawling in every direction reflecting constant change like the pulsating body of an organism in a way that contrasts with the stagnation and rigidity in the West.[9] According to Ashihara, the city of Tokyo is the dwelling of a giant, ever-expanding family, so that "each house is a private bedroom. The city becomes a mammoth cluster of 'bedrooms' interspersed with 'family rooms' (parks), 'parlors' (office buildings), 'entryways' (airports, harbors), and the like."[10] Barthes also seems to be in accord with the Kyoto school philosophy of Nishida Kitarō and his followers, who emphasize that Japanese culture is based on absolute nothingness (*zettai mu*) rather than being (*yū*), and on an intuitive grasp of the "formless and voiceless" rather than concrete things. Although Barthes does not deal specifically with the topic of familism, he apparently feels that the base of the family system is a perpetually creative void. His understanding of the relation between palace and polity, emperor and commoner reflected in his interpretation of the Tokyo ideographic map as a prime example of decentric discourse makes an important though indirect statement on the family that I will later critically discuss in light of Tokugawa era feudal hierarchy.

One of the most significant features of Barthes' approach for understanding the connection between postmodernism and Nihonism is his methodological statement in the opening pages of the book. Here Barthes makes two significant points. First, he issues a disclaimer, not only about his lack of background in Japanology, but also about his lack of interest in or need to be tied to the actuality of Japan in his comments. "I am not lovingly gazing toward an Oriental essence," he maintains, "to me the Orient is a matter of indifference, merely providing a reserve of features whose manipulation—whose invented interplay—allows me to 'entertain' the idea of an unheard-of symbolic system, one altogether detached from our own."[11] Barthes cautions the reader to interpret his writings not as a conventional historical, philosophical or literary depiction of Japan or Japanese culture, but as a deliberate attempt to invent a personal "system" that happens to use images and themes of the "other," which in this case coincides with some features of Japan. While some have ignored Barthes' warning and taken his depiction of Japan literally, and some have simply granted him license to say whatever he wants without being subject to criticism, others may have gone to another extreme of assuming that his work is not relevant to Japan at all. In a sense, Barthes is an example of latter-day "japonisme" that swept European artistic and literary circles a century before. But I think that the key to Barthes' methodology is not whether he is really dealing with Japan—after all, he is—but his effort to disclaim (several years prior to Edward Said's publication[12]) the discourse of "Orientalism" with its colonialist and racist overtones and essentialist paradigms, and to create self-consciously a set of proposals that qualifies as a postmodern narrative discourse.

It is also important to note how Barthes asserts that a main feature of his semiotic postmodern discourse is its conjunction with his demythologized view of Zen enlightenment and creative expression. For Barthes, writing and images are not "explanations" and "illustrations" but floating signs, empty of center, bringing on "the onset of a kind of visual uncertainty, analogous perhaps to that *loss of meaning* Zen calls a *satori*,"[13] which is expressed in a variety of artistic forms, including calligraphy, poetry, tea ceremony and swordsmanship. The implication is that Zen has anticipated and guided the way to the decentric postmodern perspective, and in that sense Barthes has discovered an Oriental essence in spite of disavowing just that effort.

Second Discourse: Centralization in Nihonism

While the effort to fashion a narrative that purposefully takes liberty with its source material is a matter of pride for Barthes in overcoming the Western tendency to stereotype the Orient, a similar discursive orientation also seems to underly and yet at the same time to be deliberately concealed by the Nihonist perspective on the role of *ie* in Japanese history and contemporary society. The Nihonist discourse on *ie* was initially formulated by researchers in social science, beginning first and foremost with folklore studies (Yanagita Kunio), then continuing with social anthropology (Chie Nakane), historical sociology (Murakami Yasusuke) and social psychiatry (Doi Takeo). It has also received considerable attention from intellectual historians, including Watsuji Tetsurō in his writings contrasting Japanese and Western ethics and some of his followers such as Kumon Shimpei, who has collaborated with Murakami in a major study of *ie*-ism.[14] According to this perspective, *ie*, also referred to as *kazoku-seido* (family system), *maki* (enclosed social unit), or *dōzoku* (collective family or extended kin group containing a *honke*, main family, and *bunke*, branch families), is more than a simple conjugal family in the customary sense found in contemporary Japan or elsewhere. Rather, it is an economic and political structure not strictly linked to and extending well beyond blood-line relatives, for it includes unrelated persons who are adopted or incorporated into the unit and who enjoy full privileges including the possibility of inheriting the lineage. It also functions as a pattern or model of social behavior that is considered "the basic principle on which Japanese society is built," which "penetrate[s] every nook and cranny of Japanese society,"[15] including organizations as large as mammoth prewar corporations (*zaibatsu*) and as small as local clubs and associations, as well as everything in between from baseball teams to political organizations. These are all based on a moral code involving elements from Shinto, Buddhist and especially Confucian values stressing sacred hierarchy and loyalty to ritualized authority. *Ie*-ism is especially important in artistic traditions which are transmitted by virtue of lineage inheritance, such as tea, flower arranging and martial arts, and even antistructural social organizations ranging from the *yakuza* to millenialist religious movements maintain their identity based on principles of the *iemoto* structure. In addition to group-oriented structures, the centralizing agency of *ie/ iemoto* lineage also appears in individualistic, counter-ideological trends such as meditation or mountain ascetic traditions. Both structure and antistructure derive from the sacralizing power of familism that generates an ideology demanding loyalty to persons and collectivism rather than to ideas or words.

Ie is generally credited in Nihonist works for its uniqueness, in that a similar social unit focusing on lineage rather than blood does not exist currently even in China, and for its inherent flexibility and adaptability, because it is a key to the survival and postwar success of group-conscious Japan. It is seen as the driving spiritual force of Japan's economic boom that represents a highly modernized version of the ideal Edo social unit.[16] Furthermore, *ie*, which was legally recorded in the Meiji Civil Code lasting from 1898–1947 as a microcosm of the oligarchy of the state, is said to foster values of communal loyalty and a self-sacrificing attitude that stem from an individual's affiliation with an expansive structure generating an innate mystical or intuitive unity of consciousness among all those who participate. The mystical unity is referred to in a variety of notions, including *ishin-denshin* (transmitting ideas from mind-to-mind), *amae* (intimacy and dependence), *ma* (presencing through spatial/temporal absences) and *haragei* (the unspoken way). Doi stresses that while the *ie* structure emphasizes publicness and the importance of maintaining an outer behavioral side or face (*omote, tatemae, kao*), it also helps preserve an interior world of intimacy and privacy (*ura, honne, kokoro*). These two dimensions may conflict but, when the mystical unity of *ie*-ism is preserved, they ideally result in an appropriate state of social harmony (*wa*).

One of the most detailed examinations of familism is Murakami's analysis of the four structural elements of the proto-*ie* that originally grew out of the *uji* (clan) structure, which served an earlier, agrarian or rice-cultivation culture. According to Murakami, the transition from clan to household that took place beginning in the medieval period was based on an inner developmental dynamic that generated countrywide social change, and it represents the key to understanding how Japanese "family civilization" (*bunrei toshite no ie shakai*) differs from European feudalism. The four elements he identifies are: (1) kin-tract-ship, which indicates that membership can be based either on kinship or social contract;[17] (2) stem linearity, or an emphasis on the perpetuation of the family as a corporate entity; (3) functional hierarchy, which organizes all the functionally differentiated strata in terms of a commonly shared goal; and (4) relative self-sufficiency, or the political and economic autonomy of each *ie* unit accompanied by a vertical rather than horizontal division of society as a whole. These features make the *ie*-structure a complex behavioral model tending toward achievement-mobility-homogeneity-efficiency. Ironically, the fourth feature—referring to the autonomy of each individual vertically-oriented family unit—suggests a decentralizing trend or the existence of multiple centers. Yet the third feature—the functional hierarchy of the entire system—indicates that these vertical centers are perpetually hierarchically sublated according to a horizontal orientation by more fundamental levels of authority with a diminishing number of centers until, perhaps, there is a single, well-protected center as emphasized—though for different reasons—in Barthes' Tokyo ideogram.

While there is no question about the importance of *ie* as a social unit, especially since the class-oriented Tokugawa era, the Nihonist approach has been accused of veiling itself in the pretext of a social scientific methodology in order to put forward an ideological and in many cases, especially before the war, a political agenda. For example, Murakami's arguments, which trace the roots of *ie* back to an epoch prior to Tokugawa to highlight the strength of the household in the transition Japan made into the industrial world as seen in critical comparison with Europe, are probably not really valid as sociological observations. Rather, they could largely be considered an ideological reworking and idealization of a once discredited prewar nationalist doctrine and civil code that was obedient to the imperial version of history and still has totalitarian overtones. According to Masao Miyoshi and H. D. Harootunian, the rise of Nihonism corresponds to Japanese prosperity so that

> it became evident that one of the enabling factors of this economic order was the recycling of the older elements in the national myth

of racial homogeneity and familial consensuality, symbolized by
the imperial family, that were capable of eliminating opposition
and criticism and allowing claims to cultural uniqueness.[18]

The Nihonist approach may seem like a throwback to the
quasi-mystical doctrine of the divine unity of language (*kotodama*,
literally soul or spirit of words) and nation (*yamatodamashii*) in
order to prove a cultural exceptionalism contrasting everything
purely Japanese with all forms of vulgarization that are exported by
the West.[19] Nihonism tends to overlook or dismiss the historical
impact of foreignness or of political manipulation that disrupts the
twin thesis of uniqueness and productivity—for example, the roots
of *ie/iemoto* found in Chinese Confucian-influenced lineal traditions and in Buddhist esotericism as well as the influence of the
politico-economic Heian/Kamakura *sōryō* system of leadership and
inheritance.[20] In addition, it has been pointed out that *ishin-denshin*
was originally a Zen doctrine that came to be idealized and taken
out of context by Nihonism so as to be applied to other aspects of
Japanese culture without a proper recognition of the historical context of the notion.[21] Furthermore, Murakami neglects to analyze
what may be an innate weakness in his fourth element referring to
the autonomy of discrete *ie* units which have great difficulty in
merging with other units because of an inherent vertical divisive-
ness. This autonomy, when combined with the determined pursuit
of the survival of lineal hierarchy in the second and third elements,
can result in the hardening of *ie* into an ascription-rigidity-inequal-
ity-traditionalism behavioral complex that undermines the
flexibility and adaptability Murakami and others admire,[22] resulting
in a variety of social disorders, such as high rates of stress and family
suicides.

Underlying Similarities

Despite obvious differences in outlook, there are several fundamental affinities linking the decentric postmodern and Nihonist/tradi-
tionalist discourses about *ie* in relation to the issue of centrism.
First, both viewpoints seem to constitute an "ism" in the sense that
they are not descriptive but rhetorical strategies; for Barthes'
postmodernism this is a deliberate and self-conscious choice,
whereas for Nihonism the choice is deliberately or in some cases
unconsciously concealed in an attempt to legitimate a highly
charged ideology by surrounding it with the aura of objective sociology. Also, although the premodern and the postmodern discourses
are not intended to reflect perspectives relative to actual chronol-

ogy, both perspectives could be considered a form of antimodern, neo-conservative romanticism with an ironic commitment to linear teleology. Nihonism asserts the priority of the past in terms of a declining modern civilization and postmodernism asserts the priority of the future surpassing the deficiencies of modernity.

But the main affinity is that both discourses represent a valorization of the Japanese ethos and its multiple manifestations whereby anything Japanese comes to be praised as either purely traditional or paradigmatically postmodern. Nihonism and postmodernism become mirror images that reflect and require one another: postmodernism sees Japanese traditions as an incipient form that have been ever awaiting the appropos time for fulfillment as postmodern paradigms; and traditionalism seeks to legitimate its argument concerning innate adaptability by pointing, for example, to the way *ie-shakai* anticipates postmodern "network society"[23] in the distribution of information, by emphasizing the decentralizing, vertical autonomy feature of familism. While these underlying similarities tend to diffuse the sense of polarity between the two discourses, they also suggest the need to consider an alternative approach that is unbound by the tendency to uncritical valorization.

Third Discourse: Deconstructive Postmodernism

The connections—affinities and disharmonies—between postmodernism and Nihonism are brought into focus by contrasting these discourses with another form of postmodernism that seeks to expose their links to nativist and nationalist ideologies. The second form of postmodernism (which I will refer to as postmodernism-2) shares with the Barthesian form previously discussed (or postmodernism-1) a methodological emphasis on disclosing the uncentered or groundless discursive ground at the base of all rhetorical strategies. Both types of postmodernism stress the overcoming of logocentrism through a recognition of the universality of text by virtue of the role of intertextuality seen in terms of the inseparability of author and reader as well as the interconnectedness of historiography and interpretation as forms of narrative discourse. The difference is that postmodernism-2 stresses the need for an archaeology of knowledge that emphatically and pervasively deconstructs logocentric tendencies not only in traditionalism, but in each and every discourse which claims hegemony at the expense of marginalized voices, including the ideological projections at the root of the decentric postmodern discourse. Thus, while the methodologies of the two postmodern discourses are very similar in terms of highlighting the role of disjuncture and discontinuity in evaluating traditions, when seen in light of Nihonism it seems that their conclusions are nearly opposite in that postmodernism-1 valorizes Japan and postmodernism-2 debunks this valorization. This contrast reorients the apparent polarity of centrism versus decentrism involving the postmodernism-1 and Nihonism discourses, which are based on many of the same ideological commitments that are self-validating and therefore self-negating. The real polarity, then, is not between centrism and decentrism, but rather between deconstructivism and the affinities in the decentric/centric views.

The distinction made above between two types of postmodernist discourse—one affirmative/valorizing and the other negative/refuting—does not refer only to the case of Japanology and Japanese culture but applies to the full range of topics dealt with by postmodern criticism. However, in the case of Japan, a special factor that seems to heighten the discrepancy is the prevalence of *nihonjinron* theory and the question of unconscious participation on the part of postmodernism-1 in "reverse Orientalism," "where, instead of denigrating the Other, the Other is recuperated, wholesale, often without discrimination."[24] Orientalism tends to restructure itself in many diguises and reversals, including the discourses of Occidentalism or reverse Orientialism, which makes any attempt at de-structuring or attaining a standpoint of de-Orientalism that much more difficult. From the standpoint of postmodernism-2, postmodernism-1 fails to escape the seductive grip of the tentacles of Orientalism. The aim of postmodernism-2 is to uproot the apparently mythic claims about the uniqueness of Japanese society, including those involving the role of familism, by exercising a thoroughgoing hermeneutics of suspicion or incredulity that exposes the *kokutai*-oriented source of ideological exaggerations and idealizations. According to this hermenutic approach, Nihonist claims are not only misguided, but are dangerous both for the Japanese people and for other cultures with which they wish to establish harmonious communication and productive relations.[25] For example, Roy Miller argues, "the potential of . . . Japan's modern myth for causing serious, often quite destructive, misunderstanding of contemporary Japanese life and culture still seems to be enormous . . . in generat(ing) even more serious international misunderstanding."[26] Peter Dale further highlights the political implications of the "myth of uniqueness" by maintaining that the literature on Japanese identity in which "tradition" is not understood as intellectual constructs but rather as objective descriptions of social mores . . . is the subtlest of instruments of ideological coercion, and a "self-fulfilling" prophecy since it reflects and conditions in turn manipulated categories and modes of expression diffused for the discussion of how the Japanese are supposed to perceive themselves. Such an enculturation of political discourse is potentially a more powerful form of social control than prewar "thought policing" since, though demonstrably heir to the ideological patrimony of Japanese fascism, the ideological roots of these ideas have been forgotten, while the ideas themselves are hailed as new conceptualisations and ethnological descriptions of Japanese realities.[27]

Although postmodernism-2 is often effective in probing the meta-epistemological or meta-discursive question of why, from the standpoint of gaining power and approval, all discourses, including postmodernism-1, say what they say,[28] there seem to be two limitations in the deconstructivist approach for understanding familism: methodological and historical. The methodological problematic is that deconstructivism may go to an extreme in being overly critical or negative concerning issues of Japanese identity and centrism. While postmodernism-1 seems to legitimate each aspect of Japan as incipient decentrism, postmodernism-2 tends to reject every claim as a thinly veiled political ideology. But does deconstructive postmodernism escape from, or does it in some ways recreate, the original Orientalism (prior to any recognition of the syndrome), which dismisses the expressions by the Orient about itself as so much fluff and fantasy? It is imperative to root out the weeds of one's participation, conscious or unconscious, in Orientalism or reverse Orientalism, but it is equally important to be wary of "reverse Occidentalism." The critic must not place him or her self in a privileged position that contributes to, in the name of assessing, the rhetorical and ideological damage of misplaced commitments. A middle ground may be to focus not so much on legitimating or debunking myths as on clarifying the "*enigma* of Japanese power."[29] It also appears worthwhile to focus not on the question of uniqueness—after all, Japan, like every other culture, is unique though perhaps not as unique as some Japanese like to think it is—but on a more neutrally framed issue of historical consistency as seen from the standpoint of cultural relativism rather than the extremes of cultural exceptionalism or refutation.

The second problematic in deconstructivism is historical. Postmodernism-2 accuses Nihonism of exaggerating or idealizing history by creating the image of a mythic past. It also critiques postmodernism-1 for being oblivious to the historical context of its own discourse. Yet postmodernism-2 also may also be faulted for using history selectively and presumptively, as a means to its own ends, in that it tends to put an overemphasis on discerning the roots of Nihonism in the Meiji Civil Code, when the family was legally systematized, and in Taishō *kokutai* ideology, when the family system was explicitly politicized.[30] Rather than restrict the focus to the modern period, it seems to be more fruitful to take a broader view of the historical development of familism by discovering the lines of behavioral continuity between Tokugawa and contemporary society.

Fourth Discourse: Textual and Social Scientific Evidence of the Hidden Center

The significance of the fourth area of discourse based on an attempt to carry out objective, observational studies is that it provides ample evidence of a fundamental and pervasive continuity in family behavior patterns extending from early modern to current times based on two kinds of sources. The first source is textual materials that antedate and offer a context for understanding the Meiji code, such as Tokugawa-era *zaibatsu* corporate family codes, which in stressing values such as loyalty, diligence, probity and respect for hierarchy could be considered to constitute a *chōnindō* (way of the townsmen) ethic[31] that at once incorporates and complements samurai values in the *bushidō* code of honor. The second source is twentieth-century social scientific studies, especially by non-Japanese scholars who may have been subconsciously influenced but are at least not explicitly associated with *nihonjinron* theory. These include John Embree's prewar study of rural villages, Ronald Dore's postwar study of urban neighborhoods, and Francis Hsu's account of the role of the *iemoto* in the recent economic boom.[32] By grounding its arguments in the observation of source materials, the social scientific approach is able critically to assess the pros and cons of other discourses in a way that is different from the kind of critique offered by postmodernism-2. For example, social historian John Hall, who is otherwise quite critical of Nihonism, supports the enduring influence of Murakami's four elements of familism by highlighting their impact on business practices in today's corporate houses. He points out, for example, that kin-tract-ship is analogous to lifetime employment guarantees, stem linearity to the eternal continuation of the firm, functional hierarchy to seniority and advancement systems, and autonomy to intra-firm welfare systems.[33]

But at the same time, social scientific and textual studies are not primarily concerned with verifying or refuting either Nihonism or postmodernism. Rather, they perhaps point to a way out of the debate between centrism and decentrism by suggesting the interconnectedness of horizontal and vertical dimensions (corresponding to Murakami's third and fourth elements) that indicate the role of a finely cultivated hiddenness and secrecy as the source of authority at the heart of familism. According to this perspective, it is important to recognize two main points. The first point is that there are multiple, coexisting, vertical *ie* centers. The polycentric quality is illustrated by considering the following map (figure 2) of the subcenters of Tokyo, which developed out of traditional neighborhoods and villages eventually linked by mass transit and commercial systems, with descriptions of their individual character.[34]

The second point is that the multiple centers with independent lines of authority are based on the secret knowledge (*hiden*) and protected power of the *iemoto*. Therefore, "The city is not 'empty' at the center, but is instead focused on a deeply solemn place filled with history and cultural meaning."[35] Hsu explains, for example, that the secretive traditions preserve and protect the authority and wisdom of patriarchal authority in that they are "marked by all-inclusive and nearly unbreakable command-allegiance, succoring-dependence relationships between senior and junior, or superior and subordinate."[36] Allan Grapard further describes the discursive efficacy and continuity of the rhetoric of mystery:

> Secrecy and social organization appear on the surface to be surprising companions. Nonetheless, secrecy is fundamentally tied to the spread and use of knowledge and information, as well as to power and patterns of authority such as master-disciple relationships and the formulation or manufacture of truth . . . in houses (*ie*) within which a certain type of knowledge was jealously kept and transmitted through a series of initiations.[37]

However, the phenomenon of hiddenness holds sway not only in selected mystery traditions. Rather, it is the case that the secrecy, or at least the symbolism of familial secrecy, is the fundamental paradigm that has a resonace in every level of Japanese society from the largest and most expansive to the smallest and most localized units. The *iemoto* structure fosters exclusive, hierarchical and non-rational bonding relations as found in artistic and esoteric traditions, which constitute a "way" (*dō* or *michi*) of self-discipline and

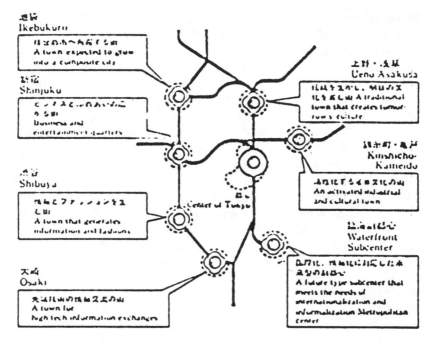

Fig. 2. Building Up of Tokyo Subcenters (From Roman Cybriwsky,
Tokyo, 211).

etiquette. But it is also evident in commercial companies, including
zaibatsu and mega-corporations, some of which have been both
praised for fostering communal loyalty and accused of exploiting
their workers by demanding excessive devotion to familist structures and values. The key factor is that the need for secrecy does not
reflect an incipient non-logocentric postmodern viewpoint but is
based on a complex array of social and political factors rooted in
Tokugawa society and extending through the war-time and postwar
periods. An interesting concrete, graphic illustration of the importance of hiddenness and secrecy in Tokugawa households is seen at
the Nijō Jin'ya estate in Kyoto. This estate was built by the Ogawa
family, which was at odds with the shogunate regime in the early
Tokugawa period. The building of the house incorporated many
ingenious devices to protect against arson and assassins, such as a
sprinkler system using water drawn from twelve interconnected
wells, trap doors, secret escape routes and hidden rooms with lad-
ders or stairs that could be pulled up to ensure the security of its
occupants.

Therefore, the family only appears to be decentric because the hidden center is overlooked by some interpreters, yet a view of monolithic centrism is also illusory because of the uncentering multiplicity of centralized units, each with a hidden center. Yet this is not a radical pluralism because the vertical expansion and addition of new *ie*, as in the development of small businesses (*kogaisha*) as branches (*bunke*) of major corportations or of numerous branches and streams (*ryū*) of religious movements, is invariably accompanied by a horizontal hierarchical sublation that reduces the number of centers to a single, all-encompassing center. According to Hsu, "all *iemoto* and independent actions are part of, or limited by, loyalty to the emperor,"[38] known in familial rhetoric as the all-pervasive "father's father" (*chichi no chichi*). In the Tokugawa era, the single center was of course Edo, which, as a castle town (*jōkamachi*), was elaborately concealed for purposes of defense. As Moriya Matsuhisa points out, "For all its economic importance as a consumption center, however, Edo was fundamentally a political city. It was a great castle town centered on Edo Castle, in which was located the bakufu, the political apparatus with the shogun at its peak.... Political and administrative information emanated from the bakufu, and the staff in every daimyo's Edo mansion collected the information and transmitted it to their own domain."[39] The town was basically designed as an extension of the castle's defenses with temples providing a maze of walls and imposing structures on the periphery, and with the spatial structure of the *shitamachi* (literally "downtown," but refers to the neighborhoods of the lower classes) and *yamanote* sectors (the central part of the city where the shogun and samurai dwelled) laid out to create a spiraling labyrinth of dead ends, T junctions, and narrow twisting lanes. The Tokugawa era map (figure 3)[40] shows how the distribution of residential areas was used to help promote lines of authority and modes of defense, with the castle surrounded by daimyo estates in the *yamanote* district that formed a buffer between the shogun and the townsmen located in the *shitamachi* district.[41]

Therefore, the concealed *ie/iemoto* structure is not to be considered a mystery cult that gives priority to initiation into a secret inner knowledge, for its primary aim is the projection of the *iemoto*'s authority from the center outward to maintain supervision and power. On the basis of this insight, the fourth discourse supports the postmodernism-2 critique of postmodernism-1, but for different reasons. It shows that in contrast to Barthes' decentric postmodernist view of Tokyo, the empty center, as revealed by

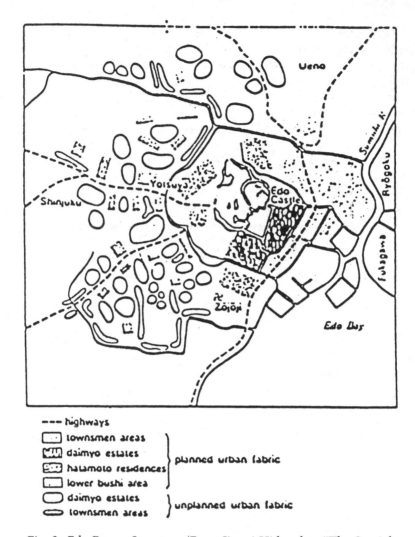

Fig. 3. Edo Power Structure (From Jinnai Hidenobu, "The Spatial
Structure of Edo," in *Tokugawa Japan*, 141).

social scientific studies, was originally a feudal castle. Furthermore,
the immaculate palace gardens were maze-like fortifications and the
expanding amoeba-like organism was a carefully crafted political
organization. The situation resonates throughout the system. Although the power of the Tokugawa shogunate was transferred to the
emperor in the Meiji era, and the imperial power is officially defunct
yet in many ways still viable since the war, this sense of the emptiness of power seems to be a far cry from what Barthes discusses as

decentrism. Thus, postmodernism-1 tends to obfuscate hiddenness and to superimpose images on a concealed center by not really asking why the center only appears to be empty.

Here, the fourth discourse's view converges with one of the main leftist critiques of the Kyoto school suggested by Asada Akira, who gained instant fame (referred to as the "AA phenomenon") in the early 1980s for his book, *Kōzō to chikara* (Structure and Power), which introduced French poststructuralist theories to Japan from a Marxist perspective heavily influenced by the works of Deleuze and Guattari. Asada points out that in the prewar work, *The Problems of Japanese Culture*, Nishida Kitarō distinguished between two forms of national power: power based on being (*yū*) reflected in European kings and nations, which contains conflict between individuals and the whole; and power based on nothingness (*mu*) as in the case of the Japanese emperor which, via the principle of absolute contradictory self-identity (*zettai mujunteki jiko dōitsu*), unifies particularism and universalism, atomism and holism from a "holonic" (*zentaishi*, in contrast to "holistic," *zentai*) standpoint ever capable of harmonizing differences. Ironically, the political power of the place of nothingness, according to Asada's critique, is perhaps best symbolized by the "empty space" of the imperial palace gardens in central Tokyo, which from this vantage point is the paradigm of the hidden, empty center (misread by Barthes as suggesting a decentric rather than totalitarian society). Asada remarks that Nishida's philosophy seems at first to be peaceful and pluralistic. But, he argues by referring to Kyoto school participation in wartime ideology that attempted to justify Japanese atrocities against other Asian countries, "when this [power of place] spontaneously spreads, the 'Great East Asian Coprosperity Sphere'—is this the absolute contradictory self-identity between liberation from European imperialism and aggression by Japanese imperialism—will be formed."[42]

Also, in contrast to the traditionalist paradigm of Nihonism, the center is deliberately displaced and disguised, or cloistered for a variety of social and political rather than mystical reasons. Since the center generally remains concealed to outside observers for reasons they do not comprehend, and their misunderstanding is compounded since they do not know what it is to which they have been denied access, it is neither the anti-metaphysical, non-logocentric text that postmodernism-1 romanticizes nor the liberating social template that Nihonists idealize. But, in contrast to the postmodernism-2 critique, the hidden center was intended originally not to be a subversive discourse inscrutable to "Orientalizing" outsiders, but to be indecipherable strategically to rivals who operated under the same hegemonic political assumptions. *Ie/iemoto* is a self-displacing horizontally hierarchical un-center, sublating yet generating multiple levels of autonomous vertical centrism. Thus the appearance of Japan as postmodernist is somewhat illusory, for Japan constitutes a multileveled con-centric interplay of centric and decentric elements, but not necessarily for the reasons described in the main discourses revolving around the complex yet disguised role of *ie/iemoto*.

Concluding Comments on Critical Methodology

To conclude, I will briefly discuss the link between the substantive issue concerning centrism versus decentrism and the methodological issue concerning the relation between competing yet overlapping modes of discourse that are used to explicate the first issue. In examining this connection, it seems that the substantive issue transforms itself into a methodological issue for two reasons. According to Nihonism, this is because the center is based not on physical but on mystical power that defies and undermines its own appearance. And according to both forms of postmodernism, the priority of the methodological issue is established because the emptiness of the center is a reflection of the lack of a central, transcendental signified in all models of interpretation. On the other hand, historical evidence suggests that an awareness of the social and political factors determining the hidden status of the center invariably grounds the methodological debate in substantive concerns.

The relation between substance and the various methodological discourses can be illustrated by the following diagram (see figure 4), which is loosely based on diagrams in an article on anthroplogical approaches to Buddhist praxis by Suzuki Masataka (figure 5).[43]

The aim of Suzuki's diagram, "Locus and Viewpoint," is to disclose the interplay of four areas of inquiry in anthropological studies of Buddhism: "armchair" or deskwork analysis stands in binary relation to "fieldwork" studies, and "text" or written materials stands in binary relation to "context" or experiential background; and looked at from another angle, text and context as "locus" or situational background stand in binary relation to deskwork and fieldwork analysis as "viewpoint" or perspective. No area exists independent of the others; each is at once displaced and clarified by the methodologcal juxtaposition.

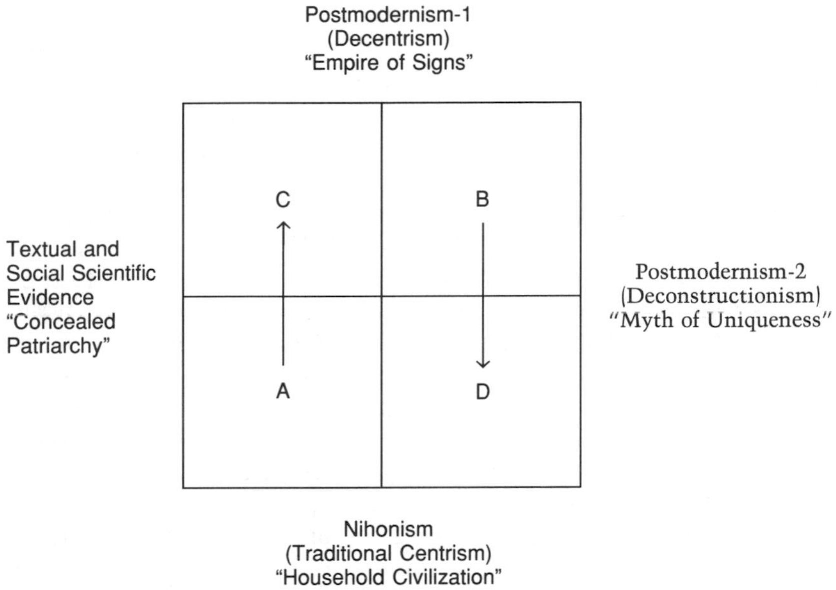

Postmodernism-1
(Decentrism)
"Empire of Signs"

Textual and
Social Scientific
Evidence
"Concealed
Patriarchy"

C

B

A

D

Postmodernism-2
(Deconstructionism)
"Myth of Uniqueness"

Nihonism
(Traditional Centrism)
"Household Civilization"

Fig. 4. Interaction of Four Levels of Discourse.

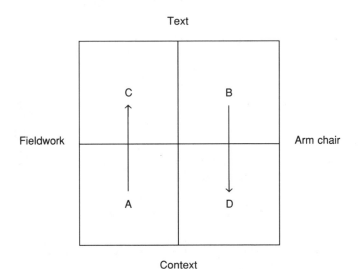

Text

Fieldwork

C

B

A

D

Arm chair

Context

Fig. 5. Locus and Viewpoint (From Suzuki Masataka, "Jinruigaku to Bukkyō," *Buddha kara Dōgen e*, 397).

Although a full explanation of Suzuki's discussion of the diagram is beyond the scope of this article, the connections I am making are based on two main points. First, the diagram in figure 4 indicates how the unlikely alliance based on the valorization of Japan of Nihonism and postmodernism-1 is complemented and potentially undercut by the equally unexpected connection based on exposing myths between social science and postmodernism-2; perhaps horizontal arrows could be added within the boxes to indicate the refutation of the valorizing standpoint. In addition, the diagram suggests that a self-critical, decentralizing methodology should be based not on judging or prefering any one particular approach, but on positing a constellation of juxtaposed discourses based on interpreting the centerless center of *ie/iemoto*. In this sense, the flexible, multiperspectival free play of shifting, displaced methodologies constitutes the decentric function of postmodernism. These discourses are neither left to stand in polarity nor promoted into an artificial synthesis, but are allowed to play off of, bisect, undermine or reorient each other in continual hermeneutic interaction. The mutual displacement of perspectives, in exposing the weaknesses of each viewpoint relative to the locus simultaneously allows the strengths or positive contributions of each—the idealism of Nihonism, philosophical depth of postmodernism-1, critical edge of postmodernism-2, and neutrality of textual/social scientific studies—to come into sharper focus.

Notes

1. Jane M. Bachnik, "Indexing Self and Society in Japanese Family Organization," in Jane M. Bachnik and Charles J. Quina, Jr., eds., *Situated Meaning: Inside and Outside in Japanese Self, Society, and Language* (Princeton: Princeton University Press, 1994), 145. This volume contains a number of interesting articles analyzing the role of language in defining *ie* from the standpoint of social anthropological studies.

2. Some of these arguments, particularly by Urabe Kuniyoshi and Iwata Ryuko, are critically discussed in Charles W. Fu's paper in this volume.

3. A prominent example is the Buddhist-Marxist critique by Ichikawa Hakugen, *Bukkyōsha no sensō-sekinin* (Tokyo: Shunjūsha, 1970).

4. I am borrowing the term "Nihonism" from Isaiah ben-Dasan, *The Japanese and the Jews* (*Nihonjin to Yudayajin*) (Tokyo: Weatherhill, 1972).

This book, which was a popular sensation when first issued in 1970s is actually a thinly-veiled pseudohistorical work by a pseudonymous author that contributes to *nihonjinron* rhetoric. Yet it contains many pertinent insights, and the use of "Nihonism" as a general designation for Japanese religiosity and conceptions of the sacred associated with nationalism is helpful.

5. Roland Barthes, *Empire of Signs*, tr. Richard Howard (New York: Hill and Wang, 1982), 108.

6. Ibid., 50–51 for a picture of Shikidai, and 31, for the photo of Tokyo. It is interesting to contrast Tokyo (Edo), created in the seventeenth century with Kyoto, created nearly a millennium earlier with perpendicular streets along the model of Chinese cities, as in the following map:

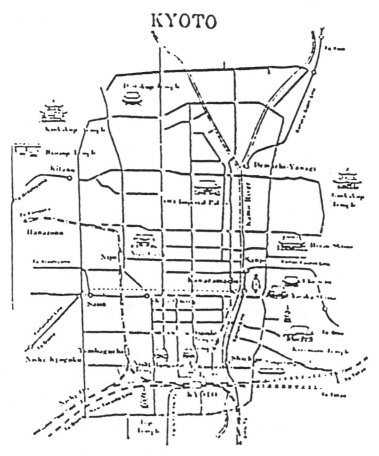

Fig. 6. The Perpendicular Streets of Kyoto.

It is also important to point out that the photo of Shikidai is not so easily invertible, as noted by David Pollack, who observes, "Once one realizes what has gone wrong, the effect of such a simple error is at once trivial and serious, comic and electrifying: this up side-down view of Japan is irremediably Western . . ." In *Reading Against Culture: Ideology and Narrative in the Japanese Novel* (Ithaca: Cornell University Press, 1992), 32.

7. Ibid., 32. He says the aim is "not in order to irradiate power, but to give to the entire urban movement the support of its central emptiness, forcing the traffic to make a perpetual detour."

8. This discussion from the video interviews is alluded to in Joseph Campbell (with Bill Moyers), *The Power of Myth* (New York: Doubleday, 1988). Campbell cites Salt Lake City as a prime example of the Western city which migrated through the three stages in less than a century and a half so that the three structures (Mormon Tabernacle, state capitol, and financial center serving both institutions) are built side-by-side. Campbell also speculates on the emergence of a new "global myth" which will replace the previous ones, and it might not be far-fetched to suggest decentric Tokyo as a harbinger of that, especially since Campbell is fond of telling how Shinto has neither theology nor ideology—a quasi-postmodernism-1 position.

9. Ashihara Yoshinobu, *The Hidden Order: Tokyo through the Twentieth Century*, tr. Lynne E. Riggs (Tokyo: Kodansha, 1989), 57–58.

10. Ibid., 45.

11. Barthes, *Empire of Signs*, 3.

12. Edward Said, *Orientalism* (New York: Vintage, 1978).

13. Barthes, *Empire of Signs*, xi. For a discussion of how Barthes' approach here fits into his overall Western philosophical project, see Lisa Lowe, *Critical Terrains: French and British Orientalisms* (Ithaca, NY: Cornell University Press, 1991), 152–60.

14. For example works by Yanagita Kunio, *Yanagita Kunio shū* (Tokyo: Chikuma Shobō, 1975), particularly *Senzo no hanashi* (Conversations About Ancestors); Chie Nakane, *Japanese Society* (Berkeley: University of California Press, 1970); Murakami Yasusuke, Kumon Shumpei, Sato Seizaboro, *Bunrei toshite no ie shakai* (Family Society as Civilization) (Tokyo: Chūō Kōronsha); Doi Takeo, *Amae no kōzō* (*Anatomy of Dependence*) (Tokyo: Kōbundo, 1971) and *Omote to ura* (*Anatomy of Self*) (Tokyo: Kōbundo, 1985); Watsuji Tetsurō, *Rinrigaku* (Ethics) (Tokyo: Iwanami shoten, 1937). See also Susan Orpett Long, *Family Change and the Life Course in Japan* (Ithaca: Cornell East Asian Series, 1987), and Steve Odin, "The Social Self in Japanese Philosophy and American Pragmatism: A Comparative Study of Watsuji Tetsurō and George Herbert Mead," *Philosophy East and West*, 42/3, 475–501. For the Tokugawa roots of this discourse,

see the discussion of Hirata Atsutane's philosophy of "household duties" (*kagyō*) in H. D. Harootunian, *Things Seen and Unseen: Discourse and Ideology in Tokugawa Nativism* (Chicago: University of Chicago Press, 1988), esp. 194–96.

15. Nakane, *Japanese Society*, 7, 4.

16. See Francis Hsu, *Iemoto: The Heart of Japan* (New York: Schenkman, 1975); Jean-Pierre Lehmann, *The Roots of Modern Japan* (New York: St. Martin's Press, 1982), 220; Fukushima Masao, ed., *Nihon shihonshugi to ie seido* (Japanese Capitalism and the Family System) (Tokyo: University of Tokyo Press, 1967).

17. Hsu may have been the first to use this term in *Iemoto*.

18. Masao Miyoshi and Harry Harootunian, "Japan in the World," in Miyoshi and Harootunian, eds., *Japan in the World* (Durham: Duke University Press, 1993).

19. Roy Andrew Miller, *Japan's Modern Myth: The Language and Beyond* (New York: Weatherhill, 1982).

20. Jeffrey P. Mass, *Lordship and Inheritance in Early Medieval Japan: A Study of the Kamakura Sōryo System* (Stanford: Stanford University Press, 1989).

21. See Miller, *Japan's Modern Myth*.

22. See John W. Hall, "Reflections on Murakami Yasusuke's 'Ie Society as a Pattern of Civilization,' " *Journal of Japanese Studies*, 2/1, 29–46.

23. See *Japanese Systems: An Alternative Civilization?* (*Nihonkei shisutemu: jinruimei no hitotsu no kata*), by the Research Project Team for Japanese Systems (Yokohama: Sekotae, 1992).

24. Eugene Eoyang, "Thinking Comparatively: Orienting the West and Occidenting the East," Comparative Literature Lecture Series, Pennsylvania State University (October 1993). Eoyang borrows the term "reverse Orientalism" from John Timothy Wixted, "Reverse Orientalism," *Sino-Japanese Studies* 2/1 (1989), 17–27. See also Bernard Faure's article in this volume.

25. Three prominent works recently have dissected the Japanese "myth": Miller, *Japan's Modern Myth*; Carol Gluck, *Japan's Modern Myths: Ideology in the Late Meiji Period* (Princeton: Princeton University Press, 1985); and Peter N. Dale, *The Myth of Japanese Uniqueness* (New York: St. Martin's Press, 1986). Of these probably only the third could be considered to use a postmodernist archaeology of knowledge.

26. Miller, viii; he refers to the *Kokutai no hongi* as the source of this.

27. Dale, *Myth of Japanese Uniqueness*, 17. On Barthes, Dale writes (4), "The ultimate form of this intellectual modesty assumes the linea-

ments of an ill-disguised, racist intimidation of theory itself when it is exploited by oriental nationalists to invalidate as tendentially imperialist any Western interpretation of Asian realitities, however benign or sympathetic. In this view, the projection of analyses derived from a Western interpretative mode is all the more insidious in its imperialism because it annuls and disguises its colonialist roots while preserving its covert values in the specifically occidental framework of modern thought."

28. See especially Hayden White, *Tropics of Discourse: Essays in Cultural Criticism* (Baltimore: Johns Hopkins University Press, 1978), and Michel Foucault, *The Order of Things: An Archaeology of the Human Sciences* (New York: Vintage, 1970).

29. Karel van Wolfren, *The Enigma of Power* (New York: Vintage, 1989).

30. See Long, *Family Change*, 15–21; in the Taishō era, "The nation came to be conceived of ideologically as one large *ie*, a 'family state' headed by an emperor-father."

31. Lehmann, *Roots of Modern Japan*, 78.

32. See John F. Embree, *Suye Mura: A Japanese Village* (Chicago: University of Chicago Press, 1939); R. P. Dore, *City Life in Japan: A Study of a Tokyo Ward* (Berkeley: University of California Press, 1963); and Hsu, *Iemoto*. See also theoretical and observational discussions in Bachnik and Quinn, eds., *Situated Meaning*.

33. Hall, "Reflections," 55.

34. From Roman Cybriwsky, *Tokyo: The Changing Profile of an Urban Giant* (Boston: G. K. Hall, 1991), 211, originally appearing in the *Planning of Tokyo* (Tokyo: Tokyo Metropolitan Government, 1990). Another feature of Tokyo that is altogether neglected by Barthes' approach is the underside represented by the slum quarters in the neighborhood formerly known as Sanya for *hinin, burakumin* and other outcasts; see Cybriwsky, *Tokyo*, 182–86, and Brett de Bary, "Sanya: Japan's Internal Colony," in E. Patricia Tsurumi, ed., *The Other Japan: Postwar Realities* (Armonk, NY: M. E. Sharpe, 1988), 112–18.

35. Cybriwsky, *Tokyo*, 156.

36. Hsu, "Iemoto," in the *Kodansha Encyclopedia of Japan* (Tokyo: Kodansha, 1983), III:260. In *Iemoto* (63–69), in which he states that "we are quite safe in stating that nearly all Japanese secondary groups partake of the essential characterisics of the *iemoto*," Hsu discusses three main features: master-disciple relationship, interlinking hierarchy, and supreme authority of the *iemoto*.

37. Allan Grapard, "The Shintō of Yoshida Kanetomo," *Monumenta Nipponica* 47/1, 36–37. An interesting comparison could be made to the

rhetoric of mystery used by the secretive guild societies of medieval Europe; see Charles Phythian-Adams, *Desolation of a City* (Oxford: Oxford University Press, 1979). However, some differences are apparent in that the guilds are based on protecting a body of knowledge (*gnosis*) rather than the authority of the patriarch (*iemoto*) who embodies wisdom, and the guilds reflect a philosophy based on valuing stasis over social change whereas Japanese familism has a built-in dynamic quality based on the transmission of lineage from generation to generation—therefore the guild system quickly broke down with the advent of modern industrial economic production while Japanese familism is considered a key to success in modernization. Furthermore, although the symbolism of mystery in guilds may have a resonance with other levels of society including the mystery of kingship in Europe, this does not appear to be an all-pervasive social paradigm in a way that parallels Japan.

38. Hsu, *Iemoto*, 227.

39. Moriya Matsuhisa, *Tokugawa Japan* (Tokyo: University of Tokyo Press, 1990), 102–3. But it is important to note that an overview of the map from the Edo period shows the same hollow space of the palace in the center; see Cybriwsky, *Tokyo*, 57.

40. Jinnai Hidenobu, "The Spatial Structure of Edo," in Chie Nakane and Shinzaburō Ōishi, eds., *Tokugawa Japan: The Social and Economic Antecedents of Modern Japan*, tr. ed. Conrad Totman (Tokyo: Tokyo University Press, 1990), 141. It should be pointed out that the amorphous structure of Tokyo sharply contrasts with the orderliness of Kyoto, originally designed along the pattern of T'ang Chinese cities with perpendicular streets emanating from a clearly defined center (see n. 6 above).

41. Therefore, rather than Campbell's view of urban centers (see n. 8), perhaps the appropos Western comparison would involve Kafka's *The Castle*, in which there is a all-pervasively dominant center but one that is hidden from view and inaccessible to non-officials unless or until they are explicitly called to do its bidding.

42. Asada Akira, "Infantile Capitalism and Japan's Postmoderism: A Fairy Tale," in Miyoshi and Harootunian, eds., *Postmodernism and Japan* (Durham: Duke University Press, 1989), 277. For a very different, sympathetic reading of Nishida's war-time activities, see Michiko Yusa, "Nishida and the Question of Nationalism," *Monumenta Nipponica* 46/2 (1991), 204. The question of the Kyoto school's involvement in the war is complex, and also involves an analysis of Tanabe Hajime's postwar philosophy of "repentance" or "metanoia" (*zange*).

43. Suzuki Masataka, "Jinruigaku to bukkyō" (Anthropology and Buddhism), *Budda kara Dōgen e* (From Buddha to Dōgen), ed. Nara Yasuaki (Tokyo: Tokyo Shoseki, 1992), 395–410.

8/1997

sees four _ie_ interpretations
(defined in first section) as
playing off one another to
illuminate the impact of _ie-ism_
in Japanese culture.

useful in illustrating defining place/
role of the _ie_ in Japanese
life; examples of traditionalist,
postmodernist, modernist
thinking; issues of Orientalism
and rhetorical constructs;
multiple and layered
interpretations; need to
identify author perspective
see particularly comments on
p 39.

Contemporary Japan
Power and Authority

Chapter Three

Intervals (*Ma*) in Space and Time: Foundations for a Religio-Aesthetic Paradigm in Japan

RICHARD B. PILGRIM

Postmodern Prolegomena

One can perhaps no more easily establish the postmodern credentials of *ma* than by linking it to Roland Barthes' *Empire of Signs*.[1] *Ma* is, of course, ultimately no *thing* but rather a poetic "remainder"; a depth on the surface; a dismembered, decentered, dislocated reminiscence; an emptied sign left over from the "fissure of the symbolic"; a pregnant nothingness; a "living in the interstices, delivered from any fulfilled meaning." Indeed, "gossamer" might be its name for it errors "on the side of the light, the aerial, of the instantaneous, the fragile, the transparent, the crisp, the trifling, but whose real name would be *the interstice* without specific edges, or again: the empty sign."[2] Exempt from meaning and its discourse, it thrives on metaphor to "carry one through" by emptying both self and other into the work at hand.

> quiet
> into rock absorbing
> cicada sounds
> (Bashō)

I. Introduction

The term *ma* (間) has only recently begun to receive the attention that it is due, both inside and outside Japan. What brought it to my attention was an exhibit relating *ma* to characteristic features of

55

Japanese artistic (especially architectural) design,[3] which, like the word itself, was rich in meaning and ambiguity but which clearly suggested that *ma* was yet another reflection of a Japanese religio-aesthetic paradigm or "way of seeing." Subsequent research has only confirmed this; the results of this research are offered here.

The word *ma* basically means an "interval" between two (or more) spatial or temporal things and events. Thus it is not only used in compounds to suggest measurement but carries meanings such as gap, opening, space between, time between, and so forth. A room is called *ma*, for example, as it refers to the space between the walls; a rest in music is also *ma* as the pause between the notes or sounds. By the same token it can also mean timing, as in the comic recitation art called *rakugo* where *ma* is quite explicitly a part of the craft and skill.

By extension *ma* also means "among." In the compound *ningen* ("human being"), for example, *ma* (read *gen* here) implies that persons (*nin*, *hito*) stand within, among, or in relationship to others. As such, the word *ma* clearly begins to take on a relational meaning—a dynamic sense of standing in, with, among, or between. Related to this it also carries an experiential connotation, since to be among persons is to interact in some dynamic way. The Japanese phrase *ma ga warui* ("the *ma* is bad"), which has overtones of being embarrassed, well illustrates this nuance.

The word, therefore, carries both objective and subjective meaning; that is, *ma* is not only "something" within objective, descriptive reality but also signifies particular modes of experience. Both the descriptive/objective (see part II below) and experiential/subjective (see part III below) aspects are important. However, the latter usage is the point at which *ma* becomes a religio-aesthetic paradigm and brings about a collapse of distinctive (objective) worlds, and even of time and space itself. As the contemporary architect Arata Isozaki says:

> While in the West the space-time concept gave rise to absolutely fixed images of a homogenous and infinite continuum, as presented in Descartes, in Japan space and time were never fully separated but were conceived as correlative and omnipresent. . . . Space could not be perceived independently of the element of time [and] time was not abstracted as a regulated, homogenous flow, but rather was believed to exist only in relation to movements of space. . . . Thus, space was perceived as identical with the events of phenomena occurring in it; that is, space was recognized only in its relation to time-flow.[4]

The collapse of space and time as two distinct and abstract objects can only take place in a particular mode of experience that "empties" the objective/subjective world(s); only in aesthetic, immediate, relational experience can space be "perceived as identical with the events or phenomena occurring in it." Therefore, although *ma* may be objectively located as intervals in space and time, ultimately it transcends this and expresses a deeper level. Indeed, it takes us to a boundary situation at the edge of thinking and the edge of all processes of locating things by naming and distinguishing.

The singular importance of *ma* in Japanese religio-aesthetics is well expressed by the contemporary Noh actor, Kunio Komparu, who in relating *ma* to Noh, notes that:

> Noh is sometimes called the art of *ma*. This word can be translated into English as space, spacing, interval, gap, blank, room, pause, rest, time, timing, or opening. . . . Of course both understandings of *ma*, as time and as space, are correct. The concept apparently first came from China . . . and was used in reference only to space, but as it evolved in Japanese it came to signify time as well. . . . Because it includes three meanings, time, space, and space-time, the word *ma* at first seems vague, but it is the multiplicity of meanings and at the same time the conciseness of the single word that makes *ma* a unique conceptual term, one without parallel in other languages.[5]

Ma seems to operate at, cross, and even deconstruct a number of boundaries. First, for some Japanese *ma* is a deep and living word that cannot even be discussed, much less analyzed and interpreted across the boundaries of culture and language. Second, *ma* operates at and bridges the boundaries between the traditional and contemporary arts, between religion and art, between one religion and another, and between religion and culture. (Paradigms tend to operate this way in cultures; they are fundamental ways of seeing or grasping the world that permeate the variety of forms of a culture and thereby cut across those divisions in culture created out of our own minds.)

Third, although *ma* ultimately deconstructs all boundaries (as mind-created constructs and orders imposed on the chaos of experience) and operates experientially at the interstices of being, some elements of its meaning and expression can be located within such constructs and orders. This article tries to be sensitive to both aspects, that is, to the location of *ma* in a descriptive world, and to the experiential meaning and power beyond locations and boundaries.

In the process of discussing *ma* I will argue that the deeper meanings of *ma* can be found most explicitly in the arts, and that the religions of Japan have influenced those meanings in significant ways. The resultant paradigm of *ma* is more clearly revealed in the arts, but it is "religio-aesthetic" in its fundamental character. Each section below, therefore, initially places *ma* in the arts but then pursues potential parallels in Japanese religions.

II. Locating *Ma* in Space and Time: Pregnant Nothings

The Arts

Perhaps the most appropriate way to begin this section is to create an image out of the Chinese characters that constitute the written word *ma*. It is made up of two elements, the enclosing radical meaning gate or door (*mon* 門) and the inner character meaning either sun (*hi* 日) or moon (*tsuki* 月). The visual image or character, therefore, suggests a light shining through a gate or door. If we were to take the gate itself as representing the things or phenomena and events of the world, the opening in the gate becomes a *ma* or interval between the things. Yet *ma* is not a mere emptiness or opening; through and in it shines a light, and the function of this *ma* becomes precisely to let that light shine through. A literary example of this image can be found in the twelfth-century novel, *The Tale of Genji* by Lady Murasaki: "It was the fifteenth night of the eighth month. The light of an enclouded full-moon shone between the ill-fitting planks of the roof and flooded the room. What a queer place to be lying in!, thought Genji, as he gazed around the garret, so different from any room he had ever known before."[6]

A more historically, descriptively concrete example, however, can be found in Noh drama. The founder of Noh, Zeami Motokiyo (1363–1443), has said the following:

> Sometimes spectators of the Nō say, "the moments of 'no-action' (*senu tokoro*) are the most enjoyable." This is an art which the actor keeps secret. Dancing and singing, movements and the different types of miming are all acts performed by the body. Moments of "no-action" occur in between (*hima*). When we examine why such moments without action are enjoyable, we find that it is due to the underlying spiritual (*kokoro*) strength of the actor which unremittingly holds the attention. He does not relax the tension when the dancing or singing come to an end or at intervals between (*hima*) the dialogue and the different types of miming. [Not aban-

doning this mind/heart (*kokoro*) in the various intervals (*himajima*)] he maintains an unwavering inner strength (*naishin*). This feeling of inner strength will faintly reveal itself and bring enjoyment. However, it is undesirable for the actor to permit this inner strength to become obvious to the audience. If it is obvious, it becomes an act and is no longer "no-action." The actions before and after an interval (*hima*) of 'no-action" must be linked by entering the state of mindlessness (*mushin*) in which one conceals even from oneself one's intent.[7]

This example is precisely an instance of *ma*—an instance in which the light (here, "spiritual strength faintly revealing itself") shines through the opening (here, the "moments of 'no-action'") in the gate (here, the actions and sounds "before and after an interval"). As Komparu says of this same example, "Zeami is suggesting implicitly the existence of *ma* that is a blank space-time where nothing is done, and that *ma* is the core of the expression, where the true interest lies."[8]

More generally, however, Komparu discusses *ma* not only as the element that gives Noh its unique character as an art but also as a "negative space" of great importance:

Nowadays space is often described as positive or negative. Negative space is enclosed and fixed, and positive space is the space taken up [or occupied] by people or things that define a negative space by their presence. Both kinds of space exist in Noh: negative space (*ma*) is the stillness and emptiness just before or after a unit of performance, positive space is produced by stage properties and by the dramatic activities of performers. . . . The two kinds of space are connected by time. . . . While there may be empty, or "negative" time, there will never be unsubstantial, uncreative or uncreated time.[9]

This negative space/time is therefore anything but a mere nothing awaiting the positive space/time; it is a pregnant nothingness that is "never unsubstantial or uncreative." To continue the metaphor, *ma* is not merely fecundative either; it glows with spiritual power, meaning, and attraction, just as a light shining through the gate or "a spiritual strength faintly revealing itself."

Others have called this an "imaginary space" (*yohaku, kūhaku*), and related it particularly to painting, tea ceremony, gardens, and calligraphy.[10] In this sense it is negative space/time "filled" by the imagination more than by some thing.

In both Noh and many of the traditional arts of Japan (and China) the negative or imaginary space functions very centrally.

Another form it takes in many of these arts, according to Komparu, is in relation to the artistic styles found in calligraphy and other arts called *shin* ("correct" or formal), *gyō* ("going" or relaxed), and *sō* ("grass" or informal). In each of these styles, Komparu suggests, the intervals or gaps serve as an empty "ground" or basis against or within which the forms or "figures" of the art function. Although present in the *shin* and *gyō* styles, one best sees this in the *sō* style, which tends to feature this emptiness.[11]

A literary example of this same affirmation of spaces between can be found, for example, in linked verse (*renga*). Writing of the Buddhist influence on this poetry, Gary Ebersole asserts that the "Buddhist essence of *renga*, then, is not to be located in the [literary] universes or scenes . . . created by the semantic relations posited between two links by the poets and the listener/reader, but in the space between the linked poems—that is, in the dissolution of the literary universe."[12] The same could be said for the Noh drama example already given: in both, narrative story and action give way to a deeper message, which shines through the cracks and gaps in those forms.

In fact, the affirmation of spaces and gaps in between the forms of things has led one commentator to suggest that the very nature of the Japanese language is itself structured in this fashion. Kemmochi Takehiko says that Japanese is characterized by a series of overlapping and associated, discrete, image worlds that are, in turn, separated by emotional spaces called *ma*. Rather than construct a logical and linear narrative order, as Western languages do, Japanese carries internal gaps and pauses (e.g., *haru wa . . .*) and fixed endings (e.g., *desu*) that create distinct spaces that are, in turn, filled with *ki* (*ke*; Chinese: *ch'i*) or emotional energy.[13] A narrative construct, or cause/effect narrative order, thus continually dissolves or deconstructs into these spaces.

A more contemporary example may well be in the film art of Ozu Yasujiro. As a series of articles has made clear, fundamentally Ozu "directs silences and voids."[14] "Codas" or "empty shots" which generally show quiet, natural scenes that contribute nothing to the narrative line or character development, figure prominently in Ozu's work: "Ozu's films diverge from the Hollywood paradigm in that they generate spatial structures which are not motivated by the cause/effect chain of the narrative. . . . The motivation [for their use] is purely 'artistic.' Space, constructed alongside and sometimes against the cause/effect sequence, becomes 'foregrounded' to a degree that renders it at times the primary structural level of the film. . . . At times spaces with only the most tenuous narrative associations (and no place in the cause/effect chain) are dominant; narrative elements may enter these spaces as overtones."[15]

At least one of these commentators on Ozu's work directly links this to *ma*,[16] and the likeness to what we have already seen is obvious. Particularly suggestive in the quote above is the relationship to the *shin*, *gyō*, *sō* structure; it is precisely an art in the *sō* style that "foregrounds" the empty spaces/times and uses the narrative actions, events, or forms of the art as "overtones." The light that thus shines through is the meaning and power of such imaginative or emotional "negative spaces" that dissolve the narrative, cause/effect world being presented.

Finally, and in particular reference to the exhibit mentioned in the introduction, certain contemporary architects are finding *ma* important for their work. The discussion of *ma* as it relates to these people, however, is more relevant to part III below since their understanding of *ma* is less obviously located within some order, boundary, and descriptive reality. Suffice it to say that *ma* (as the conjunction of space and time) is understood to effect architectural design in a number of ways: the importance of openings, bridging spaces, form defining space rather than space serving form, simplicity, asymmetry, flowing/changing forms, and so forth. All such characteristics are, Isozaki says, true of all the "arts of *ma*." All suggest that the results of affirming time/space intervals are crucial.[17]

Like the character for *ma* itself, therefore, the meaning of *ma* in many of these arts affirms the power, interest, depth or profundity that shines through the gaps, cracks, and intervals in space and time. The forms of an art often exist only to serve these interests and are often only understood in relation to them. Such intervals are thus referred to as creative/substantial negative spaces, imaginative spaces, or emotional spaces that the positive spaces, narrative sequences, or forms of an art help create but into which they dissolve.

The Religions

Although *ma* does not seem to play an explicit role in the religions of Japan, its relevance in the arts implies a strong structural/experiential parallel to, and strong influences from, Buddhism, Taoism, and especially Shinto. My interest in what follows, therefore, is to attempt to locate in these religions evidence for an affirmation of intervals and gaps as "places" of true meaning and power.

SHINTO. In this process perhaps the most interesting connection is found within Shinto. Seigow Matsuoka—writer, publisher, journalist, and student of the Japanese religio-aesthetic tradition—presents a convincing argument that "the tale of Japanese culture has been told with excessive emphasis, perhaps, on its Buddhistic core. We believe that a better understanding of Japan [and *ma*] will be gained by tracing the role played by the *kehai* of *kami* [i.e., Shinto] in this composite culture."[18]

Although Matsuoka's argument is complex and rests in large part on a kind of theology of folk Shinto found in part III below, his point here is to note the existence of *ma*-like elements, particularly in the ancient and continuing folk Shinto traditions.

Ma-like elements are best exemplified in Shinto by its sacred spaces—especially spaces thought (or designed) to be open, cleared out, and pure in anticipation of the coming and going of *kami*. Although these spaces may be located within shrine buildings or, for example, caves, their paradigmatic model is the cleared out, white rock-covered spaces surrounding shrines or even predating shrines— spaces variously referred to as *shiki, yuniwa, iwakura, kekkai,* and *tamajari*. Especially in ancient Shinto these spaces often contained a single tree, rock or pillar (*himorogi, yashiro, yorishiro, iwasaka*) into which the *kami* would come to abide temporarily. Matsuoka emphasizes that these areas are sacred precincts, borders, or boundaries (*kekkai*): "Rather than not know at all where *kami* might make its temporary appearance, our ancestors took to demarcating an 'area of *kami*' by enclosing a particular space with twisted rope thus sanctifying it in preparation for the visit of *kami*. This area was called *kekkai*."[19]

Such empty, pure, open spaces (where *kami* dwells) are also found in Japanese mythology. For example, in the myth of the sun goddess Amaterasu, her return from within a cave to renew the world takes place on the dry riverbed (*kawara*) of heaven (*takamagahara*). Beyond that suggestive parallel, however, there is evidence that the word *kekkai* may have originally meant a valley, crevice, or natural gap that then formed a border between this world and the world of *kami* in the mountains or beyond the sea—a crevice or gap into which *kami* would come.[20] Not unlike *ma* such areas might be understood as a "no-man's land," a gap or crevice between worlds, a sacred *ma* that the formless energy (*ki*) of *kami* comes into and fills.

Following the great folklorist Origuchi Shinobu, Matsuoka goes on to suggest that shrines and even homes came to be thought of as permanent or temporary *kekkai* set up to host the visiting deity (*marebito*) at New Year's.[21] More than this, however, perhaps even the object that embodies *kami* in a shrine, the *shintai*, could be considered *kekkai* since, as Isozaki says, "space was believed to be fundamentally void. Even solid objects were thought to contain voids capable of receiving *kami* that descend at certain moments to fill such spaces with the spiritual power (*ki*) of the soul (*kami*)."[22]

Finally, since the word *kekkai* refers, in Buddhism, to a special room in a temple set aside for a priest's spiritual renewal,[23] we might reasonably conjecture that *kekkai* may be related to Shinto ideas of seclusion in a sacred space for purposes of renewal (*komoru*), especially in caves, tombs, and *tama-bako* ("soul-boxes"), which—though containing nothing—are filled with sacred power to be imparted to those who have entered.[24]

A good example of this kind of sacred space is the temple Hasedera, dedicated to the Bodhisattva Kannon and a popular pilgrimage site in the Heian period. In the *Manyōshū* and other early texts, the area around the temple was originally referred to by epithets such as *komoriku no hatsuse no kuni*, suggesting a special, secluded area set apart from the everyday world. Nobutsuna Saigo argues in his book, *Kodaijin to yume*, that the original Shinto worship of a mother goddess of the mountain became synthesized later with the Buddhist cult of Kannon. Thus in the popular devotions that included temporary seclusion in the temple by lay parishioners (which is well documented in the poetic diaries of the time, such as the *Kagerō nikki*), there persist Shinto notions of mountains and caves as places of access to the spiritual world beyond. Caves, mountains, and finally Buddhist temples were sacred spaces with womblike characteristics where one could practice austerities for a spiritual rebirth.[25]

These conjectures and examples converge on a central point, that is, that Shinto affirms sacred intervals in space (and things) as those places into and within which the presence of *kami*, is experienced. When one adds to this the notion that *kami* is itself formless, the argument seems to build: "*Kami* has no physical body; its body and essence exist as a vacuum, 'a place entirely void of matter.' But 'void' does not mean 'nothing is there.' Rather, to the Japanese, 'there is a hollow there,' as 'nothing (*mu*) exists there.' This concept of *kami* as the *kehai* (atmosphere of *ch'i*) which fills a void has given the entire Japanese culture its striking quality."[26] Although this idea begins to encroach on part III below, it suggests again the affirmation of the meaning and power of the formless, empty, unseen, and intangible; it suggests that the light shining through the door is, for Shinto, the light of *kami*.

Taoism and Buddhism. Since for our purposes the potential connections of *ma* to Shinto are more interesting and less obvious than connections to Buddhism and Taoism, the latter will be only briefly discussed. As Matsuoka has already suggested, perhaps there has been an overemphasis, in fact, on at least Buddhism's connection to Japanese culture (and therefore *ma*), and it is time to redress the imbalance. (Taoism's connections await further study.)

Although not exactly a Japanese religious text, the *Tao te ching* is an important source of Taoist ideas (in China and Japan) and an important place to locate a *ma*-like element. One of its most famous passages makes this clear:

> Thirty spokes
> Share one hub.
> Adapt the nothing [*wu*] therein to the purpose in hand,
> and you will have the use of the cart.
> Knead clay in order to make a vessel.
> Adapt the nothing therein to the purpose in hand,
> and you will have the use of the vessel.
> Cut out doors and windows in order to make a room.
> Adapt the nothing therein to the purpose in hand,
> and you will have the use of the room.
> Thus what we gain is Something (*yu*, J. *yū* or *u*),
> yet it is by virtue of Nothing (*wu*, J. *mu*)
> that this can be put to use.[27]

Insofar as there is, for the *Tao te ching*, a "named Tao" or named world of twoness—nothing/something, *yin* (*in*)/*yang* (*yū*), and all distinctions—it is the emptiness, "nothing," or *yin* aspect that plays the primary role. While one must know the *yang* and the "something," one must always return to the *yin* and the nothing as the gap, interval, or *ma* by which all is accomplished. This, of course, is more a metaphoric nothing than a literal one, but nonetheless a *ma* to be located in an order of distinctions.

That such ideas have had a strong influence on Japan cannot be doubted. In fact the opening passages of both the *Kojiki* and *Nihongi* are deeply influenced by similar *yin/yang* or Taoist ideas, although perhaps reinterpreted and used in different ways for different purposes.

More obviously and perhaps more deeply, Buddhist ideas have influenced a Japanese affirmation of "pregnant nothings" that gave birth to a religio-aesthetic apprehension of the world. In the distinction between *mu* (nothing, no, nonbeing) and *u* (something, being, existence), for example, the importance of *mu* as the ground or basis for all existence is clear. In fact, to be awake to *mu* is to be liberated in *u*. As Zeami made clear, it is by entering the state of *mushin* (no-mind, *mu*-mind) that something is truly accomplished in Noh and that the actions/sounds on either side of an interval are linked. Much like the *Tao te ching*, it is thus by virtue of nothing that something is fulfilled or used.

Although the *mu/u* distinction is more appropriate for Zen, Tendai Buddhism makes the same distinction in different words by speaking of all things as being both "empty" (*kū*) and "temporarily existent" (*ke*). All such distinctions are meant to be transcended in a "third" or middle (*chū*) place, of course, but that discussion remains for part III below. Meanwhile it is important to know that within the descriptive, distinction-making world of Buddhism, such empty nothings (or nothings) are absolutely central.

The former Zen Abbot of Daitokuji in Kyoto, Kobori Nanrei, has not only supported much of this by suggesting that *ma* is importantly related to both Taoism and Buddhism, but also has said that *ma*, in Buddhism, is the *mu* that necessarily forms a background for *u*. Using the analogy of replacing flowers and pictures in the *tokonoma* (alcove) each day, Kabori explains that to clear the old ones out leaving a blank wall is *mu* (*ma*); placing new flowers or a painting back in is the *u* by which *ma* (*mu*) is expressed and lived.[28]

These suggestive interrelationships between *ma* and Buddhism, Taoism, and Shintoism only deepen and clarify the religious (if not aesthetic) character of this term. In each case, though in different ways and with different meanings, it is precisely in the gaps and intervals of time, space, and being that spiritual power is manifested or grasped. Whether understood as the *ki* (*ch'i*) of *kami's* presence or the nothingness-gnosis that liberates being, all affirm the cracks in the gate as the place of the light's shining.

III. A World in Between

The Arts

A particularly interesting and useful discussion of *ma* (in the context of architecture and city planning) can be found in an article by

Günter Nitschke, which is in turn based in large part on the work of Isozaki and others. Among other things Nitschke describes the various meanings of *ma* as (1) having objectively to do with the four dimensions of length, length/width, area/volume, and time and (2) having subjectively to do with human experience. The latter element in the meaning of *ma*, together with the former, is the focus of this part. It brings us face-to-face with *ma* as a particular way of seeing, experiencing, or being aware of the world. Nitschke suggests that this aspect of *ma* has to do with the "quality of an event . . . as perceived by an individual."[29]

In fact, for Nitschke *ma* is ultimately "place" or "place making" in that it includes not only form and nonform (i.e., *ma* as empty spaces discussed in part II) but also form/nonform as imaginatively created or perceived in immediate experience. Such place making is not merely the apprehending subject's awareness of an objective three-dimensional space continuum composed of an arrangement of things. Rather, it is "the simultaneous awareness of the intellectual concepts form + non-form, object + space, coupled with subjective experience . . . it is the thing that takes place in the imagination of the human who experiences these elements. Therefore one could define *ma* as 'experiential' place being nearer to [the] mysterious atmosphere caused by the external distribution of symbols."[30]

Such experiential "places" evoke, by their very nature, a sense of reality characterized by a dynamic, active, changing, poetic immediacy instead of being merely objective or subjective. It is in keeping with what Joseph Kitagawa has described as Japan's "unitary meaning structure" of "poetic, immediate, and simultaneous awareness" within which past and future, time and space, are collapsed into the present, and "time [is] not perceived as an independent reality from nature [or space].[31] It is an opening or emptying of oneself into the immediacy of the ever-changing moment beyond distinctions and in between the "this and that" world. It is a world in between subject and object. As Isozaki has said above: *ma* is a place in which space is "perceived as identical with the events or phenomena occurring in it; that is, space [as] recognized only in its relation to time flow."

Another contemporary architect interested in *ma* is Kurokawa Kisho. Highlighting the idea of a "world between," he discusses the *engawa* ("veranda") of a typical Japanese home as exemplifying the betweenness by which outside and inside, nature and human, are merged—blurring boundaries, distinctions, and oppositions. In more general terms, he talks about Japanese culture as a "culture of grays" saying, "*En, kū* and *ma* are all key words which express the intervening territory between spaces—temporal, physical or spiritual—and thus they all share the 'gray' quality of Japanese culture. . . . In design [*ma-dori*, 'to grasp the *ma*'], *ke* [*ki*] represents the intermediary spaces; the sense of suspension between interpenetrating spaces is the feeling described by *ke*. In design, then, *ke* is the 'gray zone' of sensation."[32]

As noted above this sensitivity to spaces in between resonates with a spiritual energy called *ke* (*ki, ch'i*) or "vital breath" and "ether," which, while formless, permeates and animates life. Such energies do not come immediately to awareness out of subject/object consciousness but are experienced in radically relational or betweenness experience within which the this-and-that-world is suspended.

Another recent book has focused on this relational character of *ma*. Okuno Takeo associates *ma* with a sense of relational ordering (*kankeiso*), or betweenness, and points out that several important words in Japanese carry *ma* (also pronounced *kan, ken, gen*) with them in compounds: *jikan* ("time"), *kūkan* ("space"), *ningen* ("humans"), *seken* ("society"). All such terms, he says, imply a relational sensitivity—a sense of standing in the midst of or between reality rather than over against reality "out there." Human relations, for example, thus become a matter of negotiating the *ma* (*ma no torikata*) between/among human beings.[33]

Okuno goes on to suggest how this betweenness experience has permeated Japanese culture and created a sensitivity to the immediately processual world; to a world of shadings and shadows, moon and mist, clouds and haze; and to *ki* (*ke, ch'i*) as an atmosphere (*kehai*) attendant to this world.[34]

Such views suggest that *ma* constitutes a "between world" as a particular sensitivity and atmosphere that arises when one empties the self (and subject/object distinctions) into the interstices of being. This world is at once temporal and spatial, aesthetic (poetic) and religious (spiritual).

The Religions

SHINTO. As was true in part II above, the parallel and connection to Shinto is suggested primarily by Matsuoka's work, especially as it relates to folk Shinto. The focus of that connection here in part III, however, shifts from *kekkai* and sacred spaces to a particular sensitivity to the atmosphere of the presence (*kehai*) of *kami*, as well as to the nature of *kami* itself. Matsuoka expresses this as follows:

> *Kami* does not abide: its nature is to arrive and then depart. The Japanese word *otozureru*, meaning to visit, is a compound of *oto* (sound) and *tsure* (bring). The ancient Japanese may truly have perceived the sound of *yūgen*, utmost mystery and elegance, accompanying the visitations of *kami*. No doubt this was what is today perceived as *ch'i* by those involved in martial arts and meditation. This "*kehai* of *kami*" has set the basic tone of Japanese culture.
>
> The *kehai* of *kami's* coming and going was to pervade the structure of homes, the structure of tea houses, literature, arts, and entertainment, and it has developed into the characteristic Japanese "aesthetic of stillness and motion." This is what we call MA: the magnetic field from which the *ch'i* of *kami* subtly emanates. . . . Space, or MA, is the very foundation of Japanese aesthetics. Minute particles of *kami*, as it were, fill that MA.[35]

This *kehai* of *kami* implies two important elements: one is the nature of *kami* as formless energy that comes and goes, and the other is the character and centrality of religio-aesthetic sensitivity to this coming and going—to the "signs of the presence" (*kehai*). Relevant to the former it is clear that the notion of *kami* operating here is closer to folk Shinto than to the classical Shinto tradition. In the folk tradition, as Origuchi and others have shown, *kami* are less the abiding, anthropomorphic deities of classical Shinto mythology and shrines than vague, formless energies or spirits (*tama*) associated with living or dead humans, or such elements of nature as particular mountains, rice, and/or simply "the other world" (*tokoyo-no-kuni*) beyond the sea. Such *kami/tama* that come and go are often associated, therefore, with the "rare visitor" (*marebito*) bringing benefits at New Year's time and returning again to its sacred locale in, for example, the mountains.

Such views might be generalized as "coming/going beliefs" (*kyorai shinkō*). They emphasize the dynamic, processual, ephemeral, and changing character of sacred reality or, as Genchi Kato suggests, a notion more typical of Shinto at its "primitive naturalistic" stage and of the sacred as *numina* than of Shinto in its "advanced naturalistic" stage and of the sacred as *deus*.[36]

Matsuoka suggests that this view of *kami* has led to a "morphology of clouds" insofar as clouds represent the moving, changing, ephemeral condensation of *ch'i/ki* as the living energy of *kami*.

This morphology (and religious structure), he suggests, is visibly expressed in the medieval Shinto mandalas which express the inter-relationship of the world of *kami* with the world of nature and the human. He believes that these mandalas express the dynamic coming and going of *kami* into and out of a shrine and carry the cloud motif as well: "The tie linking the natural with the supernatural was a morphology of clouds, their myriad changes and forms. An important element in the Japanese occult was concern with the shape, color, volume, speed and position of the clouds. With the coming of the medieval period, this physiognomy of clouds influenced the basic patterns of all decorative designs. Most Japanese designs, in fact, are based on changing forms temporarily assumed by clouds and water. In this we can discern one of the reasons . . . why Japanese culture is a 'Culture of Transformations.' "[37]

The other important element in an understanding of the *kehai* of *kami*, related to but distinct from the notion of *kami*, has to do with the particular character of the experience, sensitivity, or mode of knowing that seems important here. An "atmosphere" of sacred presence, after all, depends in part on the person who experiences it as such. As Isozaki explains it, "MA is the way of sensing the moment of movement. Originally the word *utsuroi* meant the exact moment when the *kami* spirit entered into and occupied a vacant space. . . . Later it came to signify the moment of *kami*'s sudden appearance. . . . [This] gave birth to the idea of *utsuroi*, the moment when nature is transformed, the passage from one state to another. . . . MA is the expectant stillness of the moment attending this kind of change."[38]

Ma as a "way of sensing" and an "expectant stillness" implies *ma* as a particular mode of experience or sensitivity, one that is highly attuned to the immediacy of sensual experience; one that can, for example, hear the faint sounds of *kami* presence (*otozureru*), which Origuchi relates to the coming and going of *marebito*.[39] This sensitivity has become, as Matsuoka claims, "an archetype of 'knowing' " that has informed Japanese consciousness, that is, a religio-aesthetic paradigm.[40]

This experience or sensitivity can perhaps best be related to a particular mode of waiting for the various signs (*kehai*) of *kami* presence in expectant, receptive, sensitive openness. According to the assistant chief priest of Atsuta Shrine in Nagoya, Okamoto Kenji, Shinto worship is precisely a matter of waiting for, receiving, and attending to the presence of *kami* rather than an active seeking or petitioning that presence and its benefits.[41] Others have emphasized this same kind of experience through the metaphor of a host awaiting and attending to a guest, but all of them indicate a mode of sensitivity that opens the self to the depth of the moment through a disciplined receptivity and sensual awareness. As a recent traveler to Japan has said of the rather typical environs of a shrine, "And far back in the trees, shining with pure white light, is the Shoin Jinja. . . . Inside the shrine is no altar, no image to worship, only a space in which to feel."[42]

Such an experience points to the fullness of the present moment in its intuitive, aesthetic immediacy as the locus of living reality—an experience consonant with the ancient Japanese poetic awareness of time/space collapsed into the present moment. In Isozaki we have noted that space and time were experienced as simultaneous, and space was a function of time-events that filled it. On a similar theme Ebersole has said that *Manyōshū* poetry reflects a nonlinear and ahistorical sense of time in which the past is brought into the present and time is experienced as an "eternal now (*ima*)."[43] Jean Herbert seems to be indicating the same thing when he reports that "Shinto insistently claims to be a religion of the 'middle-now,' the 'eternal present,' *naka ima* . . . [and reflects an interest in] the domain of immediate experience."[44]

This way of understanding Shinto has an interesting parallel in work done by Joanne Waghorne on the "poetic gods" of Greek and Hindu polytheism. What she finds in those traditions are two distinct notions of the gods, one positing abstract, metaphysical realities and orders and the other expressing the immediate experience of "primeval energy," an energy that is embodied, for example, in poetry and drama and that is in constant motion and changing concretization. Given these two modalities of the sacred, and the two "theologies" they reflect, "the 'sacred' was either the transcendent form of being, manifested in the material world and revealed in its perfect form in myth, or the visual and sensual embodiment of a god whose nature was connected to the very vibrational energy which gave life to this ever-unfolding world." The latter are the polytheistic "gods of the poets" and are just the opposite of, for example, Plato's God of transcendent, abiding, changeless form. They are constantly mutable and have little to do with the creation of universal orders, cosmic laws, or paradigmatic models of behavior. "These gods live in a world of sight, sound, and taste (as in *rasa*), in fleeting moments of temporal experience." They are the gods of a polytheism that is less "a mistaken belief in 'many gods,' but rather, belief in a particular understanding of the nature of God which sees no sharp distinctions between multiplicity of form, the material world, time, and divinity."[45]

Such is the case with the *kehai* of *kami* as well, where *kami* come and go into the interstices of being but leave their faint signs, and where sensitive humans, by emptying themselves into the midst of now (*naka ima*) may directly experience the time/space gods embodied—however fleetingly—in the signs, sounds, and sights of the world. It is an "experiential, mysterious place" created as a third place between all other places and as an accumulation of experienced *ch'i* beyond all distinctions, boundaries, orders, and descriptive constructs.

TAOISM AND BUDDHISM. Although the potential connection of *ma* to Shinto is the more important point of this article, both Taoism and Buddhism contributed *ma*-like elements that only deepened and reinforced the native viewpoint. These religious influences can only be briefly mentioned here.

The classical Taoism of Lao-tzu and Chuang-tzu is certainly a part of this influence since it, along with Confucianism and Buddhism, came in at the top, as it were, of Japanese society and culture.[46] As mentioned above Taoist ideas are demonstrably present in the early collections of mythology. Just where, when, and how these ideas arrived, however, is less our concern than what they were and how they might be related to *ma*.

Part II above suggested that *ma* in Taoism might be located in the affirmation of "nothing" as the function or use of "something," and as an orientation to *yin* in the polarity of *yin* and *yang* (*in* and *yū*). Here, however, we find Taoism also expressing a world in between—in this case in between *yin* and *yang* (yet incorporating both).

In his book *Myth and Meaning in Early Taoism*, Norman Girardot discusses early Taoism in China as it reflects ancient mythic themes centering on cosmogony, and as they particularly appear in Lao-tzu, Chuang-tzu, and other classical Taoist sources. At the core of this theme (the *hun tun* or original chaos theme) lies a notion of "chaosmos," incorporating both chaos as a pregnant nothing and cosmos as an ordered something while standing prior to and somehow in between *yin* and *yang* or any two-ness. It is the nameless Tao of the *Tao te ching* that is beyond or prior to the named Tao. "The Taoists affirmed that the silent, hidden, or real order of Tao embraced both chaos and cosmos, non-being and being, nature and culture. . . . The secret of life, the mystic secret of salvation, is to return to [this] primitive chaos-order or 'chaosmos' of the Tao."[47]

This chaosmos, Girardot makes clear, is a third place between all two-ness, but especially the two-ness of nothing (chaos) and something (order), or *yin* and *yang*: "All of this in early Taoist texts is rooted metaphysically in the cosmogonic mystery of the third term or central gap—the 'betwixt and between'—of chaos. This is in the trinitarian formula of liminal order. . . . Creation bears the impress of trinity, for 'if it is true that two is the number that implies opposition and discord [as well as distinctions, boundaries, and naming] three is the number of reconciliation and concord,' or as the *Tao te ching* says (chapter 42): 'Tao gave birth to the three.' Truth is three, not one."[48] The *ma* of Taoism can thus not only be located (part II) but also can be dislocated, as it were, in a place that stands "betwixt and between" all two-ness; a place emptied of distinctions, locations, and orders, yet a liberating, salvific place to be; a nameless place to which one constantly returns for renewal; a poetic place of immediate, religio-aesthetic awareness brought on, in part, by waiting and yielding (*yin*).

In other terms, Girardot follows Foucault in saying that human existence constantly finds itself at the juncture between the ordering codes of culture and language and the chaos of a pure experience of order in all its modes. This pure experience, perceived as touching an inner law or hidden network of life and self, seems to have no existence except as perceived through the grid or order created by culture (as through *ma* as empty spaces and times in the flow of being and time).[49] The issue, then, becomes one of arriving at a quality of awareness that holds fast to this deeper hidden Tao but also does not forsake the grid that lies in a third place betwixt and between being and non-being. Girardot quotes Octavio Paz on this score as follows: "The West . . . teaches us that being is dissolved into meaning, and the East that meaning is dissolved into something which is neither being or non-being: In a The Same which no language except the language of silence names." He then goes on to say that the "chaosmos" (*hun tun*) is "Paz's inherently ambivalent 'The Same' that stands between all dualities."[50]

In the light of this central Taoist mythologem and its potential relation to *ma*-like ideas in Japan, it is intriguing to note the appearance of a similar Taoist cosmogony in the prefaces to both the *Kojiki* and the *Nihongi*. In the former we find that "when the primeval matter had congealed but breath and form had not yet appeared, there were no names and no action. Who can know its form?"[51] In the latter we find that "of old, Heaven and Earth were not yet separated, and the *In* and *Yo* not yet divided. They formed a chaotic mass like an egg which was of obscurely defined limits and contained germs."[52] Interpreted metaphorically, these words could be understood in light of the *hun tun* theme discussed above. In fact, further research might show that these Taoist ideas are not a mere superficial overlay on the Shinto myths but reflect an early and serious appropriation of such ideas at the very heart of Japanese culture.

Buddhism carries very similar ideas and has demonstrably had greater influence on Japanese culture. Although the crucial ideas relevant to part II above were the pregnant no-thing (*ma*), or no-mind (*mushin*) that stand over against something (*u*) or mind (*shin*); here the focus is on a between or "middle-way" awareness and the meditative techniques for its realization. The relevant terms that express this in Japanese Buddhism are *mujō* (impermanence), *kū* (emptiness), and *chū* (middle).

Ebersole has clearly shown that Buddhism had considerable influence on *renga* poetry, not only an influence of ideas but an influence of practice as well. This is made clear in a passage from a fourteenth-century *renga* treatise: " 'Contemplating deeply the vicissitudes of life of man and body, always keep in your heart the image of transience (*mujō*), and proceeding to the mountains or the sea, feel the pathos (*awaremi*) of the karma of sentient beings and non-sentient things. . . . Through the four seasons of the plants and trees feel *hikarakuyū* [see below], being enlightened by the changes of birth, old age, illness and death.' "[53]

The realization of impermanence is the realization of the absolute relativity of all things as they arise and fall in consciousness moment to moment. In such a realization the world is emptied and filled anew in each moment, and nothing abides. As in the discussion above, the world of distinctions and boundaries, of order and semipermanence is constantly dissolving into the no-thing in between. Somewhat like Zeami's "intervals between the action as most interesting," *renga* also affirms the spaces or places between: "*Renga* proved to be a 'natural' demonstration of *mujō*, transience or ephemerality, and *hikarakuyō*, 'whirling petals and falling leaves.' The Buddhist essence of *renga*, then, is not to be located in the universes or scenes . . . created by the semantic relations posited between two links by the poets and the listener/reader, but in the space between the linked poems—that is, in the dissolution of the literary universe."[54]

Although this suggests (as in part II) that the *ma* of *renga* can be
located in the spaces between the words, it is more than that as well,
namely, an experience of betweenness and a "place" beyond distinctions. Ebersole quotes the *renga* poet Shinkei (1406–75) as saying,
" 'The mind of the true poet is not caught upon existence or nothingness, upon *shinku* or *soku*, but is like the mind-field of the
Buddha.' "[55]

Such a mode of awareness, of course, has more often been
referred to in Buddhism as "emptiness" (*kū, śūnyatā*) or "suchness"
(*shinnyo, tathatā*) awareness and as a middle awareness between
nothingness (*mu*) and being (*u*). In Tendai Buddhism this terminology is turned around a bit and "middle" (*chū*) awareness stands
between emptiness (*kū*) and temporary existence (*ke*); it is the ultimate "place" to be. However expressed, such modes of awareness
are Buddhism's salvific, liberating, enlightening middle way of "co-
dependent arising;" a mode of awareness that attaches to neither
being or nonbeing but experiences the world as absolutely relative
and simultaneously arising/falling in radical mutual dependence
and relationship. On this point it is interesting to note that William
LaFleur, in discussing the ethics of Watsuji Tetsurō, refers to *ningen*
("human being") as importantly carrying the word *ma* (*gen*) in it: to
be human is to be in relationship or betweenness. LaFleur argues
that behind this notion of mutuality and relational existence, at
least in Watsuji, is the idea of *kū* as a basic term in his system. That
is, the very reason why human beings are both individual and social
is because, according to Watsuji, the individual dimension of existence 'empties' the social dimension and, conversely, the social dimension 'empties' the individual one. . . . [Existence] is a finely
balanced mutuality of dependence."[56]

Watsuji's aesthetics, says LaFleur, are based on the same idea.
For Watsuji, he says, each of the arts (under Zen Buddhist influence)
has "a common point that the moment of negation lies at its core.
. . . This moment of negation is not merely a nothing, but the notion
of emptiness as co-dependent origination."[57] In painting, for example, "there is a relationship between the void on the canvas
where nothing is painted—a wide and deep space—and the dark
silhouette of the sparrow."[58]

Such ideas are none other than a Buddhist form of *ma*—a place
in between where the subject/object world is continually emptied
and, by virtue of that, continually filled with a radically imperma-
nent, mutually dependent reality. As the Zen master Dōgen (1200–
53) describes it: every *such* moment is the absolute fullness of

being/time (*uji*); all reality is totally present in that space/time moment.

Concluding Remarks

Without question the word *ma* can mean a variety of things depending on the context of its usage. Its rather consistent appearance in the traditional arts, however, and its apparent relationship to the religions of Japan, clearly suggest that its central or deepest meanings are both aesthetic and religious. Moreover, its distinct meaning as a category of experience, knowing, or awareness suggests that it is a "way of seeing" or a religio-aesthetic paradigm.

As a paradigm in Japanese culture it affirms the power and meaning of intervals and gaps in time, space, and being that—when properly experienced (religiously, aesthetically, directly, meditatively, openly)—reveal a rich reality of presence and place, a moonlight shining through the cracks and gaps in the gate, and a world in between.

That this paradigm might appear in other cultures, though perhaps not so centrally or consistently, seems indicated by the following suggestive parallels. For example, in speaking of Heidegger's understanding of *topos* ("place"), theologian of culture David Miller says:

> Heidegger's way . . . is a discovery of *topos* itself, a facing of the "region" or "space" which has been until now forgotten in our intellectualistic ways of thinking and being. . . . It is just in that *topos* of nothingness where we may expect to discover what is lost. As we move courageously into the various nothingnesses of our being, we may begin to discover some life there, some feeling, something we had forgotten or skipped over. The topos of nothingness (*das Nichts*) is experienced as a "rift" (*der Riss*). Yet this nothingness is scarcely known to us. It is an emptiness that is essential to our being. It is that "region" into which meaning (*Logos*) is gathered (*legein*). So the rift, however much it may seem like a "mere cleft ripped open," is not only that at all. The emptiness is full. It is a "clearing" . . . which comes now to appearance precisely in the "dark woods" of the oblivion of Being. . . . It is a dance of meaning, a dance which, according to Heidegger's description, is "time's removing" and "space's throwing open" in a "play of stillness."[59]

More literally, Annie Dillard certainly is expressing *ma* when she writes,

> Ezekiel excoriates false prophets as those who have "not gone up into the gaps." The gaps are the thing. The gaps are the spirits' own home, the altitudes and latitudes so dazzlingly spare and clean that the spirit can discover itself for the first time like a once-blind man unbound. The gaps are the clefts in the rock where you cower to see the back parts of God; they are the fissures between mountains and cells the wind lances through, the icy narrowing fiords splitting the cliffs of mystery. Go up into the gaps. If you find them; they shift and vanish too. Stalk the gaps. Squeak into a gap in the soil, turn, and unlock—more than a maple—a universe. This is how you spend an afternoon, and tomorrow morning, and tomorrow afternoon. *Spend* the afternoon. You can't take it with you.[60]

These parallels in other cultures are, of course, only "suggestive" ones. However, that mere suggestion is crucial since it strongly implies that the paradigm here articulated is not bounded by culture or history but rather belongs to being human. It is at least analogous, if not similar, to the parallels that can be found between Buddhist thought, on the one hand, and the postmodern theologies of Mark Taylor, Thomas Altizer, or Charles Winquist, on the other hand. Indeed, to the degree that a *ma* paradigm or sensitivity has the marks of the postmodern about it, it is fascinating to watch it arise, perhaps disguised, in other worlds of discourse.

That both *ma* and Buddhism have the marks of the postmodern is well argued by Steve Odin's article in this volume. He suggests that Mahayana Buddhism generally and Zen more specifically have always had elements of the postmodern, especially in a Derridean sense, and that this is particularly reflected in the aesthetic manifestations of the Buddhist paradigm in the Japanese context. Perhaps art and literature (in Japanese hands especially) are uniquely able to dislocate while locating, and thereby leave a (Derridean) "trace" of *différance*.

If so, it only remains to emphasize the role of Shinto, which may seem to be an unlikely candidate for the postmodern. However, the appropriate term for the postmodern element in traditional Shinto is to a "morphology of clouds" involved "tracing" the *kehai* of *kami*, for poetic metaphors get the job done when it is "poetic gods" with which one is working. This expectant stillness or pregnant nothing called *ma* is, after all, ultimately no *thing* but rather the poetic "remainder"; a depth on the surface, a dismembered, decentered, dislocated reminiscence marking the passing presence of the gods who have been "stalked in the gaps."

Notes

1. Roland Barthes, *Empire of Signs*, tr. Richard Howard (New York: Hill and Wang, 1982).

2. Ibid., 4, 9, 26.

3. This exhibit took place at the Cooper-Hewitt Museum in New York City in 1979. Its catalog, which in many ways is the basis for this article, is by Arata Isozaki et al., *MA: Space-Time in Japan* (New York: Cooper-Hewitt Museum, n.d.).

4. Ibid., 13.

5. Kunio Komparu, *The Noh Theatre: Principles and Perspectives* (Tokyo: Tankosha; New York: John Weatherhill, 1983), 70ff.

6. Lady Murasaki, *The Tale of Genji*, tr. Arthur Waley (Garden City, NY: Doubleday & Co., 1955), 80ff.

7. Nose Asaji, ed., *Zeami jūrokubu shū hyōshaku* (Annotated Translation of Zeami's Sixteen Treatises) (Tokyo: Iwanami shoten, 1949), 1:375ff.; as translated in W.T. DeBary, ed., *Sources of Japanese Tradition* (New York: Columbia University Press, 1964), 1:285. Words in parentheses and brackets are my additions to original text. *Hima* is an older alternate character for *ma*.

8. Komparu, *The Noh Theatre*, 73.

9. Ibid., xx.

10. See especially Teiji Itoh, *Nihon dezain ron* (Theories of Japanese Design) (Tokyo: Kashima kenkyu shuppan kai, 1974), 112–19; and Teiji Yoshimura, *Nihonbi no tokushitsu* (Characteristics of Japanese Taste) (Tokyo: Kashima kenkyu shuppan kai, 1980), 178–99.

11. Komparu, *The Noh Theatre*, 71ff.; Itoh, *Nihon dezuain ron*, 120–34.

12. Gary Ebersole, "The Buddhist Ritual Use of Linked Poetry in Medieval Japan," *Eastern Buddhist* 16/2 (Autumn 1983), 55.

13. Kemmochi Takehiko, *"Ma" no nihonbunka* ("Ma" in Japanese Culture) (Tokyo: Kodansha, 1982), 13–32.

14. Kathy Geist, "West Looks East: The Influence of Yasujiro Ozu on Wim Wenders and Peter Handke," *Art Journal* 43/3 (Fall 1983), 234.

15. Kristin Thompson and David Bordwell, "Space and Narrative in the Films of Ozu," *Screen* 17/2 (1976), 45.

16. Geist, "West Looks East," 234ff.

17. Isozaki et al., *MA*, 12–53.

18. Seigow Matsuoka, "Aspects of Kami," in ibid., 57.

19. Ibid., 57; cf. Arata Isozaki, ed., *Teien to rikyū, Nihon no bi to bunka* (Gardens and Japanese Villas: Japanese Aesthetic Taste and Culture), vol. 13 (Tokyo: Kodansha, 1983), 33–39, 149–52.

20. Folk religionist Miyata Noboru has suggested this in a private interview (Tokyo, September 1983).

21. Matsuoka, "Aspects of Kami," 56ff.

22. Isozaki et al., *MA*, 13.

23. Itoh, *Nihon dezain ron*, 51.

24. Private interview with Hirai Naofusa (Kokugakuin University, 1983); Tanaka Hisao, ed., *Kamigami to hotoke, Nihon no bi to bunka*, vol. 4 (Tokyo: Kodansha, 1984), 18–28.

25. Nobutsuna Saigo, *Kodaijin to yume* (Antiquity and Dreams) (Tokyo: Heibonsha, 1972), 87–88. This discussion forms part of his third chapter, "Dreams of Hatsuse," 75–119.

26. Matsuoka, "Aspects of Kami," 56.

27. Lao Tzu, *Tao te ching*, tr. D. C. Lau (Baltimore: Penguin Books, 1963), 67.

28. Private interview, Kyoto, September 1983.

29. Günter Nitschke, "'Ma': The Japanese Sense of 'Place' in Old and New Architecture and Planning," *Architectural Design* 36/3 (March 1966), 152.

30. Ibid., 117.

31. Joseph Kitagawa, "'A Past of Things Present': Notes on Major Motifs of Early Japanese Religions," *History of Religions* 20/1–2 (August–November 1980), 27–42.

32. Kisho Kurokawa, "A Culture of Grays," in Tsune Sesoka, ed., *The I-Ro-Ha of Japan* (Tokyo: Cosmo Public Relations Corp., 1979), 9, 17; cf. his "Rikyu Gray and the Art of Ambiguity," in *Japan Architect*, 266 (June 1979), 26–56, and Itoh, *Nihon dezain ron*, 32–51.

33. Takeo Okuno, *Ma no kōzō* (The Structure of "Ma") (Tokyo: Shuseisha, 1983), 7–29, 116ff.

34. Ibid., 397–415, 430–33.

35. Matsuoka, "Aspects of Kami," 56, 47.

36. Genchi Kato, *A Historical Study of the Religious Development of Shinto* (Tokyo: Japan Society for the Promotion of Science, Ministry of Education, 1973), 11.

37. Matsuoka, "Aspects of Kami," 56. Compare Okuno's view expressed above relating *ma*-sensitivity to a preference for clouds, mist, and moon.

38. Isozaki et al., *MA*, 14ff.

39. Origuchi Shinobu, *Origuchi Shinobu zenshū* (Collected Works of Origuchic Shinobu) (Tokyo: Chuo koron shoya, 1982), 2:33; cf. Matsuoka, "Aspects of Kami," 56.

40. Matsuoka, "Aspects of Kami," 56.

41. Private interview (Nagoya, September 1983).

42. Gregg Taylor, "Hagi: Where Japan's Revolution Began," *National Geographic* 165/6 (June 1984), 760.

43. Ebersole, 'The Religio-aesthetic Complex in *Manyōshū* Poetry with Special Reference to Hitomaro's *Aki no no* Sequence," *History of Religions* 23/1 (1983), 18–36 esp. 34.

44. Jean Herbert, *Shintō: At the fountain-head of Japan* (London: George Allen & Unwin, London, 1967), 32ff.

45. Joanne Punzo Waghorne, "A Body for God: An Interpretation of the Nature of Myth Beyond Structuralism," *History of Religions* 21/1 (August 1981), 20–47.

46. See, e.g., comments to this effect in Ichiro Hori, *Folk Religion in Japan* (Chicago: University of Chicago Press, 1968), 9.

47. Norman Girardot, *Myth and Meaning in Early Taoism* (Berkeley and Los Angeles: University of California Press, 1983), 2.

48. Ibid., 43.

49. Ibid., 2.

50. Ibid., 2ff.

51. Donald Philippi, tr., *Kojiki* (Tokyo: University of Tokyo Press, 1968), 37.

52. W. G. Alston, tr., *Nihongi: Chronicles of Japan* (London: George Allen & Unwin, 1956), 1ff.

53. As translated and quoted in Ebersole, "The Buddhist Ritual Use," 60.

54. Ibid., 55.

55. Ibid., 65ff.

56. William R. LaFleur, "Buddhist Emptiness in the Ethics and Aesthetics of Watsuji Tetsurō," *Religious Studies* 14 (June 1978), 244.

57. Ibid., 246.

58. Ibid., 247.

59. David Miller, unpublished manuscript titled "Utopia, Trinity and Tropical Topography." Cf. David Miller, *Christs: Meditations on Archetypal Images in Christian Theology* (New York: Seabury Press, 1981), 146f.

60. Annie Dillard, *Pilgrim at Tinker Creek* (New York: Bantam Books, 1974), 276.

3/97

wonderfully illustrative of
issues of cultural interaction
captured in a single
concept employed in multiple
contexts

useful in discussions of nō,
architecture and garden
design; illustrations of
"code" influences at work

Contemporary Japan
(Power and Authority)

Chapter Four

Lyricism and Intertextuality: An Approach to Shunzei's Poetics

HARUO SHIRANE

Intertextuality as it has been expounded by Western literary critics rejects the notion of the autonomous, self-contained literary work and stresses the dependence of every text on other texts. Exponents of intertextuality regard the literary text as an intertextual construct, comprehensible only in terms of other texts which it prolongs, completes, transforms, or sublimates. Julia Kristeva argues that "every text takes shape as a mosaic of citations, every text is the absorption and transformation of other texts."[1] Approaching the same problem from the point of view of the reader, Roland Barthes makes the following comment in S/Z: " 'I' is not an innoncent subject, anterior to the text. . . . This 'I' which approaches the text is already itself a plurality of other texts, of codes which are infinite, or more precisely, lost (whose origin is lost)."[2] These remarks by Kristeva, Barthes, and other exponents of intertextuality can be understood, at least in part, as an attack on certain nineteenth-century romanticist views of literature, particularly those representational and expressive readings that understood poetry in such binary terms as subject/object, inside/outside, or self/nature, and that tended to regard the primary value of "lyrical expression" as creative or individual invention. For Kristeva and Barthes, the key relationship is not between the author and the text, the "self" and "other," "self" and "nature," but rather among intersecting texts.

This notion of intertextuality forms part of a broader theory of semiotics, of the function of literary language as a system of signs and codes, referring not simply to the external world but to yet other signifiers and codes. Like sign-systems, literary texts are understood not only in relationship to the author/speaker and the external world but in reference to a wide range of other texts, signs, and

codes, without which any given text would make little sense.
Intertextuality is also closely related to the problem of interpretation. If the literary text takes on meaning in the light of previous
texts and a variety of literary and cultural codes, it follows that the
meaning of the text is not inherent, but dependent upon other texts
and the larger literary and cultural context, all of which are subject
to change.

Though the historical setting and the critical terminology are
radically different, a similar awareness of the intertextual nature
and function of literary texts emerges at the end of the Heian period,
particularly in the poetry and writings of Fujiwara no Shunzei, or
Toshinari (1114–1204),[3] one of the leading Japanese poets of the
twelfth century and a pioneer in the development of what may be
called an intertextual poetics.

The following poem by Shunzei appears in the *Senzaishū* (Autumn I, no. 258), the seventh imperial *waka* anthology, compiled in
1187 by Shunzei himself.

> Yūsareba   As evening falls,
> Nobe no akikaze   The autumn wind along the moor
> Mi ni shimite   Sweeps through me—
> Uzura naku nari   A quail raises a plaintive cry
> Fukakusa no sato   In the deep grass of Fukakusa.

At first glance, the poem simply appears to describe the poet's
observation of an autumn evening in the country. Fukakusa, which
literally means "deep grass," is the name of a secluded country
village to the south of Kyoto in the Fushimi district. The poet's
feelings of loneliness and desolation—which are expressed in the
kami no ku (5/7/5)—are embodied or projected in the *shimo no ku*
(7/7), in the image of the quail crying in the deep grass.

Konishi Jin'ichi, one of the leading scholars of medieval poetry
and poetics, regarded this poem as an example of Shunzei's *yūgen*
(幽玄), the overtones that extend beyond the immediate meaning of
the words themselves.[4] This reading is based on the assumption that
the poem is primarily mimetic, on the belief that the primary
function of the text is to represent a given setting, however mysti-
fying and complex—filled with "overtones"—that scene may be.
What happens, however, if we regard the poem intertextually, primarily in relationship to earlier texts and literary conventions, as an
"open" text in which each word or phrase refers, not to a fixed
referent (a given scene), but to other signs and signifiers?

To begin with, the opening line, "With the arrival of evening" (*Yū sareba*), immediately recalls a number of poems, such as the following two from the *Kokinshū*, that open with the same phrase.

Yū sareba	As evening falls,
Itodo higataki	My sleeves are harder
Waga sode ni	Than ever to dry—
Aki no tsuyu sae	Even the autumn dew
Okisowaritsutsu	Joins my tears.
	(*Kokinshū*, Love I, no. 545, Anonymous)

Yū sareba	As evening falls,
Hitonaki toko o	I dust and clean an empty bed—
Uchiharai	Have I become one
Nagekamu tame to	Whose fate is to grieve?
Nareru wagami ka	
	(*Kokinshū*, Love V, no. 815, Anonymous)

As these two poems in the *Kokinshū* suggest, for Shunzei and other Heian readers the phrase "As evening falls" (*yū sareba*) was closely associated with the images of autumn, tears, dew, and most specifically, that of a woman waiting in vain for the arrival of her lover. "Autumn wind" (*akikaze*) has similar implications.

Akikaze no	Now that the autumn wind
Mi ni samukereba	Has chilled me,
Tsure mo naki	I hope against hope
Hito o zo tanomu	For that cold-hearted one
Kururu yo goto ni	As each evening falls.
	(*Kokinshū*, Love II, no. 555, Priest Sosei)

In the *Manyōshū*, autumn is sometimes a time of hope and fulfillment, of vitality and renewal. In Heian poetry, by contrast, autumn inevitably takes on a melancholy hue. The autumn wind becomes a metaphor for rapid change and the impermanence of life and is associated with a group of other autumnal sounds—the pounding of the fulling block (*kunuta*), the cries of the evening cicada (*higurashi*), and the voice of the deer—all of which were considered to be lonely and mournful. Due to the homophone *aki*, "to grow weary," *akikaze* also implies unrequited love, in which the neglected lover mourns the absence of the person who has "lost interest" (*aki*).

The *kami no ku* of Shunzei's poem draws out all of these traditional associations—of the cold, loneliness, the weariness of waiting—which are then reinforced in the *shimo no ku* by the image of the quail (*uzura*) crying in the deep grass. From the late Heian period, the quail, which had become an icon of autumn, was depicted, at least in classical poetry, as loving deep grass and crying in abandoned villages and old houses. In the typical medieval *uzura* poem, the speaker expresses his or her personal regrets and sorrows (*jukkai*) through the quail which, having retreated from the world, cries in a dilapidated village or house.

It is not until the following subtext, found in the *Kokinshū* (Msc., nos. 971–92), that these pieces fall together to form a striking intertext.

> He lived in the village of Fukakusa, and when he decided to visit the capital, he sent the following poem to his lover.

> Toshi o hete   If I leave this village,
> Sumikoshi sato o   Where I have passed all these years,
> Idete inaba   Will it become a moor
> Itodo fukakusa   Of even higher grass?
> No to ya narinamu

> Her answer:

> No to naraba   If it becomes a moor,
> Uzura to nakite   I shall pass the years
> Toshi wa hemu   Crying like a quail.
> Kari ni dani yawa   Will you not come back,
> Kimi ga kozaramu   If only for a while, as a hunter?

In a footnote to this poem in the *Jichin oshō jikaawase* (1190–99), Shunzei notes that the quail (*uzura*) refers to the woman in Fukakusa village in the 123rd episode of the *Ise monogatari*, which is probably the source of the two *Kokinshū* poems.

> In times long past, there was a man who, gradually tiring of a woman who lived in Fukakusa, wrote her the following poem.

> Toshi o hete   If I leave this village,
> Sumikoshi sato o   Where I have passed all these years,
> Idete inaba   Will it become a moor
> Itodo fukakusa   Of even higher grass?
> No to ya narinamu

The woman's reply:

No to naraba	If it becomes a moor,
Uzura to narite	I will become a quail
Nakioramu	And cry in sorrow.
Kari ni dani yawa	Will you not come back,
Kimi wa kozaramu	If only for a while, as a hunter?

Deeply impressed by her poem, he lost the desire to leave.

The cluster of subtexts suggests that the speaker in Shunzei's poem is a lonely woman who has grown weary of waiting for her lover, that the cry of the quail echoes a woman in sorrow, and that the grass has grown deep as a result of the man's prolonged neglect.

In *Semiotics of Poetry*, Michael Riffaterre, one of the more innovative intertextual critics, argues that the modern reader first attempts to read a poem mimetically (that is to say, representationally), and when he or she finds that—for various reasons, particularly grammatical and semantic fracturings—the mimetic reading fails or proves unsatisfactory, he or she then attempts to read the poem semiotically, or intertextually, as a text referring to various subtexts or signs.[5] In this particular case, Shunzei's poem can easily be read mimetically—as a subjective description of pastoral scene—but the informed reader (which includes Konishi in a later interpretation),[6] realizing that the mimetic reading is of limited significance, begins reading the text as an intertextual construct, as a poem referring to other poems and literary clusters—particularly the elegant world of love found in the Heian classics—and sees the text as an inventive variation on a familiar topos found in both Heian fiction and poetry: That of the melancholy, lonely woman abandoned in the countryside.

In contrast to the traditional notion of allusion, intertextuality does not depend on the existence of a unique or fixed pretext or source. The classical concept of allusion is founded on, or at least appeals to, the notion of authorial experience and intention, as is evident in the attempts by scholars to establish which texts or sources a given author may have read or otherwise come in contact with. Intertextuality dispenses with the classical criteria of authorial consciousness or contact and replaces it with an approach which takes into account not only the literary tradition but the role of a collective unconscious. Thus, while the two Fukakusa poems in *Ise monogatari* fall under the traditional category of allusion, "as

evening falls" (*yū sareba*) or "autumn wind" (*akikaze*) do not.
Whether Shunzei had in mind the *Kokinshū* poems cited above in
connection with "as evening falls" and "autumn wind" when composing this particular poem is unclear and indeterminable. And yet
these words and phrases, with their associative clusters, form as
integral a part of the intertext as does the obvious allusion to the
Fukakusa poems.

As modern readers we are tempted to read classical Japanese
poetry either in the mimetic mode, in which the poem is seen as a
form of imitation of the external world, or in the lyrical, expressive
mode, in which the poem is regarded as a direct expression of the
poet's thoughts and feelings. In his Preface to the *Lyrical Ballads*
(1800), Wordsworth announces that "Poetry is the spontaneous
overflow of powerful feelings." We find a similar pronouncement in
the opening line of Ki no Tsurayuki's *kana* (Japanese syllabary)
preface to the *Kokinshū* (ca. 905), written around two and a half
centuries prior to Shunzei's poem.

> Japanese poetry takes the human heart as its seed and grows into a
> myriad leaves of words. The people who live in this world, aroused
> by the countless events in their lives, express what is in their
> hearts through the things that they see and hear. When we hear the
> warbler that sings in the cherry blossoms, or the song of the frog
> that lives in the water, we realize that there is no living creature
> that does not compose poetry. It is poetry that moves heaven and
> earth without effort, stirs the emotions of invisible demons and
> gods, smoothes the relations between man and woman, and calms
> the hearts of fierce warriors.

Ki no Tsurayuki argues that *waka* has an important social function,
as a form of interpersonal communication, as well as a significant
expressive, cathartic function, in releasing emotion and thought.
The expression of emotion, however, is not unmediated; it must
occur through figurative language and metaphor, particularly
through images taken from nature.

Though the *kana* preface was to become the most famous
"defense" of classical *waka*, the dominant stream of poetic activity
was eventually to go against Ki no Tsurayuki's assertion that Japanese poetry is born as a direct, emotional response to everyday
experience. The trend in the late Heian period was increasingly
toward poems on fixed, or assigned, topics. By the early medieval
period, almost all poetry considered to be serious literature and
worthy of inclusion in an imperial anthology was public poetry,

composed either for *utaawase* ("poetry contests"), for *kakai* ("poetry gatherings"), or for *hyakushu* ("verses on a hundred topics"). On these public and social occasions, the participants would be asked to write on a fixed topic, or *dai*—for example, some aspect of love, the four seasons, the moon, an atmospheric condition (e.g., snow, mist), a poetic place (*utamakura*), a particular bird, and so on. Whether the poet had ever experienced or seen the particular topic was irrelevant. In the poetry contests, two poets would compose on the same topic, and a judgment would usually be handed down determining the winner and commenting on the merits and demerits of the two poems.

A major criterion for the judgments in poetry contests was whether a particular poem was in accord with the *hon'i* (literally, "original meaning"), the "poetic essence" of a particular *dai*, or topos. The *hon'i* of Mount Fuji, for example, assumed a volcanic mountain that continually emitted smoke.[7] From as early as the *Manyōshū*, Mount Fuji had been closely associated with passionate love, a burning, unceasing, and frustrated desire for a particular member of the opposite sex. The following poem on Mount Fuji is from the *Kokinshū* (Love I, Anonymous, no. 534).

Hito shirenu	Mount Fuji in Suruga,
Omoi o tsune ni	Where the fires of love
Suruga naru	Burn forever unnoticed,
Fuji no yama koso	Is nothing but myself.
Wagami narikere	

As the *Taketori monogatari* (*The Tale of the Bamboo Cutter*) suggests, the image of unceasing desire probably derives from the phonic association of Mount Fuji with the phrases *fushi*, which means "undying," and *fujin*, which means "inexhaustible"—two associations further elaborated, as they are here, by the wordplay between *omoi*, "thoughts of love," and *hi*, "fire." Like other *hon'i*, that of Mount Fuji does not refer to the object—the mountain on the border of Shizuoka and Yamanashi Prefectures—so much as to the cluster of emotional and aesthetic attitudes and associations developed by the literary tradition with regard to this particular topic. The objective of the poet participating in an *utaawase*, or poetry contest, was to grasp this *hon'i* in his or her own individual manner, that is to say, to write on the assigned topic according to carefully defined conventions. As the practice of *daiei*, of composing poetry on fixed topics, developed, the emphasis on *hon'i* increased. Each topic (*dai*)—ranging from various aspects of the four seasons to love and personal grievances (*jukkai*)—acquired one or more poetic essences. The end result was the conceptualization of much of nature and human existence and a highly "poeticized" world.

Shunzei's poem on the quail was composed for *Sutokuin hyakushu*, a *hyakushu* sponsored by the Retired Emperor Sutoku (r. 1123–41) in Kyūan 6 (1150). For a typical *hyakushu* ("verses on a hundred topics"), different poets were asked to prepare and present their own sequence of a hundred *waka* on assigned topics. Like most extant poems of the late Heian and early Kamakura period, Shunzei's poem is both public—that is to say, it was written for public reception—and fictional, and yet, significantly, in tone and attitude, it remains lyrical. The poem is highly intertextual, depending for its full effect on the interrelationship between the work and prior texts and literary conventions, and yet the poem remains in what M. H. Abrams calls the expressive mode, focusing on the lyrical overflow of private emotions, though not necessarily those of the author.

In the *Koraifūteisho* (*Collection of Poetic Styles Old and New*, 1107), written in response to a request from Princess Shikishi, Shunzei makes the following observation about the function of poetry.

> As stated in the preface to the *Kokinshū*, Japanese poetry takes the human heart as its seed and grows into a myriad leaves of words. Thus, without Japanese poetry, no one would know the fragrance of the cherry blossoms in spring, nor would they know the color of the bright leaves in autumn. Without Japanese poetry, what would we do for an original heart?[8]

By "original heart" (*moto no kokoro*), Shunzei suggests a spirit that views and understands the world through the lens of classical poetry, particularly that of the *Kokinshū*, and that, as a consequence, can subjectively grasp the poetic essences (*hon'i*) of nature, here symbolized by the fragrance of the cherry blossoms and the color of the autumn leaves. Poetry, which Shunzei endows with the highest spiritual function, has the power to make the "human heart" (*hito no kokoro*) grasp the poetic essences of nature, or rather, it enables those poetic essences to enter into the "human heart." The resulting fusion is the *moto no kokoro*, the "original heart."[9]

In *The Anxiety of Influence*, Harold Bloom, arguing for a Freudian version of intertextuality, analyzes the different ways in which a strong poet, engaged in a form of Oedipal rivalry with a major precursor, may willfully misread or revise the poetry of a "father" poet in order to assert his originality and carve out literary ground for himself.[10] In the *Koraifūteishō* Shunzei engages in a similar act when he cites the opening line of the *kana* preface to the *Kokinshū*. Shunzei appears to be paying homage to his literary father, Ki no Tsurayuki, who argues that poetry emerges in direct response to the events of the external world, Shunzei stresses that poetry is born of poetry. It is through poetry—especially the poetry of the *Kokinshū*—that we come to know "nature," understand its beauty, and culti-vate the aesthetic/literary sensibility necessary for composing poetry. This "nature" does not exist independently of poetry but within and through it. It is not the external world that determines the standard of beauty, or the poetic/aesthetic essence of things, but the literary world of the Heian classics. Shunzei implies that the poet must possess a deep, if not unconscious, understanding of the *waka* tradition, represented by the poems that he has collected in *Koraifūteishō*. By studying these superior poems, the reader can attain the "original heart," which has been passed on over hundreds of years through poetry and which in turn can produce superior poetry.

In the opening line of the second part of the *Koraifūteishō*, Shunzei elaborates yet further on his new poetics.

> As the months pass and the seasons change, and as the cherry blossoms give way to bright autumn leaves, we are reminded of the words and images of poems and feel as if we can discern the quality of those poems. At the beginning of spring, the colors are various—the rose plum near the eaves, its blossoms emerging from beneath the snow, and the plum blossoms in the hedge of the peasant's house—and yet their fragrance is the same, penetrating the sleeve that breaks off a branch and clinging to oneself. When spring is at its height, the cherry blossoms on the hills of Yoshino become confused with the lingering snow, not to mention the cherry trees in full bloom at the imperial palace, which become one with the layers of white clouds.[11]

The poetic images established and refined by the Heian aristocratic *waka* tradition are here filtered through Shunzei's "original heart." Shunzei does not recall the hills of Yoshino as he actually may have seen them but as they exist in his literary imagination. In fact, almost every phrase in this passage echoes a poem from the *Kokinshū* or the *Genji monogatari*. For example, the reference to

Yoshino recalls the following *Kokinshū* poem (Spring I, no. 60, Tomonori).

> Miyoshino no   The cherry blossoms
> Yamabe ni sakeru   Blooming on the edges of
> Sakurabana   The hills of fair Yoshino—
> Yuki ka to nomi zo   I mistook the flowers
> Ayamatarekeru   For banks of snow.

Shunzei's description of seasonal images is no less than an elaborate presentation of *hon'i*, or poetic essences. Nature and the passage of the seasons serve only as a reminder to Shunzei of various aspects of nature as they exist as figures, tropes, and signs in classical Japanese poetry. Nature is not the object of description. It functions as the point of departure, pointing the way to literary commonplaces and nature as it appears in both early poetry and Heian *monogatari*, particularly the *Ise monogatari* and the *Genji monogatari*, which, in Shunzei's view, richly expressed the *hon'i* that had largely ceased to grow since the first three imperial *waka* anthologies (referred to as the *Sandaishū*): *Kokinshū*, *Gosenshū*, and *Shūishū*.

Shunzei does not use terms like intertextuality, nor does he engage in the kind of textual analysis carried out by modern critics—his main concern is praxis, the composition of poetry—and yet he has a profound awareness of poetry both as a highly codified object and as an intertextual construct—an awareness that was to deepen with his son and great successor, Fujiwara no Teika. Shunzei also stresses the deeply intertextual nature of perception. In contrast to Tsurayuki, who regards the "human heart" and the external "world" (*yo no naka*) in dualistic terms, Shunzei, in a manner reminiscent of the Mahayana Buddhist notions which he employs elsewhere in the preface to *Koraifūteishō*, suggests that the phenomenal world does not exist apart from individual consciousness and that this consciousness is a mosaic of citations. As noted earlier, Roland Barthes argues that the " 'I' which approaches the text is already itself a plurality of other texts, of codes which are infinite, or more precisely, lost." Shunzei likewise recognizes the "plurality of other texts" within the reader/poet, which he refers to as the "original heart," but in contrast to Barthes, who regards these pretexts and codes as "anonymous" or "lost," Shunzei specifies the Heian classics and the *Kokinshū* in particular as the source of literary codes and pretexts.

For Shunzei, the union of the "human heart" (*hito no kokoro*) and the poetic essence (*hon'i*) of things—a process suggested by the term "original heart" (*moto no kokoro*)—was critical to the recovery of the subjective lyricism that he believed had been lost in recent fixed-topic poetry. By Shunzei's time, each word in the limited canon had a specific emotional or situational connotation. The mere mention in a poem of the phrase "Bridge maiden at Uji" (*Uji no hashihime*) expressed the feeling of waiting for a lover (*Kokinshū*, Love 4, no. 689, Anonymous). The poet could respond to a given topic (*dai*)—however foreign to personal experience—by drawing on a well-established repertoire of phrases and words and their encoded situations. Poetic composition on fixed topics (*daiei*) had, to a large extent, become a game of arranging and combining words in accordance with the given topic. Even the worst poet could compose a poem on love or personal grief by mechanically drawing on the diction and phrases of the poetic canon and constructing a poetic scene with those words. One prominent method of poetic composition—sometimes referred to as *fuzei*, or "conception-oriented," poetry—consisted of studying the *hon'i* of the *dai* (assigned topic), recalling its conventional associations, and creating, with as much ingenuity and wit as possible, a new situation or image. In *Toshiyori tainō* (ca. 1114), Minamoto no Toshiyori (1055–1129) gives the following poem—on the familiar topic of expressing regret at the scattering of the cherry blossoms—as an example of a poem with "too much *fuzei*."[12]

Ōzora o	If only I had
Ōu bakari no	A sleeve wide enough
Sode mogana	To cover the sky.
Chirikau hana o	I will not leave the scattering
Kaze ni makaseji	Cherry blossoms to the wind.
	(*Gosenshū*, Spring II, no. 64)

Shunzei, who criticized this kind of poetry as being artificial, urges the poet to enter into the poetic world of the Heian classics, absorb the sensibility and diction of that world, and then compose with this "original heart."

Shunzei suggests that this "original heart" should enable the poet to achieve a more subjective, lyrical, and "natural" grasp of the *hon'i* of the topic (*dai*). A good example is the following poem (*Shinkokinshū*, Summer, no. 201), composed by Shunzei on the topic of the "cuckoo" (*hototogisu*) for a *hyakushu* in Jishō 2 (1178).

Mukashi omou	Thinking of the past
Kusa no iori no	As the night rain falls
Yoru no ame ni	On my grass hut—
Namida na soe so	Mountain cuckoo,
Yamahototogisu	Add no more tears to the rain!

In the poetic tradition, the cuckoo, a poetic icon of summer, lives in the hills and visits the capital in the Fifth Month (*Satsuki*).[13] Shunzei grasps the *hon'i* of the topic by focusing on the voice of the *hototogisu* but he does more than follow the conventional attitudes, which were waiting for, seeking out, or rejoicing at the sound of the cuckoo. The speaker instead asks the "mountain cuckoo" (*yamahototogisu*)—a cuckoo that is already singing but has not yet ventured out of the hills—not to add its tears to his own. *Yamahototogisu* also implies that the "grass hut" is in the mountains and that the "night rain" is the "summer rains" (*samidare*) of the Fifth Month, considered by the poetic tradition to be long, unpleasant, and melancholy. The interlinked images—the grass mountain hut (traditionally associated with loneliness), the damp rain of summer (which implies tears and memories), and the mournful voice of the mountain cuckoo—create a mood of unbearable loneliness, a theme further developed by an allusion to a famous poem in which Po Chü-i compares his present situation, as an official who has retired to Mount Lu, with that of his three friends, who are still flourishing in government. Two lines from this poem appear in the *Wakanrōeishū* (No. 555), which is the primary text through which Shunzei and other Japanese poets appreciated this Chinese poem.

蘭省花時錦帳下
魯山雨夜草庵中
At court, the flowers in bloom,
You bask beneath the brocade curtains,
While on Mount Lu, I listen
To the night rain in a grass hut.[14]

The opening line of Shunzei's poem—"Thinking of the past" (*mukashi omou*)—refers not only to Po Chü-i's thoughts of a happier time but to the author's memory of his days at the imperial court.

Two years earlier, in Angen 2 (1176), Shunzei, after falling seriously ill, had taken holy vows and assumed the Buddhist name of Shakua. Through an allusion, which implies that the person who is "thinking of the past" has been forced to leave the secular world, and through various pretexts and literary associations, Shunzei creates a poem that not only adheres to the "poetic essence" of the fixed topic (*hototogisu*) but that is lyrical and personal as well.

Shunzei's poetics not only links the expressive-affective poetics advocated by Ki no Tsurayuki with the intertextual poetics that was to emerge at the heart of medieval poetry (particularly that of Fujiwara no Teika), it reflects a larger tendency in classical Japanese literature. Japanese classical poetry and its generic cousins, the vernacular romance (*monogatari*), the literary diary (*nikki*), and the essay (*zuihitsu*), have often been characterized as lyrical, subjective, personal, and emotive—attitudes closely associated with nineteenth-century romanticist views of literature, which tend to regard the primary value of "lyrical expression" as creative or individual invention. Like many other Japanese literary forms, however, late Heian *waka* was also a genre that functioned within an elaborate fabric of rules, conventions, and literary associations, within a highly codified, intertextual context, and frequently in fictional or allegorical settings, in which the primary stress was not on individual invention but on allusive citation and on subtle, imitative variation of pretexts and traditional literary associations. As with Shunzei's poetry, it is often in the intersection of these two seemingly antithetical modes—a conjunction found in Shunzei's critical notion of the "original heart"—that the best and most refined of Japanese classical literature emerges.

Notes

1. Julia Kristeva, "Word, Dialogue, and Novel," in her *Desire in Language: A Semiotic Approach to Literature and Art*, tr. Thomas Gora, Alice Jardine, and Leon S. Roudiez (Oxford: Basil Blackwell, 1980), 66.

2. Roland Barthes, *S/Z*, tr. Richard Miller (New York: Hill and Wang, 1974), 10.

3. Fujiwara no Shunzei was born in Eikyū 2 (1114), the third son of Fujiwara no Toshitada. He changed his name from Akihiro to Shunzei at the age of fifty-four. When he took holy vows at the age of sixty-three, he assumed the Buddhist name of Shakua.

4. Konishi Jin'ichi, "Shunzei no yūgen-fūto shikan" (Shunzei's View of *Yūgen* and *Shikan* Meditation) *Bungaku* 20/2 (1952), 12–14.

5. Michael Riffaterre, *Semiotics of Poetry* (Bloomington: Indiana University Press, 1978), 1–6.

6. Konishi Jin'ichi, *Michi: Chūsei no risen* (*Michi*: A Medieval Principle) Kōdansha shinsho series (Kōdansha, 1975), 49–50.

7. According to a judgment by Fujiwara no Mototoshi (1060–1142) in a poetry contest (*Naidaijin utaawase*) in 1118, the *hon'i* of Mount Fuji was "a heart that never ceases to burn" (*taezu yaku kokoro*).

8. *Karonshū*, Hashimoto Fumio, et al., eds., *Nihon koten bungaku zenshū* (Collection of Classical Japanese Literature) 50.273.

9. Shunzei's subsequent references to the *Makashikan* in the preface to the *Koraifūteishō* suggest that the "human heart" concentrates upon and enters deeply into nature and that nature in turn enters into the "heart." As a consequence, the "poetic essence" and, by implication, the poetic tradition as a whole, comes to reside or live within the "heart" of the poet.

10. Harold Bloom, *The Anxiety of Influence* (New York: Oxford University Press, 1973). "Influence, as I conceive it, means that there are *no* texts, but only relationships *between* texts. These relationships depend upon a critical act, a misreading or misprision, that one poet performs upon another, and that does not differ in kind from the necessary critical acts performed by every strong reader upon every text he encounters." Harold Bloom, *A Map of Misreading* (New York: Oxford University Press, 1975), 3.

11. *Nihon koten bungaku zenshū* 50.371.

12. *Nihon koten bungaku zenshū* 50.94.

13. Shunzei's poem is included within an extended thirty-one poem sequence in the *Shinkokinshū* on the *hototogisu* which begins with the topic of "waiting anxiously for the voice of the *hototogisu*" and proceeds in temporal order to "seeking the voice of the *hototogisu* in the hills," "listening to the *hototogisu* for the first time in the capital," and "following the *hototogisu* that has returned to the hills" (*Shinkokinshū*, nos. 189–220).

14. Ōsone Shōsuke, Horiuchi Hideaki, eds., *Wakan rōeishū*, Shinchō *Nihon koten shūsei* (Tokyo: Shinchōsha, 1983), 555.

a fundamental enlargement of a basic cultural modality

Contemporary Japan
Power and Authority

Chapter Five

A Methodological Examination of the "Post-Confucian Thesis" in Relation to Japanese (and Chinese) Economic Development

CHARLES WEI-HSUN FU

Reflections on a Threefold Methodological Procedure

In one of my recent papers, "Ju-chia ssu-hsiang te shih-tai k'e-t'i chi-ch'i chie-chüe hsien-suo" ("On the Present-day Problems of Confucian Thought and the Key to Their Resolution"),[1] I have put forward two interrelated theses concerning the question of Confucianism's role in the economic development of East Asia. The first takes issue with the common assumption of a causal link existing between the phenomenon of increasing economic prosperity and the ideological structure of Confucianism. My second point proposes an alternative, more productive analysis of the phenomenon that transcends scientific theories of causality and that simultaneously serves as the starting point for an ideological revitalization of Confucianism.

To summarize my underlying argument, the role of Confucianism as the cultural or ideological "cause" responsible for the East Asian economic "miracle" has been grossly overemphasized and scantily supported. Although this position places me in opposition to the majority of scholars investigating these postwar economic success stories, it is my contention that their views represent a serious oversimplification of the situation. While it is theoretically tempting to locate a single source that is capable of explaining what has been happening in East Asia, such generalizations fail to comprehend the complexity of the situation. The inevitable result of submitting the social sciences to the Procrustean bed of rigors appropriate to the "hard" sciences is that much of the data is either distorted or glossed over.

Most importantly, in doing so, little attention is paid to the essential points of difference which undeniably exist among the East Asian societies involved (namely Japan and the four "Little Dragons"—Taiwan, Korea, Hong Kong, and Singapore). These differences arise from a multiplicity of factors, ranging from the technological to climactic-geographical, socio-political, cultural, historical, and so on. More specifically as relates to Confucianism, we must remain cognizant of how these factors transformed Confucianism from its original form as conceived in ancient China, in effect making it into a distinctive expression of the society in question. Therefore, understanding the diversity and distinctiveness of each of the traditions, especially the difference between Confucianism in China and Japan, is crucial for analyzing the decentric, dynamic nature of postmodern East Asian society.

Threefold Methodology

Given the deficiencies inherent in previously proposed approaches, the opportunity is opened for more fruitful alternatives. We must begin by modifying the questions we pose. Indeed, the most crucial question concerning the Confucian tradition's relationship (if any) to East Asian economic development does not lie in how to scientifically "discover" the assumed causal link between economy and Confucian culture stagnantly portrayed, nor in how to "interpret" the modern meaning of this link. Rather the open-ended, pluralistically oriented postmodern question we must ask is how we can ideologically revitalize ("critically inherit and creatively develop," to employ my own jargon) this great tradition, so that it will not become a mere museum piece and thus an ideological burden rather than a significant contributor to the further economic development of East Asian societies. On the contrary, our aim should be to conceive of Confucianism as a living, dynamic tradition that will be a continuing source of positive contributions in the transition of these societies into modernity and postmodernity, and beyond. Pursuant to this task, my paper poses some philosophical reflections on the problem of ideological revitalization within Confucianism as regards its epistemology, metaphysics, ethics/morality, methodology of self-cultivation and religiosity.

Continuing the current of the two main points in my previous paper referred to above, the present paper shall first attempt a critical inquiry into a threefold set of methodological procedures—the scientific, hermeneutic, and philosophical, taken in that dialectical order. I shall then critically contrast Japanese Confucianism with its Chinese roots, with a view to stimulating creative dialogue and cross-fertilization between these two main forms of Confucianism in East Asia. We need to examine the demonstrated transformational potential of Japanese Confucianism to meet the challenge of the West in the industrialization process.

In the postwar era, Japan was the first nation to lead the other Confucian-based East Asian societies in an economic explosion and miraculous growth. Following in its wake, Taiwan and Korea (and perhaps Hong Kong and Singapore) now seem set on the same course of development, emulating much of the Japanese economic system. The fact that both Taiwan and Korea were Japanese colonies prior to the end of World War II cannot be overlooked—Japanese influences in the areas of economy, culture, education, ways of thinking, and lifestyle are still indelibly present. Therefore, a comparative investigation of Japanese and Chinese Confucianism will enable a more appropriate and fruitful way for the ideological revitalization of the Confucian tradition within East Asia in general. (In this connection, I should note that my critical comparison harbors no intention of minimizing the importance of Korean Confucianism. Only my lack of sufficient knowledge of this area prevents me from including it in the comparison process, and I await those experts of Korean Confucianism to help me expand my knowledge and understanding of the various forms of East Asian Confucianism past and present.)

To begin, let us be clear as to the factors relevant to societal transformation in a broad sense. Such "transformative capacity" has been defined by S. N. Eisenstadt as "the capacity to legitimize, in religious or ideological terms, the development of new motivations, activities, and institutions which were not encompassed by their original impulses and views."[2] Methodologically speaking, it seems that our discovery, or rediscovery, of this "transformative capacity" is already inherent in our postmodern method of interpreting, or reinterpreting, a particular religion or ideology as what Hans-Georg Gadamer calls a "historical tradition" in such a way that it is relevant to economic development.

On the scientific level, the primary concern is to explain the causal links between economic development and cultural factors. It is understood as common sense by most social scientists that there is a multiplicity of factors which make up the causal link with economic development. Despite this recognition, there still are scholars who tend to develop a particular model stressing a certain set of causes as primary for economic development. Thus, it has become quite popular in scholarly circles to apply Max Weber's analysis to East Asia, thereby emphasizing motivational (religious/ ideological) variables related to economic success and, in turn, correlating these to Confucian principles.

For example, in his paper, "An East Asian Development Model?," Peter L. Berger mentions two hypotheses, one "culturalist" and the other "institutionalist." Berger states with regard to the first of these, in the form of the "post-Confucian hypothesis," that "I'm strongly inclined to believe that, as evidence continues to come in, this hypothesis will be supported. It is inconceivable to me that at least some of the Confucian-derived values intended by the hypothesis—a positive attitude to the affairs of this world, a sustained lifestyle of discipline and self-cultivation, respect for authority, frugality, an overriding concern for stable family life—should not be relevant to the work ethic and the overall social attitudes of the region."[3] If the post-Confucian hypothesis is understood only in terms of selecting these qualities, it oversimplifies the importance of Confucianism and its deeper values at work in East Asian societies. Even if we lend credence to this hypothesis, it fails to be sufficiently encompassing. Confucianism assuredly is not the only motivational factor at work in the various East Asian societies, the cultural/ideological manifestations of which are often pluralistic in nature. Furthermore, the extent of its influence on the populations in question may well be exaggerated. Berger himself seems to realize the multiplicity of cultural factors in saying, "At the same time, I strongly suspect that Confucianism is by no means the only cultural and religious factor in play. Other factors will have to be explored."[4]

Another example comes from Robert Bellah, in his early work, *Tokugawa Religion*.[5] Here Bellah investigates the *Shingaku* ("mind learning") movement of Ishida Baigan (1685–1744) and his successors along with the *Hotoku* movement of Ninomiya Sontoku (1787–1856), two of the most outstanding figures of Tokugawa religion. His argument is that each constitutes a positive ideological factor in the subsequent economic development of Japan.[6] However, eleven years later in his paper, "Reflections on the Protestant Ethic Analogy in Asia," Bellah mentions Maruyama Masao's review of his book (in *Kokka gakkai zasshi*, April 1958), containing a harsh criticism of Bellah's optimistic view of motivational factors in relation to Japanese economic development. In his response Bellah admits that he was "coming increasingly to believe that ... it becomes necessary to press beyond both the motivational and the institutional approaches and to view matters in an even broader perspective."[7] Bellah concludes that

> the whole range of problems having to do with social change in Asia would be greatly illuminated if we had a comprehensive social taxonomy based on evolutionary principles of the sort that Durkheim called for in 1895. Among recent sociologists I can think only of S. N. Eisenstadt as having made significant contributions to this end. With such a taxonomy in hand we would be in a much stronger position to *interpret the meaning* of the results obtained by those currently concentrating on motivational institutional research. We might also be in a better position to clear up profound problems both of science and policy which hover around the *definition of the concept of modernization.*[8]

It is important for me to highlight Bellah's words, because it is certainly ideal from the standpoint of the social sciences to obtain a taxonomy such as Bellah suggests. However, even if this were realistically possible (which is doubtful), the question in a deeper sense is no longer one of a scientific investigation of the causal links between economic development and factors having to do with institutions, motivation, culture, and so on. Only by overcoming biased readings of the data can we insure a correct interpretation of the meaning of these causal links. The limitations of scientific explanation are immediately exposed here as but another human way of interpreting the meaning of History. The dream of a perfectly scientific taxonomy fades into the distance and scientific methodology gives way to hermeneutics, as suggested by those words I have italicized in the Bellah passage.

Several reasons can be advanced to demonstrate why a causal explanation is, in a broader perspective, essentially a sub-project within hermeneutic studies. The first reason is that the process of constructing hypotheses or models in the social sciences must presuppose a clear definition of key concepts in order to be conventionally accepted. For instance, whether the word "modernization" should be identified with Westernization or industrialization has been a matter of ongoing controversy among scholars who deal with the economic development of non-Western countries.[9] It is interesting to note that one of the questions raised at the Hakone Conference on the "Modernization of Japan" in the summer of 1960 was whether key concepts like "democracy," "liberalism," and "socialism" should be incorporated into a broader conceptual framework as a means of dealing with the various problems of modernization. While the American participants hesitated to introduce any ideologically-charged concepts into the definition of modernization, their Japanese counterparts insisted on the inclusion of these concepts. It seems to me that such concepts arise from a hermeneutic rather than a scientific basis. In his concluding words quoted above, Bellah does not seem to fully comprehend the methodological point that ideologically charged concepts like "modernization" must be "defined"—that is, hermeneutically determined or settled upon—before or at the time the social scientists attempt to construct "a comprehensive social taxonomy."

The second reason is that the selection of the so-called primary cause concerning the causal link between economy and culture is, again, a matter of hermeneutic emphasis not to be determined with a purely scientific system of conceptualization. For example, in his book, *The Roots of Modern Japan*, Jean-Pierre Lehman lists more than a dozen causal factors relating to Japan's industrial performance and economic growth, stating "None of these factors should be seen in isolation. Rather they were strands which were woven into a common pattern and which accounted for both the causes and nature of Japan's process of transformation."[10] He continues, "While acknowledging the interplay of diverse factors and forces, the historian should nevertheless be prepared to take a stand in isolating what he perceives as the primordial cause, the *deus ex machina*, of Japan's successful transformation to modernity."[11] As primordial cause he selects the qualities (vision, determination, and flexibility) of the Meiji leadership.[12] From the standpoint of methodological procedures, as an historian Lehman apparently fails to perceive the level of hermeneutic inquiry that lies beyond scientific investigation, and hence collapses the two levels. The so-called primordial cause pointed to here is in fact a hermeneutic concept, not a scientific one.

The third reason for the deficiency of scientific causality is that the entire conceptual framework set up in the process of scientific hypothesis or model construction is also a matter of hermeneutic/thematic focus, combined with practical concerns (such as a profound urge to modernize nations like China). To introduce a heuristic concept or principle is to redirect our theoretical attention to a new hermeneutic way of seeing the human meanings of, for example, modern history, political economy, the transformative capacity of a religion or ideology, and so on. To extend the original meaning of Francis Bacon's words, "Knowledge is power," I would like to stress the practical meanings and applications of the social sciences, including historical studies, as essentially a hermeneutic enterprise manifesting intellectual power to help us change the course of history (e.g., from feudalism to modernity, or from modernity to postmodernity). That is to say, hermeneutic studies already imply our human interest in using scientific/hermeneutic explorations of all the discoverable causes, modern meanings and their implications, of the subject concerned—in our case, of Confucianism in relation to economic development.

In other words, scientific/hermeneutic explorations of our subject necessarily lead us to the philosophical quest for an ideological revitalization of the tradition under investigation here—the third level of our methodological procedure. This is what I mean by referring to the pursuit of methodological procedures on three levels in a dialectical order. Our scientific "discovery" of any new "cause(s)" leads us to a new hermeneutic way of reading the modern meanings and implications of the scientific analysis and explanation, and this interpretation of the meanings and implications in question in turn leads to the postmodern philosophical task of critically inheriting and creatively developing what Gadamer calls a "historical tradition," such as Confucianism. Dialectically speaking, the reverse order is equally true, namely that the path may lead from philosophical inquiry through hermeneutic studies to scientific analysis. In short, scientific research, hermeneutic studies, and philosophical inquiry, though provisionally distinguishable as three different kinds of theoretical enterprise, are in fact dialectically integrated with one another. This is particularly true with respect to the question of tradition in relation to economy.

Thus, in terms of my own methodological procedures, it can be said that the thematic focus necessarily shifts from a scientific analysis of the direct causal links between a religion or ideology (such as Confucianism) and capitalism (or other forms of modern institutions) to a hermeneutic inquiry into the broader transformative tendencies of the religion or ideology. In discussing the post-Weberian reexamination of the Weberian thesis, S. N. Eisenstadt seems to be tending toward a similar direction when he states that "What is required for this re-examination is a shift of attention from the allegedly direct, causal relationship between Protestantism and capitalism (or other aspects of the modern world) to the internal transformative capacities of Protestantism and to their impact on the transformation of the modern world."[13] But he stops short of saying that what he calls "the internal transformative capacities" of a religion or ideology are, in a deeper sense, a matter of interpretation (hermeneutic reading), not really of scientific explanation. In any case, this is an unavoidable hermeneutic move from causal explanations attempted by the social scientists to our human interpretations of the meaning(s) of History and its (their) implications for the future. Ultimately, however, we must proceed to the philosophical level of inquiry. Only on this third level will we be able to solve the problem of the human meaning(s) and its (their) implications of the "internal transformative capacities" of a religion or ideology. In the case of Confucianism, we must ask: How are its internal transformative capacities or potentials to be interpreted in such a way that it can be ideologically revitalized for the future economic development of East Asia? As a social scientist Eisenstadt may not wish to speak of "the transformative capacities" in hermeneutic let alone in philosophical terms; it is, however, my methodological thesis that the hermeneutic and philosophical issues must be encountered.[14]

To illustrate my methodological procedures, I would like to mention my critical review of the Chinese work, *Hsing-sheng yü wei-chi—Lun Chung-kuo feng-chien she-hui te ch'ao-wen-ting chie-kou* (Prosperity and Crisis: On the Ultra-stable System of Chinese Feudal Society), co-authored by Jin Guantao and Liu Qingfeng.[15] Partly as a result of my review, their work has aroused great interest among many scholars and intellectuals in Taiwan, and it has become a controversial topic of discussion in the fields of history, hermeneutics and philosophy. In my review, I made the following observation:

> Although I can to some extent understand and accept the point that the authors attempt to establish the unified methodology, including a theory of controls, a theory of systems, [and a theory of information], that will cut across the natural and social sciences, [I still think that] there is basically quite a distinction between natural events and historical events. Can we indeed identify our scientific investigation of natural causality with that of causal relations in history and society? Since historical events are never duplicated, they cannot be demonstrated through scientific experimentation, which requires repetition. Can we, then, only say that our historical studies, by way of applying a theory of controls and a theory of systems in the contemporary sciences, is no more than a hypothesis construction using the scientific method so as to discover the causal laws of the course of history? Can't we rather say that our

scientific inquiry into the "causal laws of history" is in a deeper sense none other than our attempt at reexamining and reinterpreting the modern meanings or implications of past history? Are our historical studies ultimately a matter of scientific, causal explanation concerning historical facts, or rather a hermeneutic inquiry into their meanings or implications as a [critical/creative] means of "marching toward the future"?

Applying my threefold set of methodological procedures, the authors' approach apparently involves (1) a scientific explanation of the causal laws governing the historical course of traditional Chinese society as an ultra-stable system, (2) a hermeneutic reading of the meanings and implications of this system, and (3) a philosophical task of transforming this system (which seems to suggest the current stagnation of the Chinese communist institution) into a modernistically dynamic social-political (as well as economic and cultural) form. Regardless of how the authors themselves interpret the nature of their work, it is a species of theoretical naiveté simply to assume that their work is purely scientific. For one thing, the concept of an "ultra-stable system" must be characterized in terms of creative hermeneutics, not of scientific method, though the authors may not have such an understanding.

Another example can be seen by analyzing a recent debate concerning the role of Confucianism in Japan. In discussing the global strategy of Japanese enterprise, Urabe Kuniyoshi is highly critical of those Japanese scholars who maintain that the uniqueness and success of the Japanese management system can be sociologically explained in terms of managerial families or hierarchical groupism deeply rooted in traditional Japanese ie-consciousness or village (mura) consciousness. According to Iwata Ryuko, for example, "In the prewar era, Japanese groupism, clad in ie-ideology, was the basis for managerial familism. With the postwar democratic revision [of Japanese social structure] as an [opportune] moment, the ie-consciousness typically manifested in the upper level of management was forsaken, and instead the mura-like way of action, that is, groupism, appeared in a more precise form."[16] Urabe points out, however, that Japanese groupism rooted in the mura-consciousness referred to the value orientation of the village community in the pre-capitalist era, and it is totally unthinkable that, despite the rapid Japanese industrialization and modernization since the Meiji period, the pre-industrial mura-consciousness has been simply inherited and has become the formative principle of Japanese management today. Against Iwata's thesis of tradition-bound groupism, Urabe puts forward his own thesis of historical evolution, according to which the management system is a product of the process of historical development, involving both historical continuity and discontinuity of any traditional culture or ideology. To illustrate his thesis, Urabe refers to the modernization of Japan's unique lifetime employment system, mentioning three directions the system has taken. These are: (1) equalization of status, (2) the introduction of a consideration of individual ability, and (3) small group activity. To Urabe, the entire modernization process with respect to lifetime employment clearly reflects Japan's gradual democratic transformation of traditional familism and groupism into a kind of humanism. This postwar form of lifetime employment, he observes, also reflects the growth of individualism (the satisfaction of individualistic motives and intentions of the employee) as a new basis for Japan's existing groupism (an expression of loyalty to the group as a means of both mutual survival and prosperity).

Urabe's thesis of historical evolution seems to directly confront Morishima's culturalist model, which strongly supports the post-Confucian thesis in explaining the economic miracle of Japan. While Urabe stresses Japan's growing individualism in its management system, Morishima tends to promote Japanese Confucianism as the key ideological factor in Japan's industrialization.[17] Interestingly, Morishima states that "Japanese society is a fiercely competitive society, but it does not produce competition between individuals; the individual has to work at the risk of his life on the battlefield of group competition."[18] He further notes, "In spite of her economic success in the postwar era, the prospects of individualism and liberalism blossoming and maturing in Japan are still remarkably remote."[19] One must be curious about what has caused Urabe and Morishima to put forth two such widely diverse views. My thesis of a threefold set of methodological procedures may enable us to find the answer.

What I wish to suggest is that, despite their original intentions of giving a causal analysis and scientific explanation of the determining factors concerning Japan's economic development, Urabe and Morishima have in the process introduced their own hermeneutic readings of the meanings and implications of the historical development of modern Japan. In introducing their preferred terms, such as "individualism" and "humanism" (Urabe) or "ethos" and "(self-sacrificing) loyalty" (Morishima), they apparently have projected their own views of what Japanese society and culture is and ought to be. In other words, their scientific investigations of the causal links between economy and culture from the outset incorporate their own hermeneutic readings. In turn, their own philosophical reflections on Japanese society and culture in relation to economic development are implicit in these hermeneutic readings. In short, the value-neutral "is" and the value-laden "ought" are intermingled in their respective approaches.

These approaches not only illustrate my methodological thesis, but furthermore suggest to us that any scientific inquiry into the role of Confucianism in relation to East Asian economic development, practically speaking, can hardly be separated from our modern/postmodern way of interpreting the meanings and implications of Confucianism as a great cultural tradition of East Asia. Our interpretations necessarily lead to the most crucial and urgent questions to be posed concerning the ideological revitalization of Confucianism for the future East Asian economic (and sociopolitical as well as cultural) development.

Critical Comparison of Japanese and Chinese Confucianism

With these illustrations of my methodological thesis, we can now turn to a critical comparison of two major forms of Confucianism in East Asia, namely the original Chinese version and the Japanese variation, which involves a nearly total ideological transformation of the original. As an ideological variant of the Confucian tradition, Japanese Confucianism shares with its Chinese relative some common characteristics, if only on the surface level. First of all, Confucian virtues, such as *jen* (benevolence or human-kindness), *yi* (righteousness or moral oughtness), *chung* (conscientiousness or loyalty), *hsiao* (filial piety), *t'i* (brotherly respect), *li* (propriety), *cheng-ming* (the rectification of names), *ch'eng* (sincerity), *chih* (uprightness), and so on, have all been known and gradually incorporated since the introduction of Chinese Confucianism to Japan via Korea in the sixth century C.E. The Confucian emphasis on political order and social harmony, ideologically intensified in Tung Chung-shu's Han Confucianism and metaphysically systematized in Chu Hsi's philosophy of the Heavenly Principle (*t'ien-li*), also suited the Japanese political ideology by providing support for the imperial court and the shogunate. It can be said that the adoption of Chu Hsi Neo-Confucianism by the Tokugawa Bakufu as the sole legitimate *Kangaku* (Sinological Learning) has much to do with this emphasis, primarily for achieving the political objective of maintaining the status quo. The Confucian promotion of the family as the basic social unit, as well as the extension of the idea of family (*chia*, J. *ka* or *ie*) to the nation (*kuo*), thus constituting the compound *kuo-chia* (the nation as an extended family), has certainly been absorbed into Japan's age-long conception of *kokutai* (national polity) reflecting the continuity of the Japanese imperial court as a symbol of national unity.

The Confucian doctrine of intellectual elitism in connection with governmental and social service has equally exercised a profound influence on the formation of Japanese bureaucracy, from the Nara period down to the present day. The four class distinctions advocated by Chinese Confucianism—the intellectual elite (*shih*), peasants (*nung*), artisans (*kung*), and merchants (*shang*)—have been absorbed into the Japanese social system with the *samurai* class traditionally occupying the uppermost position.[20] Last but not least, the Confucian emphasis on personal cultivation, moral education, and the avid search for human knowledge definitely has had a tremendous impact on the Japanese obsession with education as the foundation of meritocracy within government and society, before and after the Meiji Restoration. This in turn has influenced the extension of a modern system of meritocracy to business and economic areas.

However, if the deep structure underlying the above common surface features is exposed, significant differences begin to emerge, representing the ideological transformation of Confucianism in its accommodation to the unique features of Japanese society. First of all, while Chinese Confucianism of the Great Tradition maintained a generally universalistic system of metaphysical and moral principles, its Japanese counterpart increasingly narrowed its focus toward a nationalistic, paternalistic, and anti-individualistic ideology. As Morishima has acutely observed, "It is indeed because of this modification and transformation of Confucianism into a nationalistic Japanese version that modern Japan could pursue a course of development so completely different from China's in the same period."[21]

This extreme Japanization of Chinese Confucianism has greatly affected the Japanese prioritization of Confucian virtues. For example, while Chinese Confucianists have identified the virtue of *jen* as the governing principle of human morality, the Japanese have substituted the lesser virtue of *chung* (Jap. *chū*, self-sacrificing loyalty). It should be noted that within the context of Chinese Confucianism this ethical term always must be rendered as "conscientiousness," which discloses the essential difference between Chinese and Japanese moral judgments. In Chinese Confucianism what is motivationally right or wrong is utterly dependent upon whether or not there exists individual conscience or conscientiousness, in accordance with the principle of *jen*. In contrast, for the Japanese of the feudal period, this kind of individual motivation is always subservient to one's loyalty to one's clan, lord (*daimyō*), shogun, or the emperor. Updated in modern terms, this same loyalty is owed to one's seniors (as among one's classmates), bureaucratic or business superiors, or to a particular group or institution of which one is a member, such as one's company, factory, department, or village. As a result, Japanese society has been pervaded by gerontocracy, paternalism, and hierarchical collectivism or groupism, down to the present day.[22] The Japanese virtue of loyalty clearly reflects the basic structure of Japanese society in terms of vertical relationships (*tate no kankei*), that is, relationships between two individuals or groups, one being of a higher status than the other.[23]

The extreme dissonance existing between Japanese and Chinese Confucianists in terms of their moral priorities is aptly reflected in a story from the Tokugawa period concerning the well-known Shinto Neo-Confucian scholar, Yamasaki Ansai (1618–82). One day, while lecturing to his disciples, Yamasaki posed what was to them an unresolvable dilemma—namely, what would be the appropriate course of action if Confucius and Mencius were to lead an army of invasion against Japan. Since no responses were forthcoming from the students who were assumed to be faithful followers of the Way of Confucius and Mencius, Yamasaki answered the question himself, saying that the obvious choice was to take up arms against even the greatest Chinese Confucian teachers, if the homeland were being threatened.[24] The lines are firmly drawn here between the national loyalty, which typifies the Japanese mindset, including Japanese Confucianism, and Chinese Confucianism's universalistic sense of morality. By the same token, the Chinese criterion of "barbarism" is an absence of common human moral sense and civilized propriety, while a Japanese definition involves whatever is foreign to Japan and its immediate culture (such that even Confucius himself would fail the test).

As in the case of the virtue of loyalty, Japanese modifications of the original Confucian principle of political order and social rankings (*ming-fen*) is equally nationalistic and collectivistic in character. Thus, the Japanese notion of *ie* (house or family) is readily extendable from individual families to clans, the shogunate, and finally to the imperial court (as symbolic of national unity). While Chinese Confucianists, since the time of Mencius, have continued to speak of *ke-ming* (literally, the changing of the Mandate of Heaven) or revolution to describe periodic dynastic changes, during the Tokugawa era the Japanese maintained a hereditary system of rulership on all levels of society. Even today a similar system exists within the Japanese business world, although the basis of continuity is looked upon as *ie*, a fact well-illustrated by the common assumption of lifetime loyalty to and corresponding employment by the Japanese corporation (as discussed in Steven Heine's article in this volume).[25]

Although both Chinese and Japanese Confucianists speak of the concept of family, and *ie* represents a Japanese rendering of the Chinese term for family (*chia*), the Japanese *ie* system is vastly different from its Chinese counterpart. The Japanese sense of *ie* encompasses a hierarchical network of vertical relationships throughout social and political life, codified in the principle of *giri* (obligations), which is totally absent from the original Chinese model. By comparison the Five Relationships (three within the immediate family and two outside of it) mentioned by Mencius display a wealth of deficiencies, omitting many essential human connections that the Japanese can readily accommodate. However irrational the *ie* system may appear to an outsider, with its obsession with the rigid observance of collectivist rules or norms, it has served a key function by providing the basis for the historical continuity of the Japanese nation.

As far as Confucian elitism and its bureaucracy is concerned, unlike the Chinese reliance on a civilian government and civil service (and its disdain for the military), since the end of the Heian period the Japanese political tradition consistently maintained a military government under the name of the shogunate (derived from a phrase *shogunke*, meaning "the *ie* of the general of the army"). During the Tokugawa period, the samurai (consisting of the shogun, the *daimyō*, their retainers, and the common warriors) became the ruling elite, overseeing all aspects of the social order. Thus, in Tokugawa society a clear-cut distinction was made between the samurai class as an elite (constituting the Great Tradition) and the remaining three classes, considered commoners (constituting the Little Tradition). This is a far cry from the Chinese Confucian distinction between the Great Tradition of the scholarly elite and the Little Tradition of the commoners.

Practically speaking, this military emphasis had the salutary effect of making it possible for Japan as a nation to negotiate the transition to modernism. The action-oriented samurai (influenced predominantly by the Neo-Confucian philosopher Wang Yang-ming's principle of the Unity of Knowledge and Action) stands in sharp contrast to the contemplative Chinese scholar-bureaucrat. An eloquent personification of this difference is found in Yoshida Shōin (1830–59), a samurai loyalist of the Choshu clan, who was influenced by the diverse currents of *bushidō* (the way of the warrior), Sun Tzu's *Art of War*, and Confucian moral idealism. The result was Yoshida's call to revolution, in order to end the repression of the peasants under feudalism and to reassert the power of Japan under the imperial system through a selfless leader. After an abortive assassination plot directed against an emissary of the shogun, Yoshida was beheaded at the age of thirty. His influence nonetheless pervaded the Meiji Restoration through the agency of his equally avid students. Even in the postwar era, echoes of this same samurai spirit are to be found, notably in the figure of Mishima Yukio (1925–70), whose public act of *seppuku* (performed on the same day as Yoshida's death) was intended to protest what he considered a betrayal of Japanese culture in general, and of the imperial system in particular, to Western influences.

Another point of difference lies in the area of education. Achievement-oriented meritocracy presupposes education as a means of instilling elitism, and in both China and Japan Confucianism was the *sine qua non* for public service. However, while among Chinese Confucianists education was restricted to the scholar class, during the Tokugawa period a kind of universal education was practiced in Japan, allowing access to education by people from all classes. This period saw a proliferation of schools at various levels and for various populations—from schools commissioned by the Bakufu to perpetuate the official learning of Chu Hsi Neo-Confucianism and the clan schools (*hanko*) of the *daimyō* to small village or temple schools (*terakoya*) and private academies (*shijuku*). By 1870, 1,400 private academies and 11,000 village schools were in existence, such that nearly 43% of boys and 10% of girls are estimated to have been attending classes of some form.[26] In traditional China, however, education tended to be given through private tutors, hired mostly by the wealthy families and clans to service their younger members. There is no question that Japan's ability to rapidly modernize its economy and society has much to do with its success in promoting popular education even prior to the Meiji Restoration. As far as education is concerned the distinction between the Great Tradition and the Little Tradition in China has been far greater than in Japan, an extremely crucial factor, indeed, in relation to these two East Asian nations' respective economic developments.

These historical trends in education help explain conditions in modern Japan which have contributed to its economic success. On the one hand, a system of elite education is maintained in the "name universities" (preeminently Tokyo University), association with which constitutes a lifetime guarantee of public distinction, as well as insuring the continuation of the competitive social pressures associated with academic success (e.g., "exam hell" and the attendant rash of suicides among the young). On the other hand, the extension of educational opportunity to all levels of society has spawned the extremely high educational standard found among the Japanese people today. Public education continues to be aggressively promoted in present-day Japan, which has nearly wiped out illiteracy and remains at the top of those developed nations having reached the highest standard of education. I might add that it can hardly be denied that the success of public education in Taiwan and Korea owes much to the significant impact of Japan's education-centered meritocracy.

In relation to the Confucian emphasis on education and the pursuit of knowledge, the Chinese distinction between righteousness and profit placed merchants in an untenable position, often making them the objects of disdain among Confucian scholars. Contrastingly, in Tokugawa Japan, the rise of money economy, commercial capitalism and growing urbanization brought in its wake within Confucianism the way of *chōnin* (townsmen or merchants), explicitly denying any such conflict between righteousness and profit. Even merchants were able to distinguish themselves as Confucian scholars, among them Itō Jinsai (1627–1705), first and foremost creative thinker of the Kogaku school, and Ishida Baigan, leader of the Shingaku movement who was son of a farmer but became a merchant himself. Thus, Ishida approvingly compared a merchant's profits to a samurai's stipend.[27] It cannot be denied that the transformative capacity of the Chinese merchant class in premodern China was significantly less than that of its Japanese counterpoint, as demonstrated in Bellah's book *Tokugawa Religion*. This illustrates the negative impact of Chinese Confucianism on the ethic of economic enterprise, in sharp contrast to Japan's ideological openness toward money economy and merchant capitalism long before Japan's actual engagement in its modernization.[28] Here again, the gap between the Great Tradition and the Little Tradition in China is far greater than in Japan.

It is impossible to go on enumerating the essential differences between the Japanese variant of Confucianism and the original Chinese Confucianism in this paper. But the above contrasts should be sufficient to indicate some of the principal reasons why Chinese Confucianism has failed to ease the path to modernization, occasioning Max Weber's lamentation (though based on his misunderstanding of Chinese Confucianism) that capitalism is unable to arise from Chinese Confucianism. Simultaneously, Japan's radical modifications of the original Chinese form of Confucianism was able to create the "transformative potential," thereby paving the way for the subsequent development of Japanese business and economy. Nonetheless, in light of my proposed thesis, I want to be rather cautious, contrary to quite a number of scholars who tend to overexaggerate the ideological contributions of Japanese Confucianism in causal relationship to Japan's economic growth in modern times. The isolation of Confucianism from other cultural factors cannot be sanctioned if principles of scientific investigation are to be upheld and a sound hermeneutic inquiry is to be attempted. As I have stated in my "Japanese Spiritual Resoures and their Contemporary Relevance,"[29] no other major tradition in the world has manifested attitudinal ambiguity, pluralistic diversity, and ideological complexity as much as the Japanese tradition. In most cases, Japanese religions not only co-exist without involving any serious confrontation, but often mutually influence and assimilate each other to form a syncretic religious ideology at the expense of the original purity and integrity of each religious tradition. There are many examples: the syncretic approach taken by most of Japan's New Religions from the late Tokugawa period to the postwar era; the Christian elements of Hirata Shinto in the Tokugawa period; the mixture of Buddhism and Shinto in terms of what is called *shinbutsu shūgō* (mutual assimilation of Shinto gods and buddhas), and the Shinto elements of Japanese Confucianism and Neo-Confucianism, such as, as we have seen, Yamasaki Ansai's Shinto Neo-Confucianism which places the ideological priority of Shinto's way of loyalty to Japan's national polity over the original Way of Confucius and Mencius. Thus, to single out Japanese Confucianism as the most important ideological factor in relation to Japan's economic development, and apply the term "Confucian capitalist society" to modern Japan, as does Morishima, is to place oneself in danger of committing the reductionist fallacy. If the values of loyalty and creative vitality are emphasized, modern Japan equally may be described as a "Shinto capitalist society."

In my aforementioned English paper, I spoke of Shinto mythology that is full of gods (*kami*) whose names and activities often involve birth production, one good example being the Sun goddess and her younger brother competing with each other in the show of divine power by way of producing sons and daughters from the various parts of their bodies. This Shinto-oriented passion for creative vitality and productivity, deeply rooted in the Japanese mentality, is perhaps reflected in the enormous output of Japanese companies like Honda and Toyota.[30] And, according to Joseph Mason's insightful account of Shinto's creative spirit, "The Shinto 'path' or the ideal of life is the way the mind moves forward in everyday life, struggling to overcome the daily obstacles of progress and seeking to advance not by dreaming vaguely of some possibility of the distant future, but by day-by-day accumulation of effort and competence. It is the path of self-creative action."[31] Of course, both descriptions ("Confucian capitalist society" and "Shinto capitalist society") are one-sided and represent two hermeneutic readings of Japanese culture and its economy. Indeed, it cannot be scientifically proven that a single ideological factor, such as Confucianism or Shinto, primarily has been responsible for a particular historical development, inclusive of economic development, within Japanese society. If Weber's analysis of the causal link between the Protestant ethic and European capitalism is not convincing to many of us, how much more so with the post-Confucian hypothesis in regard to Japan, the nation of religious pluralism, as well as to China, the nation that has at least Three Teachings (*san-chiao*), namely Confucianism, Taoism, and Buddhism, making up its ideological complexity.

It is, therefore, my contention that the ideology of Japanese Confucianism cannot be severed from the many other ideological elements in traditional and modern Japan, such as Shinto, Buddhism, or various types of New Religions. Rather, Confucianism must be viewed within the ideologically pluralistic context of Japanese culture, so that a more meaningful discussion of its ideological relevance will become possible, along with other elements which have contributed to Japanese economic development. In other words, what Eisenstadt calls the "transformative capacities" inherent in the Japanese tradition must consist of a multiplicity of both Confucian and non-Confucian ideological factors. To overcome any scientific naiveté on the matter we must attempt a more careful hermeneutic reading of modern Japanese economic history in the context of ideological pluralism.

To substantiate my thesis, I should like to translate a quote from the late Japanese philosopher Watsuji Tetsurō (1889–1960). In describing Japanese culture as "multi-layered or multidimensional in structure" (jūsōteki kōzō), he states:

> In Japanese culture none of the multiple factors on different levels has ever lost its right to exist. It is one of the remarkable characteristics of Japanese culture that even those [cultural] factors which have been somewhat subjugated can still survive in the role of the subjugated [undergoing some kind of transformation]. It seems to me that there is no other race, other than the Japanese, as sensitive to the absorption of new elements [from outside], nor as faithful in preserving its own age-old [tradition]. This is true in all aspects of everyday life or in historical development on the social level, as well as in religion, art, thinking, economy and politics.[32]

Following Watsuji's characterization of Japanese culture as multilayered, I suggest that a new critical inquiry, combining both scientific analyses and hermeneutic readings, is required to discover the complex meanings and implications of the transformative potentials inherent in Japan's pluralistic religions or ideologies, whether Confucian or non-Confucian. My suggestion equally applies to the modern economic development of China, whose cultural tradition also includes the Three Teachings and some other important ideological elements as well (such as Christianity and Islam). Recognizing the fact that Confucianism has been the key tradition of China, we still must draw our attention to the importance of Taoist and Chinese Buddhist contributions and/or hindrances to China's cultural and economic development.

With the above understanding of the multidimensional complexity of Chinese and Japanese religious cultures, we can then put Confucianism in a broader (pluralistic-oriented) ideological perspective and engage in a truly meaningful philosophical quest for the ideological revitalization of this particular tradition. This revitalization involves a twofold task: firstly, a total removal of any negative elements within the tradition that may become an ideological obstacle to the further economic development in East Asian societies; and secondly, a creative self-transformation of the tradition in its various East Asian forms, in such a way that it will continue to provide the peoples of East Asian societies with abundant inspirations and ideas in seeking a higher moral and cultural standard for the qualitative improvement of individual and society. To accomplish this twofold task, the first necessary step is a creative dialogue between two or more than two forms of Confucianism by way of a critical comparison of their essential differences and evaluation of their respective pros and cons.

Conclusions

My brief examination of the essential differences between the Japanese and Chinese forms of Confucianism is intended to show how each of them can be ideologically revitalized through a process of learning from each other in terms of both positive and negative lessons. For instance, the Chinese should learn from the Japanese experience of transforming Confucianism into a new ethical culture that places emphasis on group-minded solidarity, thereby finding a proper way of overcoming what may be called "individualistic familism," which remains an ideological hindrance to the development of a healthy group spirit in China; the Japanese should also learn from the original and genuine Chinese Confucianism the universalistic principle of *jen*, thereby overcoming their traditionally nationalistic and collectivistic utilization (and even distortion) of Confucian ethics and morality at the expense of individualism and liberalism. It is an undeniable fact that the social status of Japanese women remains far lower than that of Chinese women today. In any case, just how the creative dialogue through a critical comparison/evaluation will help China and Japan successfully revitalize their respective forms of Confucianism remains to be seen.

Aside from the problem of each East Asian society's revitalization of its own form of Confucianism, there is also a universal philosophical problem concerning the overall revitalization of Confucianism as a great East Asian tradition in critical contrast to the Western tradition. In one of my recent Chinese papers, "Ju-chia lun-li te hsien-tai-hua ch'ung-chien k'e-t'i" ("On the Task of Constructive Modernization of Confucian Ethics and Morality"), I have dealt with this problem by focusing on the central theme of Confucianism, namely ethics and morality. I have proposed that a proper solution of the problem of ethical/moral revitalization of this tradition lies in finding a "middle way" between (1) the family-oriented micro-morality and the society-oriented macro-morality, (2) the ethics of human-kindness (*jen*) on the person-to-person basis and the ethics of justice as fairness on the impersonal basis, (3) the ethics of name-rectification through personal cultivation and the rule-oriented ethics of responsibility and accountability, (4) the motive-concerned ethics of *liang-chih* (innate knowledge of the good) and the consequence-concerned ethics of social utility, and (5) maxima moralia (the Confucian way of inner sagehood) and minima moralia (the legalistic observance of law and order).[33] This proposal is based on my understanding that the overall revitalization of Confucianism cannot be successfully accomplished without meeting the ideological challenge of the Western tradition. However, it is beyond the scope of this paper to attempt further reflections on this extremely difficult problem.

To conclude, in today's increasingly pluralistic postmodern world we can no longer afford to speak of East Asian Confucianism as a monolithic structure. Rather, we must recognize the Japanese, Chinese, Korean, and other variations of Confucianism in accordance with the specific needs and unique culture of each of the societies involved. As my critical comparison of Japanese and Chinese Confucianism has shown, it is only through creative dialogue and cultural interchange among the Confucian-related East Asian nations or societies that our task of revitalizing the Confucian tradition can be fulfilled. Completion of this task requires the joint efforts of social and natural scientists, historians, philosophers and religious thinkers from all of the societies concerned. Such has been my intention, at least in part, in proposing my threefold set of methodological procedures.

Notes

1. See Yang Chün-shih and Tu Nien-chung, eds., *Ju-chia lun-li yü ching-chi fa-chan* (Confucian Ethic and Economic Development) (Taipei: Yünch'en Cultural Enterprise, Inc., 1987), 1–43.

2. S. N. Eisenstadt, "The Protestant Ethic Thesis: An Analytical and Comparative Framework," in Eisenstadt, ed., *The Protestant Ethic and Modernization: A Comparative View* (New York: Basic Books, 1968), 10.

3. Peter L. Berger, "An East Asian Economic Development Model?", in Peter L. Berger and Hsin-Hang Michael Hsiao, eds., *In Search of an East Asian Development Model* (New Brunswick, NJ: Transaction Books, 1988), 7–8.

4. Ibid., 8.

5. In its first edition (New York: Macmillan, 1957), Robert H. Bellah's book, *Tokugawa Religion*, had the subtitle "The Values of Pre-Industrial Japan," which was changed to "The Cultural Roots of Modern Japan" in the most recent paperback edition (New York: The Free Press, 1985), with the author's new introduction.

6. On Ishida's *Shingaku* movement, for instance, Bellah concludes: "As a religion it taught enlightenment and the selfless devotion which was both a means toward it and a consequence thereof . . . Though a merchant class movement, it sought no direct political power for the merchants but accepted the samurai as policy leaders and attempted to assimilate the merchants to a samurai-like role in the economic field . . . Economically it reinforced diligence and economy, it valued productivity and minimized consumption. Further it advocated universalistic standards of honesty and respect for contract and gave them religious underpinnings. In these ways it must be seen as contributing to the growth of a disciplined, practical, continuous attitude toward work in the world among the city classes, important for both enterpreneurs and workers in an economy entering the process of industrialization. In doing all this it utilized one of the oldest and most powerful religious traditions in the Far East, that going back to Mencius." Ibid., 175.

7. Bellah, "Reflections on the Protestant Ethic Analogy in Asia," included in Eisenstadt, ed., *The Protestant Ethic and Modernization*, 246–47.

8. Ibid., 249 (emphasis added).

9. See Murakami Yasusuke, "Modernization in Terms of Integration: The Case of Japan," in Eisenstadt, ed., *Patterns of Modernity*, vol. II, *Beyond the West* (London: Frances Pinter, 1987), 65–88. According to Murakami, the conceptualization of "modernization" can be generally classified into two types: (1) modernization = Westernization; (2) modernization = industrialization. He observes that (2) applies in the case of Japan.

10. In addition to the contribution of Edo (Tokugawa) society in preparing Japan, Lehman gives the following list of causal factors to Japan's industrialization: (1) the political revolution and subsequent widespread institutional reform; (2) the powerful and progressive role of the state; (3) the investment in and development of the infrastructure; (4) import and diffusion of Western technology and expertise; (5) the rise of an able and dynamic entrepreneurial class with a close symbiotic relationship with the state—for example, both public and private sectors worked together in the development of the railways; (6) agricultural growth and diversification; (7) the role of silk in generating foreign revenue; (8) the advantage taken from forward linkage effects in the development of a viable and increasingly competitive textile industry catering in due course both to domestic demand and providing revenue from export; (9) the development and indeed emphasis given to heavy industry, the increased use of modern sources of energy, coal, steam, electricity; (10) cheap labor; (11) militarism and imperialism. See Jean-Pierre Lehman, *The Roots of Modern Japan* (New York: St. Martin's Press, 1982), 197.

11. Ibid., 197–98.

12. Ibid., 198.

13. Eisenstadt, *The Protestant Ethic and Modernization*, 7–8.

14. My methodological thesis here can be considered an extension or application of my "creative hermeneutics," which consists of the following five steps in that dialectical order: (1) "What *exactly* did the original thinker or text say?"; (2) "What did the original thinker *intend or mean* to say?"; (i) "What *could* the original thinker have said?", or "What *could* the original thinker's sayings have *implied*?"; (4) "What *should* the original thinker have said?", or "What *should* the creative hermeneutician say on behalf of the original thinker?"; and (5) "What *must* the original thinker say now?", or "What *must* the creative hermeneutician do now, in order to carry out the unfinished philosophical task of the original thinker?" Although my creative hermeneutics is primarily applied to hermeneutic studies of the classical texts, it can, I think, be theoretically extended to the solution of the problem of methodological procedures I am dealing with in this paper. Yet it goes beyond the scope of this discussion to relate my present thesis to creative hermeneutics.

15. See my "'*Tsou-hsiang wei-lai*' te Jin Guantao yü Liu Qingfeng" (Jin Guantao and Liu Qingfeng, 'Marching toward the Future'"), in my *Wen-hua Chung-kuo yü Chung-kuo Wen-hua* ("Cultural China" and Chinese Culture) (Taipei: Tungta Publishing Co., 1988), 229–54.

16. Iwata Ryuko, *Nihonteki keiei no hensei genri* (The Formative Principle of Japanese Management) (Tokyo: Bunshindo, 1977), 7, as quoted in Urabe Kuniyoshi's book, *Nihonteki keiei wa shinka suru* (The Evolutionary Progress of Japanese Management) (Tokyo: Chuo keizaisha, 1984), 7.

17. Michio Morishima, in *Why Has Japan "Succeeded"? Western Technology and the Japanese Ethos* (Cambridge: Cambridge University Press, 1982), 2, says in fact that "the ideology of Japan, or at least the most important of Japan's ideologies, is also Confucianism."

18. Ibid., 193.

19. Ibid., 19.

20. Although the expression "class distinctions" is used here, it should not be mistaken as social classes in the strictly Marxist sense. The Confucian term "*ming-fen*" (literally "name-distinctions"), which has been commonly accepted and used in Japanese society, particularly in the Tokugawa period, rather signifies social rankings or rank distinctions.

21. Morishima, *Why Has Japan "Succeeded"?*, 18.

22. For a detailed analysis of modern manifestations of these phenomena, see Kanji Haitani, *The Japanese Economic System: An Institutional Overview* (Lexington, MA: Lexington Books, 1976), 14–26.

23. For an interesting discussion of these vertical relationships, see Chie Nakane, *Japanese Society* (Berkeley and Los Angeles: University of California Press, 1972).

24. This story was recorded in the *Sentetsu sodan* (*The Former Philosophers' Miscellaneous Talks*), fascicle 3. See also Wm. Theodore de Bary, ed., *Sources of Japanese Tradition*, vol. 1 (New York: Columbia University Press, 1964), 360–61.

25. For an insightful observation of the essential differences between the Chinese family system and the Japanese *ie* system in relation to economy, see Ch'en Ch'i-nan's "Tung-ya she-hui te chia-t'ing yi-li yü ch'i-ye-ching-chi lun-li" ("The Familial Ideology and the Ethic of Economic Enterprise"), in the *Tang-tai* (Contemporary) *Monthly*, 34 (Taipei, 1989).

26. For a full discussion of education during the Tokugawa period and thereafter, see R. P. Dore, *Education in Tokugawa Japan* (Berkeley and Los Angeles: University of California Press, 1965); Ishikawa Matsutaro, *Hanko to terakoya* (Clan Schools and Temple Schools) (Tokyo: Kyoikusha, 1978); Richard Rubinger, *Private Academies of Tokugawa Japan* (Princeton: Princeton University Press, 1982); Dore, "The Legacy of Tokugawa Education," in Marius B. Jansen, ed., *Changing Japanese Attitudes toward Modernization* (Princeton: Princeton University Press, 1965); Herbert Passin, *Society and Education in Japan* (New York: Columbia University Press, 1965); and Nobuo K. Shimahara, *Adaptation and Education in Japan* (New York: Praeger Publishers, 1979).

27. He says, for instance, that "the profit of the merchant is like a permitted stipend . . . As for the Way of the samurai also, if he does not receive a stipend, he is not fit for service. If one calls receiving a stipend from one's lord 'greedy' and 'immoral,' then from Confucius and Mencius on down there is not a man who is moral [knows the Way]. What sort of thing is it to say, leaving samurai, farmers and artisans aside, that the merchants' receiving a stipend is 'greed' and that they cannot know the way?" In Bellah, *Tokugawa Religion*, 158.

28. The merchant spirit in relation to Confucianism and the religious ethic in pre-modern China has rarely been discussed in scholarly circles. But I should single out one recent work by Ying-shih Yu, entitled *Chung-kuo chin-shih tsung-chiao lun-li yü shang-jen ching-shen* (The Religious Ethic and the Merchant Spirit in Pre-Modern China) (Taipei: Lienching Publishing Co., 1987).

29. In the *Journal of Dharma* 10/1 (Jan.–March, 1985), 82–89.

30. Ibid., 86–87.

31. J. W. T. Mason, *The Meaning of Shinto: The Primaeval Foundation of Creative Spirit in Modern Japan* (Port Washington, NY: Kennikat Press, 1935), 189.

32. *Watsuji Tetsurō zenshū* (The Complete Works of Watsuji Tetsurō), vol. 4 (Tokyo: Iwanami shoten, 1962), 314.

33. The paper was presented at the International Conference on Confucianism and the Modern World, Taipei, November 13–18, 1987, and subsequently appeared in *The International Symposium on Confucianism and the Modern World Proceedings* (Taipei, 1988), 1213–24. It also appeared in the *Universitas* (Philosophy and Culture) *Monthly* (January, 1988).

Chapter Six

The Murky Mirror:
Women and Sexual Ethics as Reflected
in Japanese Cinema

SANDRA A. WAWRYTKO

Among the Three Imperial Treasures (*sanshu-no-shinki* or *mikusa-no-kandakara* recognized by Shinto are the imperial Sword, Mirror, and Jewels. The Mirror (*yata-no-kagami*) is said to have been created as an image of Amaterasu the sun-goddess (*Kogoshūi*) who later presented it to the Imperial Grandson, prince Ninigi, as he was about to assume rulership of "the Luxuriant Land of reed-plains."[1] A mirror also played a seminal role in saving a world engulfed in darkness after the sun goddess, outraged by the conduct of her mischievous brother, had hidden herself in a cave. Mistaking her own image in the mirror for that of a rival goddess, Amaterasu was lured from her seclusion.

Modern Japanese cinema may be said to hold up a mirror that reflects an intermingling of elements from Japanese society, past and present. Considering the association of the mirror with the primal Ancestress Amaterasu, it is appropriate to apply it to traditional and contemporary images of Japanese women. However, these celluloid images should not be hastily mistaken for a true reflection of reality—either traditional or modern. Nor are they necessarily a separate reality, as Amaterasu mistakenly assumed. As the artistic products of male directors, the films display varying degrees of sensitivity to the plight of Japanese women as victims of vastly inequitable gender roles. The empathy and feminist leanings of some of the directors who have crafted these pieces are laudable. However, the fact remains that their works represent attempts by men to portray and interpret what, for them, is an essentially alien experience—living as a woman in Japanese society. While their

121

films do express certain truths about Japanese culture, these truths are reflected in a murky mirror.

Given this caveat, is it worthwhile to peer into this mirror, clouded as it is by ancient prejudices (or the pre-judging) of women's roles? What can we expect to fathom in its depths? How is the postmodern Japanese woman to interpret the shadowy images thus presented? How can the images be decoded to reveal the source of the problems that lie at the core of Japanese gender relationships? To answer such questions we must look beyond the usual scope of film criticism and analyses of the cinematic texts using the criteria of artistic integrity. As the Japanese cinematic artists here "hold the mirror up to Nature," they often reveal more about their own psychological orientations, and those of their audiences, than they do about Nature or reality—particularly "feminine" nature or the reality of the Japanese woman.

Before pursuing this task, however, some clarification must be reached on the relationship of feminism to the modern and postmodern trends that have engulfed Japanese women for more than one hundred years. For purposes of our discussion, the "modern" period began with the inception of the Meiji Period and the restoration of imperial rule in 1868. Those events ushered in a generation characterized by cultural questioning and change as the Japanese people, and their rulers in particular, attempted to fit their society to compete successfully in a world dominated by Western technology. The postmodern period can be placed at the end of the Second World War with the collapse of the ultranationalist forces that were heirs to the Meiji agenda of global competitiveness. For the artists of Japan, including those involved in cinema, postmodernism represented a kind of post-mortem reassessment of what had gone wrong in the glittering vision of progress. The films discussed here are part of that effort. They are based on the works of authors poised at the interstitices of tradition and modernity, including the waning Edo period (in the case of *The Life of Oharu and Double Suicide*) and the tumultuous Meiji period (*Rashomon*, in which the story reflects back on the Heian era), as illustrated in table 1. These stories have then been reinterpreted by postmodern directors during the postwar period.

In these films an abiding theme of social criticism is combined with pleas and demands for a loosening of social constraints on individual behavior which are especially daunting and oppressive for women's conduct and choices. By examining dysfunctional cases, or cases in which society obviously has moved from a stabi-

Table 1: Film Selections

Theme	Films	Historical period	Death	Eros	Religion/Buddhism
Sexuality as Social Threat	*Rashomon*, dir. Kurosawa Akira, 1950	12th century Heian Period	yes	explicit	positive
	The Gate of Hell (Jigo kumon), dir. Kinugasa Teinosuke, 1953	Heiji Revolt (1159–60)	yes	implicit	positive
Woman as Social Rebel	*The Life of Oharu (Saikaku ichidai onna)*, dir. Mizoguchi Kenji, 1952	17th century Tokugawa/ Edo Period	yes	explicit	negative and positive
Obsessive Love	*Double Suicide (Shinjū Ten no Amijima)*, dir. Shinoda Masahiro, 1969	18th century Tokugawa/ Edo Period	yes	explicit	positive

lizing force to despotic tyrant, a call for a compromise arises between the trampling of human rights and the safeguarding of social
interactions. Advocates of modernization as well as their
postmodern heirs rallied behind the common cause of the plight of
women, used as a touchstone for presenting the victimization imposed throughout history by traditional social hierarchies. The
added complications of gender roles reveal cases and consequences
of women daring to defy social norms by embracing trans-social
values. The implications of these analyses for women in contemporary Japan derive from the fact that the historical settings of the
films are reinterpretations of events from modern and postmodern
vantage points. It has been argued that "A focus on women can
reveal most of Japan's inner tensions and contradictions. The changing roles of women in Japanese society and the changing nature of
their image in myth, religion, and ideology provide a good index of
Japan's cultural agenda at a given moment."[2]

Currents of feminism in Japan spanned the modern and
postmodern periods. The liberating potential of Western values was
quickly recognized by both men and women as they emerged from
the isolation that had been imposed by the Tokugawa regime. The
nascent feminist was a recurrent figure in Asian literature of the
modern period.[3] Radical Japanese writers, such as Yosano Akiko
(1878–1942), stood as role models for such efforts throughout Asia.
Yosano was especially known for her poem, "The Day When Mountains Move," presaging the awakening of women.[4] Nonetheless, two
men, Fukuzawa Yukichi (1834–1901) and Mori Arinori (1847–89),
were among the first to advocate equal rights for women in Japan,
under the influence of Christian education abroad.[5] They may be
regarded as progenitors of the film directors cited here for the feminist themes in their works.

Feminist issues are perhaps more convoluted in Japan than in
any other culture due to the corresponding complexity in gender
relationships. As the films examined here demonstrate, a certain
species of feminine power has been recognized by the tradition.
Anthropologist Hara Hiroko, a successful career woman in her own
right, has described the situation as follows:

> Japanese men look down on women in many categorical ways but
> they do not look down on women's role. She is simply the one to
> cook, bear children and keep house. For generations, most Japanese
> women have been the key person to handle not only the family
> finances but all the delicate and extremely important personal

relationships involving the family, the community, and often the business or profession. In these important areas, and others, men depend on us.[6]

In extreme forms this dependency gives rise to gynophobia or fear of women as an irresistible force to be reckoned with if not avoided. Most often women's power has been traced to their sexuality. To ameliorate this aura of danger, women have adopted a non-threatening, childlike persona. Men are thus encouraged to view their dependency (amae) on women as a natural extension of the maternal relationship and thereby they can regain a sense of security.[7] Each of the central women characters in the films examined here is in some way victimized by these cultural assumptions and accommodations.

Love and Death: The Abiding Tension between Society and Sexuality

Two stimuli seem particularly prone to precipitate conflicts across all human cultures: the experiences of erotic love and death, which are bound up with the question of religious convictions. These themes are inextricably intertwined for the Japanese, who have been wont to elevate sexuality to the status of religion and have been willing to satisfy its demands by the culturally specific practice of double suicide (shinjū). Nowhere have the seemingly contradictory demands of Eros and Thanatos—the life principle and the death instinct—melded so seamlessly as in Japanese culture. For example, the genre of "pink cinema" (soft pornography, known in the West as blue movies) effortlessly merges sexuality with political and social themes depicted in scenes and fantasies of violence and death.[8]

The depth and passion of these conflicts for the Japanese calls into question the stereotype of a stoic national temperament that unquestioningly places social values over individual integrity, blithely subverting and sacrificing personal desires for the sake of the greater good. In their own self-analysis, Japanese authors have been more sensitive to the complexity of Japanese character. On this point Inazo Nitobe observes:

> I am inclined to think that in one sense we have to feel more than others—yes, doubly more—since the very attempt to restrain natural promptings entails sufferings. Imagine boys—and girls, too—

brought up not to resort to the shedding of a tear or the uttering of
a groan for the relief of their feelings,—and there is a physiological
problem whether such effort steels their nerves or makes them
more sensitive. . . . Calmness of behaviour [sic], composure of
mind, should not be disturbed by passion of any kind. . . . When a
man or woman feels his or her soul stirred, the first instinct is
quietly to suppress the manifestation of it. . . . Personally, I believe
it was our very excitability and sensitiveness which made it a
necessity to recognize and enforce constant self-repression.[9]

If, as Watsuji Tetsurō argues, the Japanese have always "striven to
eradicate selfishness within the family and to realize the fusion of
self and other,"[10] then perhaps this betrays a suppressed reality of
willful self-assertion directly antithetical to the society's self-sacrificing ideal.[11] The intensely personal passions portrayed in our film
selections would then stand not as cultural aberrations, but rather
as revelations of a deeper social truth.

The potentially antisocial forces of Nature and the social necessity for regulating human relationships converge most poignantly in
the erotic impulse. As the least-repressible form of spontaneity that
lingers within the civilized being, sexuality has represented a
prickly thorn in the side of society, a continual reminder of the
limitations of its power to repress:

The immediate reasons for controlling it vary from the belief that
it saps virility, through proprietary rights upon women, to its
association with a complex love relationship with one woman
alone, to mention only a few. But these seem to be secondary to the
fact that sexual restraint is a principal test of the strength of the
ego, along with resistance to pain and regulation of the wanderings
of thought and feeling.[12]

Hence, debilitating mutations of societal power are most manifest
in cases involving sexual conduct, specifically society's desire and
demand to regulate that conduct within "respectable" bounds. Alan
Watts asserts: "Sexuality will remain a problem so long as it continues to be the isolated area in which the individual transcends him[or
her]self and experiences spontaneity."[13]

The total elimination of eroticism by means of celibacy has not
been a viable option for most societies due to the basic need for
continuity. Accordingly, attempts have been made to harness sexual
energy/spontaneity in the service of the community. Social roles,
including gender roles, represent an encoding of acceptable behavior

patterns. Tools of social enforcement, positive and negative, have evolved to encourage individuals to uphold those roles. External motivators include prestige and shame, and internal reinforcements include virtue, self-affirmation, and guilt. Legal codes provide a formal expression of the desired behavior patterns, with informal expressions found in social traditions and mores. Since women may pose the greatest danger to the preservation of the family by bearing illegitimate children, the highest priority has been the control of their sexuality. Oftentimes this was accomplished by physical means—such as the medieval chastity belt preventing nonmarital sexual contact or the clitoridectomy (which Islamic women continue to be subjected to) that eliminated "high risk" female orgasm. More pervasive, however, were psychological persuasions aimed at associating sexuality with women of dubious reputation, while respectable women remained "pure" (as in the Victorian advice to wives on the duty of intercourse: "close your eyes and think of England").

Uncontrolled eroticism was perceived as a threat to the very core of socially responsible behavior that has been predicated on the principle of delayed gratification and even the repression/suppression of sensual desires. Sigmund Freud, perhaps the most celebrated proponent of this doctrine, defined civilization as:

> the whole sum of the achievements and the regulations which distinguish our lives from those of our animal ancestors and which serve two purposes—namely to protect men against nature and to adjust their mutual relations. . . . [I]t is impossible to overlook the extent to which civilization is built upon a renunciation of instinct, how much it presupposes precisely the non-satisfaction (by suppression, repression or some other means?) of powerful instincts. This "cultural frustration" dominates the large field of social relationships between human beings.[14]

Thus spontaneity must be sacrificed on the altar of civilization, while its incipient resurrection foreshadows social doom. How else are we to explain the public outrage that too often is unleashed over the "private" behavior of individuals—including modern incidents of violence directed against those whose sexual preferences constitute a minority view.[15]

The neo-Confucian-based philosophy that permeated the *bushidō* ethic of Japan was quite similar in content to Freudian forebodings about the destabilizing force of rampant sexuality.[16]

Confucian priority for parent-child relations weakened male lovers and made their loved ones suffer. Suffering and passivity supported social stability by stressing obedience; however, the archetypes . . . appealed to popular sentiments, not necessarily submissive, and not only afforded psychological release from social oppression in the form of theatrical catharsis, but also presented modes of behavior for effective coping in an authoritarian society.[17]

Mainstream sects of Japanese Buddhism holding to an ascetic ideal proved to be a strong ally for the Confucian forces by touting the virtue of detachment from desires, inclusive of carnal desires.

Men projected the ominous antisocial seeds of sensuality upon womankind as the perennial "Other," allowing them the psychological ruse of distancing themselves from the natural instincts they feared to acknowledge within themselves. Consequently women, as the concrete embodiment of erotic tendencies, were deemed to be most in need of externally imposed controls and the "guidance" of clear-thinking males. Such a view reflects the feudalistic perspective in Japan, which has been described as a "limitation of spirit . . . tacit agreement (social in scope) that one *is* and cannot *become* . . . which plagues the country to this day."[18] Although men maintained greater freedom in expressing their sexual desires, they too labored under socially sanctioned limitations. In the interest of maintaining the cohesiveness of the family, men were conditioned to separate Eros from conjugal love, thereby avoiding any temptation to satisfy both with one woman.

Those who violated the "legitimate" social norms of sexual conduct within marriage had to be dealt with severely. Their appeal to a "higher" principle (e.g., love) transcendent of social stability, asserting the right of individual happiness over family obligations, was considered a direct challenge to public order. Thus, the phenomenon of "star-crossed lovers" who are doomed to pay for their personal indulgence by profound suffering, even death, may be found in virtually all cultures and is particularly prominent in Japan. The severe social repercussions of their conduct on the wider community are also emphasized—whether in the form of the destruction of an ideal society (such as the Camelot crushed by the wantonness of Lancelot and Guinevere) or the undermining of competing social ties and obligations (family, marriage, friendship). Little wonder, then, that Dante's Inferno reserves a special place in Hell for such deleterious couples.[19]

In Japanese society it also was a violation to try to "have it all"—to attempt to combine love *and* marriage within the same partnership, to seek sexual fulfillment along with social respectability. To invest so much of oneself in a single relationship and experience so much satisfaction from a single source could endanger one's single-minded loyalty to the group. This "divide and conquer" strategy required strict separation of women and men to prevent overly zealous bonding. Discussing the ideal samurai wife, Nitobe observes: "Not infrequently does it happen that a youth becomes enamored of a maiden who returns his love with equal ardour, but, when she realises his interest in her makes him forgetful of his duties, disfigures her person that her attractions may cease."[20] This strategy was so successful that it spawned its own antithesis in the all-or-nothing cult of obsessive love, *shinjū* (double suicide).

Love relationships of this depth and profundity also may serve as a point of access to other avenues of spontaneity, such as spirituality and ideological commitment, which arise from a common core experience of self-transcendence. As Freud describes it, "At the height of being in love the boundary between ego and object threatens to melt away" (a state he also links to pathological episodes).[21]

Accordingly, the women in crisis as represented in the various cinematic scenarios presented here seek and find a myriad of options to the repressive traditions of Japanese society. Despite individual failures, their examples nonetheless may point out alternative possibilities for the postmodern woman, all the more so since these traditional women seem to value the process of seeking liberation over its actual realization. For such women the unleashing of spontaneity, even momentarily, can be reward enough to compensate for the retribution exacted by a society whose control mechanisms have thereby been thwarted. The Japanese cultural context presents an ideal ground for feminist exploration in that the rigidity of Japanese social structures provides a clear focus of conflict. The role of women in Japanese society is an uneasy composite of Shinto roots with Confucian and Buddhist overlays that has been remarkably resistant to feminist pressures. Exposing these ideological roots may well serve to help disentangle them.

Each film exposes a dimension of the pervasive dilemma of fateful love triangles that grows out of traditional Japanese culture: the competing and conflicting demands of *giri* (social roles and obligations) versus *ninjō* (personal feelings and desires). The word *giri* is composed of two Chinese characters: *yi* (justice, righteousness 義) plus *li* (principle 理), denoting obligations owed to others. *Ninjō* is represented by the characters *ren* (human 人) plus *ch'ing* (feelings 情, a character made up of the heart and the color of nature), or the emotions and affections natural to a human being, one's personal preferences. Each has its claims upon the human being: *Giri* not softened by *ninjō* may seem inhuman: it denies the individual's right to be happy at the expense of society. *Ninjō* unchecked by *giri*, however, is not only self-indulgent but can in the end destroy human society.[22] How, and why, do individuals respond when forced to choose between these competing claims? Various resolutions are sought by the characters in the films, with women playing the key role of protagonist and traditional society the ever-abiding antagonist that tries to thwart their personal emotions and desires as a matter of self-defense. The elements of love, death, and religion (especially Buddhism, which serves alternately as tool of oppression and source of self-transcendence) are interwoven throughout these tales, emerging and submerging as text and subtext.

The rules of the Japanese gender game delineate the respective expectations of women and men in regard to erotic relationships. Here we find that the social threat posed by sexuality is almost exclusively deemed to be the responsibility of women. Under such conditions at least some women attempt to rebel and assert their independence from these norms of behavior. The consequences, however, tend to be devastating. Risking social condemnation and psychological stress, some couples try to choose love in defiance of the accepted rules. Those who commit themselves to this course may find they are enmeshed in a tragic situation, the doom of obsessive love. Yet, despite the inevitability of tragedy, the stimulus of alternative values and patterns for relationship may serve to give individuals a sense of choice, even if that choice ends in death or defeat.

Sexuality as Social Threat: *Rashomon; Gate of Hell*

In each of these stories a woman stands at the apex of a love triangle, and medieval Japanese society is symbolized by a decaying city gate, symptomatic of decay in society as a whole, at which dead bodies (or portions thereof) appear for public consumption. Both films demonstrate how society places the blame for aberrant male behavior on the central female figure. Both women also accept that socially imposed responsibility and attempt to rectify the situation. Kesa in *Gate of Hell* is at an advantage here since she is able to rely upon the self-transcending resources of Buddhism. Thus, although she loses her own life in the process, she also performs a bodhisattvic service for her stalker, Moritoh, that saves not only his physical life, but points the way to his spiritual enlightenment. Buddhist values are more subtly woven into *Rashomon*, most directly in the figure of the priest who intones: "Life is delicate, fleeting as the morning dew." Indirectly, they are implied in the "floating/fleeting world" quality of the various accounts of the central story, which continually shift perspectives to reflect the samsaric desires of the narrators.

Rashomon

This claim of this film, which deals with traditional Japan, to postmodern status stems from two points: its origins in two short stories by eccentric Meiji author Akutagawa Ryūnosuke (who committed suicide in 1927) and its reemergence as a film in 1950 by Kurosawa Akira; and the Nietzschean multiperspectivism (also discussed in Steve Odin's paper in this volume) expressed in the conflicting accounts of a rape by four particpants/observers (see table 2 below). James F. Davidson has suggested that Kurosawa's reworking of the original materials represents an allegory for Japan's postwar malaise and the experience of foreign occupation.[23] The bandit thus represents the predatory occupying forces, luring Japan (the woman) from the embrace of the Japanese warrior-aristocrat tradition (her husband). Both Akutagawa and Kurosawa have been described as "Western" in orientation, meaning that each of them is "concerned with truths which are ordinarily outside pragmatic Japanese morality and, being concerned with them, he questions them . . . the film is a complete opposite of the ordinary Japanese historical film in that it questions while they affirm; it is completely realistic while they are romantic; it is using its period as a pretext and a decoration while the ordinary period films aim at simple reconstruction."[24]

The two stories which inspired Kurosawa are Akutagawa's "Rashomon" ("Rashomon" or Rasho Gate) and "Yabu no naka" ("In a Grove"). Although the film takes its title from the first of these, the second story supplies the overall plot. The Rasho Gate, Kyoto's largest city gate, merely serves as a philosophical framework for the final cinematic product, symbolizing social decay. As a site at which dead bodies are abandoned it provokes a struggle between moral principle and survival. Morality and humaneness are defeated in the process. The characters in "In a Grove" are forced to confront these same competing forces, only to find their higher values trampled in the dust. Ironically, the violent events that unfold take place in the waning of the Heian ("peace") period (794–1185), an idealized golden past known for its aesthetic refinement. This sets the stage for the underlying theme that reality is not always what it seems on the surface—a delicate beauty may well be a murderous temptress, a proud warrior a weak coward, and a vile thief a man of honor.

A beautiful young aristocratic woman stands at the apex of the love/lust triangle that fuels the conflict. It has been suggested that Akutagawa intended the story, "In a Grove," as a satire of the confessional literary genre, *shishōsetsu*, popular among his Meiji intellectual contemporaries: "Akutagawa, unmoved by the exhibition of so many tedious egos, went his own way . . . [converting] an old melodramatic tale into a series of conflicting statements which undermine our prosaic confidence in distinguishing between subjective and objective, truth and fiction."[25] At one level, the story is a murder mystery, but a very atypical one in which each of the suspects (including the murder victim who confesses through a medium) admits his or her sole guilt.[26] This willingness to shoulder the guilt also seems to correspond to a sense of responsibility for the death, and a corresponding sense of personal power to cause that death at various levels. In sociological terms, the themes of honor/dishonor and shame are central to understanding the psychological impact of the action as reflected upon by the participants. As in the original story, Kurosawa never confirms the guilt or innocence of any of the characters—nor is such confirmation essential to his multiperspectival artistic intent.

The gender relationships reprise the theme of the inherent dangers of feminine sensuality—or of the woman as a scheming, duplicitous sex object who lives off her male victim(s). The woman elicits the fatal attraction that fuels the story when a seemingly innocent breeze exposes her exquisite face to the lustful bandit, Tajomaru, indolently lounging beside the road, who later remarks, "I thought I'd seen an angel."[27] To underscore the erotic tension, visual elements of Nature are woven throughout the film, including the alternation of light and shadow in the forest and the sweeping panorama of the sky during the bandit's retelling of the rape sequence. The threat posed to society by the events that transpire is not lost on film critics, who describe the forest catastrophe as "a single movement which temporarily annihilated the moral reality on which civilized human consciousness is based."[28] The impact is deepened by the setting of the film within the idyllic golden age of cultural refinement and Genji-esque romanticism of the Heian period.

Table 2: Comparison of Conflicting Characterizations in *Rashomon*

	Bandit (Tajomaru)	Wife (Masago)	Husband (Takehiro)
Bandit-lustful	calculating, bold, "honorable," lustful	seductive, fierce (catlike), disgraced, aroused	suspicious, greedy, sullen, watchful
Wife-anguished	cruel, callous, sneering	pitiful, empathetic, weak	disdainful, inhuman, unfeeling
Husband-jealous	conniving, shocked, sense of male solidarity	morose, cruel	jealous, victimized
Woodcutter-curious, larcenous?	infatuated, sincere, sympathetic to womanly weakness	distraught, contemptuous of the men, manipulative	morose, bitter, unforgiving

On recalling his capture of the husband and attempt to satisfy his lechery, Tajomaru describes the wife's reaction as fierce and catlike. This proves to be a prefiguring of her depths of passion, as he claims that what begins as a rape ends in orgasmic mutuality. Moreover, he accuses her of inciting the contest that ends in the husband's death, so that she may avoid being "doubly disgraced" by having revealed her true nature before two men. This too is a ruse, however, as she flees before the battle is won. Assuaging his wounded male ego, the bandit rationalizes his loss: "It was her temper that interested me, but she turned out to be just like any other woman." Unable to live up to his erotic fantasies, Masago is forced back into the role circumscribed by feminine honor.

This hidden dimension of the woman thus occasions both erotic arousal and fear. In his account (as relayed by a female medium) the husband comments on his wife after she is raped by the bandit, "Never had I seen her more beautiful." He also contends that the bandit excused his violent behavior as a sign of his love for her—the price of passion that must be paid when social barriers are broken through. The disgrace of his wife's dishonor drives him to the only honorable solution—suicide.

The only "impartial" witness to the crime, the woodcutter (the version presented first by Akutagawa and last by Kurosawa), is also the most scathing in his denunciation of the woman. Caught between the rapist's protestations of love and promises of reform, on the one hand, and the abusive denunciations of the husband, on the other ("You're a shameless whore. . . . I regret the loss of my horse more than the loss of you"), he claims that she exacted the revenge of a woman scorned by goading them into mortal combat. Now it is her turn to denounce the code of manly honor as a "farce" that has assaulted her integrity, and has even failed to provide her with the anticipated protection. A wanton seductress lurks within her unleashed eroticism: "A woman only loves a real man. And when she loves, she loves madly, forgetting all else." Unable to ignore the challenge to their egos, the men engage in a half-hearted battle, until the husband ignominiously succumbs. She then flees the victor, who limps off with only the husband's sword as his sole prize.

A common thread runs through the male accounts—the perfidy of the female once civilized standards have been breached. But why should they expect allegiance to a code of honor that has failed to protect her, since such protection had been the only reward for submission? Why not embrace a repentant rapist once she realizes that her previous life as a married woman cannot be regained? Why not turn homicidal once her legal spouse has contemptuously disowned her with the look in his eyes? Why not taunt two men to combat in retaliation for the contempt that has been shown you, flaunting the only power vouchsafed to a woman in the patriarchal prison, namely, manipulating the overweening pride of the male ego?

The account offered by the wife Masago, accused of mutating from rape victim to manipulatory victimizer, differs substantially from the male versions of the events. Hers is the briefest account, with the fewest details, and is related through the priest (apparently the most reliable of the narrators). The "facts" she presents obviously have been filtered through the abiding pall of gender oppression. Consciously or unconsciously, she has no choice but to fall back upon stereotypical excuses of feminine weakness as her defense.

Significantly, her story begins after the rape, omitting direct reference to it. This can be interpreted as a sign of her offended modesty[29] or a device to divert attention away from her culpability for having been seduced by the bandit's forceful eroticism. Her statement indicates that she has been most wounded not by the physical violation, but rather by the reaction it elicits in her husband: "what I saw in them [her husband's eyes] was not sorrow . . . not even anger. . . . It was a cold hatred of me." As is the case in many patriarchal cultures, the violated woman is perceived to be devoid of value, having lost her only claim to social respectability—purity. Death seems to be the only choice, but even here she claims her feminine fragility defeats her resolve: "I tried to kill myself. But, I failed. What should a poor helpless woman like me do?" Awakening from a stereotypical swoon, she finds her husband dead and assumes she herself is the murderer (although she has no recollection of the deed). She then runs off for another aborted suicide attempt, this time by drowning.

Rashomon stands as a far-reaching critique of Japanese society, "an indictment of feudal remains."[30] Time-worn but entrenched gender stereotyping persists to this day, evoking old images of the insatiable female and weak-willed male:

> young male imaginations seem haunted by a cruel, authoritarian female image. Psychological as opposed to physical masochism permeates a recurring porno movie theme, which presents the vicarious thrill of a man tied up and forced to watch his wife repeatedly raped by lusty thugs. The sadistic implications of the

rape pale before the delicious torments experienced by the hapless
voyeur, who is invariably the main character and conceived as a
vehicle for audience empathy. A consistent twist in the rape fantasy finds the victim reaching heights of sexual ecstasy that she has
never attained with her inadequate husband.[31]

Equally revealing is the fact that in the overwhelming majority of
these films the woman falls in love with the rapist, made more
jarring by portraying the stock rape victim as the image of innocence—schoolgirl, nurse, young wife. Sumiko Iwao warns that
Japan's flourishing sex industry, combined with sex crimes against
young girls, suggests "the stirrings of psychological problems engen-
dered in men who are confused and unmanned by women who are
aggressive, desire gratification of their own, know their own minds,
and can express themselves clearly."[32]

Masago and Tajomaru fit these stereotypes well—the embodiment of refined aristocracy succumbing to the brutal vitality of a
common criminal. Did the rape really unleash erotic fulfillment in
Masago, a fact she omits from her own version? Or is the inclusion
of this "fact" in the male versions actually a form of wish-fulfill-
ment? Are the events as reconstructed by the male characters primal nightmares of a destructive female, or their most closely kept
fantasies of the same? Does this uncivilized outburst of violence
justify the male's right to dominate inherently weak females? Or is
it the very strength of the female that necessitates the vindictive
social strategy of domination as an act of self-defense? Like the
murder mystery in the story, these questions remain unanswered
and perhaps unanswerable.

In Kurosawa's postmodern retelling of the story, we are left
with a glimmer of hope for humankind, sharply contrasting the deep
gloom of Akutagawa's ending.[33] This is made possible by the addition of a plot device concerning a baby abandoned at the gate. Birth
and new life counter the original story's association of the dilapidated gate solely with death through abandoned corpses. The passerby, obviously corrupted by the spiritual pollution to which he has
just been subjected, steals the baby's clothing. He excuses his immoral behavior by rationalizing that someone else would do the
same anyway, shifting the blame to the parents who placed their
offspring in such a dangerous situation. The priest cradles the baby,
becoming defensive when the woodcutter reaches for it. Expressing
sympathy for the parents who were forced to take such drastic
measures, the woodcutter offers to take in the foundling. He is not

offended by the priest's incredulity, observing "you can't afford not to be suspicious these days." Finally, the priest relents and thanks the woodcutter, crediting the latter's offer with allowing him to sustain his faith in humanity.

Gate of Hell

Our historical time frame now advances from the Heian period (794–1185) of *Rashomon* to the prelude of the succeeding Kamakura period (1185–1333) in the Heiji Revolt (1159–60). Premiered in 1953, Kinugasa Teinosuke's *Gate of Hell* was consciously modeled on *Rashomon*, and both films gained an unexpectedly positive reception in the West.[34] Both focus on a city gate as a symbol of social decline and chaos. It is also of note that the same consummate actress, Kyo Machiko, plays both females leads, manifesting the broad range of the feminine in Japanese society.

The love triangles presented in the two films also have many points in common. The pivotal role is again played by a married woman, Kesa, who is the object of the unwanted sexual advances of another man. A rivalry also arises between the two men over Kesa, but it is fought out on the more civilized, and sublimated, sports field rather than the field of mortal combat. Like Masago, Kesa also assumes responsibility for the fatal events that transpire.

There are also many significant differences between the two scenarios. Unlike the distraught Masago, Kesa's maturity and wisdom, guided by her deeply-rooted Buddhist principles, allow her to take control of a dangerous situation that the men in her society have been either unwilling or unable to defuse. Her deliberate action contrasts sharply with the unconfirmed confession of unconscious action on Masago's part. Kesa's husband, Wataru, is also quite unique, asserting full confidence in his wife throughout a difficult situation. The conflict in the *Gate of Hell* also takes place over an extended period of time, during which the level of tension is gradually escalated, as opposed to the condensed temporal context of *Rashomon*.

The film opens in the midst of a political crisis as rebels are attacking the imperial palace. The self-sacrificing courage of Kesa and Moritoh is demonstrated by their willingness to place themselves in danger so as to allow for the escape of the imperial couple. It is this valor which first draws them together in what is to become a one-sided fatal attraction. Moritoh's loyalty also is revealed by his willingness to oppose even his own brother, who has joined the rebels, to remain true to his lord (Kiyomori). Risking his life once again, he rides off to report on the dire situation to the absent lord, dispatching a traitor in the process.

Once the rebellion has been quelled and order has been restored, an accidental meeting at the Gate of Hell between the courageous couple fans the flame of love in Moritoh, who for the first time learns the identity of his mystery lady. Significantly, Kesa has come there to pray for the souls of the dead (including Moritoh's treacherous brother), a sign of her Buddhist piety and compassion. The scene then shifts to the palace of the triumphant Kiyomori, who is dispensing rewards to his troops. Moritoh goads the lord into promising him anything he asks for (except the head of the lord or his own family). When he asks for Kesa his wish is initially granted, and he is in fact commended for his forthrightness. However, the insurmountable barrier of marriage then arises to block his desire, and he is laughingly told to make another request. He remains insistent, seemingly oblivious of the social impropriety of his request. An appeal is made to his "reason," which will be unsuccessfully repeated throughout the drama, but he refuses to yield.

In contrast, Wataru, the loving husband, appears unperturbed by these matters, and perhaps even a bit triumphant in having his wife recognized as an object of desire that is his alone. He lays no blame on his wife, despite her fears of having been "careless" in her behavior. Treading a path between Buddhist compassion and male cohesion, he also initially is circumspect in his criticism of Moritoh, rationalizing his rival's forcefulness as a samurai characteristic. He seems to have implicit trust in the functionality of social rules and roles as he reassures Kesa: "You're my wife. Don't worry about it." In a later scene the couple strolls under a full moon and he promises: "I won't let anybody in the world touch you. Understand?"

Kesa's forthright rejection of Moritoh's suit exacerbates the competitiveness of the situation when he interprets it as a sign that she thinks him inferior to her husband. Moritoh makes a direct challenge to his rival through an upcoming horse race. On learning of the plan Wataru refuses to drop out of the race, but also ignores the attempts of his friends to accept the challenge as a symbolic combat. "Get mad. Hate that fool," exclaims one of Wataru's drunken comrades at a pre-race drinking party. Again Wataru expresses his sense of identification with the supposed enemy: "He is a samurai. He feels the same as I do." Here would seem to lie his fatal flaw—misjudging his rival to be the same kind of man that he is and thereby overlooking the depth of emotions (love, lust, jealousy, shame) that are propelling Moritoh.

After Kesa returns from her ordeal with Moritoh, a sympathetic Wataru listens calmly to her tale of humiliation. He invites her to the race: "Everyone has to do his best. . . . I have a feeling I'll win. . . . Be calm, keep hold of yourself. People will be watching." The reference to the social context here seems very telling, as Wataru reiterates his faith in the social system. But it also betrays his sensitivity to appearances, and his need to have everything seems correct to others. Kesa's subsequent actions indicate that she does not share his faith or his fears, and is unwilling to trust mechanisms of social control under the dire circumstances they are facing.

The race scene represents a critical turning point. The symbolic rivalry should now be resolved in a socially acceptable sublimation of aggression, especially since Moritoh wins. But at the post-race banquet charges arise that Wataru merely allowed Moritoh to win—charges that Wataru himself emphatically denies. Moritoh's elation turns to deep resentment, and he demands satisfaction. Society intervenes and he is summarily ejected as a disruptive influence, chided for "making a fool of yourself over a woman." But in this case society has overestimated its controlling force—feminine beauty has once again undermined its power. The depth of Moritoh's emotions are ignored; and the attempted social resolution has failed to satisfy him. From this point on he makes his own rules.

Rushing to Kesa's home, Moritoh is falsely led to believe that she is visiting her aunt. In fact she has taken refuge within the home's Buddhist shrine. In the meantime Moritoh has gone in search of the aunt and discovered the deception. Driven to the breaking point ("I won't give her up. . . . I'll kill anyone who stops me," he declares), he responds with his own ruse to lure Kesa away from her house on the pretext that her aunt is ill. Kesa accepts the message with some trepidation, but declines her husband's offer to go in her place.

When she arrives at her aunt's home, Kesa is met by Moritoh with an ultimatum—to go with him or be responsible for a massacre, including herself. Kesa now must confront the full force of Moritoh's passion—"Could you possibly want me at such a price?", she asks incredulously. "I can't live another day without you," Moritoh avows. Kesa realizes that his is a passion intent on obliterating the social structures in which her husband and his comrades have placed their implicit trust. Reluctantly she acquiesces to his demands. But he also insists that the husband be eliminated, and she herself is to serve as his accomplice that very night.

The moth (Moritoh) has come to the flame (Kesa), and though the flame has not intentionally bidden it, the moth can only be protected from itself if the flame is extinguished. And this is precisely what Kesa sets out to accomplish—killing both herself and Moritoh's irrational desire with one sword stroke. Luring her husband to her room, she takes his place in his room after giving the prearranged signal—extinguishing the flame in Wataru's room. Clutching her Buddhist rosary she silently awaits the inevitable.

The wisdom accompanying her compassion is vindicated by the fact that her strategy works—Moritoh is finally aroused from his self-delusions. "Forgive me!" he gasps, "What a blind fool I was! I couldn't see into your heart. I have crushed a beautiful soul." Rushing from the scene of slaughter, sword in hand, he calls for Wataru to exact his revenge: "What a beast am I. A madman who thought he could force a heart. . . . Deal with me as you please. . . . Smash this monster to pieces."

Wataru has demons of his own to confront. As compassionate as his dead wife, if not as wise, Wataru refuses Moritoh's insistence that he exact revenge by cutting off his head: "It wouldn't help. . . . Death may satisfy you." But it is no use to him; it will not bring his love back to him. In a sense he too has been unable to see into Kesa's heart, which is precisely what he had accused Moritoh of earlier.

Moritoh settles for another kind of death—and opportunity for rebirth. Cutting off his hair he vows to seek his redemption as a monk: "I must live on . . . with the torments of Hell." In fact, he and Wataru have each entered through their own Gate of Hell. Buddhist doctrine thus sounds the closing bars of the tragedy that the bodhisattvic Kesa has turned into a spiritual triumph:

> As a man who has no wound on his hand cannot be hurt by the poison he may carry in his hand, since poison hurts not where there is no wound, the man who has no evil cannot be hurt by evil.[35]

In death Kesa is not truly injured, nor has the poison of Moritoh's passion (*lobha*)—reinforced by delusion (*moha*) and anger (*dosa*)—infected her. Practicing the Buddhist virtue of self-reliance she has not only enlightened the deluded Moritoh, but saved the life of her overly optimistic husband. And she has done so despite the bumbling interference of society, overcoming its incompetence and inability to resolve the destabilizing problem. Moritoh, now set on the path of salvation, has learned the crucial lesson of karmic entanglements:

> The fool who does evil to a man who is good, to a man who is pure, and from sin the evil returns to him like the dust thrown against the wind.[36]

The cultural underpinnings of the film's story arc further clarified by a comparison with a recent American film about a very similar love triangle, *Fatal Attraction*. Both films feature a married couple whose relationship is threatened by a persistent suitor of one spouse, though in the recent film the pursuer is a woman. Both suitors are distinguished by their obsessive pursuit, which goes from harassment to violence. Both stories end in death. However the differences are much more significant. From a Buddhist perspective the *Fatal Attraction* scenario is permeated by the "poison" of anger on the part of all members of the triangle—the wife is angry with her erring husband just as his adultery points to a deep-seated anger toward her; the husband is also angry with the fatally attracted woman for failing to end things gracefully, while she is angry at him for being so abruptly jilted; and jealous anger surges between the two women over possession of the man. At bottom each of these insufferable individuals is acting solely on the basis of his or her perceived self-interest.

The Buddhist values that pervade *Gate of Hell* transform the emotional climate of its fatal attraction. Only Moritoh exhibits anger, issuing from his sense of wounded pride and ego attachment. But even his anger is never expressed in the wanton destructiveness of the fatally attracted woman—kicking the family dog is a far cry from boiling a child's pet rabbit. Wataru, the injured spouse, refuses to feel anger despite the urgings of his companions. On the contrary, he expresses empathy for his supposed rival. Kesa is likewise guided by the positive emotion of compassion (*karuna*), which leads to her self-transcending act of sacrifice.

At the same time the gory denouement of *Fatal Attraction* provides a catharsis for American audiences that eludes them in *Gate of Hell*. The latter, in fact, is prone to elicit confusion and regretful dissatisfaction. In the first case the blood bath allows for the venting of vicarious violence under the assumption that anger and revenge are justified in this case, leaving the audience secure in

Table 3: Shifting Perspectives in *Gate of Hell*

	Personal character/values	Relationship to society	View of social values
Kesa	compassion (*karuna*) plus courage through Buddhist faith; bodhisattva by Buddhist interpretation – chooses one action which can both save her husband's life and Moritoh's soul (means of stimulating his conversion)	urged by others to accept responsibility for the situation (female relative, husband)	concerned about injuring the reputation of her husband and his family (social status), but unwilling to leave resolution to society
Moritoh	courage + ego, loyal but belligerent and lacking compassion—willing to betray his own brother out of loyalty to the lord; straightforward, lack of tact	cannot bear the thought that others are laughing at him, need to vindicate himself in the eyes of his peers	takes it as a personal challenge, a point of honor, even in defiance of social order
Wataru	detached compassion, love for Kesa, empathetic toward Moritoh (male/samurai solidarity), wise, cautious, self-controlled	concern with social appearances (reminding her that people will be watching at the race); evaluates Moritoh in terms of his social role as samurai	trust in social order, his ability to protect his wife; no sense of the depths of Moritoh's passion as an individual

the feeling that justice has triumphed. The *Gate of Hell* displaces the social value of righteous anger with the socially transcendent Buddhist value of compassion. Simultaneously it exposes the superficiality of retributory justice as simply another aspect of the delusory samsaric cycle.

Woman as Social Rebel: *The Life of Oharu*

Moving now to the Tokugawa period (1600–1868), the social and political control of sexuality becomes increasingly evident in response to the perceived escalation of its threat to stability. Bowing to the inevitability of natural desires, prostitution was legalized by Hideyoshi as a means of keeping it under the watchful eye of the state. Its practice was restricted to special areas, which came to be known as the "Floating World" (*ukiyo*), that is, floating between respectability and licentiousness, social restraint and libertinism. Offering a unique meeting ground for samurai and townsmen (*chōnin*), it allowed for temporary transcendence of the otherwise rigid social caste system. It also gave free reign to the most base instincts of materialistic indulgence and exploitation, another safety valve in an otherwise rigidly controlled world, the sensual equivalent of the Roman Empire's bread and circuses calculated to forestall rebellion and dissent by means of frivolous distraction and dissipation.

To stock the brothels that were the focal point of this interim world, women and children were driven into a life of white slavery and kidnappings increased. A clear-cut double standard was subsequently generated. Women were classified in one of two categories—the wife/mother who restricted her activities to the private sphere of the home, and the whore to whom men (of means) had public access. The first type of woman contributed the stability of a family environment and continuity; the second provided sexual release and companionship.

Under such harsh conditions, where women had very little left to lose, rebellion would certainly be understandable. However, heroines of the caliber of Oharu are few and far between in Japanese cinema. Her vitality and rebelliousness—both rooted in and fanned by her sexuality—place her in sharp contrast to the feminine ideal of the long-suffering woman who patiently and silently bears her lot in life. Although she suffers much in her life, Oharu refuses to submit, time after time eschewing the easy path of social conformity for the hard road of individual integrity. The epitome of the nail that sticks up, society takes a perverse delight in hammering her ever further down into degradation.

As director Mizoguchi Kenji acknowledges, the film is based on a well-known work by Iharu Saikaku (1642–93). One of the foremost representatives of the Tokugawa *chōnin* culture evolving from among the newly prosperous merchant class, Saikaku at first described and later proscribed the lifestyle and values of his peers. The early death of Saikaku's wife reportedly led him to abandon the family business in his early thirties and embark on a life of mindless sensuality. Sexuality and money, and their interpenetrating influences, were his favored themes. Striving for realism over literary value, he was particularly noted for his portrayals of women characters. His early hedonism is reflected in *The Life of an Amorous Man* (1682), the tale of a rake without remorse or religious sentiment, and matured into an incisive social criticism. Thus Oharu, the female counterpart of the rake in *Amorous Woman* (*Kōshoku ichidai onna*), suffers from the reigning sexual double standard, in which "The courtesan's life, however, is no longer pictured in the rosy colours of the earlier works, but is revealed with full realism as a place where money rules the day and where sensual desire is rarely relieved by tenderness. . . . Saikaku evokes the dark, gloomy aspect of sex and shows us the reverse side of the medal."[37]

Mizoguchi's reworking of the story for the film emphasizes the threads of social criticism while de-emphasizing those of sexual addiction, thereby following a postwar tradition that stressed the reformist tendencies and intentions of Saikaku's work.[38] Joan Mellen has described this as "perhaps the finest film ever made in any country about the repression of women." Mizoguchi has said that "shunning didactic moralizing, [it] can only echo her pain."[39] Mizoguchi's films are noted for championing the cause of women as an oppressed class, an oppression based on gender discrimination that he views as more deeply rooted than the problems of social status.[40] The film clearly identifies the social forces which contributed to the subjugation of women, against which the heroine rebels: (1) religious, specifically the male-dominated institution of Buddhism with its misogynist doctrines, and (2) political, as embodied in the militaristic feudal clan system that valued virility to the detriment of everything feminine. Buddhism portrayed here is quite unlike the compassion-evoking faith of Kesa, embracing as it does a gynophobic view of women as sources of polluting sexual temptation, to be avoided at all costs. Its views are represented in the *Lotus*

Sūtra's claim that gender discrimination is sanctioned by cosmic forces in that women are excluded from paradise and must "earn" rebirth as men to merit that honor. Nonetheless, Oharu, like Kesa, ultimately finds refuge in her personal encounter with Buddhism, which transcends the perversions of the powers that be.

The feudal hierarchy was becoming increasingly rigid during this time period. In a society that glorified the samurai ideal, women were regarded as weak and nearly useless (save for the unavoidable need for procreation—heterosexual intercourse was in fact contemptuously referred to as "borrowing their wombs"). Women, tolerated as necessary for the propagation of the clan, were to be strictly controlled. Emulating Confucian models, emphasis was placed on the ideal feminine qualities of self-sacrifice, self-control, and complete obedience to male authority. They were to be silently submissive, devoid of jealousy, and were expected to avoid the public arena.

Oharu has risen to the peak position of lady-in-waiting at the imperial court, a member of the elite class. Yet lured on by love and the hope of personal fulfillment, she comes to question its injunctions, thus forfeiting its attendant privileges. In defiance of social standards she chooses love and sexual freedom over class consciousness, and so suffers a gradual decline in status—from concubine of a lord, to courtesan in a brothel, to servant of a merchant, to wife of a small shopkeeper, to common prostitute. Eventually she ends up as a wandering mendicant.

We first see Oharu at age fifty plying her "trade." She is questioned by her colleagues about her "lost life," as they gather for warmth around a fire near a temple (to the dismay of the priest who orders them away). But she refuses to discuss it with the others. Later, a series of flashbacks reveals her story. Significantly these come as she is seated in a Buddhist temple where images of Buddha become superimposed with the face of her first lover. The abrupt shift from religious idols to men, and the association between her past love and the Buddha, seem to signal both positive and negative connotations of worship and manipulation, or refuge and repression.

She remembers back to her early life at the imperial court where she was sought after by the lords through the Genji technique of exploratory poems. A page, Katsunosuke, has also written to her, and lured her to a meeting on the pretext that his lord has invited her. There he confesses his love for her. At first she denies having read his letter, dismissing him as a creature of humble status, thus remaining true to the social conditioning that demands the observance of rigid class distinctions, just as it imposes discriminatory gender distinctions. Gradually he wins her over by arguing that none of her noble suitors really loves her, while he is "loyal and sincere. You can despise my low rank, but you can't ignore my devotion." While others seek mere dalliance, he alone offers a honorable commitment of marriage. He also declares that "a woman can be happy only if she marries for true love" rather than for social prestige. The seeds of rebellion have been planted, to be nurtured by erotic insight.

Worried about the social impossibility of their relationship, Oharu is convinced they will be unable to obtain the needed permission to marry either from the court or her father. He suggests they elope. She finally succumbs to his persuasion, a passionate embrace followed by a swoon, as they are in a graveyard. Prophetically the camera focuses on adjacent gravestones as he carries her off.

Their joy is short-lived, for they soon are beset by the police checking allegations of prostitution. Katsunosuke tries to get out of it by lying about his name and rank; Oharu, however, gives her true name as well as that of her family. At her trial she is charged with the "crime" of "misconduct with a person of inferior rank." The sentence is exile for both her and her parents (they being guilty of "lack of parental supervision"). Katsunosuke, being of lesser rank, is executed. Oharu and her family are rudely escorted to the edge of town, and their relatives are barred from following. Relocated in a rural setting, the family lives a simple life. Oharu is verbally abused by her father for having "destroyed our family honor." Rather than submit, she pointedly asks, "Why is it immoral if a man and woman love each other?" Spouting the common wisdom of the time he counters that love without parental consent is by definition immoral.

Although Katsunosuke's appearance in the film is relatively brief, his effect on the action lingers throughout the course of Oharu's life. Despite being a member of the exploitive male gender, his low status has made him sensitive to the inequities of society and a fitting role model of erotic rebellion. At his execution he sends a last incendiary request: "Please find a good man. Be sure to marry only where there is mutual love." Before he dies he calls out for a world where people are free to love as they choose, and expires expressing his love for Oharu. When she receives the message she runs off to commit suicide, but is restrained by her mother (who has sympathetically brought the message to her, cautioning her to keep it from her father). The parting words from her beloved become a personal moral imperative and seal her fate, at least in terms of her determining subsequent attitudes and ideals.

By accepting this imperative, Oharu is transformed into an existential heroine. Like the rebel of Camus, she says both "yes" and "no"; "no" to the artificial restrictions of society and "yes" to the value of love, the inherent human right to love:

> In every act of rebellion, the rebel simultaneously experiences a feeling of revulsion at the infringement of his [her] rights and a complete and *spontaneous* [emphasis added] loyalty to certain aspects of himself [herself]. Thus [s]he implicitly brings into play a standard of values so far from being gratuitous that [s]he is prepared to support it no matter what the risks. Up to this point [s]he has at least remained silent and has abandoned himself [herself] to the form of despair in which a condition is accepted even though it is considered unjust. . . . But from the moment that the rebel finds his [her] voice—and even though [s]he says nothing but "no"—[s]he begins to desire and to judge.[41]

From this point onward Oharu's life does indeed take on the futility and frustration of Sisyphus' struggle, although her rock seems to descend ever deeper with each roll. At each step she valiantly fights a society that sees her as a mere means to an end in order to assert the intrinsic value Katsunosuke alone had seen in her. She must postpone satisfying Katsunosuke's request when she is selected to fulfill the role of concubine [surrogate] for a lord in need of an heir, as a way to redeem herself in her father's eyes (what he describes as their "good luck"). Despite her protest ("Katsunosuke won't permit me to"), she is forced to accept the position. She fits the physical criteria for the ideal woman, as gauged by an image on scroll (including specifications for fingers and nails, small feet, figure, round face, eyes, eyebrows, nose, mouth, teeth, ears, neck, lack of moles—underscoring the social emphasis on superficial traits). In a "beauty pageant" (meat market) scene several men on seeing Oharu initially react by wanting to "buy" her "for the sake of the clan" to become a surrogate mother.

Once ensconced in her new position, Oharu is inspected to insure that she can fulfill the required function. She is then taken to the barren wife, who bears a strong resemblance to Oharu. It is apparent that the wife is not fully reconciled to the arrangement. She walks out at the first official meeting with the lord, when a puppet show mirrors the new relationships of this *ménage à trois*. After Oharu is "caused to bear" the desired male heir (immediately taken away by the official wife), she becomes a political liability. Accused of being "too eager to satisfy his lordship," by sapping his energy and posing a hazard to his health, "for the sake of the clan" she is sent back to her parents. There she is greeted by paternal abuse for her failure to fulfill his materialistic dreams. Her father decides there is "no other way" than for her to become a courtesan to clear up his debts (acquired in expectation of new wealth due to her son). His wife's protests go unheeded; she empathizes with her daughter's recent disappointment and the prospect of further humiliations, but being a woman, and thus at the bottom of the social hierarchy, her protests are in vain.

Oharu does not adjust well to her new situation as a prostitute. She is not motivated by money, as are the others, exclaiming "I'm not a beggar." Her proud and defiant attitude leads to her being sent back. The brothel owner declares, "You're no different than a fish. We can prepare and dispose of you as we like," and threatens her, saying she will never be able to find work. Finally Oharu succumbs and begs forgiveness, which is refused.

A brief hope for redemption—and an abrupt reversal of the owner's attitude toward her—emerges through a free-spending man who claims to be seeking a wife. Mindful of Katsunosuke's words, Oharu offers herself to him, on the condition that he is sincere. He responds with derisive laughter, and accuses her of greed: "Money is everything. There is nothing greater." He turns out to be a fraud, nothing more than a thief and a charlatan. So much for her dreams of rescue from the male realm!

Ultimately Oharu is returned to her family deeply depressed. Her mother, happy to have her back again, tries to comfort her. On the way home they encounter a street singer who was formerly a famous courtesan, foreshadowing Oharu's own fate. Oharu gives her some money and thanks her for her elegant song. She is reduced to serving in the home of a merchant to whom her father had become indebted. At first the family is happy to have her, and refers to her as a "sister" since she is connected to the lord. They also promise to find her a husband, and the wife even suggests adopting her. But her past returns to destroy her chance for normalcy. When her experience as a courtesan is revealed by a former client, the wife is seized with jealousy, believing that her husband knew about Oharu's past and may even have visited her as a client. On his part, the lecherous husband subjects Oharu to sexual harassment attempting to take advantage of her (ironically) under the pretense of prayer: "You're a bad girl . . . just relax and play the game. . . . We can both enjoy ourselves—free of charge." The obvious assumption is, once a whore, always a whore (as logically follows from the either/or categorization of women by society). Although the victim of rape, Oharu is made to bear the guilt by the outraged wife of the merchant, and is forced out (but not before exacting a revenge of her own by exposing the wife's baldness, her deepest fear).

While working to support herself, Oharu accepts the love of a struggling fan-maker, at long last fulfilling the wishes of her ill-fated first lover. His friends intercede on his behalf, recommending him as "sincere and honest." With a sympathy born of his own experiences of discrimination, the problem of her past does not concern him: "I don't mind. I want to marry that poor, unlucky girl and make her happy." For a brief interlude they work together in his shop, where a customer describes them as an ideal couple. In a poignant twist of fate her husband is killed by a thief as he is bringing home a gift for her. It is as if she had been tantalized by bliss for the sole sake of feeling its loss all the more by a vengeful society.

Oharu seeks refuge in a Buddhist temple, where the prioress reminds her of the evanescence of life: "Even a beauty in the morning will change to bones in the evening. The world is changing without mercy." The words would seem to be a case of preaching to the converted, given Oharu's confirming experiences. The institution of Buddhism is unable, and even unwilling, to provide her shelter however. An old debt—to her former merchant employer—surfaces to destroy her peace. When he comes to collect the money he accuses her of being a "whore" and eventually exacts repayment of a different kind (she unfortunately incites his lust by an impetuous striptease to remove the kimonos which she bought with the money to return to him). Walking in on the scene the prioress misunderstands the situation and is self-righteously horrified: "Do you provide me with a visual demonstration, hoping I would join you? . . . I can't be tempted by a whore like you," she shrieks (perhaps revealing her own suppressed libidinal desires). Unmoved by Oharu's explanation, the prioress orders her out of the temple. Outside Oharu encounters an employee of the merchant, who has embezzled some money. Everyone thinks he is eloping with her, and so he forces her to go with him. When they are caught on the road, she is denounced as a "consummate whore" by his captors.

As part of her spiraling social descent Oharu is next seen earning money by singing in front of a temple (as did the once famous courtesan Oharu when encountered after being sent home from the gay quarter). A procession from the Matsudaira clan pauses briefly by her, surrounding a young nobleman, her son. Greatly moved by the scene—and her own inability to declare herself—she weeps uncontrollably. She is consoled by two passing women, who take her with them. Although common street prostitutes, they care for her in their home, and encourage her to join them: "It'd be stimulating.... Dying is the easiest way—if only we could.... Whatever you do it doesn't make any difference to the world." They also urge her to seek escape in drink. At last Oharu has found common cause with women who recognize themselves as social rejects of fast-fading extrinsic value.

Advancing age poses a barrier to her trade, but she perseveres. We see her with a potential client, who actually wants to use her as a visual demonstration of the wages of sin for his colleagues on a pilgrimage: "Take a good look at this witch, do you still want to lie down with a woman?" The final irony and injustice has found her in the form of the hypocritical religious man who portrays the female victim—repeatedly and brutally violated by social norms— as victimizer. The virtue of compassion (*karuna*) has been conveniently forgotten as society desperately struggles to reassert its control over erotic impulses. How much more comforting it is to project the dangerous sensuality on the already demeaned female gender?

Returning to the opening scene of the film, Oharu is back at the temple where she has been steeped in her memories. She soon faints and is very ill. From her mother, who has been searching for her, Oharu learns that her father has died ("He worried himself to death about you"). Despite his ill treatment of her, Oharu weeps for his passing, although her mother tells her to forget. The mother bears news that her son wants her to live with him. "You'll see happiness again," promises the mother; "It's like a dream come true," Oharu cries. Hope does spring eternal, but once again only to be brutally crushed by reality.

The clan leaders add insult to past injuries by lecturing Oharu on her "disgusting and degenerate" behavior as a prostitute—"Have you no excuse!" Fearing that they will be held accountable for this disgrace to the clan, the only option is to confine her in exile, away from the public gaze. There she can repent and seek forgiveness from the dead lord. She is allowed one last look as "a special kindness." He passes by her without even acknowledging her existence; when she tries to get closer she is forcibly held back and told to be "respectful." Invoking her maternal rights she is momentarily released, until one man denounces her as a liar (thus stripping her of natural, as well as social, rights and recognition). She eventually evades enforced exile, the netting over her intended palanquin serving as a symbol of the final social constraints she has so narrowly escaped.

The final scene finds a much older Oharu living as a mendicant nun, begging from door to door in search of food (following the original practice predating institutionalization—and subsequent perversion—of Buddhist doctrine). Underscoring gender lines once more, she is treated kindly by a woman holding a child while rudely refused by a man. As she walks into the sunset (both literally and figuratively), she stops to stare at a pagoda in the distance—at once a symbol of the misogynist Buddhist institution that refused her compassion and a phallic reminder of male dominance. Yet she simply trudges onward, following her accustomed pattern of refusing to wallow in self-pity or resentment.

In an existential interpretation, Oharu has been able to escape the "auto-intoxication" of resentment through her very act of rebellion.[42] In this Oharu has been immensely aided by the self-transcendent spirituality of the true Buddhism she practices (as opposed to the male-dominated pseudo-Buddhism that has sought to further oppress her throughout her life). Unlike the existentialist, for whom "suffering exhausts hope and faith and then is left alone and unexplained,"[43] Oharu has the in-depth Buddhist analysis of *dukkha* to draw upon. The bittersweet conclusion of her story thus need not deprive us of hope, including the hope that Camus may be correct in averring that "it is those who know how to rebel, at the appropriate moment, against history who really advance its interests."[44]

Obsessive Love: *Double Suicide*

This film is based on historical events in the Tokuguwa era involving a love triangle. The element of social pressure is overwhelming for lovers Koharu and Jihei who are torn between duty and passion and are beset by constant interference in their affair. Jihei's wife resents the intrusion of Koharu into her family, but eventually comes to support their cause, and the *shinjū* of Koharu and Jihei who run off from the floating world is deliberately done to become a public spectacle.

Koharu's passivity is reiterated throughout the film, as she depends on Jihei to resolve their dilemmas; even her attempt to break off with Jihei is merely a reaction to the emotional appeal of the aggrieved wife. Sex is something that is obviously done to her (by clients) and for her (by Jihei), most pointedly in the scenes of cunnilingus, and it is Jihei who must kill his beloved Koharu.

This poignant drama is both a retelling of a classic tale from Japanese literature and a modern critique of the social values that shaped the tragedy. It mirrors the Tokugawa morality of the original setting while exposing its feudalistic remnants in contemporary Japanese society that thwart the forces of "free love." Following the recurring symbolism of bridges in the film itself, director Shinoda Masahiro's, retelling of the well-known incident serves to bridge modern and postmodern currents within Japanese society. The basic story is taken from the 1721 play, *The Love Suicides at Amijima* (*Shinjū Ten no Amijima*), written for the Bunraku puppet theater by renowned playwright Chikamatsu Monzaemon (1653–1725). Historically it represents the theater of the emerging merchant class, the *chōnin*, and a key aspect of mass or popular culture made possible by the growing economic power of the middle class. This world was far removed from the rarefied aesthetic realm of the imperial court, the nearly claustrophobic Genji world of exquisite sensibilities presided over by an emperor god and chronicled by well-bred female literati.

Chikamatsu, the dispossessed son of a samurai family, was a perfect bridge between the subcultures of samurai elite and the expanding *chōnin* class. Increased leisure brought with it increasing demands for entertainment. After undergoing appropriate modifications, the ways of the elite samurai class were emulated by the masses. As the drama reflects, however, both groups found a common meeting ground in the "Floating World," where social distinctions were as fluid as the morality. Here merchants could mingle with hooded samurai, both groups sharing a common pursuit of pleasure. A poor girl from the country could find herself servicing a high-placed *bushi* one moment and an immensely wealthy commoner the next, just as Koharu is shuttled from a distinguished samurai client to the loathsome merchant Tahei. Along with the more obvious cultural refinements co-opted by the *chōnin* was their unique version of the samurai code of honor, now extended to love relationships. The relationship of loyalty on the part of the retainer to the lord, which necessitated the practice of *seppuku* under extreme circumstances, was now applied to male-female relationships, with love usurping the role of the lord to whom the highest fealty was rendered in the practice of *shinjū*.[45]

The change of focus in the respective practices of *seppuku* (also known as *hara-kiri*) and *shinjū* 心中 is certainly deserving of further consideration. The former involves the stomach (*hara*), while the latter is centered in the heart (*shin*). In Japanese culture, the stomach is "a vital center of our health and well-being . . . a point in our body which gives us mental and physical balance."[46] Following Chinese symbolism, the heart was the seat of emotions and thoughts, the stomach was "respository of truth."[47] Thus the contents of the heart were subjective and personal in nature, those of the stomach objective and transpersonal.

Double Suicide reveals and reinforces these interclass tensions. As is appropriate for a mercantile audience, money is the focal point of the tragedy, rather than "pure," "noble" themes of Noh theater. The rich merchant dares to compete for Koharu's favors with a samurai client declaring that he is armed with money, which is "stronger than swords." A materialistic man in a materialistic world he reveals a truth that spells doom for the lovers, "In this world money is everything."

The increasingly common practice of *shinjū* highlighted in the film and the original story evokes a "kind of tragedy which was not only appropriate to their class but their exclusive privilege, death with the woman of their choice."[48] A rash of such dramas arose during this period, an example of art imitating nature in the well-publicized actual cases known to the audiences. Eventually the authorities became so alarmed with the practice, fearing that life was imitating art, that the use of the term *shinjū* was banned in 1722.

Table 4: Cultural Convergences in the Tokugawa Period

Samurai Class	*Chōnin* Class
Noh theater	Kabuki, Bunraku
tea ceremony	pleasure quarter
sumiye (original ink paintings)	*ukiyoe* (mass produced woodblock prints)
seppeku, suicide, ultimate repayment of social obligations (*giri*)	*shinjü*, double suicide, ultimate repayment of personal debts (*ninjō*) thwarted by society

Implicit in the practice are currents of social protest compounded with a fatal striving for upward mobility. For example, the
sword carried by Jihei is nothing more than a status symbol, devoid
of any real function in his merchant's existence. Just before he uses
it for the double suicide he nearly forgets to take it with him, which
prompts another character to joke that had he been a samurai he
would have had to forfeit his life for such an offense. For the sword
of the samurai was not merely an extension of himself, but the best
of his being, his "soul." For Jihei it has been reduced to an expedient
means to escape from social constraints.

Originally the term *shinjū* referred to pledges of love made
between two people. In the film such written pledges play a prominent role in the budding tragedy. Literally the term refers to what is
inside the heart, one's innermost feelings. It came to mean a way of
revealing that inner truth through death—the only honorable way to
resolve an insoluble dilemma. Facing defeat at the hands of social
convention (especially the explicit demand that love and sexuality
be separated), thwarted lovers had no recourse but mutual destruction in their search for free expression of their passion.

From the very beginning the director has interwoven the
themes of past and present. Thus the film opens with a voice-over of
the director discussing the crucial suicide scene being staged in a
cemetery with Tomioka Taeko, the writer of the screenplay. The
space in the cemetery is to convey a sense of "emptiness," the
"vanity of life." They agree that something is wanted here besides
the beautified view of death typical of Kabuki so as to infuse realism
into the film; Shinoda emphasizes the need for "essential images"
over dialogue.

Throughout the film the theme of social control and interference is reflected in black-hooded figures, *kurogo*, the puppeteers.
Shinoda has elaborated on this point:

> The *kurogo* lead the lovers, compelled them to die, to catastrophe.
> They represent the eye of our camera and also serve as the agent for
> the viewer, who wants to penetrate into the mystery of the truth of
> the lovers' plight. And finally they represent the author,
> Chikamatsu himself. Their ominous black and silent figures might
> represent the other side of Chikamatsu, who created the anti-social
> world tinged with the melodramatic concept of double suicide, and
> who was a great sentimentalist and hedonist.[49]

Not only do these figures take care of the mundane details of stage
props, but they also are instrumental in moving the action along by

guiding the players through their scenes. Thus, they are elevated to the status of the hands of Fate, as well as the omnipresent interfering forces of society. Even in their most intimate moments, the characters are never left alone, just as their personal decisions are inseparable from broader social interests.

The chant of "Buddha's mercy . . . A net from Heaven" is flashed on the screen just prior to the title of the film. A collage of stark images follows (the entire film being done in black and white to heighten the emotional effect) to the accompaniment of bells punctuated by drums: Jihei crosses a bridge, spanning the two worlds he lives in. He encounters a white-robed funeral procession coming from the opposite direction. Jihei pauses to peer beneath the bridge, where the bodies of a man and woman are laid out, hands clasped and bound together, surrounded by the ubiquitous *kurogo*. His eyes wander into the distance where the river flows, probably thinking of his own desperate situation, whose end is prefigured in these two dead lovers.

Jihei is next seen walking through the gay quarter. A hooded figure blows out a lantern, plunging the scene into shadow. All action stops on the once bustling street, save for Jihei himself, whose way is lit by a candle-holding *kurogo*. He passes scenes of exposed female flesh, including his beloved Koharu ("Little Spring," which implies an "Indian summer"), who stands naked before a squatting tattooed man. Like all the women in the Floating World, she is appropriately presented as a piece of merchandise on display.

A group of *kurogo* step aside to reveal a lover's quarrel; Koharu bemoans the fact that Jihei has not made good on his vows to redeem her. Their tragedy is both financial and emotional. As much as he desires to do so, Jihei is unable to secure her freedom. Yet neither can he bring himself to give her up and return to his faithful wife, Osan, although he admits "I can never return all I owe Osan." Competing desires and obligations weigh heavily upon him: "Meeting is joy *and* pain." Shinoda has introduced a note of irony by having the roles of Koharu and Osan, mistress and wife, played by the same actress, Shima Iwashita (his own wife). This fact gives poignancy to Jihei's reply when Koharu asks if he loves her: "Because you are a woman and I am a man."

Of course, they do not, and cannot, exist solely as a woman and a man. The conflicting claims of *giri* and *ninjō* form a stifling network in this love triangle. Koharu and Jihei are mutually bound by their written vows of love (*shinjū*). However, Koharu also bears responsibility to Osan, as the legitimate wife; hence she must refuse

Jihei's suggestion of double suicide as their only means of escape. Such an act would not only deprive Osan of her husband, but conflict with Koharu's duty to her mother, who is financially dependent on her. Osan is obligated to Koharu for having secretly agreed to drive Jihei away. As the plot develops, this obligation means that Osan cannot allow Koharu to risk suicide by having her redeemed by Tahei, a man she hates.

The affair has not gone unnoticed by the family. Jihei's brother, Magoemon, had intervened to expose Koharu's insincerity. Significantly, he adopts the guise of a sympathetic samurai willing to resolve Koharu and Jihei's financial difficulties. Observing this, an irate Jihei screams, "She cheated me badly," and he is only prevented from abusing her by his brother. In the background we see the blood-stained wall. Tahei also has done his best to discredit his rival by disseminating rumors of his financial ruin. Tahei also plays a prominent role in Jihei's public humiliation before a crowd when he is tied up outside Koharu's place of business by the "samurai" (his own brother, who is seeking to jar Jihei back to reality). He taunts him as "Jihei, the love-sick thief."

The scene changes to Jihei's home/shop, near the bridge. The narrator notes, "He was honest by nature and his shop was reputed." In her husband's absence Osan has taken over the operation of the business, as well as the burden of caring for their two small children. She continues in this role now as Jihei escapes through sleep. Her mother (who is also his aunt) arrives unexpectedly with the brother. They demand to know about Koharu, having heard a rumor that she is about to be redeemed by a rich merchant. Osan's father, suspecting that merchant to be Jihei, has threatened to reclaim her. So even Osan, the respectable housewife, is seen to be nothing more than a piece of property. How, then, does her life really differ from that of her sisters in the Floating World?

The responsibilities of women are reiterated when Osan is accused of having allowed Jihei to stray: "Be stern and watch your husband," she admonishes. (Of course, Osan has herself appealed directly to Koharu as being ultimately responsible for her husband's entrapment—and possible release.) The aunt invokes the memory of Jihei's father, who has asked her to take care of him, knowing him to be easily led astray (the male as perennial child). As a loyal wife Osan stands behind her husband, and he denies that he has any intention of redeeming Koharu. Her mother remains skeptical and asks for a written promise to that effect, which he gives her to take back to the father. Osan thanks them for their interest and accepts the blame. Demonstrating the far-ranging effects of family interference, Osan's mother promises, "Our ancestors will help you."

After they depart Jihei again retreats to his bed, leaving Osan to settle things for the night. She expresses relief that things will return to normal, anticipating that he will resume his proper duties in the shop. Jihei is sullenly unresponsive. When she approaches him with amorous intents it is obvious he has not forgotten Koharu, for she finds that he is weeping. Reproaching him angrily it is revealed that they have not had marital relations for two years: "I don't know why you hate me. . . . It's cruel of you." Obviously overcome with emotion she shakes him and reminds him of his responsibilities as a father. Even now she seeks for a fault within herself to explain his behavior: "What have I done to deserve this? . . . your heart is gone. How cruel!" And of course she is right—Jihei's heart, his innermost heart, has been pledged to Koharu.

Jihei recognizes Osan's right to blame him and explains his "tears of regret" are about Koharu—"She's a four-legged animal, not a woman." This restriction of their relationship to sexual terms satisfies the social credo of women of that type. He claims merely to be angry that Koharu is to be redeemed so soon after the end of their relationship, recalling how she had threatened suicide if such an action were taken. Suddenly Osan stops crying, realizing that this is precisely what Koharu may be planning to do. Jihei denies it, accusing Osan of naiveté: "It's her work to use tricks to fool men." Driven by fear for Koharu's life, Osan feels obliged to confess that she instigated the break-up of their affair. In a woman-to-woman appeal, she begged Koharu her to prevent a double suicide and save their family: "Koharu is a courtesan but she is a woman." It is now clear that Koharu has not betrayed him but was motivated by love in severing their relationship. Osan also realizes this: "She's decent, with a strong sense of duty. . . . A woman in love is strong." This contrasts sharply with her befuddled husband: "You don't understand. You only talk about love."

This very sense of superiority serves to enslave Japanese women by convincing them that only they are capable of making the required sacrifices. The male is thereby absolved from reciprocal actions due to his inherent weakness. Such relationships are structured on *amae* (to depend and presume upon another's benevolence)[50] and *amaeru* (an attitude of dependency)—the relationship between the male as "eternal child" and the self-sacrificing female (originally the mother) who both indulges and anticipates his desires:

The dependency system particularly affects attitudes toward women. Since there must be some relief for Japanese men who struggle in the chilly waters of human relations, many Japanese women, after growing up, remain babyish, sweet-voiced, soft-mannered, delicate, and doll-like; girls whose inborn personalities are of the opposite kind try or pretend to be so. This is their subconscious response to the need of Japanese men who, in their mature years, retain their mother-complexes and seek spiritual as well as physical comfort in playing the baby to their women.[51]

Such stylized hyper-femininity is intended to exorcise any threats to the male ego by reproducing the ideal mother who is all warmth and devoid of any semblance of negativity or threat.[52]

Despite overwhelming difficulties, a plan is finaly devised to insure that no one dies by exhausting the household resources to redeem Koharu. Cognizant of his culpability Jihei declares: "I should be punished. Forgive me," to which Osan replies, "A husband shouldn't ask that. It's a wife's duty." That the aggrieved wife would sacrifice all to spare the life of her rival may strike the non-Japanese viewer as lunacy, but it is quite consistent with the claims of *giri* sketched out in this story:

> *Giri* was not necessarily stern-voiced duty calling a man away from the natural inclinations of his heart. Often it was a natural, internal response, directed toward another person primarily out of gratitude when fear of what society will think, or a feeling of obligation to another person, compels someone to give up what he most desires.[53]

Donald Keene warns that we should resist the temptation to judge such behavior by rational standards. Accordingly, the salvation of Jihei comes through his passionate actions, for "Purity of emotions excuses any weakness occasioned by *ninjō*."[54]

Tragically the plan fails due to the untimely intervention of society at large, in the form of Osan's father. Impatient with his son-in-law's disgraceful behavior he reclaims his property—his daughter—and drags Koharu away to the family home. The children are left behind, being recognized by society as the rightful possessions of the father. They watch the entire scene dispassionately—obviously learning a valuable lesson in the primacy of social demands over personal feeling. The fervent pleas of the couple for clemency go unheeded, as are Osan's heart-wrenching screams for her babies.

This assertion of parental authority and family honor seals the fate of the lovers—there is now no choice but suicide. A distraught Jihei drops his sword and lets out a loud, long scream of frustration and sorrow. Soon he is surrounded by the hooded figures. His emotions are unleashed in a destructive rampage as he knocks down screens, lets papers fly, and so Forth. Finally he knocks down the wall to reveal the blood-stained wall of the pleasure quarter, which turns into a shimmering surface evoking the river that plays a part in the impending suicide.

The dilemma of Koharu, the intended beneficiary of this extraordinary benevolence, is deserving of particular attention not for its uniqueness, but precisely because of its commonality. "I'm bound by money from head to foot," she exclaims, and so were many other young women at the time. Unlike Oharu, who falls from a high status into prostitution through her own rebellion, Koharu and others of her kind were innocent victims of an oppressive system. Those who were unable to find suitable marriages and were forced to support either themselves or their families had few career opportunities open to them. In most cases they signed a contract of "money-for-body," setting out the length of service (usually until age twenty-five, which even today is the expected time for women to "retire" into marriage). Fifty percent of their earnings went to the owner, one-eighth was used for her upkeep, and the remainder was applied to repay the cost of the original purchase price. Needless to say, few women were ever able to work their way out of their debt under these conditions.

These working women suffered from a high death toll due to illness and abortion. Swords were forbidden in these areas, in part to prevent suicides. Even after the original contract had been satisfied, it was difficult for women to return to their families, for they had become accustomed to an entirely different lifestyle at a much higher social level, including their tastes, customs, and use of language. It also was difficult for them to find husbands after having had such experiences. In most case they had no choice but to remain within the pleasure quarters doing menial tasks or working as common prostitutes.

Koharu and Jihei use a ruse to save her from the clutches of Tahei, to whom she has already been sold. They run off together into the night—a dishonored merchant and a piece of stolen property—intent on the final solution, which is now the only solution consistent with their previous pledges. Neither has anything left to lose. Rushing over a series of ever-symbolic bridges, they stop for rest, looking in the direction of his home. Jihei asks if she is afraid, to which she replies that fear fades when they are together. "Your wife's letter pained me the most," she admits, since Osan asked not that she return him but only that she save his life. Jihei urges her to let the past go, in light of their coming demise: "Forget it. We're going to die." The injustice of their situation is poignantly traced— "I want nothing but to be with you," says Koharu; why, she asks, is she not allowed to live—"I'm a woman like any other" who wants only simple happiness. When she asks Jihei why he wants to die with her he replies, "Out of duty to you. . . . Duty binds us all." That duty now demands nothing less than death.

The merging of sexuality and death is symbolized by the final scene (*michiyuki*, the final journey to death of lovers) in the cemetery. In accord with the director's wish, as expressed in the initial voice-over, it is not a romanticized death scene. Nor does Koharu die easily—Jihei must slash her several times. When it comes time for his own death, the hooded figures emerge once again to carry the action along. They help him position the scarf for the hanging and also remove the pedestal beneath his feet to accomplish the deed. The townspeople rush toward him, but it is too late.

Buddhism plays a pivotal role as both catalyst and antidote to tragedy. That role is foreshadowed in the initial reference to "heaven's net" or the karmic net. Following their final intercourse among the tombstones, and just prior to the suicides by the temple gate, Koharu and Jihei symbolically sever all social ties and obligations by cutting their hair, that is, committing themselves to a religious life (recalling Moritoh's act of cutting his hair in *Gate of Hell*). The social roles of father and husband, prostitute and daughter, cease to exist. Nonetheless, they discuss arranging to have their bodies found separately so that Osan will not be embarrassed, a sign of the unique socially transcendent tie that continues to bind the three people in this tragic triangle.

Seeking New Images in the Murky Mirror

> The Japanese cinema is a refuge of nonconformity. Perhaps more than any other art it expresses the living drama of a society which is the prisoner of its ghosts and is incapable of shaking them off. Never have the Japanese myths declared themselves so forcibly; never before has a people been battered by so many truths about itself. The Japanese cinema has at times been accused of sadism; it is, on the contrary, masochistic.[55]

The above remarks cast a pessimistic pall over considerations of Japanese society and its cinema, evincing no sign of hope for the future. Film is hereby reduced to an escapist playground, serving as a safety valve for otherwise antisocial attitudes to forestall their expression as behavior. Since those fantasies are primarily shaped by and for men, or at least reflect ideals determined by men, Japanese women are left devoid of any source for solace. However an alternative vision may yet be entertained.

What does the Japanese woman see in the murky mirror created on celluloid? Is it the derided Masago, the compassionate Kesa, the unrepentant Oharu, or the trapped Koharu? Or, like the imperial princess of the *Nihongi* accused of sexual dalliance, will she bury the mirror while ending her own life?[56]

Cinematic heroines in the 1980s possess a disturbing resemblance to stereotypical Western polarities of the lady or whore; the intelligent but plain woman is set in contrast to the beautiful, sexy "bimbo." For example, "the Taxing Woman" (played by Itami's wife, Miyamoto Nobuko), part one of two films by Itami Juzo (*A Taxing Woman* [*Marusa no onna*], 1987; *A Taxing Woman Returns*, 1988), presents a heroine who is undoubtedly competent, even successful, but at the price of being non-sexual. In the first film she is pitted against a tax-evading lecher, who dispenses his sexual favors to willing and beautiful secretaries as part and parcel of his larcenous business deals. His warped values are mirrored in his deformed body, but in the end virtue triumphs in the figure of the Taxing Woman.

A similar scenario is seen in Itami's early film, *Tampopo* (1987). The story centers on a latent attraction between the lead characters, a *ramen* chef (again played by Miyamoto) and a truck driver. At one level they bond as student and teacher/coach, as he prepares her for success in the wide world of noodle restaurants. But her transformation from drudge to beauty at the culmination of her training, to complement her new status, elicits not erotic desire, but mortal fear, and he is sent scurrying off into the sunset (an eight-wheeler replacing the ever-faithful horse of the western). Itami himself has admitted to being influenced by the West: "As Itami explained, his generation is more than just Japanese. . . . As a consequence, his generation of directors can step back and view Japanese society as if from the point of view of a very knowing outsider."[57]

Perhaps Japanese women should choose an older mirror in which to peer, such as that provided by the primal Shinto role models of women and sexuality that preceded Confucian and Buddhist trepidations. Two likely candidates appear in the ancient texts of the *Kojiki*[58] and the *Nihongi*: the supreme ancestress, Sun Goddess Amaterasu, and Ame no Uzume. Amaterasu is undoubtedly the more reserved and august of the two, yet she can scarcely be described as a prude. When all the other *kami* fail to tempt Amaterasu from her self-imposed isolation in a cave (occasioned by the unseemly and destructive behavior of her younger brother Sosa no wo no Mikoto[59]), Ame no Uzume is able to tempt her out by means of an erotically suggestive dance.[60] Ame no Uzume is not reproved for her exhibitionism, which includes exposure of her genitals, but is rather greeted with laughter and delight by all. Later, Ame no Uzume also is sent to clear the path for the descent of the August Grandchild of Amaterasu, Ama-tsu-hiko-hiko-ho Ninigi no Mikoto, to the Reed Plain, being especially chosen on the basis of her physical attributes. The intimidating figure of Saruta-hiko blocking the path is summarily subdued when she exposes her sexual organs to him. Again she is not condemned for her behavior but is rewarded by the August Grandson with the title of Sarume no Kimi to memorialize her conquest.[61] These actions demonstrate the perception that female sexuality was a form of power that was neither suppressed nor rebuked, but valued.

One hopeful sign recently is the model of competence and professional accomplishment combined with beauty and grace embodied in the Crown Princess, Owada Masako, a cosmopolitan Harvard graduate and career diplomat. Perhaps in her example Japanese society will be able to come to terms with the image of a woman possessed of power that does not threaten, so that the Japanese no longer need to be driven back to the regressive cycle of masochistic wallowing that is perversely expressed as sadistic violence toward women as a group. And perhaps if Japanese society learns to transcend its gynophobic past by reappropriating and refashioning its traditional view of women, it may well serve as a postmodern model to be emulated by other societies around the world.

Alternately, it has been suggested that the reactionary currents have reason to rejoice in Owada's role model: "The message is clear enough. Toying with a career is O.K., but when duty calls, the interests of family and state are paramount, and finding Mr. Right is what it's really all about."[62] Judging by conflicting reactions to the revolutionary role of Hillary Rodham Clinton among the Japanese public, Owada may be doomed to a life of circumspection. While Japanese feminist and legislator Okazaki Tomiki has hailed her as "a symbol of the changing woman," more conservative women have voiced concern over potential improprieties.[63] To determine which of the scenarios will likely come to fruition, we must continue to gaze into the murky mirror as both a reflection and evocation of the evolving postmodern Japanese woman.

Notes

1. Amatcrasu instructs her grandson to keep the mirror beside him and consider it as a means of observing and worshiping her. Accordingly it was passed down as a sign of imperial succession in the imperial line as "the living presence of the revered Sun-Goddess." See Jean Herbert, *Shintō: At the fountain-head of Japan* (New York: Stein and Day, 1967), 302, 361, 410; *Nihongi* II:23.

2. David Desser, *Eros Plus Massacre: An Introduction to the Japanese New Wave Cinema* (Bloomington: Indiana University Press, 1988), 108.

3. See, for example, the character of Cousin Chin in Pa Chin's *The Family* (1931), set in China during the period between 1916–20. See also Yi Injik's *Tears of Blood* (1906), the first modern novel of Korea, where the character Ongny dedicates herself to raising the status of women through education and marries a like-minded Korean man without parental interference.

4. The title of the volume *Mountain Moving Day: Poems by Women*, ed. Elaine Gill (Tumansberg, NY: Crossing Press, 1973), reflects Yosano's influence on American feminists.

5. Fukuzawa Yukichi's publications on women's liberation include *Nihon fujinron* (Essays on Japanese Women) in 1885, *Onna daigaku hyōron* (Criticism of the Moral Books for Women in the Tokugawa Period) in 1889, and *Shin-onna daigaku* (New Moral Book for Women) in 1898. Mori Arinori, who served as minister of education from 1885, was assassinated by fanatical nationalists for his alleged slight to a Shinto shrine.

6. Hara Hiroko quoted by John Hunter Boyle, *Modern Japan: The American Nexus* (New York: Harcourt Brace Jovanovich, 1993), 24.

7. See Robert S. Ozaki, *The Japanese: A Cultural Portrait* (Tokyo: Tuttle, 1978), 195.

8. See Desser, *Eros Plus Massacre*, especially chapter three, "Ruined Maps: Identity, Sexuality, and Revolution," 76–107.

9. Inazo Nitobe, *Bushido: The Soul of Japan, An Exposition of Japanese Thought* (Tokyo: Tuttle, 1969; orig. pub. 1905), 103–10. Nitobe also notes that terse poetic means of expression served as an emotional "safety-valve,"

borrowing images from Nature. This technique has been skillfully adapted to cinema by Japanese film-makers, adding a profound phenomenological impact to, for example, the lingering shot of falling rain.

10. Watsuji Tetsurō, *Climate and Culture*, tr. Geoffrey Brownas (Tokyo: Hokuseido Press, 1961), 14.

11. Primal archetypes for such personality traits exist in a variety of legendary figures, including the wayward brother of Amaterasu, Sosa no Mikoto, and Prince Yamato Takeru.

12. Alan W. Watts, *Nature, Man and Woman* (New York: Vintage, 1958, 1970), 145.

13. Ibid., 157.

14. Sigmund Freud, *Civilization and Its Discontents*, tr. James Strachey (New York: W. W. Norton & Co., 1961), 36, 44.

15. For example, gay-bashing and murders of homosexuals *qua* homosexuals, as well as the vocal opposition to openly admitting gays within the ranks of the military.

16. A distinctly puritanical zeal seizes hold of Confucianism as an ideology relatively late in Chinese history. In contrast, a blanket distrust of feeling and emotion is alien to the original strains of Confucian philosophy. Confucius, for example, describes his path of self-cultivation as culminating in a state where desire coincided with accepted patterns of behavior (*chü 3; Lun Yü*, II, 4), while Mencius regards moral feelings as the seeds of his ethical system.

17. Gregory Barrett, *Archetypes in Japanese Film: The Sociopolitical and Religious Significance of the Principal Heroes and Heroines* (Selinsgrove: Susquehanna University Press, 1989), 133.

18. Donald Richie, *The Films of Akira Kurosawa* (Berkeley: University of California Press, 1961), 76.

19. The Second Circle of Hell is assigned to "Carnal Sinners," of whose number Dante interviews Francesca de Rimini, who violated social mores by engaging in an affair with her husband's brother, Paolo. During their conversation she cites as the catalyst for their relationship their reading of the tale of Lancelot and Guinevere.

20. Nitobe, *Bushido*, 145.

21. Freud, *Civilization and its Discontents*, 13.

22. Donald Keene, *World Within Walls: Japanese Literature of the Pre-Modern Era 1600–1867* (New York: Grove Press, 1976), 260–61.

23. James F. Davidson, "Memory of Defeat in Japan: A Reappraisal of

Rashomon" in *Rashomon: A Film by Akira Kurosawa* (New York: Grove Press, 1969), 209–21.

24. Richie, "*Rashomon* and Kurosawa" in *Rashomon*, 223, 234.

25. Howard Hibbett in his introduction to Takashi Kojima's translation, *Rashomon and Other Stories* (New York: Liveright, 1952), 14.

26. Kurosawa's version omits testimony from the mother-in-law of the victim as well as from the arresting officer. He adds the character of a passerby ("Everyman") whose role is to review the conflicting testimonies after the inquest has been held, sheltered beneath the symbolic focus of Rasho Gate.

27. The more culturally appropriate term "bodhisattva" is used instead of "angel" in Kojima's translation, *Rashomon*, 23.

28. Parker Tyler, "*Rashomon* as Modern Art," in *Rashomon*, 201.

29. Joan Mellen, *The Waves at Genji's Door: Japan Through Its Cinema* (New York: Pantheon Books, 1976), 49. Mellen's overall interpretation of the film rests on the misogyny of Kurosawa: "After Rashomon, Kurosawa seemed to have abandoned his interest in the potential of women, as if repelled by Masago, that half-demon of his own creation. His response is parallel to that of the culture itself. And once, of course, the stereotype is elevated to a symbol in the arts, presented as an image of truth, the impact of this perpetuated myth in turn conditions the view women have of themselves. It is indeed a vicious circle, as yet unbroken by profound social change," 50.

For my part, I do not see Kurosawa's attitude to be misogynous, despite the espousal of gender stereotypes within his films. Strong female characters are not lacking in his presentations, including valiant Princess Yukihime in the *Hidden Fortress* (*Kakushi torideno sanakunin*; 1958) and the chamberlain's wife in *Sanjuro* (*Tsubaki Sanjuro*, 1962), whose understated wisdom wins over the title character.

30. Richie, *The Films of Akira Kurosawa*, 76.

31. Nicholas Bornoff, *Pink Samurai: Love, Marriage and Sex in Contemporary Japan* (New York: Pocket Books, 1991), 380.

32. Sumiko Iwao, *The Japanese Woman: Traditional Image and Changing Reality* (New York: Macmillan, 1993), 269.

33. The closing lines of "In a Grove," bringing to an end the victim's testimony about his death, read: "once and for all I sank down into the darkness of space"; translation, 33.

34. See Richie, "*Rashomon* and Kurosawa," 239. Both films garnered impressive critical acclaim outside of Japan. *Rashomon* was awarded first

prize at the Venice Film Festival, the "Grand Prix" Award, and an Academy Award as "Best Foreign Film"; *Gate of Hell* won two Academy Awards, the New Critics Award, and the Grand Prize at the Cannes Film Festival.

35. Chapter 9, "Good and Evil," verse 124, *Dhammapada*: The *Path of Perfection*, tr. Juan Mascaró (New York: Penguin, 1973), 53.

36. Ibid.

37. Ivan Morris, introduction to his translation of *The Life of the Amorous Woman and Other Stories* (New York: New Directions, 1963), 25–26.

38. Ibid., 38.

39. Mellen, *The Waves at Genji's Door*, 266–67.

40. "I've always felt that communism solves the problems of class, but overlooks the problems of men and women which still remain afterwards. So I'm especially interested in the problems between men and women"; Matsuo Kishi, "A Talk With Mizoguchi," *Kinema jumpo* (April 1952), tr. Leonard Schrader, cited by Mellen, 252.

41. Albert Camus, "Love and Rebellion," included in A. M. Krich ed., *The Anatomy of Love* (New York: Dell Publishing, 1950), 306–7.

42. Camus citing Scheler, in *The Anatomy of Love*, 310.

43. Ibid., 314.

44. Ibid., 313.

45. Michihiro Matsumoto, *The Unspoken Way—HARAGEI: Silence in Japanese Business and Society* (Tokyo: Kodansha International, 1977), p. 29. See also Steven Heine, "Tragedy and Salvation in the Floating World: Chikamatsu's Double Suicide Drama as Millenarian Discourse," *Journal of Asian Studies* 58/2 (1994), 367–93.

46. Ibid.

47. C. A. S. Williams, *Outlines of Chinese Symbolism and Art Motives*, 3rd rev. ed. (Tokyo: Charles E. Tuttle, 1974), 221, 374.

48. Keene, *World Within Walls*, 262.

49. Shinoda, as quoted by Keiko I. McDonald, *Cinema East: A Critical Study of Major Japanese Films* (Rutherford: Fairleigh Dickinson University Press, 1983), 53, as taken from Tadao Satō's *The History of Intellectual Currents in Japanese Cinema (Nihon eiga shisōshi)* (Tokyo: Sanichi Shobō, 1970), 373–74.

50. See Doi Takeo, *The Anatomy of Dependence*, tr. John Bester (Tokyo: Kodansha International, 1971).

51. Robert S. Ozaki, *The Japanese: A Cultural Portrait* (Tokyo: Charles E. Tuttle, 1978), 195.

52. Paradoxically, of course, the elementary character of the Great Mother archetype merges nurturing and destructive tendencies due to the fact that she who giveth can also taketh away, she who gives birth may also bring death. See Erich Neumann, *The Great Mother: An Analysis of the Archetype* (Princeton: Princeton University Press, 1972).

53. Keene, *World Within Walls*, 260.

54. Ibid., 261.

55. Jean-Claude Courdy, *The Japanese: Everyday Life in the Empire of the Rising Sun*, tr. Raymond Rosenthal (New York: Harper & Row, 1979), 98–99.

56. *Nihongi*, xiv, 12.

57. Beverley Bare Buehrer, *Japanese Films: A Filmography and Commentary, 1921–1989* (Jefferson, NC: McFarland & Company, 1990), 278.

58. Thirty-five direct sexual references have been found in the Kojiki, none of which censures sexual activities or expressions. See Yoneyana Toshinao, "Sex," included in *Seventy-Seven Keys to the Civilization of Japan*, Umesao Tadao, ed. (Union City, CA: Heian International Inc., 1985), 293–96. He attributes subsequent puritanical attitudes to foreign influences, preeminently Chinese Confucianism and Western Christianity.

59. Sosa comes across in the early texts as a mischievous troublemaker who neglects his assigned duties, although he undergoes a kind of self-imposed rehabilitation to become a "national culture hero" once he is banished to the earthly realm. His father Izanagi finally expels the errant son when Sosa expresses a desire to visit his mother, Izanami. One may argue that the father resented his son's affection for his estranged spouse, interpreting it as a sign of disloyalty. Donald L. Philippi speculates on the meaning of the interchange as follows: "What is the real reason for Susa-nö-wo's cosmic discontent, for his poor relations with his father, and his yearning for his "mother"? Is he an inherently evil deity, preferring the pollutions of Yömï to the ruling of his allotted ocean territory? Is he a mythical trickster, ever playing pranks and delighting in stirring up ill feelings and discord? Or is he a child deprived of motherly affection, venting his frustrations upon his father with a reply which stirs up old rancor and causes the father to disown and cast out the son?"; in *Kojiki* (Princeton: Princeton University Press, 1969), 403. In a sense he is the archetype for the physically-endowed blustering males of Japanese cinema who are in fact weak-willed and dependent on women. In terms of the films reviewed here, these would include the characters of Tajomaru, Wataru, and Jihei. Each of them brings tragedy to one or more women, but each also surrenders himself to the feminine force.

60. *Kojiki*, I, 17, 14; *Nihongi*, I, 1:39–40.

61. *Nihongi*, I, 2:17–18. In the briefer *Kojiki* account of this incident, Amaterasu credits Ame no Uzume with the ability to "face and overwhelm [others]" (I, 38:10). Matsumura (III, 567–70) explains this in terms of the use of shamanesses to confront and thwart enemy forces by means of their magical powers, as cited by Philippi, 138n. 9.

62. Andrew Gordon, "My Student, the Princess," *New York Times*, Op-Ed, 17 March (1993), A15.

63. "New First Lady Gets Mixed Reviews," *Japan Times, International Edition*, 1–7 February (1993), 3.

Chapter Seven

The Intertextual Fabric of Narratives by Enchi Fumiko

S. YUMIKO HULVEY

Every text, being itself the intertext of another text, belongs to the intertextual, which must not be confused with the text's origins: to search for the "sources of" and "influence upon" a work is to satisfy the myth of filiation. The quotations from which a text is constructed are anonymous, irrecoverable, and yet *already read*: They are quotations without quotation marks. The work does not upset monistic philosophies, for which plurality is evil. Thus, when it is compared with the work, the text might well take as its motto the words of the man possessed by devils: "My name is legion, for we are many" (Mark 5:9).

Roland Barthes

Enchi Fumiko (1905–86), who achieved fame in the 1950s by dipping into the well of the traditional Japanese canon for literary inspiration, was also knowledgeable enough about Western literature to explore paths of feminism before the concept became widely disseminated in Japan. Themes involving supernatural events situated in dreamlike, mythical settings that Enchi explored decades ago are influential and discernible in the texts of women writers of the postmodern generation, such as Yoshimoto Banana (b. 1962) and Tsushima Yūko (b. 1947). Thus Enchi can be considered a harbinger of ideas of vital concern to postmodern women writers, and it is also the case that the notion of "intertextuality," a crucial category in postmodern literary criticism, is essential for interpreting the significance of her contributions.

Spirit possession and the world of the supernatural are trademark themes for Enchi, who often utilized intertextual references to the traditional canon for subversive and transgressive applications in contemporary contexts. Enchi acquired the requisite familiarity with traditional themes by devoting a number of years translating premodern texts such as *The Tale of Genji* (*Genji monogatari*, 11th c.) into modern Japanese in her avocation as classical scholar. Her interest in the traditional canon was stimulated by the extensive premodern collection in the library of her father, Ueda Kazutoshi (1850–1937), also a classical scholar and philologist, who was professor of linguistics at Tokyo Imperial University.

Enchi's intertextual allusions to the traditional canon cover many genres: fictional tales (*tsukuri monogatari*) such as *The Tale of Genji*, poem tales (*uta monogatari*) such as *Tales of Ise* (*Ise monogatari*, ca. 950), historical tales (*rekishi monogatari*) such as *A Tale of Flowering Fortunes* (*Eiga monogatari*, ca. 1030s–40s?), war tales (*gunki monogatari*) such as *The Tale of the Heike* (*Heike monogatari*, ca. 1371), and the like, some of which she translated into modern Japanese.

The intertextual references in Enchi's texts pay homage to the tradition of writing by women of the Heian period (794–1185) whose works seem to have struck a responsive chord within her.[1] Much of her intertextual allusions refers to the Heian masterpiece *The Tale of Genji*, written by Murasaki Shikibu, a highly educated lady-in-waiting who served at the court of Empress Shôshi (988–1074) during the Heian period. In contributing a round to the chorus of voices raised by Heian women writers who expressed resentment against the subjugation of women by patriarchal society and the polygynous marriage system of the past, Enchi manages to find a literary voice of her own and help perpetuate the tradition of women writers into the modern and postmodern periods.

Enchi makes allusions to Buddhism as adhering to the patriarchal ideology involved in the subjugation of women, and she presents the indigenous Shinto belief system as a realm which granted some form of empowerment. Although the syncretic nature of Buddhism and Shinto is widely accepted, Enchi seems intentionally to set the two religions in a diametrical oppostion in order to present Buddhism as a misogynist institution which seeks to suppress women and Shinto as an avenue for females to find empowerment, albeit in the world of the supernatural. The avenue of empowerment Enchi chose to explore was spirit possession and the performance of sacerdotal functions by *miko* (female mediums or shamans).

Enchi also makes frequent reference to the all-male theaters of the Noh and Kabuki, both of which are intertextually indebted to the classical literary canon for much of their repertoire and which serve as examples of androgynous environments, a topic of interest to many women writers dissatisfied with the status quo in patriarchal society. Enchi's concept of sexuality seems to have been profoundly affected by her childhood experiences of the Kabuki theater, where the all-male cast promoted ideas of androgyny as an alternative to patriarchal situations she faced in society. Women writers, such as Ursula K. LeGuin in *The Left Hand of Darkness*, have been known to experiment with androgynous societies to highlight inequities in our society. Enchi makes frequent allusions to androgynes who do not exhibit prominent signs of either gender, but she does not develop the concept of the androgyne in detail. However, the frequency with which androgyny is mentioned attests to the importance Enchi placed on the concept of "wholeness" represented by the androgyne (Eliade, *Myths, Dreams and Mysteries*, 174–75). Enchi reaches back to the creation myths of Japan to recreate the concept of "wholeness" and androgyny. This does not suggest, however, that the image of alternate societies is the only means by which Enchi seeks to undermine the dominant power structure.

Combined with the use of intertextuality are narrative techniques that subvert the authority of patriarchy. Enchi often includes intratextual excerpts of classical Japanese literature that she has rendered into modern Japanese to further subvert the authority of the text. It is conjectured that the inclusion of an intratext has the following effect:

> An intra-textual structure within the larger structure of the complete text undermines the authority of the voice that asserts the reliability of the representational pattern on which the text is based.[2]

The incorporation of intratextual materials forces readers to reevaluate and reinterpret the function of the narrative voice itself. She also constructs complex narrative structures which, upon careful reflection, are designed to question the authority of the text she creates.

My analysis of texts by Enchi Fumiko traces the development of her trademark theme of *miko* as a vehicle to explore realms of empowerment for women in alternate worlds created in fiction. I begin with a discussion of Enchi's novel, *A Tale of False Oracles*

(*Namamiko monogatari*, 1959–65), not available in English but considered her masterpiece by some critics,[3] as one of the first texts dealing exclusively with the theme of *miko* and spirit possession. I argue that the complex structure Enchi constructs to narrate the text provides a clue to her authorial intention. She speaks in her own voice to establish herself as an unassailable authority of privileged information concerning the text she is relating, but subsequently she undermines the position of authority previously established. She also speaks in two other voices: that of a Heian-period narrator, and another voice limited to paraphrasing events that occurred in the Heian-period text being resuscitated. Ultimately, the complicated narrative structure reveals that the author is the true "false medium," undermining the authority of the text she carefully constructed.

Next, I analyze texts with similar themes of *miko*, spirit possession and the supernatural world in chronological order to hypothesize a theory of Enchi's experimentation and development of the theme of empowered women. I divide the evolution of themes into three developmental stages.[4] In the first stage, Enchi's women are depicted enduring lives of subjugation and oppression in patriarchal society with the theme of *miko* discernible only in germinal form. Texts discussed in the first stage include *The Waiting Years* (*Onnazaka*, literally, "Female Slope," 1949–57, Eng. 1971) awarded the Noma Literary Prize in 1957, "Skeletons of Men" ("Otoko no hone," 1956, Eng. 1988), "Enchantress" ("Yō," 1956, Eng. 1958), and "A Bond for Two Lifetimes—Gleanings" ("Nise no en—shūi," 1957, Eng. 1983).

In the second stage, Enchi created a host of mysterious middle-aged women who tap inner sources of strength through the shamanistic powers of the *miko*. Texts written during this stage are numerous but I list only those which I incorporate into my analysis such as *Masks* (*Onnamen*, literally, "Female Masks," Eng. 1983), *A Tale of False Oracles* and "Metamorphosis" ("Keshō," 1962). In the third stage, Enchi features a cast of elderly women who hover between illusion and reality in their endeavor to explore the nature of sexual desire. Texts written during the final stage included in the analysis are the trilogy *Wandering Spirit* (*Yūkon* consisting of "Foxfire" ["Kitsunebi," 1969], "Wandering Spirit" ["Yūkon," 1970] and "The Voice of a Snake" ["Hebi no koe," 1970]) as well as "The Old Woman Who Eats Flowers" ("Hana kui uba," 1974) and *Colored Mist* (*Saimu*, 1975). In the conclusion, I argue that Enchi's cultivation of these themes signifies a woman writer's efforts to deal with the subjugation of women in patriarchal society. Her themes tap the world of myth and fantasy, transgressing against dominant paradigms such as conventional realism and temporal progression. But before discussing the texts under investigation, an introduction to the theme of *miko* will situate readers into the heart of the matter.

The Role of *Miko*

Historically, there are a number of words which refer to young females who served at Shinto shrines to perform various sacerdotal functions such as presiding over ceremonies during Shinto festivals, receiving oracular divinations from the gods, and acting as mediums to which possessive spirits were transferred during exorcism rites. *Miko* is defined as young unmarried females who serve at Shinto shrines, perform sacred music (*kagura*), offer prayers (*kitō*) and announce the dictates of the gods. Other related words are *Saiin, Itsuki no in,* and *Itsuki no miko,* titles referring to female high priests of Kamo Shrine (also the Kamo Virgin).[5] Others are *Saigu, Itsuki no miya,* and *Itsuki no miko,* titles indicating the female high priests of Ise Shrine (also called the Ise Virgin). *Saiin* and *Saigu* were unmarried imperial princesses or high-ranking female aristocrats with close blood ties to the imperial family, who were chosen soon after the advent of a new reign to occupy official posts. After undergoing a three-year period of abstinence and purification, the Virgins finally proceeded to their posts at their respective shrines. A final related word is *Itsuki no me* which referred to young females who served at the Shinto shrines of Kasuga, Oharanō, Matsunoō, and the like.

There are differences between *miko* and *Itsuki no miko*. *Itsuki no miko,* as imperial princesses or high-ranking females with blood ties to the imperial family, presided over Shinto ceremonies related to the emperor and his exalted position as the descendent of Amaterasu Ōmikami, the female sun god. *Itsuki no miko* also presided over the Great Thanksgiving Service (*Daijōsai*) which was performed soon after the beginning of a new reign. In many instances the functions of *Itsuki no miko* and *miko* seem to overlap, but one can assume that neither imperial blood ties nor high aristocratic social standing were required for *miko*. Significantly, imperial princesses were not utilized as mediums in cases of spirit possession.

The exact nature of Enchi's contribution to the theme of *miko* results from the subversion of traditional definitions and functions of *miko*, specifically those who were employed to act as mediums in cases of exorcism. In *The Catalpa Bow: A Study of Shamanistic Practices in Japan*, Carmen Blacker defines shamans in the following manner:

> Certain special human beings . . . may acquire a power which enables them to transcend the barrier between the two worlds. . . . It is a special power to effect a rupture of plane, to reach over the bridge and influence beings on the other side.
>
> I use the word 'shaman' . . . to indicate those people who have acquired this power; who in a state of dissociated trance are capable of communicating directly with spiritual beings. These people in Japan appear in two complementary forms. The first, whom I shall call the medium or the *miko* . . . can enter a state of trance in which the spiritual apparition may possess her, penetrate inside her body and use her voice to name itself and to make its utterances. She is therefore primarily a transmitter, a vessel through whom the spiritual beings, having left their world to enter ours, can make their communications to us in a comprehensible way.
>
> The second and complementary source of power . . . the ascetic . . . is primarily a healer, one who is capable of banishing the malevolent spirits responsible for sickness and madness and transforming them into powers for good. (21–22)

Blacker describes two states of trance into which *miko* and ascetics may fall during attempts to exorcise possessive spirits. The first state is characterized by physical symptoms such as the violent shaking of a clasped hand or roaring, and the second state is a deep comatose trance during which the soul travels while the body is left behind (22–23). Further, Blacker states that possessive spirit beings can be of two kinds: divine, in which case the spirit is summoned by means of beating drums, twanging bows or playing the *koto*; or malevolent, in which case the *miko* and ascetic are employed to exorcise the malign spirits (35).

Certain tools are associated with the execution of the *miko*'s duties, such as the mirror with bells, *magatama* (comma-shaped beads), and the bow and arrows. The mirror with bells, considered a receptacle for a spirit, enabled shamans to see a dead person's soul. The mirror in ancient Japan were similarly thought to be a vessel in which the *kami* could be housed. Mirrors worn about a shaman's waist as she danced in a state of possession were intended to lure the *kami* to draw near and enter her body. Like the mirror with bells, the *magatama* was also meant as a "powerful spirit lure" (Blacker, 106). The bow and arrows, worn by the medium for Amaterasu Ōmikami, the female sun god, was prized not for its martial quality but for its magical sounds which enticed divine spirits to come. On the other hand, the bow could also be plucked to ward off malevolent spirits. In the "Yūgao" ("Evening Faces") chapter of *The Tale of Genji*, Genji has someone shout and twang the bow to ward off evil spirits when Yūgao is attacked by a malign spirit; despite all the precautionary measures taken to ward off the malevolent spirit, she succumbs and dies (Seidensticker, 71). In cases of divine possession, the bow had the further function of acting as a *torimono*, an object the *miko* held in her hand as she danced, and which served as the conduit through which divine spirits could make their way to our world.

The final point is the element of sexual union between the deity and the *miko* who in ancient times served a particular deity and delivered oracular pronouncements as "brides of the deity." During a divine possession, it was believed that the deity also possessed *miko* physically as lovers (Blacker, 123). Enchi's most notable and transgressive use of *miko* culminates in the exploration of sexual desire. Before discussing the nuances involving subversive uses of the *miko* in Enchi's texts, I would like to proceed with a discussion of her narrative masterpiece which is one of the first texts to focus exclusively on the theme of *miko*.

A Tale of False Oracles

A Tale of False Oracles is an intriguing investigation of the levels of falsehood involved in the act of creating literary texts. Enchi creates a frame in which she speaks in her own voice to establish a sense of privilege and legitimacy for the fictional metanarrative she introduces. Although Enchi also wrote the metanarrative, she claims that it was written in the late Heian period (794–1185) and states that she is attempting to recreate the tale that she had read in her youth, but which is now no longer extant. *A Tale of False Oracles*, belonging to the second stage in the development of the theme of empowered women, is characterized by women who tap inner sources of strength by relying on the shamanistic powers of the *miko*. It receives a place of prominence in my analysis due to the high regard in which it is held by many literary critics because of the complexity of its narrative structure as well as its almost exclusive focus on the topic of *miko*.

A Tale of False Oracles is set at the court of Emperor Ichijō (980–1011) and his empress Fujiwara Teishi (977–1000) that was ruled by Fujiwara Michinaga (966–1027), as de facto ruler of Heian aristocratic society. Enchi establishes a historical connection between A Tale of False Oracles and the eleventh-century A Tale of Flowering Fortunes by Akazome Emon, who wrote the first thirty chapters of the historical tale, by subtitling her metanarrative "Gleanings from A Tale of Flowering Fortunes." Akazome Emon, a lady-in-waiting in the household of Michinaga's principal wife Minamoto Rinshi (964–1053), was commissioned by her patron Michinaga to write a history of the rise of the Fujiwara clan culminating in his coveted position as the de facto ruler of court society.

While Akazome Emon, author of A Tale of Flowering Fortunes, expansively praises Michinaga for the political savvy (yamatodamashii) he exercised to achieve domination over the court, Enchi (speaking in her own voice) questions the motives of the author of A Tale of False Oracles for including sections verbatim from A Tale of Flowering Fortunes. It is at this point that Enchi departs from the original historical tale and develops the complicated narrative structure to promote the subversive message she seeks to relate. Unlike Akazome Emon who portrayed Michinaga in heroic proportions, Enchi depicts him as the epitome of evil to better contrast him with the virtuous heroine Teishi. But before beginning an analysis of the narrative structure in A Tale of False Oracles a brief plot summary will clarify the issues under discussion.

A Tale of False Oracles revolves around the polygynous marriage of Emperor Ichijō to two high-ranking females of the Fujiwara clan: the older empress was Teishi, daughter of Michinaga's older brother Michitaka (953–995); the younger was Michinaga's daughter, Shōshi (988–1074). The tale describes the efforts of Michinaga to displace Teishi as the emperor's favorite and to replace his daughter Shōshi in his affections by employing Miwa no Ayame and Miwa no Kureha, young sisters who are miko, to spy on Emperor Ichijō and Empress Teishi to uncover information which may weaken the strong bond between them. However, Michinaga does not inform the miko of his true intentions, saying that he wants information only to help his daughter Shōshi emulate the virtuous nature of Empress Teishi.

Kureha innocently serves Empress Teishi, idolizing the empress almost to the point of falling in love with her. When Michinaga notices Kureha's advanced state of adulation for Empress Teishi, he introduces a man, Yukikuni, into Teishi's service hoping that Kureha will become romantically involved with him. After Kureha falls in love with Yukikuni, she becomes jealous of Yukikuni's love for the empress and falls prey to Michinaga's trap of spying on the empress to bring about her ruin. So Kureha experiences a fall from innocence (alluded to in the title "Namamiko," which could be read as either "false or innocent shamans/oracles") and begins gathering the desired information for her employer. Michinaga convinces Kureha, the *miko*, to feign a false spirit possession in order to insinuate that Teishi's spirit is responsible for his daughter Shōshi's illness. However, the living spirit of Teishi succeeds in possessing the medium Kureha to broadcast her innocence in the alleged possession and to declare her love for the emperor. Thereafter, the false medium Kureha commits suicide in the confusion over her loyalties and the narrative winds down with a lyrical episode describing a poetry exchange between Ayame, the surviving older sister of the medium Kureha, and her younger sister's former lover Yukikuni. The lyrical interlude is followed by a brief commentary by Enchi stating that this is the point at which the extant text ended.

A Tale of False Oracles is unique on a number of levels but foremost is the narrative structure Enchi creates. She employs three voices to tell the tale: in the first, Enchi narrates in her own voice to establish herself as an unassailable authority of the tale she is resuscitating and provides relevant commentary on the canon as a classical scholar; in the second, she speaks in the voice of the Heian-period narrator as she presumably recites from memory passages from the original text; and finally, she speaks in a third voice limited to paraphrasing events that occurred in the Heian text in modern Japanese. The structure centers on a modern-day frame introduced by Enchi in her own voice which serves as a prelude to a metanarrative set in the Heian period that she ostensibly reconstructs from memory.

Enchi's purpose in narrating in her own voice is to establish herself as a privileged narrator in the frame surrounding the metanarrative of *A Tale of False Oracles* set in the Heian period. She supports her claim of being privy to "inside" information by revealing that she is the daughter of scholar Ueda Kazutoshi, who inherited the library of pioneer Japanologist Basil Hall Chamberlain, and cites an excerpt from the literary dictionary *Nihon bungaku daijiten* describing their historical relationship to substantiate her position.[6] The following is an excerpt from the opening lines of *A Tale of False Oracles*:

I had heard about Professor Basil Hall Chamberlain by the name
"Chanbaren-san" since I was young. I had come to know the name
Chanbaren-san from having heard it included in many of my
father's conversations, though of course I had never met him. Mr.
Chanbaren was my father's mentor in linguistics.

Perhaps my immature recollection of the name Mr. Chanbaren
reaches back to the time I was seven years old. My memory of this
recollection is based on the fact that we moved from Kōji-machi in
Fujimi-chō to Shitaya in Yanakashimizu-chō at that time and I
discovered a great pile of old books which I had never noticed
before on the second floor of the new house, and because many
scholars and newspaper reporters came over to see the collection at
that time. Presently as I was beginning to write this manuscript, I
consulted the *Nihon bungaku daijiten* to find the following entry
on "Chanburen" (in the Shinchōsha dictionary, his name is trans-
literated as "Chanburen," but I intend to continue using
"Chanbaren" since that is the way I heard it pronounced in my
childhood).

After establishing her position as a privileged narrator, Enchi
challenges the dictionary's authority by correcting the *katakana*
(angular syllabary) transliteration of the name of Basil Hall Chamberlain from "Chan *bu* ren" to "Chan *ba* ren," stating that at home
her father had always pronounced the name that way. She then
undermines her own authority by revealing uncertainty about the
provenance of the text of *A Tale of False Oracles* (she cannot recall
whether it was a part of Chamberlain's collection or her father's),
then further declares that the text is now lost and that she must
recount from memory a text she read forty years ago! The cycle of
falsification is apparent in the excerpt which follows the opening
lines (quoted above):

According to this entry, Mr. Chanbaren's last visit to Japan was in
1911 (43rd year of Meiji), but I suppose the arrangements for having
the library moved to my father's house were probably made in 1912
after our move. If my aged mother, who died last year at the age of
eighty were still alive, I could have confirmed these suppositions
but now it is rare to meet anyone in my circle of friends who can
clearly recall these events.

On all Mr. Chanbaren's books was a large red square seal with the
characters "Ōdō Library" imprinted on them. "Ōdō" was the
Japanized version of Chanbaren's first name "Basil Hall" but since
my father had never mentioned this episode in Chanbaren's life, I
first learned about it from this dictionary.

I knew nothing about the contents of the "rare private collection" but I still have vivid memories from my youth of having gone up to the second story to my father's study with the unpainted Japanese barrister-style bookcase and the stacks of numerous old books piled up along the three-foot long sunny hallway of *tatami* matting. Of course, most of the books were thin Japanese volumes printed on *washi* paper bound in the traditional manner,[7] and there were some which were original manuscripts copied in beautiful semi-cursive styles. There was no possibility that a little girl such as I could read those characters, so I regarded them with a curious combination of scorn and respect peculiar to children, similar to what a child feels when looking at old clothes. When books were being aired out during the summer through fall, I picked my way through books which had been left open all over the floor, and also tried leafing though pages marked by the trails of bookworms. However, when I finished elementary school and began taking calligraphy lessons, I learned how to read *hentaigana* (premodern unstandardized syllabary) and began falteringly to read books with characters I could decipher. Although I probably came across the tale I am attempting to rewrite on the second floor of my father's house in the manner described above, because I was just a child at the time I cannot recall whether it was a volume found among my father's hand-written manuscripts or whether it was from among the rare private collection of the Ōdō Library.

The narrative structure makes readers constantly gauge and recalculate the purpose of the narrators and the events being related.

One of the two other voices Enchi employs to narrate *A Tale of False Oracles* is exemplified in the following excerpt, where she presumably records the exact words of the Heian period narrator that she has memorized:

[Enchi as narrator] "If my memory is not mistaken, the opening section of *A Tale of False Oracles* was excerpted, for the most part, from the first scroll of *A Tale of Flowering Fortunes*, from the chapters "Joyful Events," "Unfinished Dreams," "The Separation of the Brothers,"[8] and the like, describing the history of the power struggle which occurred after the death of Fujiwara Michinaga's father, Kaneie, at the Higashi Sanjō mansion. Although it is natural to describe the tragedy of the familial rivalry in aristocratic society as a backdrop to relate the fortunate life of the female protagonist, the reason why the author of *A Tale of False Oracles* used verbatim excerpts to narrate the tale still remains a mystery to me; was it because the author respected the account in *A Tale of Flowering Fortunes*, or was it conversely to express rebellion

against the account? Although I think I am going to translate the
first scroll of A Tale of Flowering Fortunes into modern Japanese as
a way of introducing A Tale of False Oracles, I have a clear recollection that these were the words with which the opening paragraph of the tale began:

> [As Heian-period narrator] In the reign of Emperor Ichijō, there
> were two empresses. The first empress was Fujiwara Teishi, a
> daughter of the Naka no Kanpaku, [Regent] Fujiwara Michitaka.
> The one who came later was the eldest daughter of the Midō lord
> (Michinaga) called Fujiwara Shōshi. She was the mother of Emper-
> ors Go-Ichijō [r. 1016–36] and Go-Suzaku [r. 1036–45] known as
> Jōtōmon-in. (292; Bracketed information not provided in original.)[9]

Enchi adopts a pseudo-classical style to recreate the voice of the
Heian-period narrator. She departs from a true classical style
(though she was fully capable of reproducing it) for one that would
be more comprehensible to the majority of her modern Japanese
reading audience. She sprinkles a few classical Japanese suffixes
such as nari and keri to impart an archaic flavor to her narrative but
relies on the use of modern Japanese particles, pronouns, and
humble verbs (mairu, tatematsuru, tamau, owasu, etc.) still in
common usage to insure maximum comprehension for readers of
modern Japanese. Speaking in her own voice, Enchi informs us that
the literary intention of the author of the metanarrative is perhaps
subversive and to be taken as a corrective to the account offered in
A Tale of Flowering Fortunes. Readers would be well-advised to
heed this bit of information as an inkling of Enchi's authorial intention in this narrative.

The style Enchi adopts for the final voice relating the
metanarrative is formal modern Japanese with an abundance of
humble verbs used in relation to the high-ranking characters in the
story.[10]

> On the fifth day of the First Month in the first year of Shōryaku
> [990], Emperor (Ichijō) performed his Coming-of-Age ceremony.
> There were many people who were dismayed to see him abandon
> children's clothing since he was only about eleven years old, but he
> presented a small yet splendid figure with his hair arranged up in
> the adult manner and crowned by a man's cap.

> Because the eldest daughter of the Palace Minister Lord Michitaka
> was to be presented at court in the Second Month, the entire court
> and the Palace Minister's household were in a flurry of activity
> preparing for the ceremony. The principal wife of the Palace Min-
> ister, daughter of the governor of Yamato province Takashina

Naritada, had been called Kō no Naishi when she was in court service and was well-acquainted with the imperial court. She disliked serious and profound things and liked the splendid airs of popular songs, so everything was done in this manner for this princess's presentation to court. The princess was sixteen so she was only five years older than the emperor. On the night that she was presented to the court, she received the rank of Consort (292).[11]

The translated excerpts reveal the three types of voices employed to narrate *A Tale of False Oracles*. Enchi points out the importance of deceit and falsehood in producing texts with verisimilitude within a fictional world and undermines Murasaki Shikibu's claim that fiction fills in all the details that histories seem to lack (Seidensticker, 437). But Van C. Gessel states that "Enchi's *monogatari* is a medium through which we learn anything but the "truth about human existence' " (384–85).

In "The Medium of Fiction: Fumiko Enchi as Narrator," Gessel presents *A Tale of False Oracles* as Enchi's masterpiece. Gessel argues that Enchi depicts an atypically happy marital relationship in *A Tale of False Oracles* but intends the complex narrative structure based on several levels of deceit to undermine the metanarrative. He claims it is Enchi herself who is the false "narratorial medium": she weaves a tale of purported happiness in the marital relationship between Ichijō and Teishi, but creates the complicated narrative structure to undermine the message of the metanarrative she has related (384). Gessel concludes that the complex narrative structure suggests that the only truth which can be divined is that "no form of narrative can be regarded as the final word." He also maintains that the "false" unreliable text launches a major attack against the male-dominated genre of I-novels whose raison d'être is completely dependent upon the "truthfulness" of narrated events (384–85). The brilliant reading by Gessel of this complex work ferrets out the subversive purposes of the author, and renders the message it conveys consistent with those in Enchi's oeuvre in which unhappy marriages are the norm. Let us now return to the first stage in the development of the theme of empowered women in which the topics of *miko* and spirit possession are discernible only in germinal form.

First Stage of Development

Enchi's oeuvre in Japanese consists of at least sixteen volumes in a "complete collection," much of which still remains unavailable in

English.[12] One of the first texts to be translated into English from the
first stage of development featuring women who endure lives of
subjugation and oppression is *The Waiting Years*. This work helped
to establish Enchi as a serious writer and was awarded the Noma
Literary Prize in 1957, but is in many ways regarded as "atypical"
and criticized for exhibiting "fundamental weaknesses in its structure and mode of narration" (Gessel, 380). Viewed in terms of the
development of the theme of empowered women, perhaps it is more
constructive to think in terms of a germinal stage before the theme
reached fruition in the second stage rather than labeling *The Waiting Years* as atypical.

The Waiting Years

Structurally, the work is divided into three parts: the first chapter
with three subtitles, "First Bloom" ("Hatsuhana"), "Green Grapes"
("Aoi budō"), and "Handmaid" ("Saihishō," Colorful Maidservant
Selection); the second also with three subtitles, "Moon of the
Twenty-Sixth Night" ("Nijūroku ya no tsuki"), "Purple Ribbon"
("Murasaki tegara," Purple Hair Ornament), and "Unripe Damsons"
("Aoi ume shō," Unripe Plum Selection); and the third with only
two subtitles, "The Stepsisters" ("Ibomai," Half-sister) and "The
Waiting Years" ("Onnazaka," Female Slope)—roughly covering a
period of thirty years from the end of the Edo period (1600–1867)
to the early Meiji period (1868–1912). Leaps in the chronology of
the narrative are often accompanied by shifts in points of view
and altered levels of accessibility to the interior thoughts of the
characters.

The perceived flaws in the mode of narration may refer to the
shifts in emphasis which occur as the narrative progresses—from
the wife, Tomo, to the mistress, Suga, and then back again to the
wife at the conclusion. Swings in the emotional and sympathetic
level of the narrative are bound to leave readers frustrated. The
stoicism expressed by Tomo as she sets out to search for a young
mistress for her husband, Shirakawa Yukitomo, greets readers who
ready themselves to "see" the story from her point of view. Yet as
the story proceeds, readers are given more interior views of the
mistress, Suga, and are denied those of Tomo, thereby creating an
aesthetic distance between the reader and the character of Tomo.
Just at the height of sympathy for Suga, the entire narrative turns
away from both women, and converges on a new generation of
youngsters, returning only at the conclusion to the wife, Tomo.

Despite its inconsistencies, the narrative focus is on the psychological damage inflicted upon women living in a polygynous household in a patriarchal society which allowed such injustices against women.

Woven into the fabric of *The Waiting Years* toward the end of the work is Tomo's hope that reliance on Buddhism will prove a source of strength to her. However, Enchi perceives Buddhism as part of the inherently misogynistic scheme to perpetuate the subjugation of women and depicts Tomo discarding Buddhism for a chance to tap the hidden, inner resources of shamanistic strength. Challenging male fears of feminine mystique and intuitive powers, Enchi clearly opposes the religious system of Buddhism as well as the Confucian ethical system which sought to oppress women by maintaining the status quo.

There are typical elements in this "atypical" work, the label most likely resulting from the fact that Enchi had not fully developed her theme over the period of eight years (1949–57) it took to complete its publication. For example, there are germinal signs of Enchi's pet images and themes in the making, such as the phrase "the utterance of medium" in the first chapter which betrays her fascination with this topic, and descriptions of the mask-like faces of women who strive to conceal inner emotions which reached fruition in Enchi's *Masks*.

Despite its technical problems, some scholars have noted an affinity between the eleventh-century masterpiece, *The Tale of Genji* and *The Waiting Years*. In "The Medium of Fiction: Fumiko Enchi as Narrator," Van C. Gessel suggests that *The Waiting Years*, *Masks*, and *A Tale of False Oracles* form a trilogy written by Enchi as a tribute to *The Tale of Genji*. Gessel interprets *The Waiting Years* as "a view of a modern fallen *Genji* world as seen through the eyes of a long-suffering Lady Aoi" (Genji's first principal wife), *Masks* to be a "shift to the perspective of Lady Rokujō" (a high-ranking, proud woman scorned by Genji), and *A Tale of False Oracles* to be to a "certain degree a re-creation of the ideal, a reenshrinement of the Shining Prince as seen through the eyes of the faithful, loving Murasaki" (Genji's second wife).

Other scholars have suggested that *The Waiting Years* may be the closest Enchi ever came to writing in a semi-autobiographical vein—the story of a woman oppressed by patriarchal society reflected, in part, the life experiences of her beloved grandmother, Ine, who lived in the Meiji period and endured a polygynous marriage with a man from a samurai family. The jealousy, insecurity, and mental anguish caused by polygyny is of primary importance in the narrative, and echoes like a familiar refrain in some of her other works. Even the literal translation of the title *Onnazaka*, "Female Slope," suggests the uphill battle women faced in patriarchal society and the polygynous marriage system which rendered women's homes veritable "harems."

The similarity in polygynous situations between the Heian and Meiji periods has caught the attention of others who study Enchi's works. Yukiko Tanaka and Elizabeth Hanson in an introduction to Enchi's "A Boxcar of Chrysanthemums" ("Kikuguruma," 1967, Eng. 1982) allude to "subtle influences" from *The Tale of Genji* in *The Waiting Years* (70). But what exactly is the nature of the suggested affinity between the two texts? Is it in the similarity of topics, that polygyny is detrimental to the female psyche? Or is it the episodic nature in the structure of the two works?

In light of the suggested affinity of the classical work and Enchi's *The Waiting Years*, a study of its publication record reveals some hesitation on the part of Enchi to conclude the narrative she had been writing for a number of years. Before concluding the novel, Enchi produced the short narrative, "Skeletons of Men," which may have been written as an experimental conclusion to the narrative. It has an almost identical plot for the metanarrative of the two-layer story and takes advantage of the focus on the mistress which had been developed extensively in the second chapter of the narrative. Written in 1956, it preceded the conclusion to the narrative by almost a year and may have provided Enchi with a chance to conclude the work focusing on the mistress instead of the wife.

"Skeletons of Men"

"Skeletons of Men" displays Enchi's penchant for using a double-layered structure of a metanarrative within a frame. The frame is presented by an "I" narrator and the metanarrative is related to the "I" narrator by her closest friend, Mikanagi Shizuko, a classical scholar-poet. The metanarrative by Shizuko reveals her discovery of a "blood-letter" written by a woman called Chise sewn into the folds of her grandmother Ritsu's antique *obi* (sash). The metanarrative revolves around Shizuko's grandmother, married to Sagane Yoshimitsu who kept mistresses within the home and who conducted other affairs outside the polygynous harem he maintained. The metanarrative describes the torment Shizuko's grandmother endured from Yoshimitsu's selfish indulgence in mistresses and lovers. The events of the metanarrative very closely parallel those found in *The Waiting Years*, but provide a poignant glimpse of the fate of the mistress character after the death of both the wife and the husband.

Plot parallels in the metanarrative and *The Waiting Years* are striking. Sagane Yoshimitsu is described as a man of samurai background receiving a stipend from the Hosokawa domain and working as a government official in Tokyo in the Metropolitan Police Department (419). Shirakawa Yukitomo in *The Waiting Years* fits the description almost exactly (55). Both male characters were raised in Kyūshū, a place noted for "its powerful traditions of male dominance and female suppression" (421). The two resident mistresses in each narrative are described with parallel lives: Shiga, the primary mistress of Yoshimitsu, was about thirty years younger than he and outlived the couple by a number of years; the other mistress was married off and went to live elsewhere not long after she was purchased. In *The Waiting Years*, Suga is the primary mistress of Yukitomo purchased by Tomo in Tokyo to become his mistress. The secondary mistress, Yumi, is married off to a distant relative of the Shirakawa family, and leaves the Shirakawa household to start a family of her own. Ritsu, after having been denied physical intimacy with Yoshimitsu from the time the first mistress entered the home, dies ten years before Yoshimitsu (420). Similarly, Tomo dies at the conclusion of *The Waiting Years*, after having endured years of neglect by her husband Yukitomo in his indulgence with women from various quarters. Although the details concerning the mistress Suga are not provided, one assumes that she lived for many years after Tomo's death at the end of the narrative.

In "Skeletons of Men," Shizuko surmises that her grandmother Ritsu kept the "blood-letter" sewn into the folds of her obi because she empathized with Chise, the married woman scorned by Yoshimitsu (425). After mistresses entered Ritsu's home, Yoshimitsu severed physical relations with her, making her feel that she too was a "scorned woman" even though she retained her social position as his official wife. Shizuko felt compassion for the plight of the mistress by stating that "Shiga endured many long years with Ritsu, the legal wife, like a heavy weight pressing down on her head" (421). We are told that after Yoshimitsu's death Shiga was "given enough stock certificates to allow her to manage independently and was set up living with her niece in a Sagane family rental house. But just before the war became severe she died of pneumonia. . . . [I]n all likelihood Shiga's bones were interred here in this grave as one of the Sagane family, right along with the urns of Yoshimitsu and Ritsu" (424).

Characters in both narratives are described in a similar manner and given names that resemble one another. Shiga and Suga are cast as lackluster personalities for the fates they shared as mistresses without the hope of escaping lives constrained by polygynous relationships; Ritsu and Tomo are portrayed as characters who have acquired distinction through torment due to the unhappiness and oppression of living in a patriarchal society. Yoshimitsu and Yukitomo blatantly pursue their selfish desires in callous disregard for the psychological damage they inflict on women.

Patriarchy is condemned as creating a "living hell" for women by condoning polygyny in the second metanarrative related to Shizuko by her grandmother Ritsu in an allegorical tale about Katō Saemon Shigeuji (421–22). Katō Saemon Shigeuji realizes the anguish and jealousy he caused his wife and resident mistress after seeing the hair of his sleeping wife and mistress turn into fighting serpents. Later Katō Saemon Shigeuji repents and enters the priesthood, but the narrator notes that "most men, in real life, wouldn't actually take up priestly practice because of something like seeing women's hair turned into serpents" (422). Shizuko thought in retrospect that her grandmother Ritsu told her the story of Katō Saemon Shigeuji because she felt an empathy for women who had to share men in polygynous marriages: "She could envision how, just as an author introduces emotions into a plot, Ritsu, for all her self-control, was including her own emotions in the telling of this story" (422).

"Skeletons of Men" exhibits a greater freedom than The Waiting Years to play with the supernatural themes with which Enchi later became associated. The addition of the frame piques our interest when one of the narrators, Shizuko, claims that she has "been manipulated by the spirit of this sash" (418). Further, an eerie atmosphere pervades the description of the "blood letter" found in the obi written by Chise, the married woman spurned by Yoshimitsu. The second metanarrative in which the hair of the rival women battle one another like those on Medusa's snake-like crown also enhances a sense of the macabre. Unlike The Waiting Years, which only hinted at spirit possession as Tomo's niece announced her wish that her corpse be "dumped" into the sea in the final scene, the conclusion of "Skeletons of Men" leans more decidedly toward the supernatural when "the white bones beneath the grave seemed to fade dimly and it was as if the haze congealed into the form of Minami" (425), as it reveals that even Shizuko had an affair with a younger man which caused her to uncharacteristically chase after a man whose passions for her had cooled. Jealousy and resentment against the injustices of polygyny form the core of both works, but it seems clear that Enchi, struggling to achieve public recognition at the time, wanted *The Waiting Years* to be free from controversial topics which may have inhibited its reception with the public.

"Enchantress"

"Enchantress," another short narrative published in 1956, shows a significant development of the theme of empowered women toward the maturation of the topic in stage two. Narrated in the third person from the point of view of the female protagonist Chigako, "Enchantress" contains elements more representative of a work by Enchi: a world inhabited by classical Japanese scholars, a woman enduring a loveless marriage, a woman attempting to regain her lost youth by fantasizing about an affair with a younger man, an obscuring of the distinction between the past and the present, and hints of the supernatural. Chigako, a middle-aged translator of classical Japanese works into English, proclaims that she "believe[s] their spirits [women writers of the Heian period] have taken possession of her" and have induced her to write "romances" of her own. (One is tempted to draw parallels to Enchi who also functioned in the dual role of classical scholar and writer.)

As in most texts by Enchi, the narrative is related from the point of view of the female protagonist Chigako. After a description of her residence beneath a slope (a topic she pursued in *Onnazaka*, which literally means "Female Slope"), we learn that Chigako has just seen her youngest daughter off on a ship to California where her husband, a physician, is to work for the next four years. Chigako's eldest daughter had moved to Kyūshū with her husband some time ago. Chigako, who felt that her daughters had acted as a buffer between her and her husband Keisaku, is intimidated when her husband tries to reestablish intimacy with her now that their daughters are no longer at home. She retreats to the annex building beneath the hill to isolate herself away from her husband's attempts to renew conjugal relations. She has unpleasant memories of her husband forcing her to translate Edo period (1600–1867) pornographic literature to make ends meet during the war, but recalls with nostalgia that the pornographic works awakened a new sense of sensuality in her that she had never known she possessed.

When Keisaku advises Chigako to apply hair tonic to replenish the hair loss he has noted, she immediately reacts to his criticism by engaging in a ritual of applying make-up to mask the signs of aging. She treats the application of cosmetics as if it were a religious ritual while at the same time indulging in fantasies about keeping assignations with younger men. After translating Episode 63 of the *Tales of Ise* into English, Chigako feels that the description of the old woman's thinning hair in the *Tales of Ise* might have been an apt description of her own thinning locks. Her revelations shock Tōno Shigeyuki, a male Heian literature specialist, because he had thought of her as an older woman past the age of sensuality (*Ise monogatari*, 183–185). The reference to Episode 63 also reflects Enchi's interest in love affairs between older women and younger men, which is further echoed in the main theme of Chigako's fictional "romance" in which she imagines a young music student having a love affair with an older married woman. Chigako confesses that she felt she exacted a form of revenge on her husband Keisaku by fantasizing about an affair with the younger man in the fictional story she creates and by having the wife in the story break a prized Ming vase belonging to her husband. It is obvious that Keisaku, who is an antique collector, is the target of Chigako's revenge in literary form (91). (One might also draw parallels to Enchi as a writer who invented a host of weak and unattractive male characters as a form of revenge for the partner in her own unhappy marriage.)

"Enchantress" centers on the unhappy twenty-year marriage of Chigako and Keisaku, dwelling on factors such as the physical loss of teeth, hair and youth, and on the psychological deprivations caused by misunderstanding, distrust, and ennui. In contrast to the pessimistic conclusions of *The Waiting Years*, Enchi injects a touch of humor into the conclusion by focusing on the comic effects of the toothless mouths of the couple. On the other hand, Enchi surprises readers by suggesting that a story from Chigako's dreams and fantasy world had suddenly manifested itself in reality. The contrast between the amusing image of the toothless married couple and the melding between the worlds of fantasy and reality makes for one of the most unusual and memorable conclusions for Enchi. We will return to the idea that fantasy can become reality when Enchi began exploring this topic in earnest in the 1970s.

"A Bond for Two Lifetimes—Gleanings"

A conflation of the world of reality and illusion occurs with a vengeance in the brilliant short work, "A Bond for Two Lifetimes—Gleanings," displaying once again a double-layered narrative consisting of a frame and this time an intratext. The intratext features Enchi's modern translation of the story "Nise no enishi" ("A Bond for Two Lifetimes") from the collection *Tales of Spring Rain* (*Harusame monogatari*, 1809) by Ueda Akinari (1734–1809), a writer noted for his tales of ghosts and supernatural occurrences. The frame is related in the first person by a World War II widow acting as an amanuensis to her former professor, a specialist in Edo period literature, who is in the process of translating Ueda Akinari's tale. The intratext that Enchi chose to translate was the story of Jōsuke, a Buddhist priest who was interred while in a state of trance and whose desiccated body was exhumed when a man heard the sound of bells coming from beneath the ground. The priest is reverently revived, but has no memory of his previous life and becomes sexually involved with the female village idiot, and proves, at least to the family who harbored him, the futility of living piously. The agility with which the two texts are woven together, blending the past and the present, lends a surreal air to the conclusion, when reality and dreams mingle, making readers wonder what actually occurred.

In "A Bond for Two Lifetimes—Gleanings," an investigation of the existence of sexual drive without the guiding hand of intelligence is set into motion in the guise of the resuscitated priest Jōsuke. Enchi's penchant for this topic is clear in the staging of similar scenarios portraying mentally deficient characters with normal sexual drives in other works—Harume in *Masks*, Shirakawa Michimasa in *The Waiting Years*, and Ichige Masatoshi in "A Boxcar of Chrysanthemums." Enchi was evidently intrigued by the idea of the persistence of the sexual drive devoid of intelligence as an opportunity for exploring the psyche, especially since she had already investigated the antithetical position of the existence of the sexual drive without sexual organs in the course of writing other works.

The use of explicitly sexual language in "A Bond for Two Lifetimes—Gleanings" brought notoriety to Enchi. The line in question, "my very womb cried out in longing," describes the widow's desire for her husband who was killed during the war (44). The use of explicit language continued during the first stage of development while Enchi was dealing with the physical loss of having undergone mastectomy and hysterectomy surgeries, losing aspects of womanhood she considered essential for female identity. During this stage she revealed in her texts that she considered herself neither a man nor a woman, but some grotesque monster devoid of gender. Under the circumstances it is not difficult to see Enchi's fascination with concepts of androgyny and homoeroticism which appear frequently among the themes she addresses in the course of her narratives. In "Eroticism and the Writings of Enchi Fumiko," Yoko McClain states that Enchi said that some women write about sex from a deep-seated need while others write for sensational or commercial reasons (33). McClain concludes that Enchi belonged to the first category and attributes some of the motivation for writing about sex to the physical deprivation Enchi experienced in her life through a mastectomy and a hysterectomy.

Second Stage of Development

The first stage of development of Enchi's female characters is followed by a host of enigmatic women who reach into hidden inner sources of strength by tapping shamanistic powers. The image of the *miko*, often combined with those of the *Itsuki no miko*, provide another forum for Enchi to investigate concepts of sexual desire in the second stage of empowered female characters. Enchi reaches into the traditional canon for suitable material to serve as a backdrop for the updated, subversive message she seeks to convey.

Masks

Perhaps one of the most intriguing works by Enchi is *Masks*, which introduces readers to the world of the supernatural through a woman who may be a modern-day *miko*. Toganō Mieko, the protagonist of *Masks*, comes closest to fulfilling the ideal of a strong, enigmatic woman who manipulates a host of minor players on a stage choreographed to create a surreal atmosphere. Mieko, a widow in her fifties, is an accomplished poet who is keen about classical Japanese literature, especially concerning spirit possession in *The Tale of Genji*, the masterpiece of the Heian period. The members of Mieko's entourage are: Toganō Yasuko, the widow of Mieko's son, Akio, who died in a mountaineering accident; Harume, the retarded twin sister of Akio, sent away by Mieko to be raised in a temple in the country; Ibuki Tsuneo, a married Heian literature professor; and

Mikame Toyoki, a bachelor psychologist and amateur folklorist. The characters are bound by their shared interest in the study of spirit possession and by the acquaintance of Toganō Akio, who before his death had been conducting research on Heian spirit possession as a professor of literature. After Akio's death, Mieko persuaded Yasuko to continue his research, thereby establishing a link with Akio's colleagues Ibuki and Mikame. (Harume did not possess the necessary intellect required for meaningful interaction with the group studying spirit possession and remains in the background until the latter part of the narrative.)

The theme of spirit possession is entwined with images of female masks worn in the Noh theater. The image of masks appears in the title of the novel, *Onnamen* ("Female Mask") and the three chapters titles bearing the names of specific female Noh masks—the first chapter, "Ryō no onna" (lit., spirit woman) for the vengeful spirit of a woman tormented beyond the grave by unrequited love; the second chapter "Masugami" (lit., a length of hair) for young women plagued by madness; and the third chapter "Fukai" (lit., deep well or deep woman) for middle-aged women beyond the age of sensuality. Masks of the Noh theater play a substantial role in the novel with direct correlation to the three female characters: the mask for "Ryō no onna" may refer to Mieko, the one for "Masugami" to Harume, and "Fukai" again to Mieko. Images of ghosts who roam the world telling woeful tales full of tormented memories are *de rigueur* for Noh performances and find resonance in the novel in the form of malign spirits who, during exorcism rites, reveal causes for lingering in the world.

Ghosts and spirits are not the only things to cloud the readers' understanding of the novel—the lack of narratorial guidance in *Masks* makes it a difficult work to comprehend. In "Twin Blossoms on a Single Branch: The Cycle of Retribution in *Onnamen*," Doris G. Bargen states that a simple process such as recapitulating the plot in a chronological fashion, becomes, in the case of *Masks*, an interpretation of the work (148). Bargen's twenty-four page analysis is the most extensive work done on the interpretation of *Masks* to date and reveals a good deal of thought extracted from clues embedded in the text. Without guidance from the narrator, there is little readers can do but seek clues along the way to make sense of the narrative and hope to discover the message it seeks to relate.

A further complication in reading *Masks* arises from the lack of a central point of view from which the narrative unfolds. The reader is allowed little access to the interior thoughts of the major characters and when glimpses are made available, readers must occasionally suspect their reliability. Enchi was much enamored of works by Tanizaki Jun'ichirō and Akutagawa Ryūnosuke, whose works played with unreliable narration, and Enchi seems to have adopted their techniques and fashioned them into an elevated art form. She conceals everything from us and only hints at things she wishes us to grasp, never approaching us directly but always proceeding obliquely with hidden motives and veiled purposes. Even Enchi's intertextual references to the Heian classics are imbued with mystery.

Masks contains significant references to *The Tale of Genji, The Tale of Nezame,* and *the Tales of Ise. The Tale of Genji* occupies so central a role in the work that one ponders the significance of reading *Masks* without having read the eleventh-century masterpiece beforehand. The inclusion of an essay in *Masks* by Mieko on the significance of Lady Rokujō depends heavily on the intertextual knowledge of the character's role in *The Tale of Genji.* Lady Rokujō, an accomplished, high-ranking woman scorned by the hero Genji, found that the repression of her emotions caused her spirit to leave her body to torment her rivals through spirit possession. The essay reflects Enchi's extensive research on the topics of spirit possession and *miko,* reveals the depth of the attraction the character held for her, and seeks to reevaluate the importance of the character of Lady Rokujō. The empathy Mieko displays for the character of Lady Rokujō in the essay is reflected in turn by Enchi for the characters of Mieko and her classical predecessor, Lady Rokujō (Pounds, 176).

Strong undercurrents of references to Buddhist misogyny are evident in the essay "An Account of the Shrine in the Field" ("Nonomiya ki"), an intratext purportedly written by Mieko in *Masks.* While recognizing the syncretic nature of Buddhism and Shintoism in Japan, I argue that Enchi intentionally places the two religions at polar opposites in order to attack Buddhism as part of the dominant ideology involved in the continued subjugation of women and to uphold Shintoism as a realm where women found empowerment through the image of *miko.* The two attacks against Buddhism in the essay by Mieko are carefully worded:

> Commentators generally agree that the Rokujō lady was jealous and vindictive—traits, they say, which Genji abhorred and which drove him from her. This view is colored by Buddhist teaching. As passion transforms the Rokujō lady into a living ghost, her spirit taking leave of her body again and again to attack and finally to kill

> Genji's wife Aoi, the commentators see in her tragic obsession a classic illustration of the evil karma attached to all womankind. (*Masks*, 51)

> In our own day, shamanism seems to have withered and died. Yet does it not, on second thought, offer a partial explanation of the power women still have over men? Perhaps it is true, as Buddhism teaches us, that this power constitutes woman's greatest burden and delusion—and ultimately her greatest sin. But the sin is inseparable from a woman's being. It is a stream of blood flowing on and on, unbroken, from generation to generation. (*Masks*, 57)

Enchi insinuates that Buddhism considers the essential nature of womankind to be evil, and that sin is an inherent part of women. The wording concerning Buddhism is subtle enough to be mistaken for the author's own attitude, but it is clear that Enchi does not uphold the view that women are evil. Enchi's use of the image of blood flowing on from generation to generation is also reminiscent of the fear and mystery attached to women during menses as procreators of life.[13] At the conclusion of Mieko's essay, the text launches into Ibuki's analysis of her essay with the following ideas from Shinto:

> Ibuki was intrigued by Mieko Toganō's theory. From his readings in the *History of Japanese Shamanesses* and elsewhere, he was familiar with the idea that the ancient Yamato tribe might have brought Ural-Altaic forms of shamanism to Japan. And in Japanese folklore, the prominence of the sun goddess Amaterasu Ōmikami suggested that the gods had spoken through shamanesses in prehistoric times. Supporting evidence could be found in the *Kojiki* episode concerning Emperor Chūai, in which a deity enters the empress Jinjū [*sic*] Kōgō and through her decrees the invasion of Korea. (*Masks*, 57)

I believe there is considerable significance in having Ibuki's ideas concerning empowered images of women in Shinto mythology placed immediately after the essay expressing negative Buddhist attitudes toward women. I hold that Enchi's literary endeavors utilizing the *miko* have been drawn from the same well of Shinto tradition from which empowered female images of the past were derived.

Apparently Enchi's fascination with *miko* is related to her desire to recapture the empowered role played by women in Japanese history. The female sun god, Amaterasu Ōmikami, plays a key role in the Shinto creation myth, according to the account in the *Record of Ancient Matters* (*Kojiki*, ca. 712). Further, the matrilocal nature of Heian society granted women the right to remain with their families after marriage, to inherit property, and to retain custody of children after divorce (McCullough, 1967). Moreover, the role of high-ranking women (Naishinnō: imperial princess) as female high priests of Ise and Kamo Shrines confirm their sacerdotal connections to the divine in Shinto. Finally, *miko* who served as mediums acted as receptacles for possessive spirits during cases of exorcism in malevolent possessions. However, Enchi's trademark use of *miko* is a subversion of the traditional definition of a medium as a passive recipient of a possessive spirit in that she empowers her *miko* with the ability to possess others, not to inflict bodily harm as tradition would have it, but to seek sexual assignations with younger men. But we must delay discussion of this aspect until we reach the third stage of development in the theme of empowered women, and will now continue tracing further allusions to the traditional canon.

Intertextual references to *The Tale of Nezame* and the *Tales of Ise* are limited to cases which directly support either the topic of spirit possession or *miko*. *The Tale of Nezame* is cited for the express purpose of bringing to light a case of spirit possession used for political ends. In *The Tale of Nezame*, the heroine Nezame is falsely accused of being the spirit responsible for possessing a high-ranking female rival. Later it is revealed that Nezame's political rivals hired a false medium and instructed the medium to implicate Nezame as the malign spirit possessing the lady and causing her illness (*Masks*, 76–77). The idea of employing false mediums for political ends was developed in the narrative, *A Tale of False Oracles*, which specifically addresses this issue—mediums who were motivated by the promise of material compensation to divine the origin of a malign possession to effect political change or to acquire personal emoluments. This further suggests the idea that some shamans in a heightened state of sensuality during trances were especially susceptible to sexual advances, placing them in the vulnerable position of falling prey to bribes on the promise of sexual or material favors.

Classical literature brims with accounts of royal princesses who, while serving in the capacity of vestal virgins or high priests, *Itsuki no miko* at Kamo and Ise Shrines, kept clandestine assignations while ostensibly in seclusion for purification rites. Episode 69 of the *Tales of Ise* preserves a famous poetic exchange between Ariwara Narihira (825–80) and his cousin, the incumbent Ise Virgin.

In this episode, sexual ecstasy is blamed for the confusion between the world of reality (waking) and the world of dreams (sleeping), the relevant factor being the sexual encounter bordering on the divine because of the official post held by the Ise Virgin (*Ise monogatari*, 191–93; *Masks*, 77, 111–12). Along this line, *Masks* makes direct reference to Narihira's sexual encounter with the Ise Virgin, who of her own accord goes to Narihira's bedchamber, confirming the idea that shamans view sex as sinless, and reinforcing the idea of divinely inspired sex as proposed in the stage-three text *Colored Mist* (*Masks*, 77). Significantly, the assignation exacted no retribution for either party.

Other sexual issues at stake in *Masks* are the concepts of twins (similarity), androgyny, homogeneity, and homosexuality, attacking the system of patriarchy which supports the concept of difference. The twins, embodied by Akio (lit., autumn male) and Harume (lit., spring female), foster the concept of androgyny, in the concept of male and female counterparts of one being. While still in the womb, Akio kicks his sister in the head, causing mental retardation and signifying the woman as victim. Homosexuality is suggested in the relationship between Mieko and Yasuko, is complemented by the androgynous nature of different-sex twins, and could be interpreted as exploring an alternative to the patriarchal system. Masks from the Noh theater constitute another element suggesting androgyny in that the all-male cast dons female masks to portray women on stage. Twins, androgyny, and homosexuality are combined with masks from the Noh theater to further obscure the traditional distinctions between male and female (*Masks*, 25–26). The birth of Harume's child at the narrative's conclusion may imply a spiritual reunion of the male and female aspects of the damaged twins, Akio and Harume, bringing to full circle the concept of androgyny implied by twins.[14] Although *Masks* is a richly complex narrative that has drawn the attention of scholars from varied fields,[15] my analysis of the work has been limited to the topics of *miko*, intertextual allusions to the classical canon, and the concept of androgyny. A complete analysis of *Masks* is beyond the scope of this study focusing on the second stage of development toward images of empowered women.

"Metamorphosis"

Another narrative from stage two is "Metamorphosis" in which Enchi employs narrative techniques which intentionally subvert the authority of the text presented from a male perspective and propose an alternative world, albeit a fictional one, inhabited by empowered women. Enchi's narrative seeks to subvert the authority of traditional masculinist paradigms in the textual world she constructs, featuring empowered women who take control of situations unimaginable in reality, but which becomes the fictive reality of her texts.

"Metamorphosis" was written in 1962, only five years after Enchi had achieved fame as a writer. It focuses upon the relationship between a middle-aged couple with hereditary ties to the Kabuki theater. The short narrative is narrated from the third-person perspective of a male character, Sanogawa Shinsha, a fifty-year old Kabuki actor. Shinsha has been married for a number of years to Chisa, a forty-year old woman from a family of equally famous Kabuki actors. While Shinsha performs on the stage of the all-male Kabuki theater, the talented Chisa is denied an outlet for her dramatic skills because she was born a woman. However, she seizes the opportunity to covertly display her talent with the world as the stage upon which to perform.

Most of Enchi's works are narrated from a female perspective, thus "Metamorphosis" is unusual for sustaining a male perspective from the opening lines up to the final paragraph of the text. Readers are privy only to the speculations and limited perceptions of Shinsha, the husband, concerning the true feelings of his wife, Chisa, for her brother-in-law Kikuo, a twenty-year old Kabuki actor with whom she had been conducting a love affair for a number of years. Neutral narration sprinkled throughout the text offers background information on the main protagonist Chisa, but readers are denied access to her inner thoughts. Therefore, when the perspective is suddenly switched to Chisa's privileged viewpoint in the last paragraph of the text, readers are forced to reevaluate the information provided from the husband's (male) perspective.

Information from the husband's perspective focuses on his inability to fathom the true depths of his wife's feelings for his younger brother Kikuo. Shinsha would like to believe that Chisa was using the younger man Kikuo as a "plaything," rather than accept the humiliating fact that she might really have loved his younger brother. Readers, who have been exposed to the skeptical, egotistical perspective of the husband, must decide which is more reliable: what one is told or what one is shown. The shift in perspective in the last paragraph of the narrative provides the final word. A succinct overview of the main events will provide the necessary background for the following analysis.

After a brief descriptive passage setting the scene, the scenario is set in motion. There is a phone call in the middle of the night informing Chisa that her brother-in-law Kikuo has been killed in an automobile accident. Chisa awakens her husband, then immediately collapses on the floor beside the bed, trembling violently. After Shinsha admonishes Chisa to regain control of herself, a passage of neutral narration reveals Shinsha's previous knowledge of the affair between his wife and his younger brother. After he was informed of their affair by Torisu Kishi, a spinster housekeeper who manages the Sanogawa household, he deduced that this may have been Chisa's covert way of avenging herself on him for the affairs he has had with various women throughout their marriage.

Speculations concerning the affair are presented from the point of view of Shinsha, and his ally, the housekeeper Torisu Kishi. Shinsha is busy nursing his wounded ego because he had been rendered a cuckold but expresses admiration for his younger brother, Kikuo (who is also referred to by his nickname, Kiichan, and his Kabuki stage name of Tojaku), for the maturity and discretion he displayed in conducting the love affair. From the perspective of Shinsha's ally, the housekeeper Torisu Kishi, we learn about the latest developments in the affair by her keen intuitive sense and tenacious quest for relevant information. Just a few days before Kikuo was killed in the auto accident, Kishi reported that he had kept a secret rendezvous with Chisa in the couple's own bedroom while Shinsha and Kishi were out attending the opening of a new theater.

The text situates the unhappy marital relationship as belonging to a part of the gender conflict. Shinsha feels sympathetic toward his younger brother Kikuo, first because he died an untimely death, and further because they were men bound by common life experiences. But when the wife Chisa is described with negative metaphors from the husband's perspective, such as possessing "white, puffy lips which resemble silk worms" and having "shoulders which reminded him of dead fish," the adversarial conflict based on gender difference is set in motion. That Shinsha should ally himself with the man who violated the sanctity of his marital relationship may be thought illogical until the gender identity factor has been taken into account. Shinsha's identity with males becomes blatantly apparent, setting the wife apart as the opponent (or member of the female gender) who must be conquered and vanquished.

Concepts of homosexuality and androgyny in the Kabuki theater are suggested in the cross-gender role playing. Toying with gender identity is given further scrutiny in passages describing the curious relationship shared by Shinsha and Kikuo on the Kabuki stage, where the elder brother in a male role sometimes embraced and kissed the younger brother in a female-lover role. Furthermore, for readers who are cognizant of a notion among fans of the Kabuki theater who believe that male actors who habitually play women's roles (onnagata) embody feminine ideals better than do biological females, a reconsideration of same gender relationships between the elder and younger Kabuki actors is emphasized.[16]

Ironically, the female protagonist Chisa was denied access to the stage because of her gender. However, throughout the narrative we are provided with clues from the housekeeper Torisu Kishi that Chisa is a much better actor than Shinsha. Although Shinsha acts on the Kabuki stage, he is no match for the performance Chisa gives with the world as the stage in upholding the character of the devoted wife she seeks to portray. Chisa gives the performance of her life, transforming herself from the trembling wretch who received word of her lover's death to the respectable matron who calmly oversees the four-day funeral service as the wife of the deceased's elder brother. The title of the story refers directly to Chisa's transformation. But what does the title really mean?

The Chinese characters in the title, keshō 化性, could not be located in any dictionary consulted, therefore, one must conclude that Enchi invented the compound, not so much to confound readers (although that is also possible), as to suggest a number of alternative and equally relevant meanings of the word. The literal meaning of the characters comprising the Chinese compound are as follows: ける bakeru ("to appear in disguise"), also pronounced bakasu ("to bewitch, to enchant, to delude, to confuse"), or kasuru, kasu, kesuru ("to change into, convert into, transform"); and 性 sei, shō ("sex, gender; nature"). Thus, the meaning for the compound keshō could mean "disguised, changed or bewitched, sex/gender/nature," all of which could be applied to the transformation Chisa undergoes in the course of the narrative and the gender conflict depicted in the marital relationship.

There are also homophonous words which offer semantic clarification of the word keshō. First, there is the homophonous word, 化粧 keshō ("make-up") with connotations to the world of the Kabuki stage, where the application of cosmetics enables actors to transform their gender and appearance to match the roles they are to play. Next, there may be a visual play on the characters for another homophonous 化生 keshō here with Buddhist connotations to the world of spirits involving a metamorphosis before entering another realm of existence. Reference to the world of spirits is explicitly made in the text in two distinct passages, one describing Chisa's drastic metamorphosis as resembling someone who was possessed by spirits, and another revealing Shinsha's interior monologue in which he felt he had entered the world of ghostly spirits when he saw his wife and another female character, Yukiko, touch Kikuo's cheek, thus supporting the theory on the visual play of similar Chinese characters. Enchi's frequent incorporation of the supernatural in other texts supports the suggested connections with the otherworldly in "Metamorphosis." Her venture into the supernatural is often accompanied by a fluidity in time and the distortion in the perception of reality.

The narrative weaves its way back and forth through time, winding back to reveal background information and rolling forward into the narrative present to deliver effective and dramatic scenes as the occasion demands. As fluid as the flow of time is the flexibility between illusion and reality in texts by Enchi. The confusion which arises in Shinsha's mind when he gazes at his brother's face in the casket is typical: Shinsha and Kikuo often played roles on stage in which the younger brother died, thereby leading Shinsha to ponder whether the dead face he sees in the casket is the illusion or whether the dead face he saw on stage was reality. Through the conflation of time and the confusion between illusion and reality, Enchi succeeds in making a ripple in the readers' sense of reality as well.

The authority of the traditional masculine paradigms inherent in the all-male Kabuki theater is subverted when Chisa, a woman who is not allowed to act in Kabuki, is declared the winner in the adversarial relationship in the spheres of both marriage and gender. If Chisa, a woman who is not permitted to perform on the Kabuki stage, is a better actor than Shinsha who actually does perform, then the ultimate authority of the theater controlled and dominated by men is undermined. The adversarial relationship between husband and wife in the unhappy marital relationship eventually spawns a conflict in gender as well, exemplified by the male perspective sympathizing with other males and forming alliances against a common foe, the female gender.

The masculine view maintained throughout the narrative is given the final subversive blow in the last paragraph, when readers are exposed to the glaring truth behind the speculations concerning Chisa's true thoughts and feelings. Chisa's perspective is revealed with a touch of irony and defiance: she knew of her husband's feeble attempts to pit her against the younger woman, Yukiko, with whom

Kikuo had been concurrently conducting an affair, in order to gauge the depth of her feelings for her lover, and although she wanted to laugh at the simple-minded antics of her husband at the end of the narrative, she managed to suppress her emotions and demurely wiped tears from her eyes. Hidden in the subtle gesture is the realization that Chisa as the wife has achieved victory over her husband in the marital relationship, and Chisa as the woman has worsted her enemy in the gender conflict exacerbated by the use of subversive narrative techniques.

In addition to narrative techniques aimed at undermining the authority of the male perspective is Enchi's trademark utilization of intertextual allusions to the traditional canon. The most significant intertextual reference employed in "Metamorphosis" is an allusion to the chapter "The Death of Atsumori" ("Atsumori no saigo") in the medieval war tale The Tale of the Heike (Heike monogatari, ca. 1371). Enchi makes an oblique yet blatant reference to the historical character Taira no Atsumori (ca. 1168–84), who was killed by Kumagae no Naozane, a warrior fighting for the Minamoto clan at the battle of Ichinotani, by using the words usu geshō (light application of make-up) to describe the young actor Tojaku's dead face in the casket during the funeral wake. Those familiar with the traditional canon recall the famous episode in The Tale of the Heike in which the young aristocrat Atsumori, wearing a light coat of facial powder and having blackened teeth, is killed by a low-ranking barbarian from the East.

In "The Death of Atsumori," Kumagae no Naozane beckons Taira no Atsumori to engage in combat as the young aristocrat was retreating on horseback to reach a ship in which he hoped to make his escape. After defeating his opponent in a seaside battle, Kumagae removes Atsumori's helmet to find a young courtier about the age of his own son. Kumagae's sympathy for the younger man is a perfect foil for the contempt with which the high-ranking Atsumori holds his enemy. However much Kumagae would like to spare the young man's life, all avenues of escape evaporate when the Minamoto cavalry arrives on the beach. Then Kumagae resolves to kill Atsumori, but only after having sworn a solemn pledge to pray for Atsumori's afterlife by becoming a Buddhist monk to atone for his sin of being a warrior whose sole purpose in life is to kill. This pivotal scene is incorporated into Enchi's narrative to highlight the theme of mujōkan (the evanescence of human life) and to suggest an affinity in the tragic deaths of the aristocrat Atsumori and the actor Tojaku, both of whom died in the bloom of youth.

However this intertextual allusion is characteristically utilized for subversive purposes. For although Atsumori and Tojaku both died young, the narrative woven by Enchi reveals Tojaku to have been a tainted youth. That he was killed in an automobile accident en route to visiting one of his lovers subverts the full force of tragedy accorded the death of Atsumori in *The Tale of the Heike*. The themes of *mujōkan* featured in the medieval war tale and the romantic notion of dying in battle are placed against the backdrop of Tojaku's affairs of the flesh. Enchi's narrative ultimately seeks to subvert the authority of the male-dominated world of warriors depicted in *The Tale of the Heike*.

Enchi Fumiko's use of subversive narrative techniques in "Metamorphosis" ultimately seeks to undermine the authority not only of the text itself presented from a male perspective, but also dominant masculine institutions and ideologies which seek to sustain the subjugation of women in society in both the past and the present. By allowing the female viewpoint to override the previous legitimacy attributed to the information gleaned from a male perspective, Enchi confers victory upon women at the end of the narrative. Let us now consider stage three in which aged female protagonists confront reality in a surreal manner.

Third Stage of Development

The third stage in the development of female characters is characterized by sojourns into the world of fantasy by elderly women who deal creatively with their lingering sexual desire. When Enchi began translating *The Tale of Genji* into modern Japanese in 1967, she began searching for new avenues to channel her creative energies. In 1968, she wrote an article "Monogatari to tanpen" ("Tales and Short Stories") for the journal *Gunzō* in which she stated that she was looking for a method of creating a new form of literature she had not yet written:

> Recently I have been perplexed because I have reached a point of exasperation with conventional fiction. Some people may suggest that I write autobiography, but the scope one can write about is limited and it does not agree with my nature as a writer. I wanted to try writing in some form that I had not yet written up to now, which allowed me to remain comfortably and unreservedly within myself while creating a fantasy world. Although I have always been

captivated by such wild ideas, I have not been able to discover a
method for creating it (Kamei and Ogasawara, 91).[17]

I argue that Enchi's sojourn into fantasy and antirational occurrences found in the third stage is the solution to the method she had
sought in the quote above. The trilogy *Wandering Spirit*, consisting
of "Foxfire," "Wandering Spirit," and "The Voice of a Snake," pays
tribute to the classics but subverts the traditional role of *miko*
within the context of spirit possession. The three narratives comprising *Wandering Spirit* are connected by characters in similar
circumstances: an aged woman, who lives with her daughter and her
son-in-law, with each narrative developing the nature of the aged
woman's desire for her son-in-law, and eventually causing the
woman's spirit to leave her body to enjoy the embraces of the
younger man.

Wandering Spirit

The name of Suo, the aged female protagonist in "Wandering
Spirit," means "burgundy," alluding to a deep purplish-red color
restricted to the use of the high nobility in the premodern period and
which has connotations to sexuality inherent in the word *iro*
("color" or "passion"). Suo tries to suppress her desire but finds her
spirit wandering off to men who are the objects of her sexual desire.
Not only is this a subversion of the concept of spirit possession per
se with its usual intention of inflicting bodily harm, but it is also an
imaginative way for aged women without partners to achieve sexual
fulfillment. Curiously, the men who share Suo's sexual fantasy in
"Wandering Spirit" retain total recollection of the encounter,
thereby creating the familiar conflation between the world of
dreams and the world of reality found in many of Enchi's works.

In the article "Enchi Fumiko and the Hidden Energy of the
Supernatural," Wayne Pounds draws attention to Enchi's aberrant
use of the word *miko*. In the classical tradition, *miko* are used as
mediums to exorcise malign spirits from the victim's (i.e., the possessed person's) body. However, Enchi has chosen to subvert the
traditional use of the word *miko* from medium to the possessing
spirit that in many cases must be expelled from the victim's body.
This subversive redefinition, detected in many of Enchi's works,
may be interpreted as a transgression against the former role of
woman as a passive vehicle in exorcism rites transformed into a
empowered woman with a sense of control, albeit in a supernatural
context.

Colored Mist

Colored Mist shares with *Wandering Spirit* the topic of old women (in their sixties and seventies) linked to the supernatural. It examines female sexuality which lingers into old age, coupled with a venture into the world of *miko*. In the long narrative *Colored Mist*, Kawai Yukiko is described as a female descendant of the chief priests of the Kamo Shrine who possesses an erotic picture scroll called "The Maiden in Service of the Kamo Shrine." The picture scroll, which is never explicitly described, apparently depicts the sexual union between a shrine maiden and a lowly shrine caretaker whose body is possessed by a god to consummate sexual relations with his "shrine maiden." The narrative suggests that the person in possession of the picture scroll becomes endowed with prodigious sexual powers historically linked to the role played by *miko* in Shintoism. Sano, the second female protagonist, is a woman writer in her sixties who is a neighbor of Yukiko in Karuizawa. Before Yukiko dies, she bequeaths the erotic picture scroll to Sano, thereby propelling her to the center of action.

Men who have coupled with Yukiko describe the experience in ecstatic, almost religious terms, but subsequently they succumb to unnatural deaths. After Yukiko dies toward the end of the work, Sano inherits the picture scroll from her, and shortly thereafter, begins to resemble Yukiko physically and to mimic Yukiko's erotic behavior, suggesting that Yukiko's spirit has taken possession of Sano. Enchi hints at the relationship between sex and the divine in the figure of the *miko*, albeit in the form of an old woman instead of the virginal maidens of antiquity, once again subverting the classical allusion to explore the concept of lingering sexuality in aged females. In *Colored Mist* the traditional image of *miko* as Shinto shrine maidens and the amoral role of sexual relations is given a subversive turn by Enchi's imagination. In the following, reference will be made to both *Wandering Spirit* and *Colored Mist* in discussing the final narrative in stage three.

"The Old Woman Who Eats Flowers"

The final narrative in the third stage of development, "The Old Woman Who Eats Flowers" discards comfortable notions of reality to venture into the world of myth and fantasy. The short narrative places little value in conventional realism and temporal progression, but still manages to support a modicum of Enchi's trademark themes such as visitations from the supernatural world, conflating the distinction between the past and the present, challenging accepted notions of reality, and exploring the nature of sexual desire. But why does Enchi defy conventional realism and turn to the worlds of myth, fantasy and irony? And is this short narrative so unlike others from Enchi's oeuvre?

I propose that in this state of development, Enchi turned away from conventional realism toward an exploration of the alternate worlds of myth, fantasy, and irony, which recent feminist critics have identified as a "literature of subversion." In "The Old Woman Who Eats Flowers," Enchi also challenges cultural myths by tapping the sources of the mythologies of the East and the West. She investigates the concept of aging within the context of mythology and in doing so promotes a reinterpretation of patriarchal cultural myths designed to thwart the desires of women.

Before beginning the analysis, a brief plot summary will facilitate the discussion which follows. There are two elderly female protagonists in this work narrated by a first person "I." There is a description of a veranda on which a potted plant with flowering blossoms is placed which draws the attention of a white-haired old woman. The old woman, the referent in the title "The Old Woman who Eats Flowers," is blessed with radiant skin and eyes which shine with a "mysterious brightness like those of a young girl." No description of the "I" narrator is offered at any point in the narrative, except that the narrator, like the old woman, shares the same affliction which limits the ability to see.

The potted plant is described in great detail by the narrator, focusing on her interest in nurturing the flowering plant. The crab cactus becomes the focal point of the narrative as the old woman shocks the narrator by wantonly plucking off a cluster of three flowers and eating them. Then the narrator and the old woman embark upon a metaphysical discussion on the nature of desire (with connotations of sexual desire) and the means to satisfy that desire. After discussing the nature of the desire which impels the old woman to eat the flowers that the narrator had carefully nurtured for a number of years, the narrative leaves the dialogue between the two elderly women and begins describing the narrator's psychological state since loosing "her windows to the outside world" to an eye disease. The narrator mentions various ghostly images which began manifesting themselves in her daily life at the deterioration of her sight and begins reminiscing about the past when a bundle of letters written in her youth fell onto her lap late one night as she was straightening up items in her closet.

The bundle of letters was written by the narrator in her youth to a man who was a distant relative a few years older than she. Apparently the narrator was not romantically involved with the man but had maintained correspondence with him until he moved to a foreign country. Thereafter, correspondence between the man and the narrator was severed. However, many years later the narrator heard of the man's sudden death from a heart attack while he was playing golf as a retiree in England. Soon after his death, the narrator received a package from his widow containing all the letters she had written to the man in her youth. The narrator feels nothing but scorn for the man who valued the immature sentiments of a young girl written in a clumsy hand, but at the same time she cannot help but feel a bit nostalgic for the memory he retained of her as a youth who was at that time unsullied by the world.

The man's widow sent the letters back to the narrator because her husband had valued them all his life and now that he was gone, the widow felt that the narrator should have them back as keepsakes of her husband. However, the narrator was annoyed by the memories they evoked and without a second thought placed them in the bottom of a letter box, stuffed them into the closet and promptly forgot about them. In the course of cleaning out her closet years later, somehow the letters had worked their way from the bottom of the box where she knew she had placed them, and onto her lap, making her dwell on the past against her wishes. At this point, the narrative returns to the conversation between the two old women.

The old woman speculates that the narrator also wants to eat flowers but will not allow herself to indulge in her desire for fear of public censure. The old woman suggests that they go out for a walk to the park, and the narrator readily agrees to the outing. As they begin their walk, the narrator begins to doubt the sincerity of the old woman's assertions that she also has impaired vision because the old woman walks so assuredly, even going so far as to guide the narrator at busy intersections and the like. Once they arrive at the park, they observe an androgynous-looking couple openly displaying their affection for one another in public and recall the strict upbringing which prohibited women of their generation from exhibiting such behavior. Then the old woman spies a young man and urges the narrator to approach him. When the narrator stands up, a flock of pigeons fly off at her sudden movement, creating a flurry of feathers and dust, obscuring her already reduced vision.

In the next instant, a young man in a black suit appears suddenly before her eyes as the dust stirred up by the pigeons settles. He speaks to her in a familiar manner, yet the narrator does not identify the youth for readers. Apparently the young man is a friend of the narrator's older brother and had gone over to visit the older brother who had gone on a fishing trip. The young man asks the narrator what she has been reading, and she replies that she had come to this particular library because this was the only branch to have translations of foreign plays, and that the one she had read that day was a play called "Strife" by English playwright John Galsworthy. The young man expounds his hatred of faces of women who have been reading books and warns the narrator against reading books and admonishes her not to look for happiness in the world of books. This angers the narrator who is tempted to say that the young man probably likes the faces of women who have been performing domestic duties in the kitchen all day long, but manages to suppress the urge as being a sign of immaturity. The young man invites the narrator to have coffee and sweets at a cafe, but the narrator refuses him thinking that it would be inappropriate. After the young man leaves her, she becomes upset at the words the young man had spoken to her about hating the faces of women who had been reading books. She finds his remarks about women being obsessed reading books ridiculous, but the thought suddenly occurs to her that perhaps she had become just as he had warned her about. She read all the books she felt she ought to read all through her life and as a result of overindulging in her love of reading, the books she loved to read had actually succeeded in robbing her of her sight. This irony is not lost on the narrator but she states that if that youth were still alive today, he could no longer tell her not to read books because she, in fact, was not able to read books anymore with her disability. The only thing that the youth could do, the narrator says, was to drop a bundle of letters onto her lap, making her recall the past.

As the narrator looks about, the sun has set and the old woman with whom she had gone on the outing is nowhere in sight. She begins picking her way along the dusky path looking for the old woman in the flower garden with chrysanthemums. The narrative breaks off at this point.

As Enchi grew older, the age of her female protagonists kept pace with the author's own aging process. Many narratives by Enchi focus on aged female protagonists who possess a mysterious, youthful quality in some physical attribute or aspect of their personality.

The youthful element in old women placed against a background of women's role in the Shinto tradition seems to suggest connotations with religion. But what is the significance of the religious connotation of women in Shintoism?

The white-haired old woman in "The Old Woman Who Eats Flowers," with radiant skin and a "mysterious brightness in her eyes like those of a young girl," harks back to a theme from traditional Japan which treated elderly white-haired people as those with divine connections. For example, in the introduction to the translation of the historical tale Ōkagami (The Great Mirror, ca. 12th c.), Helen Craig McCullough makes the following connection between elderly white-haired people and the divine:

> Indigenous Japanese divinities (kami) appear with remarkable frequency in the guise of white-haired old people. We find them in Takasago, Hakurakuten, Chikubushima, Awaji, and many other Noh plays; in setsuwa collections; and in other written and oral literature of all kinds, including The Great Mirror. Yanagita Kunio has observed that such deities usually turn out to be associated with water, as in the well-known case of the Sumiyoshi gods; that it was once customary in parts of northeastern Japan to refer to floods as "white hair waters" and that there is still a tendency among his countrymen to seek a hidden meaning in premature white hair (for example, by calling it "lucky white hair"), which, in his view, may be traceable to a feeling that such people were in touch with the gods. However that may be, the connection between old age and the supernatural seems to have been a powerful one, and we are probably justified in concluding that the author has it in mind, at least subconsciously, when he calls Yotsugi utatage, a word that might be translated as eerie. (19)

Enchi's use of an elderly woman with white hair falls within the parameters described by McCullough, however Enchi subverts the traditional application of white hair to the divine by alluding to elements of youth within aged women. By utilizing a white-haired old woman as an embodiment of a kami, perhaps Enchi is proposing that one should follow one's desire rather than worry about societal censure. Not only does Enchi tap traditional Japanese sources in this short narrative, but her reference to Greek mythology in the discussion conducted by the two old women concerning flowers and their relationship to human beings suggests further symbolic significance.

Flowers symbolically refer to the evanescence of life, and to the transience of beauty, youth, and spring. Further, colors symbolically signify specific ideas, with the color red indicating a relationship with blood, passion, and animals. The fact that the "I" narrator imagines that the mouth of the old woman appears "blood-stained" when she was eating the red crab-cactus flower suggests the relevance of this particular color symbolism. This, combined with the fact that both the "I" narrator and the old woman are aged and perhaps seeking to recapture lost youth, brings the symbolic use of flowers into further prominence. Moreover, the metaphysical discussion on the nature of desire by the old women supports the concept that flowers suggest passion, or more specifically, the attempt to gain that which has been lost. The symbolic use of flowers as a connotation for lost youth can be discerned in narratives from other ancient cultures. The fact that the white-haired old woman eats the mottled red blossoms of the *shako shaboten* (crab cactus), suggests an attempt to recapture that which has been lost.

In *The Epic of Gilgamesh* (ca. 3000 B.C.E.), Gilgamesh is informed of a flower growing at the bed of the sea, which if eaten, would grant immortality. The following recounts the revelations of the wife of Utnapishtim the Faraway, the only human beings granted the status of immortality in the tale:

> Gilgamesh, I shall reveal a secret thing, it is a mystery of the gods
> I am telling you. There is a plant that grows under the water, it has
> a prickle like a thorn, like a rose; it will wound your hand, but if
> you succeed in taking it, then your hands will hold that which
> restores his lost youth to a man. (Sandars, 116)

Gilgamesh laboriously retrieved the flower from the water and began the journey home to share the flower with the old men who lived in his hometown of Uruk, naming the flower "The Old Men Are Young Again." However, while resting beside a well of cool water, a serpent ate the flower before Gilgamesh could take it home. Thus Gilgamesh was denied the chance to eat the flower which would have granted him everlasting life and which would have restored the vitality of youth to the old men of Uruk. Gilgamesh's attempt to ward off the effects of aging and to escape the inevitability of death are reminders of the fate that awaits all human beings. However, Enchi's reference to the Greek myths seems to indicate cases of metamorphosis from human into botanical form.

There are a few cases in Greek mythology where human beings are transformed into botanical form.[18] In the case of Hyacinthus, a flower springs forth from the blood of the beautiful youth who was accidentally killed when he was hit on the head by a discus thrown by Apollo. Unlike the flower called by that name today, the hyacinth of Greek legend was shaped like a lily and was blood-colored, either a deep purple or splendid crimson. Hyacinthus represents the death of youths just as they approach the full bloom of their beauty.

Next is Adonis, from whose blood sprang forth a blood-red flower called the anemone. The handsome blossom of the anemone matures quickly but flourishes only briefly, supporting the concept that the flower is similar to Adonis who died in the full bloom of youth. Adonis met his end while hunting a wild boar although he had been warned by Aphrodite to avoid ferocious beasts. Adonis hit a boar with an arrow but succeeded only in wounding it, after which the maddened boar tore him to pieces.

Finally, there is Narcissus, a youth loved by countless women for his beauty, but who cruelly rejected the love of all who approached him. As retribution the goddess Nemesis (righteous anger) caused him to fall in love with his own reflection in a pool of water. He pined away from unrequited love and after his death, a flower of deep purple color sprang from where his body had lain, signifying a connection with death in the bloom of youth. Edith Hamilton conjectures that the connection of the color red may denote the blood spilt during the ancient practice of human sacrifice to propitiate the gods (85–91). This may have formed the basis of a symbolic connotation between red flowers and the images of blood and passion.

It is significant that in both the Sumerian epic and Greek myth flowers are symbolically linked to youth: in *Gilgamesh* a flower, if eaten, enabled an aged individual to recover lost youth, and in the Greek myths, red flowers sprang forth from the blood of Hyacinthus, Adonis, and Narcissus, all of whom died in the bloom of youth. The symbolic use of flowers with the same ties to youth is also to be found in the myth and folklore of the East.

The final allusion made to flowers within the narrative is to the chrysanthemum, with its origin in Chinese tradition. In Chinese culture it was believed that if chrysanthemum dew, collected by placing cotton covers over the flowers at night, were rubbed over the body, it would ward off old age and prolong life. This belief was adopted by the Japanese aristocracy during the Nara (710–94) and Heian (794–1185) periods, and appears in literary texts of the Kamakura period (1185–1333) as well.[19] Because the author of this narrative was a noted classical scholar, the aged "I" narrator's search for the garden with chrysanthemums at the end of the narrative may suggest an attempt to ward off old age, to prolong life, or more specifically, to recapture lost youth.

Enchi's allusions to the mythology of the West combined with traditional themes from the mythos of premodern Japan point to her concern to explore the idea of lost youth as she faced the process of aging and accompanying physical limitations. The symbolic use of flowers as a major motif in the narrative emphasizes the ephemerality of spring, beauty, and youth. As the body begins to fail in old age, the narrator and the white-haired old woman in this narrative begin a foray into hyper-reality.

Although Enchi usually conjures up the supernatural world through the image of *miko* (medium, shaman), in this narrative she uses the physical ailment of an old woman's impaired sight as the vehicle to transport readers to the "other" world.[20] In the opening paragraph of the narrative, we are told that the two elderly female protagonists share the physical ailment of impaired sight which causes the "I" narrator to feel that "various kinds of ghostly apparitions which dwelt within [her]" had begun to manifest themselves in her daily life. The narrator's imagination becomes overactive as "the windows to her outside world" begin to close.

The narrator's impaired sight acts as a catalyst for several other antirational occurrences. For example, the narrator's reduced vision leads her to recreate events from her past without indicating to us that the events being described have departed from the ebb and flow of the narrative present. Clues in the narrative read in hindsight confirm the fact that although the narrator does not want to dwell on the past, ghostly apparitions succeed in subverting her intention not to do so and creating images from the past in a vivid and seductive manner. Antirational occurrences can create confusion for readers who breeze through the narrative.

Not only is the narrator faced with ghostly images conjured up by her faulty vision but she is also faced with supernatural occurrences which are presumably caused by the spirit of a former "boyfriend" from her youth. The narrator begins an attempt to deconstruct personal cultural mythologies involving marriage, romantic love, respectability, and the like, within the narrative.

I propose that the metaphysical conversation between the two old women is actually a dialogue between two opposing aspects of the narrator: one who does what she pleases and the other who is hindered by public opinion. Enchi once said that "I claim no clear understanding of existentialism or mysticism, but I have come to cultivate a hypothesis that there exists another me and another object of my life in a realm apart from the one which this body of mine inhabits" (Sodekawa, 94).

In the trilogy *Wandering Spirit*, it is clear that Enchi began exploring fantastic themes as she grew older and faced the physical constraints of failing eyesight. In the narrative "Wandering Spirit," Enchi delves into the world of fantasy with the character Suo, a female writer in her late sixties who by chance encounters the "other woman," an aspect of herself that is not bound by social constraints. Readers are made cognizant of the fact that the "other woman" of Suo is actually her "real self," one whose spirit leaves her body to fulfill assignations with younger men. However, Suo's double is quite considerate and never fails to ask Suo's permission before going off to substitute for Suo at assignations.

The theme of two aspects of a female protagonist that interact with one another is further developed in "Foxfire." When the aged protagonist Shio is gazing at a reflection of herself in a three-sided mirror, she sees an image of herself as a young girl of about seventeen or eighteen while looking at her present self as an old woman. As Shio gazes at a reflection of herself in a mirror and sees herself as she was in the past and as she is in the present, the distinction between the past and present is conflated, producing an eerie atmosphere and supporting the premise that the dialogue between the two old women in "The Old Woman Who Eats Flowers" may have been a discussion between two aspects of one character, one who is free to pursue her desires and one who is constrained by social censure.

It is important to recognize the historical connection between foxes and the supernatural. In premodern Japan, it was believed that foxes had the capacity to bewitch human beings, that is, they were capable of transforming themselves into human form, having sexual relations, producing offspring, and the like. In Japanese folklore, foxes were thought to be messengers of the Inari god, one of the myriad gods of the indigenous Shinto religion. It was also believed that foxes emitted fire from their mouths, which could be seen late at night in remote recesses of the countryside. This "foxfire" is semantically related to the English definition which denotes a phosphorescent glow. Further connotations of "foxfire" reveal extensions into a "foolish passion," a "delusive or misleading goal," or a "mysterious fire."

Another striking similarity of "Foxfire" to "The Old Woman Who Eats Flowers" involves an uncanny event which befalls the female protagonist Shio (Sodekawa, 71). On Shio's wall there was a Hiroshige woodblock print on which white foxes were depicted cavorting around a catalpa tree "like graceful nude women." Sud-

denly the foxes take on material form and "fall down on Shio
without a sound." Similarly in "The Old Woman Who Eats Flowers," the "I" narrator is startled when a bundle of old letters falls
onto her lap while she was straightening up her closet, because she
knew that she had placed the bundle of letters into the bottom of the
letterbox. The narrative leads readers to believe that the young man
from the narrator's past caused the letters to somehow work their
way from the bottom of the letterbox and fall onto the narrator's lap,
making her recall her past and consequently recall the person to
whom the letters were addressed. In a similar vein, there is a scene
in "The Voice of a Snake" in which the female protagonist enters a
scene depicted in a woodblock print hanging on the wall of her room
and begins interacting with the girls in the print, heightening the
sense of departure from conventional realism. "Foxfire," "Wandering Spirit," and "The Voice of a Snake" deal specifically with contrasts between free and restrained aspects of a person, aspects of the
young and the old within a character, and antirational and rational
occurrences.

The use of fantasy and the reliance on antirational elements in
literature by women has drawn the following comment from critic
Rosemary Jackson in *Fantasy: The Literature of Subversion*:

> Anti-rational, it is the inverse side of reason's orthodoxy. It reveals
> reason and reality to be arbitrary, shifting constructs and thereby
> scrutinizes the category of the 'real'. Contradictions surface and are
> held antinomically in the fantastic text, as reason is made to
> confront all that it traditionally refuses to encounter. (21)

Further, literary critic Anne Cranny-Francis in *Feminist Fantasy:
Feminist Uses of Generic Fiction* interprets science fiction writer
Ursula K. LeGuin and critic Rosemary Jackson's ideas on fantasy in
the following manner:

> Both LeGuin and Jackson present a case for fantasy as a potentially
> subversive literary form, subversive not only of other literary
> forms, but also of the means by which we construct and verify the
> real. Those means are the discourses which are encoded in the
> narrative and generic conventions of texts and which categorize
> experience in crucial ways, validating or denying it in relation to
> dominant ideologies. In a patriarchal society the experience of
> women is commonly denied, invalidated, by reference to the domi-
> nant gender discourse of sexism; the sphere of activity open to
> women is severely circumscribed, while women's experience of
> injustice is denied a voice. Women, the experiential subjects rather

than the idealist construct, are not only invisible; they are entirely imperceptible. Feminist fantasy explores the problems of being for women in a society which denies them not only visibility but also subjectivity. It scrutinizes the categories of the patriarchal real, revealing them to be arbitrary, shifting constructs: the subjugation of women is not a "natural" characteristic, but an ideological process. Feminist fantasy explores the contradictions elided by the (patriarchal) real; for example, that women are both inside patriarchal ideology, as the essential Woman, and outside it, as the (repressed and denied) experiential subjects. In this encounter women as active subjects become perceptible, and the feminine construct of patriarchy, Woman, is revealed as a negotiation inimical to women as subjects. (77)

Fantasy defamiliarizes and deconstructs the real, creating the necessity for readers to reevaluate the societal norms of their culture, casting aside the familiar and forcing an objective view of one's own culture in a way that a stranger might view an alien culture.

Literary critic Nancy A. Walker states the following about deconstructing cultural mythologies in her work, *Feminist Alternatives: Irony and Fantasy in the Contemporary Novel by Women*:

the contemporary woman novelist understands the power of language to both control and subvert the control of authority. Not only do irony and fantasy depend for their force upon a recognition of verbal constructions, but authors must maneuver around the language of dominant discourse in order to deconstruct cultural mythologies, including the myths that women construct about their own lives. (8)

If the use of fantasy in literature by women is considered by feminist critics to be a subversive activity, then the theme of "The Old Woman Who Eats Flowers" does not differ radically from those found in the majority of Enchi's oeuvre. In fact, the use of fantasy, the antirational, and the lack of temporal progression obscures the subversive intention of the narrative which challenges the validity of certain cultural myths. The notion of romantic love, for example, is deconstructed by reducing the relationship between the narrator and the young man to a foolish and immature infatuation. Further deconstructing that notion is the fact that the young man continued with his obsession with the narrator until his old age, prompting his widow to return the letters the man had kept throughout the years as a precious keepsake. Yet ironically the narrator clings to the image that the man retained of her as a young girl who was then still unsullied by the world. The dilemma between intention and action hangs precariously in the balance.

The most notable use of irony is poignantly leveled at the narrator's love of books. She notes with biting irony that the books she had indulged herself in reading throughout her life had in the end caused her to loose her sight. She then recalls the words spoken by the young man admonishing her in her youth not to become obsessed by books. Now the narrator states that she *couldn't* read books even if she wanted to because her eyes were too damaged to read. At this point, it is tempting to state that the irony expressed by the narrator could be applied as well to Enchi Fumiko, who in 1973 had been operated for the second time for a detached retina. The operation never succeeded in restoring her sight so that she had to resort to the use of an amanuensis to continue producing her narratives. Whether Enchi Fumiko really believed that over-indulgence in books had caused her to loose her sight or not, the application of irony in the case of the aged female narrator in this narrative serves to deconstruct another cultural myth, one that reflects the Confucian morality of the Meiji period (1868–1912) during which Enchi was born. Enchi succeeds in debunking the cultural myth that women would be better off without acquiring too much knowledge or education. The narrator never regrets the path she has chosen for herself, despite the fact that women of the Meiji period were often faced with the dilemma of choosing between personal desires and the dictates placed on them by Confucian morality.

A conflict between the fulfillment and the suppression of desire is posed for the sake of deconstructing the cultural myth of respectability, addressed in the course of the dialogue between the narrator and the white-haired old woman as two aspects of a single character. The white-haired old woman can be taken as an aspect of the narrator that acknowledges the need to fulfill her desires, while the narrator is too conscious of social censure to make an attempt to fulfill her desires. When at the end of the narrative, the narrator walks toward the chrysanthemum garden in search of the white-haired old woman, not only is she seeking the "fountain of youth" contained in the image of the chrysanthemum but she is also hoping to reclaim the more impulsive part of her personality, the side which actively seeks to fulfill her desire. Without the more daring side of her personality, the aged narrator is left "picking her way along the dusky path" unable to see clearly and without the independent part of her character that could help lead her toward a resolution.

The exact nature of desire is not addressed in the narrative but during the metaphysical discussion between the two aspects of the narrator, desire is couched in terms of the "way a man loves a woman." The trademark theme exploring the nature of sexual desire is still apparent in this text written in the author's old age, but here it has been placed into the realm of metaphysics and takes into account a fate which awaits all human kind. The process of aging has reinforced the concept of ephemerality which impelled Gilgamesh to seek a balm to cure the malady that is the bane of all human beings. In the same way that mythic heroes of the distant past sought immortality through brave deeds to be sung by bards, Enchi chose to make her mark in the world of language in a unique and expressive manner, defying convention for the sake of personal expression and art.

Summary

In summary, I have discussed the texts of Enchi Fumiko in terms of the development of female characters from stage one in which women were depicted bearing oppression in a stoic manner on the outside while inside they longed to find a means of revenge for injustices suffered in polygynous households in patriarchal society. In stage two Enchi developed a host of female characters who delved deep within themselves to find a core of strength and empowerment through the shamanistic powers of the *miko*. Due to the nature of *miko*, Enchi's fictional world in stage two became an eerie place visited by spirits and ghosts from the "other" world. In the final stage, Enchi tired of conventional realism and began exploring the world of myth and fantasy, producing texts in which the antirational and the transtemporal was the norm, creating a ripple in our sense of reality and a warp in the normal flow of time.

Woven into the texts featuring the development of empowered females are the ever present references and allusions to the classical literary canon. Enchi's avocation as a classical scholar is never far below the surface of her literary fabric and her erudition often serves as a springboard for her creative fabrications. Enchi proclaims her literary debt to the tradition of women writers of the Heian period promoting the dissemination of their literary endeavors through her fiction and her scholarly articles and translations of their canon into modern Japanese. Occasionally Enchi expanded the scope of her literary allusions to the mythologies of the West to enrich the well of tradition she tapped.

Enchi's literary masterpiece, *A Tale of False Oracles*, stands as a testament to her skill as a narrator and a storyteller. She works on multiple levels of fabrication and deceit, weaving a work as complex as any wrought in the classical period. She takes up where the women writers of the classical period laid down their brushes, painting a horizon with its roots in the past but which also expressed concerns for the contemporary world in which she lived.

One of Enchi's most significant accomplishments is that she found a literary voice of her own, one which pays conscious tribute to the pioneer voices of women writers of the Heian period. In exploring their works for literary inspiration, she played the role of medium conjuring up their memory for modern readers, but she often subverted the original message to fit the needs of women in a postmodern context. She has made an enormous contribution to the literary tradition she inherited from the women writers of the Heian masterpieces and has established a contemporary tradition of excellence which will be hard to surpass. Although her literary creations are difficult to decipher, it is indeed a worthy venture to invest time in divining the true purpose behind the texts she weaves so skillfully. Enchi is a rare genius, one of the most memorable writers of modern Japan, and no doubt further discussion of her works will appear in the future as scholars begin to explore her collection.

Bibliography

Works in Translation

Enchi Fumiko. "A Bond for Two Lifetimes—Gleanings" ("Nise no en shūi," 1957). Tr. Phyllis Birnbaum. *Rabbits, Crabs, Etc.* Ed. Phyllis Birnbaum. Honolulu: University of Hawaii Press, 1983.

————. "A Boxcar of Chrysanthemums" ("Kikuguruma," 1967). Tr. Yukiko Tanaka and Elizabeth Hanson. *This Kind of Woman: Ten Stories by Japanese Women Writers 1960–1976.* New York: Putnam, 1982.

————. "Enchantress" ("Yō," 1956). Tr. John Bester. *Modern Japanese Short Stories.* Comp. the Japan Quarterly Editorial Board. Tokyo: Japan Publications, Inc., 1960, 72–93.

————. *Masks* (*Onnamen*, 1958). Tr. Juliet Winters Carpenter. New York: Knopf, 1983; Tokyo: Tuttle, 1984.

————. "The Old Woman Who Eats Flowers" ("Hana kui uba," 1974). Tr. S. Yumiko Hulvey. *Mānoa* (Winter 1994).

————. "Skeletons of Men" ("Otoko no hone," 1956). Tr. Susan Matisoff. *Japan Quarterly* 35/4 (1988): 417–26.

————. *The Waiting Years* (*Onnazaka*, 1949–57). Tr. John Bester. Tokyo: Kôdansha International, 1971.

Mishima Yukio. "Onnagata" in *Death in Midsummer*. New York: New Directions, 1966.

Murasaki Shikubu. *Tale of Genji* (*Genji monogatari*, ca. 1010). Tr. Edward Seidensticker. New York: Knopf, 1978.

The Epic of Gilgamesh. Tr. N. K. Sandars. London: Penguin, 1960.

Critical Writings

Bargen, Doris G. "Twin Blossoms on a Single Branch: The Cylce of Retribution in *Onnamen*." *Monumenta Nipponica* 46/2 (1991), 147–71.

Barthes, Roland. "From Work to Text," in *Textual Strategies: Perspectives in Post-Structural Criticism*. Ed. Josue V. Harari. Ithaca: Cornell University Press, 1979.

Blacker, Carmen. *The Catalpa Bow: A Study of Shamanistic Practices in Japan*. London: George Allen and Unwin, 1986.

Cranny-Francis, Anne. *Feminist Fiction: Feminist Uses of Generic Fiction*. New York: St. Martin's Press, 1990.

Crumbley, Deidre Helen. "Impurity and Power: Women in Aladura Churches." *Africa* 62/4 (1992), 505–22.

de Man, Paul. "Genesis and Genealogy in Nietzsche's *The Birth of Tragedy*." *Diacritics* 2 (Winter 1972).

Eliade, Mircea. *Mephistopheles and the Androgyne: Studies in Religious Myth and Symbol*. Tr. J. M. Cohen. New York: Sheed and Ward, 1965.

————. *Myths, Dreams and Mysteries: The Encounter Between Contemporary Faiths and Archaic Realities*. Tr. Philip Mairet. New York: Harper Torchbooks, 1957.

Gessel, Van C. "The 'Medium' of Fiction: Fumiko Enchi as Narrator." *World Literature Today: A Literary Quarterly of the University of Oklahoma* 62/3 (1988), 380–85.

Grapard, Allan G. "Visions of Excess and Excesses of Vision—Women and Transgression in Japanese Myth." *Japanese Journal of Religious Studies* 18/1 (1991), 3–22.

Hamilton, Edith. *Mythology: Timeless Tales of Gods and Heroes.* New York: New American Library, 1940.

Hulvey, S. Yumiko. "Enchi Fumiko," in *Japanese Women Writers: A Bio-Critical Source Book.* Ed. Chieko Mulhern. Westport, CT: Greenwood Press, forthcoming.

———. "The Nocturnal Muse: A Study and Partial Translation of *Ben no Naishi nikki,* a Thirteenth-Century Poetic Memoir." Ph.D. Diss., University of California, Berkeley, 1989.

Jackson, Rosemary. *Fantasy: The Literature of Subversion.* London: Macmillan, 1981.

Knapp, Bettina L. "Fumiko Enchi's *Masks:* A Sacred Mystery," in Knapp, ed., *Women in Twentieth-Century Literature: A Jungian View.* University Park: Pennsylvania State University Press, 1987.

McClain, Yōko. "Eroticism and the Writings of Enchi Fumiko," *Journal of the Association of Teachers of Japanese* 15/1 (1980), 32–46.

McCullough, Helen Craig. *Ōkagami: The Great Mirror.* Princeton: Princeton University Press, 1980.

———. *Tales of Ise: Lyrical Episodes from Tenth-Century Japan.* Stanford: Stanford University Press, 1968.

McCullough, William H. "Marriage Institutions in the Heian Period," *Harvard Journal of Asiatic Studies* 27 (1967), 103–67.

——— and Helen Craig McCullough. *A Tale of Flowering Fortunes: Annals of Japanese Aristocratic Life in the Heian Period,* 2 vols. Stanford: Stanford University Press, 1980.

Pounds, Wayne. "Enchi Fumiko and the Hidden Energy of the Supernatural." *Journal of the Association of Teachers of Japanese* 24/2 (1990), 167–83.

Sodekawa, Hiromi. "Enchi Fumiko: A Study of the Self-Expression of Women." M.A. Thesis, University of British Columbia, 1988.

Walker, Nancy A. *Feminist Alternatives: Irony and Fantasy in the Contemporary Novel by Women.* Jackson: University Press of Mississipi, 1990.

Texts in Japanese

Enchi Fumiko. "Hana kui uba." Vol. 5 of *Enchi Fumiko zenshū* (Complete Works of Enchi Fumiko). 16 vols. Tokyo: Shinchōsha, 1978 [hereafter EFZ].

———. "Keshō." Vol. 5 of *EFZ.*

———. "Monogatari to tanpen." Vol. 16 of *EFZ*.

———. *Namamiko monogatari* in *Enchi Fumiko shū*. Vol. 37 of *Shinchō Nihon bungaku*. 64 vols. Tokyo: Shinchôsha, 1971.

———. "Nise no en—shūi." Vol. 2 in *EFZ*.

———. "Otoko no hone." Vol. 2 of *EFZ*.

———. *Onnazaka* in *Enchi Fumiko shū*. Vol. 37 of *Shinchō Nihon bungaku*.

———. *Onnamen*. Tokyo: Shinchōsha, 1966.

———. *Saimu*. Vol. 13 of *EFZ*.

———. "Yō." Vol. 2 of *EFZ*.

———. *Yūkon*. Vol. 5 of *EFZ*.

Heike monogatari. Vols. 29–30 of *Nihon koten bungaku zenshū*. 51 vols. Ed. Ichiko Teiji. Tokyo: Shōgakukan, 1975.

Ise monogatari. Vol. 8 of *Nihon koten bungaku zenshū*. Ed. Katagiri Yōichi, Fukui Teisuke, Takahashi Shōji, and Shimizu Yoshiko. Tokyo: Shōgakukan, 1972.

Kamei Hideo and Ogasawara Yoshiko. *Enchi Fumiko no sekai* (The World of Enchi Fumiko). Tokyo: Sōrinsha, 1981.

Murasaki Shikibu. *Genji monogatari*. Vols. 12–17 of *Nihon koten bungaku zenshū*. Ed. Abe Akio, Akiyama Ken, and Imai Gen'e. Tokyo: Shōgakukan, 1976.

Ueda Akinari. "Nise no enishi." *Harusame monogatari*. Vol. 48 of *Nihon koten bungaku zenshū*. Ed. Nakamura Yukihiko, Takada Mamoru, and Nakamura Hiroyasu. Tokyo: Shōgakukan, 1973, 511–17.

Yoru no nezame monogatari. Vol. 19 of *Nihon koten bungaku zenshū*. Ed. Suzuki Kazuo. Tokyo: Shōgakukan, 1974.

Notes

1. There are numerous extant works by women writers of the Heian and Kamakura (1185–1333) periods available in English translation: *The Gossamer Years* (*Kagerō nikki*, ca. late 10th c.) by Fujiwara Michitsuna's mother, tr. Edward Seidensticker; *The Pillow Book of Sei Shōnagon* (*Makura no sōshi*, 11th. c.) by Kiyowara Motosuke's daughter, tr. Ivan Morris; *The Murasaki Shikibu Diary* (*Murasaki Shikibu nikki*, 11th c.) by Murasaki Shikibu, tr. Richard Bowring; *The Izumi Shikibu Diary: A Romance of the Heian Court* (*Izumi Shikibu nikki*, 11th c.) tr. Edwin A. Cranston; *A Tale of Flowering Fortunes* (*Eiga monogatari*, ca. 1030s–40s?)

by Akazome Emon, tr. William H. and Helen Craig McCullough; *As I Crossed a Bridge of Dreams* (*Sarashina nikki*, ca. 1060) by Sugawara Takasue's daughter, tr. Ivan Morris; *The Tale of Nezame* (*Yowa/Yoru no nezame*, ca. 1060) attributed to Sugawara Takasue's daughter, tr. Carol Hochstedler; *The Emperor Horikawa Diary* (*Sanuki no Suke nikki*, ca. 1107) by Fujiwara Nagako, tr. Jennifer Brewster; *The Poetic Memoirs of Lady Daibu* (*Kenreimon-in Ukyō no Daibu shū*, ca. late 12th c.) by Fujiwara Koreyuki's daughter, tr. Phillip Tudor Harries; Kamakura period: *The Journal of the Sixteenth-Night Moon* (*Izayoi nikki*, ca. 1280) by the nun Abutsu, tr. by Helen Craig McCullough in *Classical Japanese Prose: An Anthology*; and *The Confessions of Lady Nijō* (*Towazugatari*, ca. 14th c.) by Minamoto (Koga) Masatada's daughter, tr. Karen Brazell.

2. Paul de Man, "Genesis and Genealogy in Neitzsche's *The Birth of Tragedy*," 51.

3. Van C. Gessel in "The 'Medium' of Fiction: Fumiko Enchi as Narrator," 380–85, suggests that *A Tale of False Oracles* (*Namamiko monogatari*) is Enchi's masterpiece. Gessel supports his high regard for the text by citing similar opinions expressed by scholars Takenishi Hiroko ("Namamiko monogatari ron," *Tenbō*, January 1967, 171) and Saeki Shōichi (conversation with Gessel soon after Enchi's death in November 1986). The complex trifold level of narration introduced by Gessel in his article inspired the present study. I also adopted Gessel's translation of *A Tale of False Oracles* for *Namamiko monogatari* for use in my study. Typical readers are likely to disregard the significance of Enchi speaking in her own voice to establish legitimacy in the text she is constructing, thereby promoting a misreading of the author's intention in creating the complicated narrative levels. Such a reading of the text will produce an atypically happy marriage between Ichijô and Teishi, quite out of keeping with Enchi's preoccupation with unhappy marriages as the norm in her textual worlds. Finally, *Namamiko monogatari* was awarded the Women Writers' Prize in 1966, further substantiating the claim by critics that this is her literary masterpiece.

4. For the idea of treating Enchi's themes along developmental lines, I am indebted to Hiromi Sodekawa, "Enchi Fumiko: A Study in the Self-Expression of Women," M.A. thesis, University of British Columbia, 1988. Although the idea of analyzing Enchi's works in terms of developmental lines was inspired by Sodekawa's study, I do not agree with the conclusions drawn in her analysis. We differ most sharply in the analysis of the final stage of development in which Sodekawa concentrates on the inspiration of themes due to the effects of old age, loneliness, and the fear of death. Sodekawa fails to consider Enchi's conscious decision to adopt antirational techniques in order to create a fantasy world and to challenge conventional realism by departing from temporal progression. Enchi's quest to create a new type of writing, I suggest, was fulfilled in the 1970s by delving into the

world of myth and fantasy through the image of empowered women in the third stage of development.

5. *Ituski no in, Itsuki no miya,* and *Itsuki no miko,* derived from the verb *itsuku* (to observe purification rites in reverence of the gods or the emperor), refer to those who in their capacity as the Kamo or Ise Virgins observe a period of abstinence and purification prior to performing sacerdotal functions for the gods or emperors.

6. The following is a translation of the *Nihon bungaku daijiten* quoted in *A Tale of False Oracles:* "Chanburen (Basil Hall Chamberlain) linguist. Born in Portsmouth, England in 1850 (3rd year of Ka"ei) and died on 25 February 1936 at the age of eighty-six. In his youth he studied many languages at a school in Versailles, France and devoted many years to the study of literature, but at the age of eighteen he went to work for a bank in England. However, he became ill due to overindulgence in the pursuit of his studies, and on the advice of a doctor embarked on an ocean voyage for Tokyo where he diligently began the study of Japanese literature. . . . In 1887 (19th year of Meiji) he was employed by the Ministry of Education, then became a university lecturer at the Tokyo Imperial University where he was the linguist in charge of Japanese classes. But in 1891 he had to resign his post due to an illness and returned to England. . . . Thereafter he frequently visited Japan to continue his research but in 1911 he set out on his final research voyage, and in 1912 announced his farewell to Japan after having lived there for almost forty years. . . . After having returned to England, he felt that the 11,000 'rare private collection' of Chinese and Japanese books that he had collected over a number of years for his library should be returned to Japan where they would be of more use than in Europe, so he bequeathed the entire library to Ueda Kazutoshi, a testament to Chamberlain's eloquence and character as a scholar."

7. *Fukurotoji,* traditional Japanese book binding method in which sheets of paper folded in half are bound with the loose ends collected together to form the "spine" of the book. The volumes are held together by a string that is threaded through tiny holes drilled through the paper and bound securely by tying the string. The exterior edge of the page in Japanese binding was folded, unlike Western binding in which edges of the page consisted of loose sheets of paper.

8. English titles for chapters 3, 4, and 5 were adopted from McCullough and McCullough, tr. *A Tale of Flowering Fortunes,* vol. 1 (Stanford University Press, 1980).

9. The language employed by Enchi in the original: Ichijō no mikado no ontoki, kisaki futari owashimashikeri. Saki no kisaki wa, Fujiwara Teishi, kore wa Naka no Kanpaku Michitaka kō no onmusume nari. Nochi yori mairitamaishi wa Midōdono (Michinaga) no Ōhimegimi, Fujiwara

Shōshi to mōshitatematsuru. Go-Ichijō, Go-Suzaku no onhaha, Jōtōmon-in kore nari.

10. Enchi's modern Japanese style reflects the standard dialect of the Kantō district, the dialect native to Enchi born in Tokyo. It differs greatly from the dialect spoken by the aristocracy of the Heian period who resided in Kyōto, in the heart of the Kansai district. Writers such as Kawabata Yasunari (1899–1972) and Oda Sakunosuke (1913–1947) born and raised in the Kansai exhibit signs of the southern dialect in their texts, signs of which are missing in writers from the Tokyo area such as Akutagawa Ryūnosuke (1892–1927) and Mishima Yukio (1925–70). Tokyo-born author Tanizaki Jun'ichirō (1886–1965) resorted to hiring native speakers of the Osaka dialect to edit his written attempts to capture dialogue in the southern dialect. By way of contrast, Enchi made no attempt to adapt her style to fit the mold of the Kansai.

11. The original language Enchi used: Shôryaku gannen no shōgatsu itsuka ni mikado (Ichijō mikado) wa genpuku asobasareta. Mada jūichisai no shōnen de, dōgyō ga outsukush ikatta noni to oshimi au hitobito mo atta ga, mikushi o agete kakansareta osugata mo ochiisai nagara totonotte rippa ni omie ni natta.

Nigatsu ni wa Naidaijin Michitaka kō no ōhimegimi ga judaisareru node, sono onreigi no junbi ni dairi mo Naidaijinke mo bōsatsusareteiru. Naidaijin no Kita no kata wa, Yamato no kami Takashina no Naritada no onmusume de mukashi Kō no naishi to itte miyazukae mo shita kata nanode, kyūchū no yōsu nado ni wa yoku tsūjiteirareru. Omo-omoshiku okubukai yō na koto wa okirai de, imayō ni hanabanashii fū o okonomi ni naru kara, kondo no himegimi no onjudai mo banji sô iu yarikata de aru. Himegimi wa jūroku ni onari ni natteiru node, mikado ni wa itsutsu bakari no otoshiue de irassharu. Judai asobashita sono yo, nyōgo no kurai o ouke ni natta.

12. See bibliography of this chapter for works available in translation, most of which are discussed in this study. *Enchi Fumiko* zenshū (A Complete Collection of Enchi Fumiko, 16 vols.) was published in 1978. However, because Enchi continued to write for eight more years until her death in November 1986, this collection is by no means "complete."

13. Menstrual blood, along with death, was considered a source of pollution and defilement in Shintoism. In *Masks*, Enchi has a male character espouse the following view about menstrual blood: "Because of that trait you seemed at once incomprehensible and unclean to me" (I admit to the unreasonable fastidiousness of the Japanese male, to whom the blood of menstruation is of all blood the dirtiest) (104–5).

In the article "Impurity and Power: Women in Aladura Churches," Deidre Crumbley notes that some men in Yoruba culture hold similar views that menstrual blood is "unclean." Crumbley states that her view of the "uncleanliness" of menstrual blood was revised by Olabiyi Yai who suggested that menstrual blood "commands respect and distance" due to its recognition that it is *the* blood from which life originates (515). This view acknowledges female power and occasionally is accompanied by a fear of the procreative power of women by men.

In "Visions of Excess and Excesses of Vision—Women and Transgression in Japanese Myth," Allan G. Grapard's interpretation of women in the Japanese creation myth is stated in the following manner: "I would submit that the fact that early Japanese cosmography was the spatial projection of certain types of experiences of violence and transgression is of more than passing interest to the historian of religions. In each of the cases analyzed above, this violence ended up codifying women as the natural locus of pollution and as the cultural bearers of propriety in virtue of their having posted the first no-trespassing sign, and men as the perpetrators of a transgression that is deeply rooted in desire—in Japan a desire to see" (21).

14. The concept of "androgyny and wholeness" was derived from chapter 7, "Mother Earth and the Cosmic Hierogamies," of Mircea Eliade's *Myths, Dreams, and Mysteries: The Encounter between Contemporary Faiths and Archaic Realities*, which promotes the idea that "androgyny is an archaic and universal formula for the expression of wholeness, the coexistence of the contraries, or *coincidentia oppositorum*. More than a state of sexual completeness and autarchy, androgyny symbolises the perfection of a primordial, non-conditioned state. It is for this reason that androgyny is not attributed to supreme Beings only. Cosmic Giants, or mythical Ancestors of humanity are also androgynous. Adam, for example, was regarded as an androgyne. The *Bereshit Rabbā* (I.4, fol. 6, col. 2) affirmed that he was "man on the right side and woman on the left side, but God has cloven him into two halves." A mythical Ancestor symbolises the *commencement* of a new mode of existence; and every beginning is made in the wholeness of the being" (174). For further details, see chapter 2, "Mephistopheles and the Androgyne or the Mystery of the Whole," in Mircea Eliade, *Mephistopheles and the Androgyne: Studies in Religious Myth and Symbol*.

15. For further critical articles focusing exclusively on *Masks*, see Doris Bargen, "Twin Blossoms on a Single Branch" and Bettina Knapp, "Fumiko Enchi's *Masks*: A Sacred Mystery."

16. For a literary interpretation of this notion, see Mishima Yukio's "Onnagata" in *Death in Midsummer*.

17. The essay "Monogatari to Tanpen" originally published in *Gunzō*, is also included in vol. 16 of *Enchi Fumiko zenshū*. I had access only to the *zenshū*.

18. Although the image does not correspond exactly (from that of a flower to a tree) and is the creation of the Roman poet Ovid, there is a related episode in *Metamorphosis* in which Daphne, a female nymph, chose

to transform into arboreal form to ward off the unwanted amorous atten-
tions of Apollo. Thereafter, Apollo chose the laurel as his sacred tree to
commemorate his unrequited love for Daphne and adopted the practice of
adorning the heads of heroes with laurel wreaths.

19. In section 11 of *Ben no Naishi nikki* cotton covers to catch dew
were placed on chrysanthemums at night. For details, see S. Yumiko
Hulvey, "The Nocturnal Muse: A Study and Partial Translation of *Ben no
Naishi nikki*, a Thirteenth-Century Poetic Memoir."

20. In 1968 Enchi endured the first of two operations for a detached
retina, just a year after she had begun translating *The Tale of Genji*, a project
which occupied six years of her life. The second occurred in 1973 at the age
of sixty-eight after which Enchi never fully regained her sight. Thereafter
Enchi continued to write by dictating to an amanuensis until her death at
the age of eighty-one in 1986.

Chapter Eight

Tradition, Textuality, and the Trans-lation of Philosophy: The Case of Japan

JOHN C. MARALDO

Part One: Questions

Is Pure Philosophy Free of Tradition?

Philosophers are so accustomed to reflecting on the presuppositions and relevance of their own discipline that this self-reflection seems as essential to philosophizing as anything else. In current debates about the nature of philosophy, the role of tradition looms large as a bone of contention. Does the philosophical tradition serve as a voice of authority, a sounding board for the cogency of present speculation, a model for how to think, and how not to—or a harness to be cast off, just so much baggage to be unloaded, before one is free to philosophize today? All these questions, dealing as they do with one's stance towards past philosophizing, reveal the immense influence of the history of philosophy on the education of philosophers, whether they would recognize or repudiate that history. Those who accept the history of philosophy as authoritative may endeavor to dismantle it, deconstruct its conceptual edifices and expose hidden assumptions that have controlled the way problems are raised. Those who renounce it may discount certain traditional problems altogether and strive to raise and solve others in the name of philosophical progress. Between these two attitudes is an ambivalence about the identity of the philosophical tradition itself, about what counts as past, as well as present, philosophizing. Today among philosophers in North America there is a lively dispute over the issue of tradition. Many so-called pluralists claim that the big questions of the tradition have been picked to death by linguistic analy-

sis, and proclaim that philosophy has become impoverished by lack
of attention to literary and speculative approaches. Some so-called
analysts, whose traditional hegemony in the American Philosophical Association and in academic departments of philosophy is increasingly being challenged, counter that the first business of
philosophy is to address the questions directly and logically, not to
interpret the work of others or of old. "The tradition up to Kant was
analytical," Professor Ruth Barcan Marcus of Yale University announced recently, implying that the less logical, more literary approach to questions is not philosophy.[1] The political acrimony of the
dispute aside, it must be ironic for both sides that the meaning of
tradition itself has become as big a question for philosophy as the
issues of truth, knowledge, reality, and the good.

Although the disputants are at odds over the role and the constitution of the philosophical tradition, more often than not they
equally assume that there is, or should be, *one* tradition and that
this one tradition is simply a matter of what has been handed down
from past philosophers, whoever may be counted among them. Even
when "pluralists" recognize the existence of a plurality of traditions, so as to include Indian or Chinese philosophy, for example,
they tend to take each of these traditions as a fixed body of literature
to be tapped for its historical interest or potential insight. Seldom
considered is the possibility that traditions are shifting entities, and
that the traditionalizing of a select group of texts has become a
condition for doing philosophy.

The problem of the identity of the Japanese philosophical tradition is particularly instructive. For most Japanese philosophers that
tradition begins only with the Meiji-era (1868–1912) introduction of
Western philosophy, while for a few it stretches back into antiquity
and includes Buddhist and Confucian thought. Again for some it
consists of all the work done by academic philosophers in Japan,
while for others only original contributions count, and for still
others only works with a distinctively "Japanese" or "Oriental"
character count as original.[2] In this identification of a Japanese
philosophical tradition the overtly operative criteria are those of
influence, originality, and uniqueness—the uniqueness of philosophy vis-à-vis other forms of thought, and the uniqueness of Japanese
thought vis-à-vis that of other traditions. The problem, however,
also has a hidden side: the transmission of texts, past and present,
that permit the venture unique to philosophy to be shared by a
community. This aspect of the problem is by no means unique to
Japan, but the case of Japan, because of its explicit struggle with the

question of a philosophical tradition, can serve to expose one of the basic preconditions of philosophizing.

Philosophy as a practiced discipline emerges when certain methods, problems and terminologies are advanced by a community of trained people. One learns to philosophize by critically reading written texts, listening to spoken texts, and constructing texts of one's own. Since texts are the mediators of the philosophical endeavor, they form a precondition for philosophizing that may be termed its "textuality." Similarly, the process of mediation by which texts convey philosophical methods, problems and terminology may be called the "trans-lation of philosophy." I use this term to designate not only the transference of texts from one natural language to another, but also the *transformation* of textually embedded problems, methods, and terminologies both across and within natural languages. The "trans-lation" of philosophy is thus both an inter-lingual and an intra-lingual transmission, and it entails the formation of textual traditions. This "trans-lation" constitutes, I will maintain, a *sine qua non* for the practice of philosophizing. Nowhere is this precondition more noticeable, and yet less acknowledged, than in the terminology of those who purport to be doing philosophy freed from dependence on a tradition, who argue about arguments about arguments. Here, however, I return to the case of Japan where the issues of philosophical tradition and translation have been more explicit, and controversial, themes.

The controversy over the meaning and scope of philosophy in Japan began with the Meiji era importation of texts that were taken as examples of a discipline considered novel, even without precedent, in Japanese tradition. One matter in this long-term controversy, the question of whether there is any such thing as *Japanese* philosophy, is widely thought to have been laid to rest by the acceptance of Nishida Kitarō as Japan's first original philosopher. The conditions under which philosophy was established in Japan cannot be made explicit, however, unless we re-open this matter as a question. I begin, therefore, not with the early Meiji controversy, but with the question of Nishida's status as Japan's first philosopher.

Was Nishida Kitarō Japan's First Philosopher?

Raising the question of the reputation of a philosopher would seem a rather academic matter removing us from the *philosophical* issue at hand, the philosopher's work and thought itself—were it not for evidence suggesting that the matter of Nishida's status entails the questions of what philosophy is, and in what sense it existed in premodern Japan or Asia in general. Critics, disciples and neutral reporters alike have shown a remarkable unison in acclaiming Nishida Japan's first original philosopher. Takahashi Satomi's lengthy, critical review of Nishida's pioneer work, *An Inquiry Into the Good (Zen no kenkyū)* in 1912 called it "the first, and only, philosophical work in post-Meiji Japan," "overflowing with *original* thought [with] its own hue and aroma."³ Takahashi's was but one of the first voices to proclaim Nishida's "originality" or "creativity" (*dokusōsei*) without being able to define it structurally. The great historian of Meiji philosophy, Funayama Shinichi, echoed the conviction of a whole generation of scholars when he wrote in 1959, "with Nishida's *An Inquiry Into the Good,* Japan's philosophy moved from the stage of the enlighteners (*keimōka*) to a stage of originality."⁴ Later Nishida's disciple Shimomura Toratarō reinforced the reputation of his master by linking it to the relative lack of Japanese philosophy both before and after Nishida: "A philosophy that has grasped the rigorous methods and concepts of Western philosophy and yet possessed *a distinctive Eastern or Japanese originality* has been an extremely novel development. Nishida became a model in this regard."⁵ Even recent works more critical in tone proclaim Nishida the first philosopher. Nakamura Yūjirō writes: "One had to wait for Nishida for a work that could disprove [Nakae] Chōmin's judgment [in 1900] that there was no philosophy in Japan . . . Nishida's work is *the first* to deserve the name of philosophy."⁶

If Nishida was the first to open to Japan the possibility of philosophizing in a new way, his reputation implied a double closure: premodern, indeed pre-Nishida Japanese (and Asian) thought was excluded from the title of philosophy, strictly speaking; and philosophy in Japan after Nishida was bound to take a stance toward him, be it emulation, inspiration, outspoken criticism or silent rejection. Nakamura's prologue quotes the prophecy of the apostate, Miki Kiyoshi, uttered in the year of the master's death, 1945: "I do not think that Japanese philosophy can arise in the future unless it fundamentally confronts Nishida-philosophy."⁷

The elusive notion of a philosopher's originality is supplemented by the notion of influence; usually the two notions are parasitic upon one another. Since originality cannot mean creativeness ex nihilo, formative influences are sought, and then the original and the merely influential are defined in difference from one another. Japanese historians of philosophy recognize that Nishida had his teachers and mentors in Japan and drew upon their thought in formulating his own. Yet current consensus has it that Meiji intellectuals like Inoue Enryō and Inoue Tetsujirō were not original thinkers but philosophers only in a derivative sense, people who conveyed Western philosophy to a Japanese audience, who were primarily translators of Western thought and sometime syncretists of West and East. Nishida, then, is considered Japan's first philosopher in the scnsc that his achievement exceeded, if not entirely preceded, the philosophical endeavors of other Japanese. Some scholars see Nishida as first in the further sense that his thought gave rise to the first, and allegedly only, genuinely Japanese school of philosophy, the "Kyoto school."

Was There No Philosophy in Premodern Japan?

As we have seen, the claim that Nishida was the first really to philosophize in Japan implies not only that his contribution was original in comparison with that of other Meiji intellectuals, but also that philosophy did not exist in premodern or pre-Meiji Japan. In fact, a heated controversy among Meiji intellectuals centered on the question of whether there was anything in traditional Japanese thought that could be called philosophy. The actual content of the controversy is not as instructive for the defining of philosophy as is the rhetoric, that is, the style and vocabulary, of the contributions. It would be a mistake to understand the importation of philosophy in the early Meiji era simply as an introduction of new, language-neutral subject matter, for there was no way to separate subject matter from language. Likewise, our reexamination of this importation must not be understood simply as an exercise in the past history of Japanese philosophy; it leads, rather, to the elucidation of tradition and textuality as fundamental conditions for present philosophizing.

The rhetoric of Meiji-era texts by Nishi Amane, Kiono Tsutomi, Nishimura Shigeki, Inoue Enryō, Miyake Setsurei, and Nakae Chōmin all indicate an ambivalence towards linguistic usage that lay behind the ambivalence towards premodern Japanese and Asian thought.[8] This underlying ambivalence arose not only from the struggle to modernize the Japanese language and reduce the difference between its written and spoken forms, but also from a perplexity in face of the alien language of philosophy. In order to convey Western philosophical texts, Meiji writers invented neologisms, left many terms untranslated, and used old words in new ways; but they also had recourse to native Confucian and Buddhist categories and occasionally reverted to a *kambun* (classical Chinese, Japanese-style) of writing. The question of whether there was anything in traditional Japanese thought that could be called philosophy was linked to that of how to translate the Western discipline.[9]

After several attempts at translating the term *philosophia* in the 1870s, Nishi Amane finally settled on the neologism *tetsugaku*. Most of those who introduced what came to be denoted by this term differentiated it from traditional Japanese thought because of its insistence on *logical, systematic* knowledge. What they took to be the defining characteristics of philosophy was determined in large part, of course, by the particular philosophers they began to read: John Stuart Mill, August Comte, and later the German idealists and reigning Neo-Kantians. Had Nietzsche been their model, they would have seen philosophy's search for logical, systematic thought in a different light.[10] But they still would have found ample contrast between Nietzsche's critique of Western philosophy and their own traditional, "unphilosophical" thought.

A sign of the predominant use of the term *tetsugaku* in Japanese academia today is the division of university departments. In addition to "pure philosophy" and the "history of Western philosophy," there may be academic programs in "Chinese philosophy" and "Indian philosophy" (not in "Japanese philosophy"!); but these latter programs in fact comprise the philological and historical study of classics and require no training in Western philosophy. The term "Western philosophy" is used primarily to make the distinction between the two sides clear rather than to imply the existence of a complementary "Eastern philosophy," that is, *tōyō-tetsugaku*. Appellations like "Eastern philosophy" and "Buddhist philosophy" are frequent today only because of the authority of the Western category and the search for the likes of it in Asian traditions.

Is Philosophy a Universal Science? Is Logic a Universal Method?

An old way to identify philosophy is to regard it as the "first science" (*proto episteme*) that precedes and exceeds all other sciences or bodies of knowledge by serving as their parent and foundation. We need not trace this idea to Aristotle but only to men such as L. Busse and Raphael von Koeber who transmitted it to prospective Meiji-era philosophers.[11] The irony is that Japanese intellectuals since the Meiji era who have accepted the universalist definition of philosophy have regarded science itself (G. *Wissenschaft*) as something lacking in Japanese tradition; not only the "first science," but the individual sciences as well are regarded as imports from the West. The question of the universality of philosophy would be summarily solved by the distinction between the universal validity of science and the extent of its occurrence as a practiced discipline, were it not for the concomitant claim that human reason, the recipient or even guarantor of this universally valid knowledge, is itself universal.[12] If universal reason had not been exhibited in previous Japanese tradition, then why not? The situation of the Meiji intellectuals brings us face to face with the tension between philosophy as universal science and philosophy as a product, and producer, of "Western" culture.

Current modes of relativizing philosophy do not eliminate the problem of its universality. Some scholars propose to leave philosophical problems to the particular sciences, the problem of the mind-body relation to the neurosciences, for example. But that proposal tends to redefine the terms in question operationally and to discard denotations that cannot be handled by the particular sciences. Hence this tactic cannot treat the question of how universally applicable its solutions are. Others regard philosophy as the record and continuing act of the great conversations of mankind; but that approach does not provide a way to determine the geographical and cultural range of these privileged conversations. Still others appeal to Heidegger's pronouncement of the "end of philosophy" in order to fix its temporal bounds; but they tend to forget the other half, the "task of thinking," that Heidegger bequeaths to those who would call themselves philosophers. Part of this task will be to judge to what degree Japanese tradition reached an end with the Meiji importation of Western ideas and technology, and to investigate as well—contra Heidegger's ethnocentrism[13]—in what sense philosophy can be said to extend into Japan's past, forming some sense of "Japanese philosophy." Other thinkers would deconstruct traditional philosophy, exposing its "logocentrism" or reliance on the priority of presence and the spoken word, for example. That approach may help discover its difference from traditional Japanese thought, but it will have to take seriously the claim of universality that Meiji thinkers heard philosophy make.

At the same time that the Meiji intellectuals appropriated the claim of universality, they located the specific difference from traditional Japanese thought in philosophy's logical character. In fact, it was logically constructed knowledge that gave philosophy its universal character. Today even apostate analytic philosophers like Richard Rorty who would relativize philosophy do not seem to question the universal validity of formal logic. To relieve logic of its parochial origins in ancient Greek thought and language, the tendency has been to find equivalents of formal logic in other traditions,[14] rather than to follow the lead of Hegel and Heidegger in questioning its ontological neutrality, and therefore its universal applicability.[15] Much of Nishida's claim to the honor of being Japan's first philosopher, on the other hand, is due to his attempt to formulate a new logic based in part upon Asian Buddhist concepts. Yet we would misconstrue Nishida's intent by calling his achievement an "Oriental" or a "Japanese logic," for Nishida understood his logic of *basho*, or "place" (*topos*), as a universally applicable critique of all previous logic. Nishida's drive to develop a new logic implied a questioning of the universal validity of the logic imported from the West, but this skeptical stance was possible only after Japanese thinkers had become competent users of the Western import.

Up to now I have outlined a series of problems that range from the historical rank accorded Nishida Kitarō in Japan to the cultural extent of philosophy and the universal validity of logic. In order to resolve these problems I will advance the thesis that philosophy can be understood as a textually transmitted idiom. Following my attempt to define philosophy as an idiom, I challenge the widespread view that Japan's trans-lation of philosophy was unique.

Part Two: Resolution

Philosophy as Idiom

Given the plurality of philosophical styles today it would seem presumptuous to try to bind them all under one definition of philosophy. They do not even all share the supposedly perennial task of self-definition, of asking, "What is philosophy, anyhow?" Yet recognizable patterns of language used by philosophers make it possible to speak of a "philosophical" idiom, the forms of discourse used by certain communities of people regarded as philosophers. Again, actual practice would seem to warrant speaking of a plurality of philosophical idioms, for different communities of philosophers use quite different terminologies and compositional styles, and often accord each other only the slightest nod of understanding. The singular term "idiom," however, captures rather than precludes variance within philosophical language, for "idiom" contrasts with any notion of a "universal tongue," and emphasizes instead dependence upon a community. "The philosophical idiom" should be understood to include disputes about what problems and forms of argument are philosophically legitimate. This purely functional definition does not deprive philosophers of the pleasure of defining philosophy ever anew, but rather is inclusive of its various "self-understandings" throughout history. Acknowledgment of an idiom by outsiders and its mastery by competent users, moreover, do not depend upon the linguist's descriptions that would localize the idiom. It will not be necessary, then, to try to discover the defining features of the philosophical idiom from the outset in order to apply this definition to our problem.

Philosophy as an Idiom of Trans-lation

Philosophy is recognizable as an idiom in large part because it is formed by a tradition of certain texts and reactions to those texts. The canon of texts taken as classical is a shifting entity, but currently certain works are mandatory reading for philosophy students in universities throughout the world. Kant's *Critique of Pure Reason* is an example of such a text. These texts, even when read in the original language, are examined, affirmed, and contested in the light of current interests that differ historically from those of the original. Heidegger's *Kant und das Problem der Metaphysik*, and Strawson's *The Bounds of Sense*, are examples of the trans-lation of Kant's classical text. Poststructuralists today would have us see not only canonical collections but also texts themselves as shifting entities by focusing on the interdependence or "intertextuality" that governs the writing and reading, and thus the identity, of every text. A discussion about Heidegger's reading of the "B" edition of *The Critique of Pure Reason*, in contrast to the "A" edition, is an example of such intertextuality. Regardless of how determinate or indeterminate texts may be, however, and of whether they are read in the original language, the reading process that sustains them can be regarded as a process of translation. It is an active and transformative process that includes deletion and distortion as well as "faithful" rendering. Rarely a matter of matching up words within an existing repertoire, trans-lation entails transference and transposition, incorporation and expulsion, creation and destruction, writing and rewriting.

To the extent that philosophy is formed by the transmission and transformation of texts, then, it can be defined as an idiom of translation, of the trans-lation of philosophical texts. This definition is deferential rather than circular; it does not presuppose the meaning of "philosophical," but takes this term as a floating signifier whose significance defers to the interests of controlling communities. Some communities may insist that certain texts are by nature philosophical, and that the essence of what is it to be philosophical must be determined before one can speak of a philosophical idiom. In that case as well, the philosophical idiom would eventually be defined by a tradition of texts, and the specification of what makes these texts philosophical would be an empirical matter of investigating what criteria are actually employed in selecting certain texts over others. There are ample examples of texts regarded as philosophical by some but as "merely" literary by others. Nietzsche's writings are a case in point; some philosophers do not consider them to be philosophical, others obviously do, and disagreements exist even over whether there can be philosophical treatments of non-philosophcial works or problems. Ironically enough, Nietzsche himself questioned whether the term "philosophy" denotes what we today call a "natural kind." Bernd Magnus notes that Nietzsche gave a genealogical account of how we came to believe that philosophy must have a transcendental standpoint with a meta-historical agenda.[16]

The term "philosophy" in my proposal always awaits completing definition, but this open-endedness means we can finally recognize without chagrin that people called philosophers have perennially disagreed about what counts as philosophy and which texts deserve study. The definition of philosophy as an idiom of translation also has the distinct advantage of allowing us to focus on concrete items such as terminology and grammatical style, instead of groping for some more abstract approach or set of problems that supposedly defines (a) philosophy. Even where a particular set of problems is identified as perennial, that set must be transmitted and shown, by way of trans-lation, to be current as well as traditional. If there is a perennial philosophy, its very existence provides support for the notion of an idiom of trans-lation.

The Signifying and Critical Power of the Philosophical Idiom

It is important to realize that the philosophical idiom does not simply consist of a set of texts and their translations, but has the power of an idiom to signify. Unlike logical sets, idioms can without paradox include themselves and other idioms as signified terms. Using the English idiom, for example, I can speak of the English and Hungarian languages, even if I cannot use the latter. Or, to use the Wittgensteinian idiom, philosophy can itself be considered a "language game" without losing its ability to signify other language games and examine their role in its its own significations. Philosophy does not need to be some kind of meta-idiom or meta-language in order to take a critical stance.

It may not be apparent that the definition of philosophy as an idiom of trans-lation does allow for reasoned critique, which is often taken to be the heart of philosophy. The process of translation obviously calls for critical decisions and for making distinctions, but it is not as evident that it promotes critique in the sense of challenging one position from the standpoint of another. This kind of critique requires of the disputing parties a clear understanding of the disputed positions, and it is precisely a task of translation to promote understanding. Understanding, in turn, becomes a task only when there is some initial difference, disparity or disagreement between people; understanding occurs only when differing standpoints exist. Beyond understanding and difference, however, philosophical critique usually implies judgment and justification. How does a signifying idiom of trans-lation make judgment possible? How does it give rise to justification? I propose that the trans-lation of texts, written and spoken, makes judgment and justification possible in the practical sense that it teaches one how to judge and what counts as justification. It signifies, and thus provides, models of good judgment and justification; indeed, many texts are understood only when the models are learned and imitated. Textuality is, to be sure, not the only precondition of critique, but it is an indispensable mediating condition.

Proper reasoning would seem to be an equally important precondition of justification. Yet reasoning too is mediated and conveyed; that is, it is trans-lated, namely by way of logic or modes of argumentation. Logic might be regarded as the grammar of the philosophical idiom. To view logic as the grammar of the philosophical idiom, however, is to take it as historically, not transcendentally, necessary; it binds together certain communities of competent users, and delimits them from other communities with different styles of thought. More importantly, this view acknowledges the fact that logic has a history and changes over time, and that there exist a plurality of modes of argumentation.

The logical grammar of the philosophical idiom can partially define this idiom in differentiation from others, but we should also distinguish between the grammar or mode of philosophizing and what we philosophize about. The emphasis on textuality would seem to undermine the significance of *"die Sache"* of philosophy. Husserl, on the contrary, exhorted philosophers to bypass merely textual analysis and get back to the issues themselves (*"zu den Sachen selbst"*). Of course, we in turn take up this task in deference to the texts of Husserl that so exhort us, and Husserl himself drew the phrase from Hegel's preface to the *Phenomenology of Spirit*. That text *spoke* to Husserl, as it were; its problematic became for him an issue (*Sache*) of philosophizing. When the object of philosophy *speaks* to us, that is, is a text, then it has the power to inform our philosophizing. Even when that object is not a text, our manner of speaking about it is informed by a tradition of texts that teach how to see or analyze *"die Sache."* The present essay is an attempt to make texts and traditions a *"Sache"* of philosophy, similar to the way in which the "linguistic turn" of this century made language a primary issue of philosophy. Language, the medium through which we philosophize, became the primary object of philosophical reflection. Philosophers reflected not only on what words refer to but on the fact that they do refer and on how they do so; and further, at least in the case of Heidegger, on what else language can do besides referring. I have suggested that texts and traditions have shifted to the center of philosophical issues. As such my suggestion itself is conditioned by a set of texts, that is, by textuality. It remains to be seen how this textuality relates to traditions of philosophy, particularly to the Japanese tradition.

Philosophy as a Trans-lation of Tradition

Defining philosophy as a trans-lation of texts allows us to agree with those Meiji intellectuals who could find no "philosophy" in Japanese tradition, and yet to concur with much current usage that speaks of premodern "Japanese philosophy." This seeming contradiction is overcome because *the range of texts defining the philosophical idiom has changed* since the Meiji era and now includes, for some philosophers at least, premodern Japanese texts.

Thirteenth-century Zen Master Dōgen's *Shōbōgenzō* is a significant example.[17] It would be possible to show how modern philosophical treatments of Dōgen differ in style and terminology from both traditional and contemporary sectarian studies, and from historical-critical studies as well. Philosophical reflection on the writings of Dōgen does not in itself make these writings *philosophical*, to be sure; it is rather their translation into the body of texts appropriated by philosophers that brings them under the sweep of the philosophical idiom and makes them formative of this idiom. Two recent writings by contemporary philosophers illustrate this point. Arifuku Kōgaku has used passages from the *Shōbōgenzō* to point out subjectivist presuppositions in the notion of the self in modern philosophy. He reads some of Dōgen's texts as an implicit critique of the identification of self with mind and reason, a critique he finds explicitly in Nietzsche. Yet Nietzsche presupposes the individuality of self, an assumption that Dōgen's text likewise exposes.[18] A similar exposé of assumptions and presentation of alternatives is at work in Yuasa Yasuo's *Shintai (The Body)*,[19] another study that has incorporated Dôgen into the modern philosophical idiom. Yuasa employs Dōgen (and Kūkai as well) to present a theory of the formation of the self through bodily practice or *shūgyō*. By transferring the context of Dōgen's writing, Yuasa presents an alternative both to theories of "personality development" and to the body-mind problem. Dōgen's notion of cultivation, *shūgyō*, integrates the body more completely than theories that separate motor control and mental capacity. It also allows us to understand body-mind unity as an achievement rather than an unchanging fact to be corroborated or disputed. Still other recent works have brought Dōgen into dialogue with contemporary philosophy[20] and drawn upon his texts to present alternatives to traditional philosophical notions such as those of time and temporality.[21] It is noteworthy that all these works, whether by Japanese or non-Japanese philosophers, and despite their differences in linguistic competence, share the methodology of transferring Dōgen's texts to a twentieth-century and more global context. Because of their work, Dōgen now belongs to the philosophical tradition.

Other philosophers have used premodern terms, if not texts, to reexamine modern problems. Ōmori Shōzō's essay "Kotodama ron" is an example of the rehabilitation of an ancient category to reexamine the relation between words and things, or mind and matter.[22] *Kotodama*, roughly "the power of words," is a term found in premodern texts such as the ancient poetry collection, the *Manyōshū*, and alluded to in Motoori Norinaga's eighteenth-century commentary on the *Kojiki* or Record of Ancient Matters. *Kotodama* referred to the spiritual power that words (*koto* 言) possess in their ability to convey the original (sacred) sense (*kokoro*) of things (*koto* 事, a different *kanji* than the one mentioned above for words) and thus make things present. Ōmori, a philosopher of language, does not give a philosophical analysis of this primitive belief, but rather reawakens the belief to have us rethink contemporary theories about language and reality. He reminds us of the power, more commonplace than mystical, of words to evoke things whether considered real or not, present or absent, mediated through symbols or directly perceived. The reality of things evoked by words is a multiplex, varying reality that includes dreams, illusions, misunderstandings, and the imaginary. Words take their meaning, and things their reality, from a system of relations organized practically, for the sake of living, not according to an epistemological standard of truth or real existence. Truth and real existence are selectively defined within a living and changing system that connects words and things together.

Ōmori argues for the superiority of a monist theory of meaning, according to which "objects" and "meanings" come to appear directly whether in perception or imagination, over a dualistic theory in which symbols that mediate (real) objects appear to the mind. "Reality wavers. So words, irrespective of wavering reality, evoke being and let it appear. This is the functioning of *kotodama*."[23] We can contrast Ōmori's pragmatic analysis with Ernst Cassirer's more transcendental reflections on myth and language. Cassirer distinguishes between mythic thought and discursive or logical thought, and suggests that the former remains limited to the immediate appearance of things. For Cassirer, therefore, mythic thought, unlike language, cannot give rise to a theory of meaning.[24] Ōmori identifies *kotodama* as a mythic conception that suggests how words present things before logical distinctions are formed, but he also shows in detail how his monistic theory better resolves issues of truth and reality. Ōmori has not so much analyzed a prephilosophical term as employed it in the service of philosophical analysis.

The extension of philosophy into the past, that is, the incorporation of pre- or un-philosophical texts into a *philosophical* tradition, has by no means been confined to Japan.[25] The renewed treatment of the "Pre-Socratics" in this century, for example, or the attention given to legal and medical texts and practices in current applied ethics, have enriched the philosophical idiom. Heidegger's interpretations of Hölderlin and other poets, or Derrida's readings of Rousseau and Condillac have not been without effect at least on the formation of their own idiolects. More importantly, however, philosophers such as they have opened up new ways to "read" Western tradition; and their readings have rendered the tradition problematic, its definition a task instead of a fixed entry in the dictionary of time. Foucault's detailed excursions into long overlooked, narrow alleys of European culture have begun to erode the established and all-too broad avenue of "the tradition."

A tradition can no longer be understood as some fixed set of ideas and texts handed down from the past, like a suit of clothes that wears with time. Traditions are created and re-created, formed and reformed by, among other things, the translation of texts—a translation as much into the past as of it. In the order of time, traditions are not continuous streams flowing forward to the present, but rather they stretch backwards from junctures that reintegrate a past and redefine the present. History is replete with examples both within and outside philosophy. The medieval translations and incorporation of Aristotle into Christian philosophy, the Re-formation of Christianity and vernacular translation of the Bible by Luther; the reconstruction of the earliest "classical" literature of Japan, that is, Kamo Mabuchi's translation of the *Manyōshū* and Motoori Norinaga's of the hitherto unreadable *Kojiki*; the literally anachronistic creation of *bushidō* (the way of the warrior) by Yamaga Sōkō and Yamamoto Tsunetomo, or by Victorian Inazo Nitobe, when samurai had long ceased being warriors—each of these is a variation of the post-factum creation of a tradition.

Traditionalizing, moreover, as Nietzsche would remind us, is a process of forgetting as well as of recalling. The effective content of "the tradition" varies from era to era as well as from community to community. Which philosophers get read, and which fall by the wayside, is often a matter of prevailing, and ever shifting, academic interests. Even when other, "unphilosophical" or "alien," texts come to be influential, this inclusion is not straightforwardly an expansion or universalization of philosophy; it is, on the contrary, a reminder of philosophy's parochial heritage.

The process of traditionalizing is twofold also in the sense that it acculturates as well as spreads philosophy. The trans-lation of "Western" philosophy into Japan obviously helped bring about a transformation of Japanese culture often called "westernization" or "modernization." This trans-lation, moreover, also entails the transformation of philosophy by the addition of Japanese perspectives, and these perspectives apply to the reading of traditional texts and of texts yet to be traditionalized. Heidegger, Derrida, Foucault, and Rorty, each in their own way, have argued that the entire "tradition" must be reread in a way that opens philosophy to the future. I have maintained here that the "entire tradition" which must be radically reread has come to include pre-Meiji, as well as contemporary Japan. Not only do Kūkai, Dōgen, and Shinran now belong to philosophy, but Plato, Augustine, Descartes, and Kant now also belong to Japanese tradition. "Japanese philosophy" is not to be identified simply with the thinkers in twentieth-century Japan who achieved a "distinctive Eastern or Japanese originality"—as Shimomura put it—any more than American and German philosophy are defined by thinkers with a "distinctive American or German originality."

I previously raised the question of in what sense Nishida Kitarō, to whom Shimomura referred as the original Japanese philosophy, can be called the first philosopher of Japan. If Nishida is a great Japanese philosopher, it is not because he achieved an independent system of "distinctive individuality," as Shimomura wrote, but because he became a co-creator of a tradition in Japan. It remains a task to show just how his mastery of the philosophical idiom allowed him to accomplish this trans-lation of philosophy.

Epilogue

The presentation of my essay is a good example of my thesis. What I have written are conclusions based upon an examination and translation of old texts in Japanese (the texts mentioned in note 9). These hundred-year-old texts, furthermore, consist in part of attempts to translate Western philosophical language, to create a philosophical idiom in Japanese. Today, as professional philosophers, we take that idiom for granted; but its creation is not a finished business, and neither is the content of this essay. If anything new and insightful is to come of all these translations and retranslations of texts within texts, it will necessarily include the new text that we create by reading and critiquing this essay.

Notes

1. Quoted in a newspaper report by Richard Bernstein, "Philosophical Rift: a Tale of Two Approaches," *The New York Times*, 29 December 1987. A rejoinder to this view was offered by David Hoekema: "everywhere [in the 1987 APA meeting] there was evidence that political and philosophical animosities within the profession are giving way to a spirit of mutual respect and cooperation," in *Proceedings and Addresses of the American*

Philosophical Association 61/3 (January 1988), 521. Hoekema may be right about the atmosphere of the conferences, and in fact the movement for pluralist representation in the APA has since then been successful in getting non-analytical philosophers elected to the presidency and to more committee positions. Nevertheless, many philosophy departments, including Yale University's, remain deeply divided at the time of this writing, 1993.

2. Indicative of the problem is the influential *Encyclopaedia Britannica* (1966 edition) two-part article, "Japanese Philosophy." The division of the article into "Traditional Japanese Philosophy," by Joseph M. Kitagawa, and "Modern Japanese Philosophy," by Takeuchi Yoshinori, reflects not so much two historical periods as rather a split in the meaning of "philosophy." Kyoto-school philosopher Takeuchi notes that many scholars restrict the term in Japan to modern, Western-influenced thought, and then proceeds virtually to identity Japanese philosophy with the thought that grew up around the work of Nishida Kitarō.

3. "Ishikigenshô no jijitsu to sono imi—Nishida shi chô *Zen no kenkyū* o yomu" (The Reality and Meaning of Phenomena of Consciousness—Reading Nishida's *An Inquiry into the Good*) in *Takahashi Satomi zenshū*, vol. 14 (Tokyo: Fukumura shuppan, 1973), 153–54.

4. *Meiji tetsugaku shi kenkyū* (Studies in the History of Meiji Philosophy) (Tokyo: Minerva shobō, 1959), 33–34. Funayama of course does not neglect to point out the influences on Nishida's thought, especially in his summaries in the sequel volume, *Taishō tetsugaku-shi kenkyū* (Studies in the History of Taishō Philosophy) (Tokyo: Hōritsu bunkasha, 1965).

5. *Nishida Kitarō—hito to shisō* (Nishida Kitarô—The Person and his Thought) (Tokyo: Tōkai daigaku shuppan kai, 1977), 201.

6. *Nishida Kitarō* (Tokyo: Iwanami shoten 1983), 20.

7. Ibid., 5.

8. For a more detailed account of these ambivalences, see John C. Maraldo, "Contemporary Japanese Philosophy," in *Encyclopedia of Asian Philosophy* (London: Routledge, forthcoming).

9. Although an analysis of these ambivalences is beyond the confines of this article, I can point to the following textual evidence: Nishi Amane, "Seisei hatsu-un"; Kiono Tsutomi, "Tetsugaku jii hensan no koto o ronji awasete yo no gengo kairyōka ni tsugu"; Nishimura Shigeki, "Jishiki roku"; and Enoue Enryō, "Tetsugaku isseki wa"—all reprinted in *Meiji tetsugaku shisōshū, Meiji bungaku zenshū*, vol. 80 (Tokyo: Chikuma shobō, 1974). In addition, see Miyake Setsurei, "Tetsugaku kenteki," *Miyake Setsurei shū, Meiji bungaku zenshū*, vol. 30 (Tokyo: Chikuma shobō, 1967); and Nakae Chōmin, "Ichi nen yūhan," *Nakae Chōmin zenshū*, vol. 10 (Tokyo: Iwanami shoten, 1983).

10. In fact, between 1901 and 1903 some sixty newspaper and journal articles were published in Japan in a lively controversy centering on Nietzsche's thought. Philosophers to be, such as Kuwaki Genyoku, and literary critics such as Takayama Chogyū, debated Nietzsche's morality and individualism, rather than his critique of the Western tradition, and knew his works largely secondhand. See H.-J. Becker, *Die fruehe Nietzsche Rezeption in Japan (1893–1903)* (Wiesbaden, 1983). Even with Watsuji Tetsurō's *Nietzsche Studies* in 1913 and Abe Jirō's *Interpretation and Critique of Nietzsche's Zarathustra* in 1919, Nietzsche did not become a model for philosophical thinking.

11. Dr. L. Busse, *Introduction to Philosophy* (Tokyo, 1892), 21: "Philosophy [is] the universal science which investigates the ultimate data and laws of Reality and gives . . . a comprehensive and satisfactory view of the Essence and Significance of all Reality."

12. Professor Raphael von Koeber, *An Introduction to Philosophy* (Tokyo, 1895), 1, 4, 5: "One of these faculties, by which man distinguishes himself from animals, is the *reason*, the logical thinking, which is the source of language, science and philosophy . . . reason . . . is *every where* . . . Reason (*Logos*) produced and rules the world. It is the first and the last principle . . . the *universal* wisdom (*sofia, Weisheit*) and our particular (individual) wisdom is nothing but to recognize the universal wisdom."

13. Not only are ancient Greek and modern German philosophical languages par excellence for Heidegger, but philosophy itself is restricted to the Greek tradition and its modern heirs; there is no such thing as traditionally Indian or Chinese, not to speak of Japanese, philosophy. See *Was heißt Denken* (Tübingen: Max Niemeyer, 1961), 136.

14. Compare the many expositions of the Indian Buddhist logic of Dignāga and Dharmakirti, for example, or for Chinese examples, Hu Shih's *Development of the Logical Method in Ancient China* (Shanghai: the Oriental Book Co., 1928) and A. C. Graham's *Later Mohist Logic, Ethics and Science* (Hong Kong: The Chinese University Press, 1978).

15. See Heidegger's remarks about Hegel in "Die Grundsätze des Denkens" (translated by Maraldo as "The Principles of Thinking") in *The Piety of Thinking* (Bloomington: Indiana University Press, 1976), 51, and about the dependence of logic on ontologies in his 1925/26 lectures, *Logik: Die Frage nach der Wahrheit*, published in the *Gesamtausgabe*, vol. 21 (Frankfurt: Vittorio Klostermann, 1976), 16.

16. Bernd Magnus, "The Use and Abuse of *The Will to Power*," in Robert C. Solomon and Kathleen M. Higgins eds., *Reading Nietzsche*, (New York: Oxford University Press, 1988), 232.

17. The group of texts known as *Shōbōgenzō* serves as an example on several levels: it exemplifies (1) a work whose identity (contents!) changed

through the centuries, and (2) a work just recently incorporated into not only (2a) philosophical circles but also (2b) Japanese traditional thought itself. Dôgen's work remained confined to the Sōtō sect for the most part until Watsuji Tetsurô's 1919 essay, "Shamon Dôgen" (Dôgen the Monk).

18. Arifuku Kōgaku, "The Problem of the Body in Nietzsche and Dōgen," in Graham Parkes, ed., *Nietzsche and Asian Thought* (Chicago: Chicago University Press, 1991), 214–25. This incorporation of Dōgen's texts into modern philosophy contrasts with Arifuku's own philosophical interpretation of Dōgen in his book, *Dōgen no sekai* (Dōgen's World) (Osaka: Osaka shoseki, 1985).

19. Yuasa Yasuo, *Shintai: tōyōteki shinshin-ron no kokoromi* (Tokyo: Sōbunsha, 1977). Translated as *The Body: Toward an Eastern Mind-Body Theory*, tr. Shigenori Nagatomo and T. P. Kasulis (Albany: SUNY Press, 1987), 111–24. See also David Edward Shaner, *The BodyMind Experience in Japanese Buddhism: A Phenomenological Study of Kūkai and Dōgen* (Albany: SUNY Press, 1985); and Maraldo, "The Practice of Body-Mind: Dōgen's *Shinjingakudō* and Comparative Philosophy," in William R. LaFleur, ed., *Dōgen Studies*, (Honolulu: University of Hawaii Press, 1985), 112–30.

20. Masao Abe, *A Study of Dōgen: His Philosophy and Religion*, ed. Steven Heine (Albany: SUNY Press, 1992).

21. Heine, *Existential and Ontological Dimensions of Time in Heidegger and Dōgen* (Albany: SUNY Press, 1985); and Joan Stambaugh, *Impermanence is Buddha-Nature: Dōgen's Understanding of Temporality* (Honolulu: University of Hawaii Press, 1990).

22. Ōmori Shōzō, *Mono to kokoro* (Objects and Mind) (Tokyo: Tokyo Daigaku shuppankai, 1976), 103–54.

23. Ibid., 154.

24. Ernst Cassirer, *Language and Myth*, tr. Susanne K. Langer (New York: Dover, 1953), 56–57.

25. A comprehensive example in Japan is the twelve-volume prewar collection, *Nihon tetsugaku zensho* (Tokyo: Saigusa dainichi shobō, 1936–37). Pre-Meiji texts account for about half of the the more recent, twenty-volume *Nihon tetsugaku shisō zensho* (Collection of Japanese Philosophical Thought), ed. Saigusa Hiroto et al. (Tokyo: Heibonsha, 1955–57).

Chapter Nine

The Kyoto School and Reverse Orientalism

BERNARD FAURE

> When all is said, Nishida belongs to the East.
>
> D. T. Suzuki, Preface to *An Inquiry into the Good*

Much of the recent Western discourse on Japanese philosophy has focused on the so-called Kyoto school. As is well known, this school was founded by the Japanese philosopher Nishida Kitarō (1870–1945) and the main themes of "Nishida philosophy" (*Nishida tetsugaku*) continued to serve as a rallying point after his death. I will not attempt to address the strengths of the philosophical ideas of the "most demanding thinker Japan ever produced" (Piovesana 1963, 91), but merely try to assess the "Nishida effect" on the current "philosophical" discourse about Zen and note the recurrence of a certain Orientalist *esprit simpliste* in the interstices of Nishida's complex thought. Although the question of the ideological elements in this thought will lead us to examine briefly Nishida's political positions in a way that cannot do justice to his philosophy, it should be clear that my reading differs from recent political readings of Martin Heidegger, Paul de Man, or Mircea Eliade.[1] Much of the criticism levelled at Nishida by Japanese and Western historians derives from the same scapegoating mechanisms that have been at work in the denunciation of Orientalism. On the other hand, while I am primarily concerned with the Zen rhetorical elements in Nishida's discourse, I will at the same time question the readiness with which this rhetoric can lend itself to appropriation by nationalist ideologies. Without falling into sociopolitical reductionism, it remains necessary to protest against the prevailing tendency among Western scholars to read the works of Nishida and of the Kyoto school as expressions of a "pure philosophy" stemming from a "pure experience."

245

Despite a number of recent publications, Nishida's thought is just beginning to have some impact on Western philosophy.[2] It is much more complex and rigorous than that of D. T. Suzuki, although, as we will see, it has often been presented by exponents of the Kyoto school as paralleling Suzuki's. It is not Nishida's philosophy *per se*, but the extent to which the Kyoto school and D. T. Suzuki have served the "Orientalist" purpose that is of interest to us here. Although I will also address briefly the work of Nishitani Keiji (1900–91), a disciple of Nishida who co-authored several books on Zen with Suzuki, for our present purpose, it can be said that in most cases Nishida's disciples have merely amplified tendencies already present in his work.

Nishida and Suzuki were schoolmates, and their friendship lasted until Nishida's death in 1945. Taking their cues from Zen, the two men offered opposite responses to the challenge of Western philosophy. Whereas Suzuki underscored the anti-systematic nature of Zen and relentlessly expressed his contempt for Western philosophy, Nishida attempted to systematize Zen insights in a way compatible with Western philosophy. Thus, *Nishida philosophy* has sometimes been read as a "Zen philosophy" based on the notion of "pure experience" (*junsui keiken*).

Nishida's search for harmony through philosophy appears to be an attempt to come to terms with his existential problems. At least at the beginning of his philosophical career, Nishida was too aware of Suzuki's example to feel satisfied with his own meditative practice or intellectual achievements.[3] He eventually managed to gain some degree of spiritual realization, but shortly before his "insight" (*kenshō*), he noted that he had been "mistaken to use Zen for the sake of scholarship" (Knauth 1965, 342). Although the fact that he chose to have his grave in a Zen monastery in Kyoto does not in itself imply a deep faith in Zen, it has been read as a significant symbol of the connection between the Kyoto school and Zen.

While Nishida has been sharply criticized after the war for lending his support to the imperial(ist) ideology of the Japanese government, these criticisms have not led—as in Heidegger's case—to a thorough questioning of his philosophy. The Marxist characterization of Nishida's conservatism as belonging to the "cringing harmony type" has not prevented "Nishida philosophy" from knowing a growing success in recent years.[4] On the other hand, this type of criticism may explain a poem written by Nishida: "It is because of Marx/ That sleep comes hard to me" (Nishitani 1991, 30).

One might argue that this judgment reflects a sociopolitical conception of philosophy that fails to do justice to Nishida's philosophical position. Lothar Knauth, for example, feels that Nishida "responded totally to an intellectual and historical challenge," and that, unlike his friend Suzuki, he "tried to do away with the simplistic counterposing of tradition and modernization" (Knauth 1965, 358). David Dilworth also thinks that "Nishida's thought as a whole remained remarkably free of those currents [i.e., ultranationalist ideologies] despite the attempt to coopt his name on occasion. If anything, Nishida's text may be rather atypical in that respect." However, Dilworth adds: "Nevertheless, a comparatively mild strain of chauvinistic definition does appear in Nishida's writings during those years. It is only [*sic*] a *leitmotiv* in the overall corpus of his writings" (Nishida 1987, 129).

Nishida did write some fairly ambiguous pages on the condition of the "national polity" (*kokutai*) and he lectured in 1941 to the emperor on the philosophy of history. *The Problem of Japanese Culture* (*Nihon bunka no mondai*), originally delivered in 1938 as a series of lectures at Kyoto University, was an attempt to emphasize the affinities between Japan and the West and caused him to be attacked as pro-Western during the war. In particular, his reservations concerning the adventurism of the Land Army made him the subject of criticism from the extremist faction, which succeeded in censoring several of his writings before publication (Knauth 1965, 348). Although Nishida asserted that, "underlying the Oriental view of the world and humanity, there has been something equal, if not superior, to Occidental conceptions," he asserted, against the nationalists, that "we cannot take any culture and call it *the* culture" (Tsunoda, de Bary, and Keene 1964, 2:352, 353). Against Orientalism, he argued that "the Orient, though it is spoken of as one, cannot be regarded as one in the sense that the European countries constitute one world" (ibid., 354). Yet, he set out to discover the logic underlying Oriental culture. Although he did not, like Suzuki, reject Western logic in the name of Oriental intuition, he contrasted Occidental logic—a logic that takes things as its objects—with Oriental logic—a logic that takes the mind as its object (ibid., 356).

On the other hand, Nishida's ideal of harmony, derived partly from the Kegon/Zen philosophy, and the accompanying tendency to shun all conflict, could all too easily have perverse effects. Western readers may be attracted by his conception that individuals are "creative elements of a creative world" (ibid., 359), a world in which "each of us, as the individuated manyness of a world of absolutely contradictory self-identity lives with free will" (ibid., 361). However, the ideological effect of Nishida's conception becomes disturbingly clear when his theoretical individualism eventually turns into an apology for the imperial system: as a solution to the conflict between individualism and holism, Nishida suggested that, in the particular case of Japanese history, which is centered on the Imperial Household, both the individual and the whole "mutually negate themselves" for the emperor (Arima 1969, 11). Nishida's lectures to the emperor in 1941 on the philosophy of history were taken by his followers as a testimony of his denial of Japan's "divine mission" and of his courageous stress on individualism at a time when the individual was being sacrificed on the altar of patriotism. However, this interpretation is bluntly contradicted by Nishida's assertion of *kokutai* ("national polity") ideology, according to which there is an essential identity between the divine realm of the *kami*, the divine Emperor, and Japan, the "divine land" (*shinkoku*). These ideas find their most complete expression in two specific essays, *The Problem of Japanese Culture* (*Nihon bunka no mondai*, 1940) and *The National Polity* (*Kokutai*, 1944) (see Tsunoda, de Bary, and Keene 1964, 2:350–65).

We will continue to be confronted with a variety of readings of Nishida. For someone who is fortunate enough to have direct access to the realm of "pure experience," the point of view of ultimate truth in which the subject/object dichotomy does not obtain, historical values of the conventional level must appear rather meaningless. Even if one remains at the level of conventional truth, to interpret the truth-claim of philosophy in terms of sociopolitical determinism is perhaps unfair. Nishida would probably have argued, as he did about earlier (philosophical) criticism: "It has not been a criticism from within my own standpoint. A criticism from a different standpoint which does not truly understand what it is criticizing cannot be said to be a true criticism" (Nishida 1987, 128). Of course, the same standard could be applied to Nishida himself, for example, in his criticism of the Western religious tradition. In such a conflict, or rather *différend*, of interpretations, no single interpretive approach can pretend to defeat the others definitively. The fact remains that, once a philosophical discourse becomes the sign of some orthodoxy, it lends itself to ideological appropriation. Was Nishida an "accomplice of silence," or even an active supporter of the *Dai Nippon* ideology, or was he merely an ardent defender of Japanese culture? While it is too early to pass judgment in the actual state of the documentation, we should be aware that Nishida's statements, whatever their extenuating circumstances, are highly problematic and have grave consequences for his philosophy. The ideological component of Nishida's philosophy is so explicit that philosophers can no longer overlook it.

Pure Experience

Since it is not my purpose to focus on moral and political issues, let us turn to the epistemological aspects of the so-called Nishida philosophy and note some of its problematic aspects. First, a brief discussion of the notion of "pure experience" is in order. One of the claims of the Kyoto school is that "pure experience," being, like Suzuki's notion of *prajñā*, the realization of "absolute nothingness," is independent of any sociocultural context. However, the negative terms in which it is described are reminiscent of the description of awakening in the Mahayana tradition—and also, of the neo-Platonic tradition of Meister Eckhart, to which Nishida constantly referred. This leads us to suspect that "pure experience" itself, and not only its *a posteriori* description, is from the outset informed by expectations specific to Buddhism. According to Steven Katz, "there are *no* pure (i.e. unmediated) experiences. . . . That is, *all* experience is processed through, organized by, and makes itself available to us in extremely complex epistemological ways" (Katz 1978, 26). While Katz's argument is somewhat weakened by its dogmatic tone, the point remains valid, and one could find similar conclusions in Wittgenstein. Ultimately, even nothingnesses "are texts" (Boon 1982, 234), and Nishida's epistemological claim lacks philosophical validity. Furthermore, whatever the subjective reality of the experience, it does not legitimate the performative use of the expression "pure experience" in the texts of the Kyoto school.

   This expression also recalls Christian mysticism and Protestant theology. Religious experience was first and foremost "an event of the soul" for Nishida, who writes: "Just as color appears to the eye as color, . . . so too God appears to the religious self as an event of one's own soul" (Nishida 1987, 48). One might argue however, as Marcel Mauss did in his critique of William James, that "This theory of religious experience, as source of religion, considers only states rarely given, exceptional, that is, in last analysis, it rests on a pathological religious psychology" (Mauss 1968–69, 1:59).

   Formulated in terms influenced by William James's philosophy, as well as Fichte's notion of "absolute will" and the Greek "logic of place," Nishida's notion of "pure" or "immediate" experience seems to find its source in an experience that he had as a high school student in Kanazawa. The active role played by memory in this case brings to mind Freud's concept of *Nachträglichkeit* (*après-coup*, "differed action"), that is, the retrospective manipulation of "memory traces" (*Erinnerungsspuren*), the active reconstruction of the meaning of the past in terms of its function in new situations, and ultimately, the possibility to remember an event that may have never have been experienced as such, and yet exerts potent psychological effects (Laplanche and Pontalis 1967, 33). One of the consequences of Freud's hypothesis is that there is no pure present in which such an experience could take place, since the present, or the full presence to things, are always derived, reconstituted (see Derrida 1967, 314).

At any rate, the main influence on Nishida's formulation of "pure experience" is clearly that of Zen.[5] It is well known that Nishida, following Suzuki's example, practiced Zen for about a decade, beginning in 1897, at various monasteries in Kamakura and Kyoto, eventually achieving some insight at Daitokuji in the summer of 1903. In a short piece entitled "How to Read Nishida," Suzuki claimed that "Nishida's philosophy of absolute nothingness, or his logic of the self-identity of absolute contradictions is difficult to understand, I believe, unless one is passably acquainted with Zen experience. Nishida . . . thought it was his mission to make Zen intelligible to the West. . . . [He] experienced [the] Ultimate and then, desiring to give it an intellectual analysis to his own satisfaction, reflected on the experience so as to make it intelligible to the sophisticated mentality as well as to himself, and the result was 'Nishida philosophy'" (Viglielmo 1960, iii–vi). Suzuki apparently toned down his anti-intellectualism to introduce his intellectual friend's first book. Although Nishida himself never felt the urge to respond to the claim made by Suzuki on his behalf, Suzuki's statement, despite its problematic aspects, became the basis for the later readings of Nishida's philosophy in the Kyoto school.

However, if there is some truth in the Zen dictum that the finger pointing at the moon is not the moon, it follows that the notion of "pure experience" is by no means the pure experience itself. Assuming that such an experience can be found, any attempt to characterize it, even the least reifying one, will betray it. Thus, as a philosophical category used by the early Nishida and his disciples in various discursive contexts, "pure experience" came to function performatively and to produce specific effects outside the field of philosophy. According to the Marxist critic Arima Tatsuo, for instance, "with all its logical embellishments, [it] was used to preach social resignation as a means of achieving individual enlightenment" (Arima 1969, 13). Like Heidegger's ontology, the ontology of pure experience is political in its origin as in its effects. However, it needs to be deconstructed, not only politically, but also philosophically.

Thus, assuming that pure experience itself is ontologically "pre-critical," that is, anterior to any discrimination between subject and object, Nishida's *philosophy* of "pure experience" remains nevertheless ideologically uncritical. As Nishida's former disciple, Tanabe Hajime, pointed out, Nishida "evidently draws illegitimate conclusions from premises taken from the field of religion and transferred to the field of philosophy, thereby transgressing the bounds of philosophy" (Waldenfels 1966, 372). For Tanabe, "the religious experience of absolute nothingness cannot become the principle of a philosophical system," and therefore the combination of Eastern "mystical" experience with Western logical thought was bound to be a failure (ibid., 373).

Such need not always be the case, provided that the religious commitment be clearly spelled out and that the categories in use be carefully chosen. To be sure, the categories used by Nishida were not sufficiently elaborated to avoid Tanabe's criticism, and it was necessary to point out their epistemological limitations; but this does not mean that a larger rationality cannot include the religious dimensions of human experience. Just as there is, since Kant, an "analytic of finitude" according to which "the limits of knowledge provide a positive foundation for the possibility of knowing" (Dreyfus and Rabinow 1983, 30), might there be someday an "analytic of infinitude"?

Whereas Nishida was primarily interested in Zen, and only later in his life in Pure Land, Tanabe was from the start a Pure Land believer. In some ways, Tanabe and Nishida seem to replay in highly philosophical terms the old Zen/Pure Land controversy between "self-power" (*jiriki*) and "other-power" (*tariki*). Nishitani claims that Tanabe misunderstood Nishida (Nishitani 1991, 1966, chap. 9), and that both men were actually closer than they thought. For one thing, "their philosophies share a distinctive and common basis that sets them apart from traditional Western philosophy: absolute nothingness" (ibid., 161). The implication here is that, in contrast to the empty mental constructs of Western philosophy, their philosophy is grounded in ultimate reality, or "absolute" emptiness. Another common basis that Nishitani, for obvious reasons, could not point out, is their participation in *nihonjinron* ("Japanism") discourse.

The East-West Dialogue

Because Nishida's borrowings from the languages of Zen and of the Western mystical tradition were not sufficiently qualified, they generated semantic difficulties that became more obvious in the writings of his successors. For instance, inasmuch as meaning is contextual, it is highly problematic to translate the Japanese term *mu* as "Nothingness" and to equate it with the *Nichts* of the German mystics, or conversely to confuse the Western connotations of "Being" with those of the Japanese term *yū* ("to have," "there is"). This "linguistic-cum-ontological confusion," which led Nishida to contrast "Oriental Nothingness" with Western "Being," has also prompted comparativists to compare Heidegger's *Being and Time* with Dōgen's conception of *uji* (usually "translated" as "being-time").

The problem arises as to whether Nishida actually set out to "explain Zen to the West" and compare it with Western spirituality, or whether he was merely perceived as doing so. According to his disciple Nishitani: "In fact his thinking was a continuation of his Zen meditation, which for him meant the quest for the self or enlightenment. . . . I should think that he maintained to the last the conviction that his own philosophy was an unfolding of Zen within himself, a new manifestation of the Zen spirit" (Nishitani 1991, 24).

It is clear from Nishida's diary and other writings that his understanding of the Zen and Christian traditions remained relatively superficial. His interpretation of Buddhism is very idiosyncratic, and he himself admitted that his Zen was rather different from the teaching of the Zen tradition. His quotations from Ch'an/ Zen texts such as *The Platform Sūtra of the Sixth Patriach* (*Liu-tsu t'an ching*), *The Emerald Cliff Record* (*Pi-yen lu*), *The Essentials of Mind Transmission* (*Chuan-hsin fayao*), *The Record of Linji* (*Lin-chi lu*), *The Record of National Master Daitō* (*Daitō kokushi goroku*), and Dōgen's *Shōbōgenzō*, are indeed very free and eclectic, as are his quotations from Christian mystics and theologians such as Scotus Erigena, Meister Eckhart, Jacob Boehme, Cusanus, Luther, and Kierkegaard. However, Nishida never seems to question his "performative" use of Western and Buddhist sources to illustrate his theses. Although Nishida illustrates his conception of the non-dual identity of the absolute with quotations of these (mostly neo-Platonist) Christians, I strongly doubt that, as Dilworth claims, "if anything, these cross-cultural analyses are one of the strengths of Nishida's text" (Nishida 1987, 130).

It is only late in his life that Nishida explicitly identified his standpoint with Zen (and Pure Land). In his last work, he even attempted to correct popular misunderstandings about Zen: thus, for him, Zen has nothing to do with mysticism—although mysticism is something extremely close to Zen! (ibid., 108–9). Nishida contended that, despite the closeness of Zen and of what has been called mysticism in Western philosophy since the time of Plotinus, Western mysticism was never able to transcend the standpoint of "object logic": "Indeed, the One of Plotinus stands at an opposite pole to the Zen experience of nothingness. Neo-Platonism did not in fact attain to a religious celebration of the ordinary and the everyday as we find it in the Zen tradition" (ibid., 109).

Significantly, it is also toward this time that Nishida took his most nationalist stand in essays such as *The Problem of Japanese Culture* and *The Logic of Place and the Religious Worldview* (*Bashōteki ronri to shūkyōteki sekaikan*) (see Nishida 1987; Yusa 1986, 1987). He was perhaps influenced on this point too by Suzuki, who wrote his nativist books on *Japanese Spirituality* and *Zen and Japanese Culture* in the mid-forties. As noted earlier, Nishida eventually placed the formulas borrowed from Western philosophy and Buddhism in the service of nationalism, apparently espousing the *kokutai* ideology. He interpreted, for instance, the cardinal Zen notion of "no-mind" (Ch. *wu-hsin*, J. *mushin*) and the Pure Land notion of *jinen hōni* ("natural spontaneity in accordance to the Dharma") as the purest manifestations of the Japanese spirit. He identified this Japanese spirit, "which goes to the truth of things as an identity between actuality and reality," that is, "the realization of this absolute at the bottom of ourselves" (Tsunoda, de Bary, and Keene 1964, 2:364), not only with Mahāyāna Buddhism and its Japanese variants, Zen and Amidism,[6] but also with Shinto ideology, the so-called Way of the Gods (*kannagara no michi*). The following passage is worth quoting at some length in this respect:

> As for the characteristics of Japanese culture, it seems to me to lie in moving from subject to object (environment), ever thoroughly negating the self and becoming the thing itself, becoming the thing itself to see, becoming the thing itself to act. To empty the self and see things, for the self to be immersed in things, "no-mindedness"

(*mushin*) or effortless acceptance of the grace of Amida (*jinen hōni*)—these, I believe, are the states we Japanese strongly yearn for . . . . The essence of the Japanese spirit must be to become one in things and in events. It is to become one at that primal point in which there is neither self nor others.[7]

Without blaming Nishida for what he could not possibly have foreseen at the time, can one forget that this "point of high fusion" found its ultimate expression in Hiroshima? Interestingly, the translator of this excerpt, Masao Abe, the best known representative of the Kyoto school in the West, has omitted the following sentence: "This [process] seems to have as its center this contradictory autoidentity that is the Imperial Household" (Nishida 1965, 6: 104; see also Nishida 1991, 74).

The expression "to empty the self and see things, for the self to be immersed in things" (*Onore o kū shite mono o miru, jikō wa mono no naka ni botsu suru*) is reminiscent of Dōgen's *Shōbōgenzō Genjō kōan* fascicle (T. 82, 2582:23c; see also Faure 1987, 114). Nishida frequently quotes Dōgen in this nationalist and expansionist context. To give just an example: "Today, the problem of our national culture can only be considered as that of its broadening to a horizontal "universality" (*mondialité*), while retaining of the vertical "universality" that has characterized it for millennia. This amounts necessarily to promoting a culture of flexibility of mind (*junanshin*), a culture of dropping off body and mind (*shinjin datsuraku*). . . . And it is necessarily to establish in a contradictorily self-identical way one single world entrusted to things. It is this, I believe, in which resides the Japanese mission, that is, to construct the Eastern mind" (Nishida 1965, 6:107; 1991, 76–77). Nishida, however, nuances this statement with what sounds like a critique of Japanese imperialism: "If, as subject, we assimilate the other by negating it, this is no other than imperialism, this is not the Japanese spirit" [ibid.].

Despite Nishida's fondness for Dōgen, his understanding of Zen, like Suzuki's, may be considered biased or reductionistic in several respects. Apart from references to Dōgen, Nishida was greatly indebted to Suzuki, particularly in his later writings. Although Nishida desired to elaborate a philosophy of the "concrete," his concepts of "pure experience," "absolute nothingness," and so on, remained fundamentally abstract and dualistic. If applied thoroughly, the Mahayana logic of non-duality would deny the possibility of "pure experience," or even the linguistic pertinence of the expression, since the very distinction between pure experience and the "impure" ordinary experience, or between philosophical/metaphysical language and ordinary language, remains, not only dualistic, but utopian. There is no metaphysical or metalinguistic position available to the philosopher, only values that become ideological when they are denied as such. Even the "concrete world" of which Nishida speaks so often is an abstraction, an idealistic product without much resemblance to any sociocultural reality. Perhaps this impossibility to return to the "real thing" is the price that Nishida, like most philosophers, had to pay to establish the philosophical authority of his discourse. Ironically, when he tried to apply the Buddhist notion of the "actual *qua* absolute," Nishida ended up equating the "actual" with the *kokutai* and the Imperial House. Although Nishida was a product of Japanese modernity, he was unable to accept this fact and to overcome his nostalgia for Japanese and Western orthodoxies. His philosophy appears more like an exorcism than like a set of operative notions enabling him (and us) to understand and act upon reality. While he was more influenced by Bergson, in certain aspects Nishida resembles Durkheim, whom he mentions only in passing when arguing, in his last writings, that "every historically crystallized society begins from a religious ground—from what Durkheim has called *le sacré*" (Nishida 1987, 116). In his case too, the individualism of the beginning gave way to a mystical conception of society (or nation). According to Nishida, "Each nation is a world that contains the self-expression of the absolute within itself" (ibid., 122). After a final quotation from Suzuki, he closes his book with the following statement: "The nation is the mirror image of the Pure Land in this world" (ibid., 123).

Already in the preface to *From Acting to Seeing* (*Hataraku mono kara miru mono e*, 1927), Nishida stated his desire to "supply philosophical foundations" for traditional Oriental culture. In this work, he refers to "the form of the formless, the voice of the voiceless which lies at the basis of Eastern culture, transmitted from our ancestors for thousands of years" (ibid., 127). Their common interest in Western mystics like Meister Eckhart led both Nishida and Suzuki to misrepresent Christianity as some kind of inferior version of Mahayana Buddhism, thus reversing the old schemas applied to the East by Westerners. Like Suzuki's work, Nishida's entire attempt to elaborate a "logic of the East" based on the notion of "contradictory identity" (*mujunteki dōitsu*), the so-called logic of *sokuhi* ("is" and "is not"), is governed by Orientalist categories and reveals a "nativist" bias.[8] Nishida was indebted to Suzuki for his discovery of the logic of *sokuhi* in the *Diamond Sūtra* (Nishida

1987, 70). In his final essay in particular, he repeatedly quoted Suzuki and used Zen anecdotes in the style of Suzuki—a style which was to become characteristic of much of the production of the later Kyoto school. Suzuki is invoked in particular to support the contrast drawn by Nishida between East and West: "If the concept of compassion has not been foundational for Western culture (as Suzuki Daisetsu maintains), then I think there is a basic difference between Eastern and Western culture in this regard."[9] Although many important philosophical insights remain, the ideological function of such simplistic assumptions undermines the validity of "Nishida philosophy" (*Nishida tetsugaku*). As David Dilworth remarks, "The danger of confusing the socio-historical and metaphysical spheres when defining things 'Eastern' and 'Western' potentially remains, I think, in some aspects of *Nishida tetsugaku*" (Dilworth 1970c, 212). Because he is more nuanced and subtle than other nativist thinkers—including Suzuki—Nishida has exerted and continues to exert a greater seduction on intellectuals, a faculty which has allowed him to rally a number of them to the nationalist ideology (see Nishida 1991, 14–15).

Nishitani Keiji and the Postwar Kyoto School

The dichotomic framework established by Nishida's (and Suzuki's) logic of contradictory identity and its use of "Oriental Nothingness" (J. *mu*) as an ideological weapon paved the way for the kind of theological/philosophical confrontation of "East" and "West" that has occupied much of the "philosophical" activity of the postwar Kyoto school and resulted in a rather sterile "dialogue" between Zen and Western philosophy, or Zen and Christianity.[10] This state of affairs, however, is due as much to Suzuki's as to Nishida's influence on the Kyoto school.

The label Kyoto school is by no means precise. Although this school was identified with "Nishida philosophy," Tanabe Hajime, a former disciple of Nishida who became one of his strongest critics, is usually counted as one of its members—and sometimes as its true leader. As noted above, Nishitani argues that Tanabe's criticism misses the point, and that both philosophers had actually much in common. Various aspects of "Nishida philosophy" have been developed by his disciples, most notably by Nishitani, but also by Ueda Shizuteru and Masao Abe. In particular, the development of the nationalist tendencies in Nishida's thought reached its full expression in the symposia organized in 1942 on the philosophy of world history, by the so-called right wing of the Kyoto school, Kōsaka Masaaki (1900–1965), Nishitani Keiji (1900–1991), Kōyama Iwao, and Suzuki Shigetaka. These symposia advocated total war as the unification of all dimensions of human life. In the January 1942 symposium entitled "The Standpoint of World History and Japan" [Sekaishiteki tachiba to Nihon], Nishitani, an authority on Zen who later coedited several books with D. T. Suzuki and was until his recent death perceived as the main representative of the Kyoto school, commented: "[I]s it not that the political consciousness of the Germans is more advanced? I believe too that in people such as Hitler the consciousness of the necessity to restore an interior order is clearer than in Japanese rulers . . . . Although today the various peoples of the East have no national consciousness in the European way, this is perhaps a chance for the construction of the Co-prosperity sphere . . . , because it means that they are being constituted as people of the Co-prosperity sphere from a Japanese point of view."[11] Admittedly, Japanese intellectuals like Nishitani did not commit any war crime and perhaps they knew little about those committed in the name of the Japanese emperor. Nishitani's political position, like Nishida's, remained very abstract, removed from actual political events. But it is precisely this tendency toward abstraction, which will characterize his later religious and "supra-historical" thought—that could be seen as a withdrawal from the sphere of concrete action, a kind of *trahison des clercs* that leaves the field open to fascism—if it does not actively endorse and legitimize it. It is the same tendency toward abstraction or idealization that could make the imperial mystique (or the Nazi mystique for Heidegger) look so seductive, and that allowed them to regard as incidental the violence that followed (cf. Lacoue-Labarthe 1987, 21). Nishitani's "abdication" of the nation, which Maraldo sees as occurring after the publication of *The Self-Overcoming of Nihilism* in 1949, might already be found in his wartime writings (Maraldo 1993). Unfortunately, the irony in the title of Notto Thelle's "profile" of Nishitani, "The Flower Blooms at the Cliff's Edge," is inadvertent (see Thelle 1984).

The Hermeneutical Dilemma

One may argue that this short excerpt from a "political" text inspired by specific circumstances does not do justice to Nishitani, who has written extensively on religion and philosophy after the war—the best-known example of his later thought being *Religion and Nothingness*. But the question is precisely: can justice be done in such a case? Is one being just when one tries to present a more nuanced account of his philosophy—or is one already framing the question and silencing it by diluting the scandalous passages among more benign and innocent philosophical statements? Can there be any neutral ground in these matters? Can one avoid taking sides between those whom Heisig calls "the side-swipers and side-steppers, the one trying to apportion blame, the other resisting the effort" (Unno and Heisig 1990, 14). Can anything short of a strong criticism—a fundamental rejection of the position represented here—take the proper measure of the scandal? Can injustice toward a particular author be entirely avoided, if one is to check the ideological effects of discourse? How much does this injustice weigh, compared with the massive injustice that this discourse, consciously or not, may have endorsed or simply failed to denounce? Nishitani's intentions may have been as good as those of his defenders and prosecutors—but we know that hell is paved with good intentions. Besides, what could justice be in such a case, which is what Lyotard calls a *différend*, a situation in which the protagonists do not even share the same frame of reference? From what kind of ideological or non-ideological space, from what vantage point, could one see equally and adjudicate objectively these two irreducible interpretations? There is no mountain top from which one can one see—and by so doing implicitly reconcile—these two thoughts, because they are not the two versants of the same mountain. Thus, it requires some naiveté to believe in the possibility of a hermeneutic of retrieval that would do justice to the author. What we have, in our "history of effects," are partial—limited and biased—readings, specific ways to mobilize a given text. What we need are alternative ways to mobilize the text—and their very partiality will reflect the urgency of counterbalancing the dominant interpretation; it will also reveal the ideological nature of any writing or reading—in particular when dealing with the writings of prominent philosophers like Nishida and Nishitani who, as Dilworth puts it, "confuse metaphysical and cultural predicates to some degree in their works" (Nishida 1987, 146).

Beside the philosophical or hermeneutical naiveté, which believes that one can keep one's hands pure as long as one remains in the enchanted circle of philosophy, there is the critical naiveté, which holds that one can denounce philosophical discourse from the outside, without actually exposing oneself to the seduction of deep meaning—let alone to the possibility of an irruption of that most elusive experience of emptiness. Is it possible to avoid both pitfalls of complaisance and reductionism? Referring to the Heidegger case, Bourdieu argues that "we must abandon the opposition between a political reading and a philosophical reading, and undertake a simultaneously political and philosophical *dual reading* of writings which are defined by their fundamental *ambiguity*, that is, by their reference to two social spaces, which correspond to two mental spaces" (Bourdieu 1991, 3). But how can one sustain such a dual reading? Are we not reproducing here a kind of theoretical "self-contradictory identity"? In the end, Bourdieu himself fails to live up to his ideal, and gives a sociological reading of Heidegger that is clearly biased, if slightly less polemical than some others.

Whatever their theoretical irreducibility or self-contradictory identity, the two approaches are necessarily intertwined. In the case of Nishitani, the convenient division of his work into two parts and/or periods (political vs. religious), although it finds some support in his biography (the fact that all his political works were written prior to the 1950s), has allowed critics and epigones too conveniently to ignore and dismiss each others's points (Maraldo 1993). A similar hermeneutical strategy has been used in the case of Dōgen, whose harsh sectarian statements seem to contradict too bluntly the best philosophical parts of the *Shōbōgenzō*. The strategy consists in downplaying the scandalous parts by excizing them from the main body as accidents, or external growths, after dividing the body into two different parts to contain the cancerous growth; or, on the contrary, in underlining the unity of the text while letting the sectarian metastases, to continue using this metaphor, disseminate throughout the body. However, the real challenge is to see how the two parts might have always coexisted, and to consider to what extent Nishitani's interest in—or escape into—the "supra-historical" is not a continuation of the same metaphysical nostalgia that allowed him to posit the transcendence of Japan as nation-state. We seem to have here a replay of the logic of place or emptiness which, according to Nishida, found its ultimate expression in the imperial house.

We have already discussed this point regarding Nishida. Clearly, judging a philosophical statement, or even a political statement made by a philosopher, according to purely political criteria is what philosophers call a "category mistake," that is, judging a language game in terms of another. Nishida himself, as noted above, was precisely making this point. But the question is even more complicated in the case of Nishitani and others (like Heidegger, de

Man, Eliade) who have survived the war, and thrived in the postwar period. In the light of subsequent history, some sentences carry much more weight, have much more resonance than others, and a single word can discredit the rest of a discourse, turn it into mere noise, make it sound almost irrelevant.

We have to address three different yet related questions, at three levels—author, discourse, reader: (a) How does the failure of a person—allegedly a master—undermine his or her philosophy; (b) To what extent does the logic that allows his or her nationalist stand pervade his later teaching; (c) How are these ideological effects reproduced in reading, either in a reactionary reading of a progressive text or vice versa (as in the case of Nietzsche)? We need therefore to shift the responsibility from the author to the reader. It then becomes important to ask what effects the prevalent interpretation of the Kyoto school has had on our understanding of Japanese philosophy, and, through it, on our understanding of Buddhism and Ch'an/Zen. Thus, when we simply denounce the *nihonjinron* ideology, making a scapegoat of it, in a certain sense we participate in it, and tend to reproduce the same nativist structure of thought.

Should we then, in all candor or blissful ignorance, accept Robert Thurman's characterization of Nishitani as a Mañjuśrī, the great Bodhisattva, or "spiritual Messiah," because of his alleged penetration of the standpoint of emptiness (Unno 1990, 144)? Obviously not. One of the many horns of the hermeneutical dilemma could be expressed as follows: by what right could one put him on trial? And yet, how could one avoid doing so? As far as I know, Nishitani has never manifested any regret for such youthful errors, nor has this aspect of his work ever been discussed among his disciples. As Lacoue-Labarthe points out in his discussion of the role of Heidegger and German intellectuals, "The question is that the said intellectuals . . . said nothing after the war, publicly and within their own sphere of responsibility" (Lacoue-Labarthe 1987, 33). Likewise, Nishitani's wartime commitment cannot simply be dismissed as an error or accident, a poor judgment, because it produces statements that are philosophical, and therefore it produces philosophical, and ultimately ideological, effects (ibid., 13).

It is hard to avoid the suspicion—the "great doubt," to use a Zen expression favored by Nishitani—that his silence is due to a lack of self-examination and courage, and that the teacher's flaw would cast a shadow over his teaching. Compared with Nishitani's "thundering silence," Tanabe's self-criticism seems at first glance more appropriate, although it might be partly strategical (Heisig

1990, 284). As is well known, Tanabe's whole project of metanoetics stems from his repentance over his abuse of philosophy for nationalistic ends (ibid., 289). Nishitani expressed no grief or sympathy for Asian people who suffered under Japanese rule.

In his book, *An Ideal Portrait of Twentieth-Century Japan* (1954), Kamei Katsuichiro denounces his former "conqueror mentality": "I could as an overlord of Asia preach with equanimity the love of Asia" (Tsunoda, de Bary, and Keene 1958, 2: 397). He does not shrink from the realization that "Japan slaughtered people while preaching the love of Asia and the Way of the Gods" (ibid.). Finally, he argues that "the true meaning of what (he is) attempting to discuss under the theme of 'return to the East' may be said in the final analysis to be the product of a sense of guilt towards the East"—particularly towards China and Korea (ibid., 398). This emphasis on "the East," however, implies a critique of the very same type of "soft nativism" still present in the postwar Kyoto school: "However, in so doing we must free ourselves from any infantile notions such as the simple schematization formerly in vogue here, according to which the East stood for the spirit and the West for material things. . . . In fact, it should result in the destruction of the very sense of opposition between East and West which figured so prominently in our former ideas" (ibid., 399).

By contrast, it is somewhat ironical that the only sympathy expressed in *Religion and Nothingness* toward other sentient beings is toward mosquitoes (here again a Buddhist topos, found in haiku). "Does not our immediate intuition of the distress in the sound of the mosquito [that, in his example, he has just squashed in the palm of his hand] take place on a field of psychic sympathy?" (12)

In *The Self-Overcoming of Nihilism*, Nishitani blames the war on Western nihilism and its influence on Japanese imperialists, and he advocates a return to the Japanese tradition, without ever realizing that the ideology of tradition was itself a cause of the war. In the same way, Suzuki blames Hiroshima on the Western lack of love for nature. In a footnote to *Zen and Japanese Culture*, he places all the responsibility on Western intellectualism: "The intellect presses the button, the whole city is destroyed" (Suzuki 1970, 337). Apparently, Suzuki was unaware that perhaps the chief cause of war and its fuel were found in the same warrior mystique (*bushidō*) that he exalted in several chapters of the same book.[12]

What should one think of someone like Nishitani, who reproaches Kant for not going far enough in his understanding of ethics (Unno 1989, 183), that is, for not realizing that true ethics is based on emptiness? Before taking the high moral ground, we would do well to realize that we live in a glass-house. One could excuse Nishitani's wartime statements on account of youth. But what is more disturbing is that Nishitani, like Heidegger, Eliade, or de Man, while assuming the status of *maître à penser*—and in his case even of an enlightened spiritual master—for later generations, remained silent about his past.

Is the acknowledgment of the ideological problem just a preamble to the serious discussion of "purely" philosophical issues— the antechamber in which the critical scholar must wait whereas he does not have, like the philosopher, access to the inner sanctum. Or must it become, assuming that it is not already in a certain uncanny (*unheimlich*) way, the core of the philosophical discussion itself, a constant reminder (and remainder, residue) of the danger of metaphysics? *Revenons à nos moutons* (Let's get back to the subject, literally, "to our sheep"), an impatient (French) philosopher would say at this point, without realizing that in the meantime his philosophical sheep have turned into ideological goats—assuming that they have not always been wolves in sheep's clothing.

It is time to question the guardians of orthodox interpretation— of Zen or Nishida philosophy, and to reveal what Bourdieu calls "the blindness of the professionals of insight." Nevertheless, a number of questions arise: how can one evaluate this ideological discourse without falling in the opposite extreme of counter-ideology? Is the nationalist episode a mere loss of vigilance, or does it reflect a more fundamental aspect of his thought? How do the ideological commitment to wartime effort and the lack of any later disavowal affect the thought of Nishitani? Are they merely accidents, temporary failures, that leave his philosophy basically intact, or do they leave an indelible stigma? How can such statements be made, from a philosophical viewpoint? Do they not afflict or shatter the whole system by revealing its blind spot? In other words: is nativism an ideological outgrowth, or is it essential to the thought of the Kyoto school? How does the notion of "pure experience" lead to the possibility of a commitment to nativism, of essentializing Japan and leading to a discourse on Japaneseness? Is this relation a necessary, structural one?

It is important to acknowledge the possibility of a "continuity between Nishitani's wartime writings and his postwar exercises in an apolitical and thereby 'innocent' philosophy of religion."[13] One must consider seriously the idea that these intellectual stands are perhaps not mere accidents or mistakes, but reveal something essential about those who hold them. The logic of Japanese imperialism is essentially a spiritual one, sustained as it is by the imperial mystique and the myth of Japanese uniqueness. This effect of "spirituality," however, of the hegemony of the spiritual as it is still claimed by the Kyoto school and other advocates of cultural uniqueness, has not yet been thought through. If Tanabe may have coined the term metanoetics (*zangedō*) in an attempt to "purge philosophy of its tainted innocence," then, in Nishitani's case too, one should contemplate the possibility of a camouflage and retreat into religion.

Having raised this "preliminary" question—not simply to exorcise it but to let it resonate throughout the discussion, let us nevertheless bracket it and turn toward Nishitani's "philosophical" statements. We need not rehearse too long his philosophical theses, because, although they are in many respects quite original and provocative, they obey the same constraints as "Nishida philosophy." In particular, both authors set up as a foil to Japanese spirituality a simplified Western philosophy or mysticism; they make a constant idiosyncratic use of vague, at times simplistic, and utterly demythologized Buddhist notions; and they advocate a kind of "militant syncretism" between Japanese and Western traditions, at the expense of the latter, and of the rest of Asian culture.

First of all, we encounter the basic issue already discussed in the case of Nishida, that of a philosopher resorting authoritatively to the claim of a privileged access to pure experience or absolute emptiness—a normative rather than descriptive statement. Once again, we can observe a confusion between theology and critical philosophy. As the following passage makes clear, the field of *śūnyatā* or emptiness remains a working hypothesis, a distant ideal: "It would appear as the field of wisdom that we might call a 'knowing of non-knowing'. . . . And lastly, it would be a standpoint where knowledge and praxis are one, a field where things would become manifest in their suchness" (Nishitani 1982, 121, 122). However, Nishitani soon becomes more dogmatic in his assertions: "The standpoint of emptiness is altogether different: it is absolute nothingness" (ibid., 105). "Only on the field of emptiness does all of this become possible. Unless the thoughts and deeds of man one and all be located on such a field, the sort of problems that beset humanity have no chance of ever really being solved" (ibid., 285). Thus, the only way for one to escape nihilism is to pass to the deeper, transpersonal level of *śūnyatā*, which lies on the "absolute near side" of his life. In Nishitani's own words, "Emptiness is the field on

which an essential encounter can take place between entities normally taken to be most distantly related, even at enmity with each
other, no less than between those that are most closely related"
(ibid., 102). But except for a few allusions to meditation, Nishitani
never reveals how this transition from "nihility" to emptiness is to
be achieved.

There appears to be some kind of a drift between asserting the
logical (or rather, spiritual) "necessity" of an absolute standpoint,
and asserting it as privilege and foundation for one's own philosophical discourse, let alone using it as a polemical weapon in a
game of oneupmanship vis-à-vis Western thought. It seems easy to
forget that the word emptiness is not the thing (or the no-thing):
despite the subtitle of Taitetsu Unno's book on Nishitani, "Encounter with emptiness," what we have is an encounter with the notion
or ideology of emptiness—quite different indeed. In the process, the
awareness of the dialogical or performative use of the notion gets
lost. Thus, one may wonder if the wrong view of emptiness that
Nishitani attributes to heterodox Buddhists might not apply to him
as well: "Nothingness may seem here to be a denial of self-attach-
ment, but in fact that attachment is rather exponentialized and
concealed (ibid., 33). One cannot help wondering with what authority he speaks. Is there anything else than a bricolage, an ingenious
(or disingenuous?) montage of Buddhist clichés in passages like the
following: "The reality that appears at the bottom of the Great
Doubt and overturns it is none other than our 'original countenance'" (Nishitani 1982, 21)? Where is this much-vaunted Great
Doubt, when all his assertions sound so dogmatic?

In a number of passages, Nishitani elaborates on the intellectual affinities between the Kyoto school and Zen Buddhism. He
admits his free use of standard Buddhist notions: "From the viewpoint of traditional conceptual determinations, this way of using
terminology may seem somewhat careless and, at times, ambiguous" (Nishitani 1982, xlix). To him, Zen is less a religious tradition
in the conventional sense than a guarantee of intellectual freedom:
"We consider it necessary for our philosophical inquiry to maintain
a fundamental religious attitude that accords with the spirit of free
and critical thought of philosophy. Since Zen has no dogmatics to
speak of and wishes to have none, it is easy to understand why many
of us keep rooted in the experience of Zen practice" (Nishitani 1982,
xxxv). Admittedly, Nishitani's brand of non-sectarian Zen and demythologized Buddhism has little to do with the living tradition:
"Here, however, no firm stance is taken on any particular religious
view. My aim is rather to inquire into the original form of reality,

and of man who is part of that reality. . . . If I have frequently had occasion to deal with the standpoints of Buddhism, and particularly Zen Buddhism, the fundamental reason is that this original countenance seems to me to appear there most plainly and unmistakenly" (ibid., 261). Like Dōgen, who rejected even the term Zen, Nishitani's Zen is allegedly non-sectarian, and culminates in the quasi-Nietzschean notion of emptiness: "(Nietzsche's standpoint) might also be interpreted as one of the currents of Western thought that come closest to the Buddhist standpoint of *śūnyatā*. We seem to be breathing here the same pure mountain air that we felt in approaching the standpoint of Dōgen through the words: 'We meet a leap year in four./ Cocks crow at four in the morning.'" And again: "I do not have a single strand of the Buddha's dharma. I now while away my time, accepting whatever may come" (ibid., 215). In practice, one knows how fiercely sectarian Dōgen was, and one cannot help wondering about Nishitani's idealized vision of Dōgen, and about his own lack of dogmatism.

Like Nishida and Suzuki, Nishitani contrasts the Eastern spirit with the spirit of the West. (Nishitani 1991, 49). As he puts it, "things are different in the East" (ibid., 52). Although he does not suscribe to a simplistic brand of nativism, as is obvious from the following passage, he plays an active role in the *nihonjinron* ideology: "We Japanese have fallen heir to two completely different cultures. . . . This is a great privilege that Westerners do not share in . . . but at the same time this puts a heavy responsibility on our shoulders: to lay the foundations of thought for a world in the making, for a new world united beyond differences of East and West" (xxviii). Even when he acknowledges his debt to the West, he wants to make this inheritance an aspect of Japanese uniqueness. A new world united beyond differences of East and West will nevertheless be guided by Japan, since this new unlocalized ideology will be located in Japan. In the title of the translation of his book on European nihilism, *The Self-Overcoming Of Nihilism*, the bold initials form an acronym that reads: SOON. Is this subliminal message appropriate in a "philosophical" work? The eschatological tone of this book, originally written several years after the war, is disturbingly close to that of Nishitani's wartime writings.

The New Kyoto School and Its Critics

Although not directly related to Nishida, Umehara Takeshi's School of Japanese Studies, also known as the "New Kyoto school," has contributed to the expansion of a discourse initiated by Suzuki's *Zen and Japanese Culture*. The ideological agenda of this school was advanced with the nomination of Umehara Takeshi as director of the International Center for Japanese Culture (better known as Nichibunken) in Kyoto, a center created in 1986 by the Nakasone government. The nativist thinking of Umehara appears openly in a dialogue he had with Prime Minister Nakasone Yasuhiro in 1986. In this dialogue, published in *Bungei shunjū*, both interlocutors marvel at the pantheistic love of nature and other perennial characteristics of the Japanese. In response to Nakasone's assertion that Japanese culture is the oldest in the world, Umehara explains that he has never regretted abandoning the study of Western philosophy to return to that of Japanese thought.[14] At times, his declarations remind us of passages in Nishitani's *The Self-Overcoming of Nihilism*: "At the same time that we are attempting to make strides as an international nation, it is very important for us to reexamine our own identity and unity as Japan." Likewise, Umehara's characterization of Japanese culture as peaceful and based on the notion of "harmony" (*wa*) is reminiscent of Nishida's statement, quoted above, on the yearning of the Japanese for "naturalness" (*jinen hōni*)—and of the imperialist propaganda of the *Kokutai no hongi*.[15] More than ever, Zen and Japanese culture appear as ideological instruments to promote a cultural image of Japan in the West and as an essential component of the so-called "uniqueness of the Japanese" (*nihonjinron*). This co-optation of Zen as a cultural phenomenon, and of cultural studies in general, in the name of an unchanging cultural essence, is also found in governmental institutions such as the Japan Foundation, whose motto of internationalization paradoxically amounts to little more than an affirmation of Japaneseness.

If the philosophical impact of Umehara's ideas is not comparable to that of Nishida or Nishitani, their ideological implications should not be underestimated. The Nichibunken has attracted Western and Japanese scholars of different political horizons—such as Lévi-Strauss, Donald Keene, Masao Miyoshi, Amino Yoshihiko, or Ueno Chizuko. It has thus gained momentum and tended to use Japanology as an alibi, an ideological commodity—hard to dissociate from *nihonjinron* discourse and to some extent legitimizing it. Thus, whereas many scholars argue that their presence at the Nichibunken does not affect their moral integrity, one must question the overall ideological effects of their participation in this institution.

The same can be said, *mutatis mutandis*, about the Kyoto symposia in Zen philosophy led by Nishitani, which in a spirit of "dialogue," have brought together Japanese and Western scholars (including myself)—*ad majorem [Kyoto] scholae gloriam*. The apparent tolerance shown by the representatives of the Kyoto school to criticism can be construed as a sign of indifference to the ideological critique, a critique which serves as an alibi to a thriving *nihonjinron* ideology. Thus, the much-vaunted "internationalization" (*kokusaika*) turns out to be a cover for nationalism. For instance, the opening "international" conference of the Nichibunken in 1988, on "Japan in the World," featured Claude Lévi-Strauss, Donald Keene, and Umehara Takeshi. The conference turned into a glorification of Japaneseness: Lévi-Strauss in particular delighted his hosts when he expressed his uncritical admiration for the uniquely aesthetic character of Japanese culture, a character which he sees as remaining unchanged from the Jōmon period to the present age. Obviously, we have to face the problem of our participation in *nihonjinron* discourse—even when we believe that we can remain critical. Thus, even a project like the present book—admittedly a hybrid collection of scholars—raises questions: for it is not clear whether the outcome will be a genuine critique or another attempt at containment.

Like Umehara's "New Kyoto school," Nishida, Nishitani and the Kyoto school have provided arguments to the *nihonjinron* ideology. Paradoxically, even recent critics of these trends end up contributing in a strange way to this ideology—not unlike Nishida himself when he thought that "a point of union between Eastern and Western culture could be sought in Japan." Karatani Kōjin (b. 1941), for example, argues that Japanese thought, as exemplified by Motoori Norinaga, was postmodern and poststructuralist *avant la lettre* (or *avant la Grammatologie*),[16] or rather, that it does not need poststructuralism and postmodernity, since it has never known a "rationalist" phase (with the benign exception of *karagokoro*, "Chinese mind," a term under which Motoori Norinaga includes Buddhist philosophy) against which to react (Karatani 1985a,b).

On the other hand, virulent *nihonjinron* critics like the Buddhist scholars Matsumoto Shirō and Hakamaya Noriaki adopt a reverse ethnocentrism which denies the authenticity of Japanese Buddhism (and most of Chinese Buddhism). Their criticism of the *tathāgatagarbha* theory and of its Japanese variant, the *hongaku shisō* ("inherent awakening" theory), is made in the name of "pure Buddhism"—a conception almost as narrowly essentialist and reifying as the nativism they denounce (see Matsumoto 1989, Hakamaya 1989). Hakamaya in particular, by taking the polemical high ground, has rapidly made a name for himself and stirred a tempest in the bowl of Japanese Buddhology—in particular in the Komazawa University *vase clos*. His attack on *hongaku shisō* leads him to reject out of hand Mahayana classics such as the *Vimalakīrti-sūtra*, Ch'an and Zen, and many aspects of Japanese culture deriving from the notion of the immanence of a Buddha nature. By attempting to give a normative definition of Buddhism as a teaching based on a few basic dogmas such as no-self (*anātman*) and co-dependent origination (*pratītya-samutpādā*), and selfless action, he intends to deal a heavy blow to traditional Buddhist scholarship.

Whatever its critical value in the Japanese context, this kind of polemics constitutes a regression for Buddhist scholarship—particularly when it is reproduced and thereby uncritically legitimized by Western scholars. Paul Swanson concludes his review of Hakamaya's book as follows: "The old clichés concerning Japanese religion can never again rest so comfortable or unquestioned. The academic world in Japan needs more books like this."[17] Although I agree that the Buddhist establishment deserves some challenge, this one seems counter-productive. It appears that we are here trading clichés—those of traditional Japanese Buddhology—for others— those of nineteenth-century, philosophically oriented, Western scholarship—and our understanding of Buddhism does not benefit much from this. Such normative, foundationalist conceptions of Buddhism are precisely what recent Western scholarship in Religious Studies has attempted, with some degree of success, to relegate to the section of Antiquities. It is sadly ironic that there still are Western scholars who see this as the very latest thing in Buddhist studies. Even if Hakamaya's criticism of the Kyoto school seems at first glance warranted, it is done for the wrong reasons, in the wrong way, and it has a very high cost. His view is as fundamentalist as the one it attemps to demolish, and its polemical thrust leads to rather unpleasant scapegoating mechanisms. Hakamaya works on the same premises as the best (or worst) of the Japanese scholarship that he so violently denounces: in particular, this bickering and rather elitist scholar of Yogācāra Buddhism, intent on settling accounts with the Komazawa University establishment, shows the same contempt for everything that is not purely textual, philological, and doctrinal. Paradoxically, his conception of religion as founded on a few intangible dogmas is strongly influenced by

Western and Christian (mis)conceptions about religion as pure *doxa*, orthodoxy. His denunciation of Ch'an/Zen as "not being true Buddhism," and his *ad hominem* attacks against Zen scholars such as Yanagida Seizan, are staged as a replay of Dōgen's denunciation of the "naturalist heresy" (*jinen gedō*). Thus, while presenting himself as a *nihonjinron* critic, he ends up, in good Sōtō orthodoxy, raising Dōgen as the true heir of Śākyamuni—while practically ignoring the entire Mahayana tradition. In order to achieve this dubious *tour de force*, he establishes the superiority of the so-called "twelve chapter *Shōbōgenzō*" over the better-known edition in seventy-five chapters. His reason for so doing is that, in the sermons of his later years, Dōgen (like Chi-tsang, Tsung-mi, and other Buddhists before him) criticizes the "substantialist" interpretation of the Buddha-nature, which he compares to Vedantist, Taoist, and Confucian conceptions. Hakamaya fails to point out that the same text also reveals a Dōgen advocating, not only the Buddhist theory of karmic causality (which Hakamaya admires), but also "superstitious" practices such as the cult of *stūpa*, of icons, of relics, and of the *kasāya* (the sacred patriarchal robe transmitted from Bodhidharma to Hui-neng, two "heretics" of the worst kind).[18] In other words, Dōgen was a pious Buddhist as different from Hakamaya's idealized conception of Dōgen the "critical thinker" as from the "incomparable philosopher" exalted by the Kyoto school. There is no need to discuss Hakamaya's theses in detail here. The weaknesses of this—hopefully short-lived—form of intellectual terrorism (compelling some colleagues to redirect their research) warns us against the temptation to localize the effects of ideology in a specific discourse, in contrast to which one's own discourse is assumed to be ideologically neutral.

Conclusions

Thus, despite its potential *esprit simpliste*, an ideological critique remains more than ever necessary, if only because ethnocentric categories are operative, despite a radically different historical context, in the thought and the rhetoric of contemporary Kyoto school philosophers and of their detractors (see Asada 1988, 633–34). Furthermore, as in the case of Heidegger, one cannot help asking to what extent the "philosophical text" is affected in its content by the ideological and political "context." In other words, how essential are these Orientalist and nationalist stigmata, not only to "Nishida philosophy," but also to "Zen philosophy" as it is championed by the Kyoto school and its Western admirers.

To repeat, I am not concerned here with "Nishida philosophy" as such, but with its long-lasting effects on the constitution of an authorized discourse on Zen and Japanese culture, a discourse monopolized by the later Kyoto school and vehicled by journals such as *The Eastern Buddhist* or *Philosophy East and West* and by institutions such as the F.A.S. ("For All Mankind Society"), an idealistic and rather grandiloquent lay movement founded in 1958 by Hisamatsu Shin'ichi (1889–1980) and dedicated to "universalism, individual self-awareness, critical spirit and a will to reformation."[19] My initial purpose in this essay was not to criticize philosophical or political ideas, but a certain rhetoric that remains trapped in Orientalist and nativist structures. However, I ended up raising two different sets of questions concerning the ideological role of "Zen philosophy" and the epistemological status of Zen Orientalism. This is in part because the philosophy—religious or otherwise— cannot be divorced from the rhetoric and its ideological effects.

Admittedly, only a discourse blind to its own conditions of production could blame Nishida and Nishitani for using Orientalist categories and chauvinist rhetoric at the time they wrote—a time when the opposition of East and West had become an all-powerful collective representation—in the Durkheimian sense. As the Heidegger controversy has shown, the mere denunciation of past errors might easily lead to good conscience while reproducing the scapegoating mechanisms it denounces. However, the attempt at objectivity is flawed in its presupposition (or wishful thinking) that a neutral ground may be found between the two conflicting approaches or entrenched positions variously defined as the hermeneutical and the ideological, or the philosophical and the political. Indeed, a charitable interpretation and a nuanced sense of context help explain, if not always justify, the motivations of these philosophers. Yet, by diffusing, contextualizing, framing, or simply deleting the most incriminating parts of their nativist discourse, one risks lending a hand to the forces of ideological recuperation still at work. Thus, in order to check the ideological effects and prevent them from reinforcing the *nihonjinron* ideology, one cannot avoid turning these philosophers into ideologues, and reducing the rich tapestry of their philosophical thought to what some may see as accidental slips, others as its woof.

With Suzuki, Zen, a demythologized product of the Meiji Buddhist reformation, attempted to co-opt the whole field of Japanese culture and, imposing on Japanese ideology the myth of transparency, claimed the status of a transcendental spirituality. With Nishida and the Kyoto school, Zen acquired a cross-cultural philosophical status. Thus, through the work of Suzuki, Nishida, and their successors, a new field of discourse was created, one that differs markedly from the earlier Ch'an/Zen discourse(s) it claimed to replicate or interpret. Even if the leitmotiv of transparency and purity are not mere alibis, they are the product of what one might, using Bourdieu's terminology, call a Zen *habitus*—that is, the perfect adequacy to values that seem "transparent" only because their conditions of production have been occluded (Bourdieu 1991, 53). For those who enter this field, everything may appear spontaneous or natural. The success of this discourse is proved by the fact that, for Suzuki's critics as well as for his Japanese and Western followers, the existence of something called Zen thought is always taken for granted: comparative philosophers manipulate the ideas of Dōgen, Nishida, or Heidegger, as if they were algebraic signs in an equation or discrete entities represented in diagrammatic form (see, for instance, Abe 1985). Not only do "Nishida effects" lead one to believe in the existence of Zen, they also can lead to the acceptance of the spiritual hegemony of pure experience, and implicitly of its advocates—a move that is never innocent in its nostalgia of tradition and emptiness. One can perhaps underscore with Heisig the creativity of the Kyoto school, and argue that its teaching cannot be simply reduced to traditional Buddhist doctrine (Heisig 1990). The problem, however, is that this school tends to co-opt Buddhism and is increasingly (and wrongly) perceived in the West as the authorized interpreter of Zen. *Zut à ce Zen-là*, as Etiemble said about Suzuki's watered-down, idealized, demythologized version of Zen—which, in his characteristic fashion, he labelled and spelled "Zaine" (see Faure 1993, 72–74). Furthermore, it is necessary to distinguish original thinkers like Nishida, Tanabe, and to some extent Nishitani, from their epigones—in whom the ideological "effects," no longer counterbalanced by originality, are strongest and most noticeable.

The recent increase of interest in the philosophy of the Kyoto school in the West makes this ideological critique more urgent. However, rather than accusing or excusing individual authors, we should shift the focus to ourselves, and realize that our accusing or excusing, excluding or including, is never neutral; that our reading these texts, our reception, is always verging on deception. The Nishida effects are alive in us, and this "effective history" is never simply critical or ideological, but also ideological while critical, or critical while ideological. For instance, it may be relatively easy to denounce the *nihonjinron* ideology, while it is harder to see the *amerikajinron* (or *furansujinron*) ideology at work in this very process. We need to become aware of our own "political ontology," even as we perform the necessary task of deconstructing that of "philosophical" movements like the Kyoto school. But certainly one cannot ignore the issue and continue to talk and write ad nauseam about "religion and nothingness," as if nothing ever happened.

If Nishitani is the full master of his discursive game, he must be held accountable for his early statements. Even if they occupy comparatively little space in the totality of his work, their murmur can be deafening. But this is asking claivoyance of an author—even an allegedly enlightened one—and we should rather admit that he, like so many others, became the mouthpiece of a specific ideology, one which still exists, in a different guise. We tend to endorse it when we listen to the seductive song of "pure philosophy." Perhaps it is time to shift the emphasis from the fallible individual philosopher to his gullible audience—ourselves—and from his perfected doctrine to the conditions of production and reproduction of his and our social and mental space. It is important to recognize the prejudice (in the Gadamerian sense) of this philosophy, to see, not only its insights, but its oversights—and blindness; while remaining aware of the existence, if not of the specifics, of our own.

Bibliography

Abe, Masao. 1985. *Zen and Western Thought.* Honolulu: University of Hawaii Press.

Arima, Tatsuo. 1969. *The Failure of Freedom: A Portrait of Modern Japanese Intellectuals.* Cambridge, MA: Harvard University Press.

Asada Akira. 1983. *Kōzō to chikara: kigōron o koete* (Structure and Power: Beyond Semiotics). Tokyo: Keisō shobō.

———. 1988. "Infantile Capitalism and Japan's Postmodernism: A Fairy Tale." *South Atlantic Review* 87/3, 629–34.

Boon, James A. 1982. *Other Tribes, Other Scribes: Symbolic Anthropology in the Comparative Study of Cultures, Histories, Religions and Texts.* Cambridge: Cambridge University Press.

Bourdieu, Pierre. 1991. *The Political Ontology of Martin Heidegger.* Cambridge: Polity Press.

Carter, Robert E. 1989. *The Nothingness Beyond God: An Introduction to the Philosophy of Nishida Kitarō*. New York: Paragon House.

Cook, Francis H. 1985. "Dōgen's View of Authentic Selfhood and its Socio-ethical Implications." In William R. LaFleur, ed., *Dōgen Studies*, 131–49. Honolulu: University of Hawaii Press.

Cooke, Gerald. 1974. "Traditional Buddhist Sects and Modernization in Japan." *Japanese Journal of Religious Studies* 1/4, 267–330.

Dale, Peter N. 1986. *The Myth of Japanese Uniqueness*. St Martin's Press.

de Bary, Brett. 1988. "Karatani Kōjin's *Origins of Modern Japanese Literature*." *South Atlantic Quarterly* 87/3, 591–613.

Derrida, Jacques. 1974 [1967]. *Of Grammatology*. Tr. Gayatri C. Spivak. Baltimore: Johns Hopkins University Press.

———. 1989. *Memoirs for Paul de Man*. New York: Columbia University Press.

Dilworth, David A. 1969a. "The Initial Formations of 'Pure Experience' in Nishida Kitarō and William James." *Monumenta Nipponica* 24/1–2, 93–111.

———. 1969b. "The Range of Nishida's Early Religious Thought: *Zen no Kenkyū*." *Philosophy East and West* 19/4, 409–21.

———. 1970a. "Nishida's Early Pantheistic Volontarism." *Philosophy East and West* 20/1, 35–49.

———. 1970b. "Nishida's Final Essay: The Logic of Place and a Religious World-view." *Philosophy East and West* 20/4, 355–67.

———. 1970c. "Nishida Kitarō (1870–1945): The Development of his Thought," Ph.D. dissertation, Columbia University, 1970.

———. 1978a. "Suzuki Daisetz as Regional Ontologist: Critical Remarks on Reading Suzuki's *Japanese Spirituality*." *Philosophy East and West* 28, 99–110.

———. 1978b. "The Concrete World of Action in Nishida's Later Thought," in Nitta Yoshihiro and Tatematsu Hirotaka, eds., *Japanese Phenomenology: Phenomenology as the Trans-cultural Philosophical Approach*, 249–70. Analecta Husserliana 8. Dortrecht: D. Reidel.

Dreyfus, Hubert L. and Paul Rabinow. 1983. *Michel Foucault: Beyond Structuralism and Hermeneutics*. Chicago: University of Chicago Press.

Durkheim, Emile. 1965. *The Elementary Forms of the Religious Life: A Study in Religious Sociology*. Tr. Joseph W. Swain. New York: Free Press.

274 *Bernard Faure*

Farias, Victor. 1991. *Heidegger and Nazism.* Temple University Press.

Faure, Bernard. 1991. *The Rhetoric of Immediacy: A Cultural Critique of Chan/Zen Buddhism.* Princeton: Princeton University Press.

―――. 1993. *Chan Insights and Oversights: An Epistemological Critique of the Chan Tradition.* Princeton: Princeton University Press.

Griffiths, Paul. 1985. "On the Possible Future of the Buddhist-Christian Interaction." In Minoru Kiyota, ed., *Japanese Buddhism: Its Tradition, New Religions, and Interaction with Christianity,* 145–61. Tokyo: Buddhist Books International.

Hakamaya Noriaki. 1989. *Hongaku shisō hihan* (A Critique of Original Enlightenment Theory). Tokyo: Daizō shuppan.

―――. 1992. *Dōgen to bukkyō: Jūnikanbon 'Shōbōgenzō' no Dōgen* (Dōgen and Buddhism: The Dōgen of the *Shōbōgenzō* in Twelve Chapters). Tokyo: Daizō shuppan.

Harootunian, H. D. 1988. "Visible Discourses/Invisible Ideologies." *South Atlantic Quarterly* 87/3, 445–74.

Heidegger, Martin. 1962. *Being and Time.* Tr. John Macquarrie and Edward Robinson. New York: Harper and Row.

―――. 1971. *On the Way to Language.* Tr. Peter D. Hertz. New York: Harper and Row.

Heisig, James W. 1990. "The Religious Philosophy of the Kyoto School." In Taitetsu Unno and James W. Heisig, eds., *The Religious Philosophy of Tanabe Hajime: The Metanoetic Imperative,* 12–42. Berkeley: Asian Humanities Press.

Hisamatsu Shin'ichi. 1960. "The Characteristics of Oriental Nothingness." Tr. Richard DeMartino. *Philosophical Studies of Japan* 2, 65–97.

Ishii Shūdō. 1990. "Recent Trends in Dōgen Studies." Tr. Albert Welter. *Annual Report of the Zen Institute* (*Komazawa Daigaku Zen kenkyūjō nenpō*) 1, (1)–(46).

Karatani Kōjin. 1985a. *Hihyō to posuto-modan* (Criticism and Postmodernity). Tokyo: Fukumu shoten.

―――. 1985b. "Généalogie de la culture japonaise." Tr. Nakamura Ryōji. *Magazine littéraire* 216–17: 18–20.

―――. 1988. "One Spirit, Two Nineteenth Centuries." *South Atlantic Review* 87/3: 615–28.

Kasulis, Thomas P. 1978. "The Zen-Philosopher: A Review-article on Dōgen Scholarship." *Philosophy East and West* 28, 353–73.

———. 1982. "The Kyoto School and the West: Review and Evaluation." *The Eastern Buddhist* (n.s.) 15/2, 125–45.

Katz, Steven T. 1978. "Language, Epistemology, and Mysticism." In Katz, ed., *Mysticism and Philosophical Analysis*, 22–74. New York: Oxford University Press.

Knauth, Lothar. 1965. "Life is Tragic: The Diary of Nishida Kitarō." *Monumenta Nipponica* 20/3–4, 335–58.

Kōsaka Masaaki, Nishitani Keiji, Kōyama Iwao, and Suzuki Shigetaka. 1942. "Sekaiteki tachiba to Nihon" (The Viewpoint of the World and Japan). Tokyo: Chūō kōronsha.

Kracht, Klaus. 1984. "Nishida Kitarō (1870–1945) as a Philosopher of the State." In Gordon Daniels, ed., *Europe Interprets Japan*, 198–203. Tenterden, Kent: Paul Norbury.

Lacoue-Labarthe, Philippe. 1990. *Heidegger, Art, and Politics*. Oxford: Basil Blackwell.

LaFleur, William R., ed. 1985. *Dōgen Studies*. Honolulu: University of Hawaii Press.

———. 1990. "A Turning in Taishō: Asian and Europe in the Early Writings of Watsuji Tetsurō." In J. Thomas Rimer, ed., *Japanese Intellectuals during the Interwar Years*, 234–56. Princeton: Princeton University Press.

Laplanche, Jean, and J. B. Pontalis, eds. 1967. *Vocabulaire de la psychanalyse*. Paris: Presses Universitaires de France.

Lavelle, Pierre. 1990. *La pensée politique du Japon contemporain*. Paris: Presses Universitaires de France.

———. 1994. "The Political Thought of Nishida Kitarō." *Monumenta Nipponica* 40/2, 139–65.

Maraldo, John C. 1989. "Translating Nishida." *Philosophy East and West* 39/4, 465–96.

———. 1993. "Nishitani Keiji's Abdication of the Nation." Paper presented at the Stanford Symposium "Imagining Japan: Narratives of Nationhood," May 13–14, 1993.

Matsumoto Shirō. 1989. *Engi to kū: nyoraizō shisō hihan* (Pratītyasamutpāda and Śūnyatā: A Criticism of Tathāgatagarbha Thought). Tokyo: Daizō shuppan.

Mauss, Marcel. 1968–69. *Oeuvres*. 3 vols. Paris: Editions de Minuit.

Miyajima Hajime. 1960. "'Junsui keikensetsu' no hassō ni kiyōshita shoshisō" (The Various Philosophical Contributions to the Formulation of the Conception of "Pure Experience"). *Risō* 326/7, 1–12.

Nakamura Yûjirō. 1987. *Nishida tetsugaku no datsu kōchiku* (The Deconstruction of Nishida-philosophy). Tokyo: Iwanami shoten.

Nakasone Yasuhiro and Umehara Takeshi. 1986. "Shōwa rokujūichinen o mukaete: Sekai bunmei no nagare to Nihon no yakuwari" (The Flow of World Culture and the Role of Japan). *Bungei shunjū*, 297–300.

Nishida Kitarō. 1949. "Bashoteki ronri to shūkyōteki sekaikan" (The Logic of Place and the Religious Worldview). In *Nishida Kitarō zenshū* (The Complete Works of Nishida Kitarō), vol. 11, 371–464. Tokyo: Iwanami shoten.

———. 1953. *Nihon bunka no mondai* (The Problem of Japanese Culture). In *Nishida Kitarō zenshū*, supplementary volume [*bekkan*] 6. Tokyo: Iwanami shoten. Reed. 1965–1966. *Nishida Kitarō zenshū*, vol. 12, 277–394.

———. 1960. *A Study of Good.* Tr. V.H. Viglielmo. Tokyo: Ministry of Education.

———. 1965. *Nishida Kitarō zenshū* (The Complete Works of Nishida Kitarō). 19 volumes. Tokyo: Iwanami shoten.

———. 1987. *Last Writings: Nothingness and the Religious Worldview.* Tr. David A. Dilworth. Honolulu: University of Hawaii Press.

———. 1990. *An Inquiry into the Good.* Tr. Masao Abe and Christopher Ives. New Haven: Yale University Press.

———. 1991. *La culture japonaise en question.* Tr. Pierre Lavelle. Paris: Publications Orientalistes de France [see Nishida 1953].

Nishitani Keiji. 1982. *Religion and Nothingness:* Tr. Jan Van Bragt, Berkeley: University of California Press.

———. 1990. *The Self-Overcoming of Nihilism.* Tr. Graham Parkes with Setsuko Aihara. Albany: State University of New York Press.

———. 1991. *Nishida Kitarō.* Tr. Yamamoto Seisaku and James W. Heisig. Berkeley: University of California Press.

Noda, Matao. 1955. "East-West Synthesis in Kitarō Nishida." *Philosophy East and West* 4, 345–59.

Ogawa, Tadashi. 1978. "The Kyoto School of Philosophy and Phenomenology." In Nitta Yoshihiro and Tatematsu Hirotaka, eds., *Japanese Phenomenology: Phenomenology as the Trans-cultural Philosophical Approach*, 207–21. Analecta Husserliana 8. Dortrecht: D. Reidel.

Piovesana, Gino K. 1968. *Recent Japanese Philosophical Thought, 1862–1962: A Survey.* Rev. ed., *Monumenta Nipponica* Monographs 29. Tokyo: Sophia University.

Sakai, Naoki. 1988. "Modernity and its Critique: The Problem of Universalism and Particularism." *South Atlantic Quarterly* 87/3, 475–504.

Sharf, Robert H. 1991. "Occidentalism and the Zen of Japanese Nationalism," presented at the national meeting of the American Academy of Religion, November 1991 [published as "The Zen of Japanese Nationalism," *History of Religions* 33/1 (August 1993), 1–43].

Shibata, Masumi. 1981. "The Diary of a Zen Layman: The Philosopher Nishida Kitarō." *The Eastern Buddhist* 14/2, 121–31.

Stone, Jackie. 1990. "A Vast and Grave Task: Interwar Buddhist Studies as an Expression of Japan's Envisioned Global Role." In J. Thomas Rimer, ed., *Japanese Intellectuals during the Interwar Years*, 217–33. Princeton: Princeton University Press.

Suzuki, Daisetsu (D. T.). 1960. "How to Read Nishida." In Nishida Kitarō. 1960. *A Study of Good*, iii–iv. Tr. V. H. Viglielmo. Tokyo: Ministry of Education.

———. 1970 [1959]. *Zen and Japanese Culture*. Princeton: Princeton University Press.

———. 1972. *Japanese Spirituality*. Tr. Norman Waddell. Comp. the Japanese Commission for UNESCO. Tokyo: Japanese Society for the Promotion of Science.

Takeuchi, Yoshinori. 1959. "Buddhism and Existentialism: The Dialogue between Oriental and Occidental Thought." In W. Leibrecht, ed., *Religion and Culture: Essays in Honor of Paul Tillich*. New York: Haprper and Row.

———. 1982. "The Philosophy of Nishida." In Frederick Franck, ed., *The Buddha Eye: An Anthology of the Kyoto School*, 179–202. New York: Crossroad.

Tanabe Hajime. 1986. *Philosophy as Metanoetics*. Tr. Takeuchi Yoshinori. Berkeley: University of California Press.

Thelle, Notto R. 1984. " 'The Flower Blooms at the Cliff's Edge': Profile of Nishitani Keiji, a Thinker Between East and West." *Journal of American Religion* 13/3, 47–56.

Tillich, Paul, and Hisamatsu Shin'ichi. 1971–73. "Dialogues, East and West: Conversations between Dr. Paul Tillich and Dr. Hisamatsu Shin'ichi." *The Eastern Buddhist* (n.s.) 4/2, 89–107; 5/2, 107–28; 6/2, 87–114.

Tsunoda, Ryusaku, Wm. Theodore de Bary, and Donald Keene, eds. 1964. *Sources of Japanese Tradition*. 2 vols. New York: Columbia University Press.

Ueda Shizuteru. 1983. "Ascent and Descent: Zen Buddhism in Comparision with Meister Eckhart." *The Eastern Buddhist* (n.s.) 16/1, 52–73; 16/2, 72–91.

——. 1990. "'Experience and Language' in the Thinking of Kitarō Nishida." Paper presented at the Annual Meeting of the American Academy of Religion in New Orleans.

Unno, Taitetsu, ed. 1990. *The Religious Philosophy of Nishitani Keiji: Encounter with Emptiness.* Berkeley: Asian Humanities Press.

Unno, Taitetsu, and James W. Heisig, eds. 1990. *The Religious Philosophy of Tanabe Hajime: The Metanoetic Imperative.* Nanzan Institute for Religion and Culture. Berkeley: Asian Humanities Press.

Viglielmo, Valdo Humbert, tr. 1960. *A Study of Good.* Tokyo: Japanese Government Printing Bureau.

Waldenfels, Hans. 1966. "Absolute Nothingness: Preliminary Considerations on a Central Notion in the Philosophy of Nishida Kitarō and the Kyoto School." *Monumenta Nipponica* 21/3–4, 354–91.

——. 1980. *Absolute Nothingness: Foundations of a Buddhist-Christian Dialogue.* New York: Paulist Press.

Wargo, Robert J. J. 1972. *The Logic of Basho and the Concept of Nothingness in the Philosophy of Nishida Kitarō.* Ann Arbor: University Microfilms International.

Yamada Munemutsu. 1978. *Nishida Kitarō no tetsugaku: Nihonkei shisō no genzō* (The Philosophy of Nishida Kitarō: The Development of Japanese Thought). Tokyo: San'ichi shobō.

Yusa, Michiko, tr. 1986–87. "The Logic of *Topos* and the Religious Worldview." *The Eastern Buddhist* (n.s.) 19/2, 1–29; 20/1, 81–119.

——. 1991. "Nishida and the Question of Nationalism." *Monumenta Nipponica* 46/2, 203–9.

Notes

1. Concerning Heidegger, see Farias 1991; Bourdieu 1991; Lacoue-Labarthe 1990. Concerning Paul de Man, see Derrida 1989. Mircea Eliade's participation in the Iron Guard, although well documented, has not been the object of much debate at Chicago and elsewhere.

2. Western language literature on Nishida and the Kyoto school has steadily grown in recent years. On Nishida, see in particular: Noda 1955; Dilworth 1969a, b, 1970a, 1970a, b, c, 1978b; Waldenfels 1966; Maraldo 1989 and Nishitani 1991. On the Kyoto school, see also: Ogawa 1978; Waldenfels 1966; Kasulis 1982; Maraldo 1989, 1993.

3. In his diary, Nishida appears as a rather unsatisfied and almost culturally alienated individual, obsessed with his smoking habit and writing to himself in snatches of German and various other Western languages. On Nishida's diaries, see Knauth 1965 and Shibata 1981.

4. See Miyajima Hajime, *Meijiteki shisōzō no keisei*, Tokyo (1960), 376–82; quoted in Knauth 1965, 357. On the ideological elements in Nishida's thought, see Pierre Lavelle, "The Political Thought of Nishida Kitarō" (unpublished paper), and Lavelle 1990, 78–81. On Nishida's political ideas, see also: Yamada Munemutsu, *Nishida Kitarō no tetsugaku: Nihonkei shisō no genzō*, Tokyo: San'ichi shobō (1978); and Nakamura Yūjirō, *Nishida tetsugaku no datsu kōchiku* (Tokyo: Iwanami, 1987).

5. For a critique of the Ch'an/Zen "rhetoric of immediacy," see Faure 1991.

6. As can be seen from the following excerpt, Nishida was strongly influenced by Amidism: "Even Mahayana did not truly attain to the world-creatively real in the sense that I have just indicated. I think that it was perhaps only in Japanese Buddhism that the absolute identity of negation and affirmation was realized, in the sense of the identity of the actual and the absolute that is peculiar to the Japanese spirit. Examples of this realization are found in such ideas of Shinran as 'in calling on the name of Buddha non-reason is reason' and 'effortless acceptance of the grace of Amida.' But even in Japan, it has not been positively grasped. It has only been understood as an absolute passivity to Amida, or as some non-discriminating wisdom in a merely irrational, mystical sense" (Nishida 1987, 102). Shinran's notion of "natural conformity with the Dharma" (*jinen hōni*, a term rendered by Dilworth as "effortless acceptance of the grace of Amida") recurs often in *The Problem of Japanese Culture*, and Nishida points out that this notion has nothing to do with the Western concept of nature [Nishida 1965, *bekkan* 6, 127–29].

7. Nishida 1965, *bekkan* 6, 104; Tsunoda, de Bary, and Keene 1964, 2, 362; see also Nishida 1987, 102. Nishida 1991, 73–74.

8. See for example, the notion of "self-identity of absolute contradictories" (*zettai mujunteki jikō doitsu*), Nishida's version of the Buddhist logic of dialectical identity (*sokuhi*), in *On the Philosophy of Descartes* (*Dekaruto no tetsugaku ni tsuite*), 1943; in Nishida 1965, 11. 189. See also *Zen bunka no mondai*, in Nishida 1965, *bekkan* 6, 104.

9. See Nishida 1987, 107–8. Already in *Fundamental Problems of Philosophy*, in an essay entitled "The Forms of Culture of the Classical Periods of East and West Seen from a Metaphysical Perspective," Nishida had determined that, whereas the ground of reality was Being for Western philosophy, it was Nothingness for the East.

10. On this "irenically polemic" dialogue, as Cooke calls it (Cooke 1974, 276), see Takeuchi Yoshinori, "Buddhism and Existentialism: The

Dialogue between Oriental and Occidental Thought," in W. Leibrecht, ed., *Religion and Culture: Essays in Honor of Paul Tillich* (New York: Harper and Row 1959), 291–365. For a more open "dialogue," see Waldenfels 1980; for a critique of the concept of "Oriental Nothingness," see Wargo 1972.

11. Kōsaka, Nishitani, Kōyama, and Suzuki 1943, 201. Similarly, in the April 1942 symposium entitled "Ethics and Historicality of the Great Asian Co-prosperity Sphere" ["Tōakyōeiken no rinrisei to rekishisei"], Kōsaka Masaaki declared: "The Sino-Japanese war is also a war of morality. Now that we have entered the Great Asian War, the war is much larger in scale now, namely, a war between the Oriental morality and the Occidental morality. Let me put it differently, the question is which morality will play a more important role in the World History in the future." [*Chūō kōron*, April 1942, 120–21; qtd. in Sakai 1988, 492–93].

12. For a critique of Suzuki, see Faure 1993, 52–74. On the relation of the warrior mystique to Japanese imperialism in Asia, see *Kokutai no hongi* [Foundamentals of Our National Polity], a propaganda tract drafted in 1937 by the Japanese Ministry of Education: "It is this same *bushidō* that shed itself of an outdated feudalism at the time of the Meiji Restoration, increased in splendor, became the Way of loyalty and patriotism, and has evolved before us as the spirit of the imperial forces" [Tsunoda, de Bary, and Keene 1958, 2, 285].

13. William Haver, "review of *Nietzsche and Asian Thought*," *Journal of Asian Studies* 51/3 (1992), 630; and Maraldo 1993, 9.

14. See Nakasone Yasuhiro and Umehara Takeshi, "Shōwa rokujūichinen o mukaete: Sekai bunmei no nagare to Nihon no yakuwari" [The Flow of World Civilization and the Role of Japan], *Bungei shunjū*, February 1986, 297–300. He elaborates on these ideas in various books such as *Japan's Deep Strata, The Philosophy of the Forest Will Save Mankind*, or *The Spirit of the Japanese*.

15. See the following passage of *Kokutai no hongi*: 'Harmony is a product of the great achievements of the founding of the nation, and is the power behind our historical growth; it is also a humanitarian Way inseparable from our daily lives . . . Harmony as in our nation is a great harmony of individuals who, by giving play to their individual differences, and through difficulties, toil and labor, converge as one. . . . War, in this sense, is not by any means intended for the destruction, overpowering, or subjugation of others; and it should be a thing for the bringing out of great harmony, that is, peace, doing the work of creation by following the Way" [Tsunoda, de Bary, and Keene 1958, 282–83].

16. Derrida, *Of Grammatology*, 1974.

17. Paul Swanson, "review of Hakamaya Noriaki, *Hongaku shisō hihan*," in *Japanese Journal of Religious Studies* 17/1 (1990), 89–91.

18. See Yūhō Yokoi, *Zen Master Dōgen: An Introduction with Selected Writings* (New York: Weatherhill, 1976).

19. According to Hisamatsu, *"F"* also stands for *formless* self, *"A"* for the stand of *all* mankind, while *"S"* points to the obligation to create a *suprahistorical* history. Therefore, these three letters symbolize the three dimensions of human life: self, world, and history. See Cooke 1974, 303.

Chapter Ten

Tradition Beyond Modernity:
Nishitani's Response to the Twentieth Century

DALE S. WRIGHT

Born in rural Ishikawa prefecture in the year 1900, educated in Tokyo, and established as professor of philosophy in Kyoto, Nishitani Keiji has recently gained prominence in an international philosophical context as Japan's best-known and perhaps foremost thinker. Moreover, his longtime study of Nietzsche and his years of study with Martin Heidegger in Germany have contributed to the idea that Nishitani may also be Japan's representative "postmodern" thinker. It is certainly true that much of Nishitani's work is a focused response to Japan's emergent modernity as well as a critique of paradigmatic modern forms of thought. What makes Nishitani's response to modernity exceptionally interesting, however, is that his resources for this response are essentially twofold, each source appearing on the opposite side of modernity. On the one hand, Nishitani was educated and trained as a specialist in European thought with a focus on German philosophy. Particularly attracted to Nietzsche and Heidegger, the two thinkers most critical of the modern Enlightenment project and most often cited as the precursors of postmodern thought, Nishitani had access to powerful critiques of the modern world. On the other hand, Nishitani's later work shifts its focal point from Europe to Japan in search of indigenous resources in response to the westernization and modernization of Japan. Here Nishitani's sources are the premodern tradition of Zen Buddhism set in the context of East Asian Mahayana Buddhist thought. Having immersed himself early in life in the former (European thought), Nishitani set as his goal a retrieval of the latter (East Asian thought) under postmodern circumstances.

In this chapter I seek to understand Nishitani's response to modernity by examining ways in which his premodern Buddhist and postmodern European sources enable him to articulate positions on three focal issues which have emerged in Western debates on modernity. These three, each integrally tied to the others, are: selfhood, nihilism, and historical consciousness. On these bases I will reflect, in conclusion, on the question of the applicability of the category "postmodern" as applied to Nishitani's thought.

Selfhood and Modernity

I shall begin with Nishitani's critique of the modern form of selfhood because it is here, in Nishitani's view, that modernity is most clearly manifest. The modern era makes available to us a particular way to be a self as well as a particular interpretation of that mode of being.

What is the distinctively modern mode of being? Nishitani locates the origins of the modern self in the Cartesian *cogito*, the self which takes its own independent and indubitable being as the point of certainty from which all else can be interrogated. Upon this foundation of comprehensive self-knowledge, the modern self understands itself to be capable both of the kind of detachment essential to scientific observation and of unlimited progressive enlightenment. Asserting itself over the world, the self structures its activities around the pursuit of power through knowledge. Nishitani's quest for an understanding of selfhood begins with an effort to question and challenge these dimensions of the modern self.

Nishitani undertook this challenge because he concluded, early on in his career, that the self is not fully transparent to itself, and that there are unknown depths to the self that foil any effort of the "I" to pose as a foundation or ground. These depths are unknown largely because they originate beyond the self; they are the presence of otherness within the self. Perhaps partly because of the collectivist character of Japanese society, it was clear to Nishitani that no self is independent of society at large, and of history, culture, and language. For these reasons the self, for Nishitani, is less an independent and self-conscious unity than a plurality of confluent traces. In his view the Cartesian non-social self is an illusion generated by the history of a desire to make the self graspable by constructing sharp boundaries between self and world. For Nishitani, these "boundaries" are unclear and evasive to structural metaphysics because they are always porous to outside intervention, and always in flux.

One consequence of Nishitani's view on the relational qualities of the self is that modern freedom, understood as the autonomy of the self, becomes questionable as well. Nishitani came to conclude, no doubt under both Buddhist and Western influences, that the free choice of the rational modern subject is itself dependent upon a prior shaping of individual identity in an intersubjective setting.[1] Human choices presuppose the complex cultural and historical background which makes them possible and which are ultimately inscrutable to any form of methodical knowing. For Nishitani, the real issue is not so much the "autonomous self" as it is the self's non-autonomous background. Therefore the heart of his intellectual project comes to be understood as the quest for "a true attainment of our background."[2]

Thus far, Nishitani's doctrine of the self coincides with the early Heidegger of *Being and Time* as he no doubt understood it from the first translations of Heidegger into Japanese in the 1930s and directly from Heidegger in class and as a guest in conversations at Heidegger's home in Freiburg. Nishitani understood the relational and non-substantial concept of the self as Dasein (*gensonzai*) and he nods approvingly in his own writings at Heidegger's efforts to break the subject-object separation of modern self-awareness. The self is not encapsulated within an inner sphere and need not, therefore, go out of itself to encounter the world. We already are, Nishitani says in antimodern rhetoric—that is, from the standpoint of a postmodern critique of modernity—"being-in-the-world."[3]

From there Nishitani follows both Heidegger and Buddhist thought a step further: it is not enough to live as the unself-conscious, socially determined self. Becoming truly ourselves, we must, on our own, face what he calls "the *koto* [matter] of life and death." "It is our own affair," he writes, "not anybody elses".[4] The Kierkegaardian/Heideggerian critique of the inauthentic "crowd" or *das Man*, which inspired mid-twentieth century existentialism, was rendered into Japanese as *seken no hito*, "society's person," or one who is unable to take the project of being onto oneself as one's own. Faced with submersion in cultural anonymity, Nishitani calls upon the modern self "to become a question mark" (*gimonfu to naru*), to problematize oneself and enter into the path of self-inquiry.

The questioning self is the self that discovers two shocking truths: that "finitude constitutes our innermost essence" and that human being has "Nothing at its ground."[5] Here, however, Nishitani tends to differ from at least one prominent line of postmodern Western thought represented by Nietzsche and Foucault. Rather than trace the self into its complex multiplicities that are determined by historical, sociological, or psychological factors, Nishitani treats this background as a nonsubstantive unity. Rather than a social/historical plurality, he refers to it as "nothingness" or "the void." On this point, in every essay in *Shūkyō to wa nani ka* (What is Religion?, translated as *Religion and Nothingness*), Nishitani reverts to the language of Zen Buddhism and to stories about the masters of the void. And quite understandably, Nishitani begins to sound pre-(post)modern in his language of the "True Self." It is clear that Nishitani is well aware of the rhetorical choice he has made. After all, he had access to Buddhist versions of "dissemination" without needing to allude to Western texts at all. Kegon (Ch. Hua-yen) thought in Japan, which as Nishitani occasionally notes appears as a primary philosophical influence in Zen texts, shows the source of the self to be everywhere and essentially untraceable. Nevertheless, he prefers the simpler and more powerful language of Zen. It is "not that the self is empty," he says, "but that emptiness is the self."[6] In Nishitani's view, Cartesian or modern self-doubt only reaches its true conclusion in the "Great Doubt" of Hakuin from the perspective of which the self stands "over the deep chasm" of nihilism.

Nihilism

The second issue—nihilism—continues Nishitani's inquiry into modern selfhood and it is on this topic, more than any other one, that Nishitani focuses attention. A number of interesting historical connections between Japan and Germany stand behind Nishitani's analysis of modern nihilism. In 1936 Nishitani arrived in Germany to spend two years studying with Martin Heidegger. Picture the political intensity of that historical moment in Germany and Japan, as both nations were rapidly advancing on a collision course with the rest of the world. Recall also that this was the moment subsequent to Heidegger's now infamous political failure as rector of the university and in his relation to the National Socialist Party. Withdrawing from the political arena, Heidegger turned his philosophical interests toward Nietzsche's diagnosis of the modern condition of nihilism. Nishitani, who had long been an avid reader of Nietzsche, immersed himself in Heidegger's attempt to use Nietzsche as the catalyst in a thoroughgoing reevaluation of the modern age.

Another intriguing historical link was the arrival in Japan, also in 1936, of the prominent German philosopher, Karl Löwith.[7]

Löwith settled into Sendai University for what turned out to be a five-year stay, leaving Japan in 1941 when the worldwide implications of the European and Asian wars began to be felt. Löwith had also been a student of Heidegger and was the first twentieth-century European thinker to focus his work specifically on the issue of nihilism. In 1933 he had written a book on Kierkegaard and Nietzsche subtitled "The Theological and Philosophical Overcoming of Nihilism." In the early 1940s, he published further on the issue of nihilism, based on work he had written while in Japan. Finally, in 1948, the year before Nishitani delivered his lectures entitled *Nihirizumu* (Nihilism), a translation of a monograph by Lowith appeared in Japan under the title "Yoroppa no nihirizumu" ("European Nihilism").

Against all of this historical background, and no doubt much more, Nishitani began to lecture on the topic of nihilism in 1949. Although this work, recently translated into English as *The Self-Overcoming of Nihilism*,[8] focuses heavily upon European thought, the seeds of Nishitani's subsequent conversion to Buddhist thought are already clearly there. The primary theme is that of "nihility" (*kyomu*), the hollowness or negativity manifest in modern life, and the possibility of overcoming this negativity in some deeper form of human praxis. Nihility becomes manifest in the modern West, and subsequently, according to Nishitani, in Japan, as a consequence of the destruction of traditional forms of life, particularly religious life. Nishitani connects nihility to the "mechanization of human life"[9] and to a way of thinking that, rather than standing in awe of the world, seeks to conquer and to transform it in accordance with human desire. Moreover, human beings are constructed to understand themselves in terms of this conquest and to orient themselves toward the "pursuit of desires."[10] For Nishitani this transformation is no less than a loss of world undermining the possibility that any form of human excellence will be achieved except through an overcoming of the modern.

Of course, not everyone experiences this modern form of selfhood as a loss. But, according to the early Nishitani, anyone who "resolutely strives to be oneself and to seek the ground of one's actual existence"[11] comes to be aware of the hollowness, the nothingness at the root of all things. "On the field of nihility," Nishitani writes, "all that is ordinarily said to exist or to be real . . . is unmasked as having nihility at its ground, as lacking roots from the very beginning."[12] Awareness of "no ground," Nishitani's notion of *mutei*, is clearly related to what we now call the "end of metaphysics," the awareness that there is no primary reality from which all other realities can be derived. The dawning of this nihilistic possibility is the source of modern anxiety, a form of anxiety correlate to the sense that we human beings stand on no foundation whatsoever.

Nishitani's point in all this, however, is that the experience of nihility is "transitional," a sign of the possibility of transcendence.[13] That we may overcome nihility is, for Nishitani, a religious possibility. It is something "quite beyond the control of the consciousness and arbitrary willfulness of the self,"[14] which is the reason, presumably, that Nishitani's Japanese volume *Nihirizumu* has been translated under the title *The Self-Overcoming of Nihilism*. It is also for the same reason that Nishitani names the deepest form of modern self-questioning the "self-presentation of the Great Doubt."[15] Rather than something we do, these events occur to us beyond our control as possibilities determined by larger historical forces.

Especially in his early work, Nishitani thinks that this religious possibility makes its first modern appearance in the work of Nietzsche as a new form of religiosity. He writes, "A fundamental conversion in the human way of being in the world . . . shows up in Nietzsche as the impulse to a new religiosity—basically different from former religions but nonetheless a new religiosity."[16] As Nishitani's articulation of this new religiosity gains maturity, it is increasingly informed by a retrospective reading of the Buddhist tradition and less and less by Nietzsche, who in later writings, begins to be submitted to critique.[17] Now asserted in the language of classical Mahayana as interpreted by Nishitani's mentor Nishida Kitarō, the religious possibility beyond the experience of nihility is called *zettai mu*, "absolute nothingness," or *kū no tachiba*, the "standpoint of emptiness." Although the groundlessness of reality and the loss of self are first experienced nihilistically in anxiety and dread, facing this nihility allows one to pass through it to "the Great Affirmation,"[18] where emptiness, the infinite interpenetration of all beings, enables the groundless self to keep its balance.[19]

The juxtaposition of "emptiness" and "the self" opens up extraordinary possibilities. Most significant is the possibility of a new posture for human life beyond or even from within the loss of metaphysical grounds, a form of thinking and experience no longer insistent upon absolute foundations. "The total loss of ground and structure becomes the basis for creative freedom, a freedom unfixed on and unattached to anything else, an ecstatic self-detachment."[20] Nishitani relishes in the Zen/Kegon tendency to name this basis in paradoxical terms. It is a "groundless ground," a "foundationless foundation." Attaining the form of self-awareness behind these paradoxical claims entails a monumental conversion in religious terms. "It is nothing less," he writes, "than a conversion from the self-centered mode of being, which always asks what use things have for us . . . to an attitude that asks for what purpose we ourselves exist. Only when we stand at this turning point does the question 'What is religion?' really become our own."[21]

But what is the connection between this experience, available through the practices of traditional East Asian Buddhism and the modern world? If this transformation from "nihilistic emptiness" to "relational emptiness" reinstates a traditional account given by Buddhists of their highest realization, in what kind of relation does it stand to history and to the modern era? If, in Western postmodern thought, nihilism is first and foremost a historical phenomenon, how can Nishitani locate this same problematic in traditional Buddhism?

Historical Consciousness

These questions take us to our third issue: historicity, or the kind of historical consciousness present in Nishitani's thought. Is nihilism a historical phenomenon, peculiar to modernity, or is it a perennial metaphysical issue, something intrinsic to human being as such? Nishitani's answer is occasionally one, occasionally the other, and, in at least one place, ambiguously both. In the early essays on nihilism, he writes that "nihilism as we understand it today is the product of a particular epoch, the modern period in Europe. It represents the current achievement of the European spirit, a provisional outcome of the whole of history in a modern European expression."[22] Some years later, in the essay "Śūnyatā and Time" included in *Religion and Nothingness*, he writes: "This is not to say that the awareness of the abyss of nihility found in nihilism appears only in the West. Quite to the contrary, it has been present in the East, particularly in India, since ancient times as a perennial and fundamental issue."[23] Bringing these two positions together, Nishitani writes: "On the one hand, nihilism is a problem that transcends time and space and is rooted in the essence of human being, an existential problem in which the being of the self is revealed to the self itself as something groundless. On the other hand, it is a historical and social phenomenon, an object of the study of history. The phenomenon of nihilism shows that our historical life has lost its ground. . . . Viewed in this way, one might say that it is a general phenomenon that occurs from time to time in the course of history. The mood of postwar Japan would be one such instance."[24]

The upshot of this convergence seems to be that nihilism is a metaphysically determined structural possibility for human beings as such and that historical circumstances will determine the extent to which the phenomenon is manifest in the lived experience of any particular epoch. Our problem with this explanation, however, is that it seems to assume a separation between metaphysical essence and historical manifestation. But Nishitani has anticipated our critique. In *The Self-Overcoming of Nihilism* he writes: "The metaphysical essence of human existence and its historical manifestations are correlatives. . . . The habit of separating essence and phenomenon is a residue of the tendency to separate the subject of inquiry from its object. Even when life is taken as the central problematic of history, there is still a chance that one is not yet questioning in a truly historical way."[25]

Nevertheless, we may still suspect that Nishitani's correlation implies that he "is not yet questioning in a truly historical way."[26] Whatever can be correlated can also be separated, and this separation is just what postmodern historical reflection—from Nietzsche to Derrida and Foucault—has called into question. These philosophers ask: What is "metaphysical essence" beyond a connection which we are inclined to make between selected elements of historical manifestation? And they respond: There is nothing—no essence—standing beyond historical manifestation as its ground. Nishitani is clearly aware of the issue, as the previous quote shows, but he may not have seen it through to the conclusions that, for us, a full historical awareness would require.

Nishitani's attention is clearly elsewhere, however. By the time he had appropriated European historical thought to the point that he could see modernity as a meaning-bearing sign pointing beyond itself to some further, transcendental possibility for human being, he had already come to understand a demythologized Buddhism as the referent of that sign. Although nihilism is indeed the malady of modern self-consciousness that the Japanese are quickly learning from the West, traditional Buddhist thought—even though currently dormant in Japan—holds the key to forms of experience able to push through nihilism to positive, albeit still groundless, forms of human experience. Nishitani pictures this historical epoch beyond the modern as a third stage in the development of human history that is analogous to three stages of progression in Zen practice. This triad has traditionally been expressed in numerous ways, and Nishitani calls many of them into reflection. For example, there is the classical Mahayana account of the bodhisattva's movement from *saṃsāra* to *nirvāṇa* and then back to a transformed *saṃsāra* synthesized with *nirvāṇa*. There is also the Kegon movement from phenomenal form to emptiness to true emptiness inseparable from forms, and the Tendai movement from things to emptiness to "the middle way." Moreover, Dōgen expresses a trichotomy of thinking, non-thinking, and without-thinking (or the prethought), and a Zen narrative attributed to Ch'ing-yüan Wei-hsin and westernized in verse by the popular singer Donovan suggests that "first there is a mountain, then there is no mountain, then there is," and so on. Nishitani's own version of this threefold development is the movement from "the field of consciousness" to "the field of nihility" (relative nothingness) and through it to the "field of emptiness" (absolute nothingness).[27]

Individual Buddhist saints are understood to have moved through these three stages. Our epoch is different, however, in that modern nihilism places virtually all of us in the second stage from which we have no choice but to learn how to live in the midst of impermanence and relativity—thereby beginning to transcend to the third stage—or fail to survive at all. The breakthrough to stage three—the bodhisattva's reemergence into the samsaric world after having attained *nirvāṇa*—is now not just a structural possibility for us but a historical necessity, a matter of survival through the self-overcoming of nihilism.

"On this field of emptiness," Nishitani writes of stage three, "modern man's standpoint of subjective self-consciousness, which had been opened up by Kant's Copernican Revolution, has to be revolutionized again. We appear to have come to the point that the relationship in knowledge whereby the object is said to fashion itself after our *a priori* patterns of intuition and thought has to be inverted yet again so that the self may fashion itself after things and correspond to them. The field of emptiness goes beyond both the field of sense intuition and rational thinking."[28]

The rhetoric of this passage and others demonstrates an inclination toward something like progressive historical understanding. Nishitani claims that transcendence "signals an advance to the final frontier" and that it "has to advance a stage deeper in its development." His language is deeply influenced by the Hegelian rhetoric of overcoming in addition to the notion of paradigm-shifts now so fully ensconced in twentieth-century thought. Nishitani clearly thinks

Buddhist thoughts within a newly emerging historicized framework. Significant new possibilities for thinking emerge out of this cross-cultural juxtaposition.

On the other hand, there are several places where limits to the historical dimension of Nishitani's thinking come into view. Meister Eckhart, for example, a medieval German mystic and theologian, is regarded as having attained the third stage to which Nietzsche and twentieth-century thinkers, including Heidegger and Sartre, would aspire but fail to attain. Eckhart's negative theology is understood by Nishitani as having lifted him, not only out of medieval metaphysics, but beyond the abyss of modern nihility as well. More telling perhaps is the fact that when Nishitani writes about Buddhism, very little historical articulation enters the picture. When referring to premodern Buddhist figures, Nishitani follows the Japanese custom of alluding to "the ancients," as if all Buddhist saints from every era could be included within this one historical category. Buddhism as a whole—with the exception of a weak Hinayana phase—appears always and everywhere to demonstrate the full development of religious form.[29] This privileging of Buddhism is perhaps inevitable in that it cannot be separated from Nishitani's reliance on transitional East Asian sources for the overcoming of nihilism. Japanese Buddhist thought—even in its modern form—tends to be ahistorically conceived. Although Buddhist texts are currently being submitted in Japanese scholarship to philological, form-critical, and historical analyses learned from the West, this was not the case in the early postwar period. Even now these critical methodologies tend to focus more on individual historical issues than on an historical overview or the deconstruction of layers of development in the Buddhist tradition. Nishitani's Buddhism is, for the most part, an ahistorical phenomenon.

Another indication of limitations in Nishitani's historical sense is that in two crucial essays on this topic—"*Śūnyatā* and Time" and "*Śūnyatā* and History" (the concluding chapters of *Religion and Nothingness*)—Nishitani does not engage the most significant Western philosophical literature on these topics. For example, "*Śūnyatā* and Time" is clearly modeled on Heidegger's *Being and Time*. Yet, in spite of influences on rhetorical style and language, Heidegger's thinking on temporality nowhere enters Nishitani's text. Instead, Nishitani takes Dōgen as the fully realized historical thinker and chooses Arnold Toynbee as the Western historical thinker with whom to enter into debate. Not surprisingly, Dōgen runs circles around Toynbee.

In saying this, however, I do not mean to imply that Nishitani's choice of Toynbee invalidates his project. Toynbee's historical sense is no doubt exemplary of Western—especially Anglo—historical consciousness. Toynbee is also fully "modern" in overall orientation and therefore open to Nishitani's "deconstruction." But it is well worth noticing his choice. If Nishitani had wanted to write on historical temporality and to test the viability of Dōgen in a contemporary, cross-cultural setting, he could have done no better than to place Dōgen in relation to *Being and Time*—the text which was then rapidly transforming historical awareness in the West, and not incidentally, calling modernity into question.

Once again, however, Nishitani makes a move that seems to anticipate possible criticisms of his historical understanding. In "*Śūnyatā* and Time" he acknowledges, with both humility and a call to action, that "a consciousness of history . . . remains largely undeveloped within Buddhist teaching." Continuing, he asks, "Why is this? It is surely an issue of importance for us today to retrace the causes of this failure."[30] In other words, Nishitani has called upon his contemporaries to submit their own Buddhist tradition to a far-reaching reflection on the process through which its historical understanding has been constructed. That call, I suspect, will be central to Japancsc philosophy in the twenty-first century.

Conclusions

I have surveyed Nishitani's response to modernity based on three themes of analysis which have been central to Western debates about postmodernity. Should we, on the foregoing grounds, consider Nishitani a postmodern thinker? I consider the question itself problematic for three reasons. First, the category "postmodern" is vague at best and currently undergoing heavy critique. Historians of ideas have shown a broad range of ways in which to align the traits of "postmodernism" with the modern project. In the texts of Habermas, for example, "postmodernism" is simply a name for the heightened complexity of our particular moment within modernity. Others claim that postmoderism is merely the most recent phase in the Romantic reaction to Enlightenment rationality and the dogmatism of science.[31] The upshot of these divergent views is that we do not yet know what to mean by "postmodernity" even in relation to our own culture. This should at least make us skeptical about its applicability elsewhere.

A second reason for not dwelling on Nishitani's status within postmodernity is that we risk turning our Western categories into bases for the proclamation of our own superiority. If Nishitani as a Japanese thinker does not voice our currently acceptable doctrines, we judge him "behind the times," "still modern," and therefore not yet up to our level of historical advancement. This line of thinking is one of the more arrogant features of modernity. It foresees a single linear progressive movement from primitivism to sophistication which runs directly through ruts already established by our own culture. In doing so it overvalues our own doctrinal inclinations and fails to take Nishitani and other non-Western thinkers seriously as suggestive of alternative courses for our own thought. Surely we will not insist that initiation into our canon is based on the sole criterion that writers demonstrate orthodoxy. It may be preferable just to drop the modern/postmodern hierarchy and get on with the task of thinking.

Finally, a third reason for skepticism about the cross-cultural applicability of the term "postmodern," is that Japan's historical course is not a duplicate of our own or any other. We each have our own histories and therefore require different schemes of periodization. This is not to say that Japanese history is entirely independent of ours—the two are more and more intertwined in the emerging unity of cultures. But the differences remain crucial. Consider how modernity in the West is linked to democratic revolutions and to the emergence of particular forms of government, to the development of free-market capitalism, and to individualistic forms of selfhood. If Japan is a modern nation it is so without having actualized any of these traits, at least not in a way that is identical or even parallel to the West. Nor do the Japanese seem to be on the way to doing so. Furthermore, we must all be aware that broad historical categories refer not so much to objective realities as to ways of ordering our thinking which are more adequately judged on the basis of their heuristic viability. Although the thought that we may be standing at the threshold of a new era is certainly intriguing, reifying that thought may prove to be more self-deluding than illuminating. Clearly, our categories of periodization are problematized in their application to any non-Western culture. But it is precisely in rendering our categories questionable, or in contextualizing them, that the value of our encounter with thinkers like Nishitani is actualized. Not only does he show us a different path of reflection, he poses directly to us an important and disconcerting question: How will you respond when you discover that your deepest thoughts—even your new postmodern ones—lack solid foundations and succumb to the dismantling effects of impermanence foretold by the Buddhas of history?

Notes

1. The issue of freedom was central to Nishitani's career from the very beginning when he undertook translating Schelling's *Treatise on Freedom* into Japanese.

2. Nishitani Keiji, "Scicncc and Zcn" in Frederick Franck, ed., *The Buddha Eye: An Anthology of the Kyoto School* (New York: Crossroad Publishing Co., 1982), 128.

3. There are limits, however, to the influence of Heidegger's "Dasein" on Nishitani's understanding of selfhood. Although the vocabulary of *gensonzai* is common to the later essays contained in *Shūkyō to wa nani ka*, the references to selfhood are more often Zen influenced than hermeneutically determined. No critique of Heidegger on this issue can be found there, however, and it is not yet clear to me how to sort out the limits of each influence on Nishitani's understanding of the matter.

4. Nishitani, *Religion and Nothingness*, tr. Jan Van Bragt (Berkeley: University of California Press, 1982), 230.

5. Nishitani, *The Self-Overcoming of Nihilism*, tr. Graham Parkes with Setsuko Aihara (SUNY Press, 1990), 168.

6. Nishitani, "The Standpoint of *Śūnyatā*," *Religion and Nothingness*, 138.

7. The historical links summarized in this paragraph are gleaned from various locations in *The Self-Overcoming of Nihilism*.

8. Parkes draws our attention to an interesting thought, one which shows the significance of the emerging intellectual influence of German thought in Japan. This is that in 1949, whcn all these converging lines came together in Nishitani's lectures on nihilism, no major discussion of Heidegger, and no work at all on the issue of nihilism, had yet appeared in the English language (*The Self-Overcoming of Nihilism*, xxiii).

9. Nishitani, "Nihility and *Śūnyatā*," in *Religion and Nothingness*, 87.

10. Ibid.

11. Nishitani, *The Self-Overcoming of Nihilism*, 2.

12. Nishitani, *Religion and Nothingness*, 122.

13. Masao Abe, "Nishitani's Challenge to Western Philosophy and Theology," in Taitetsu Unno, ed., *The Religious Philosophy of Nishitani Keiji* (Berkeley: Asian Humanities Press, 1989), 25.

14. Nishitani, "What is Religion?" in *Religion and Nothingness*, 18.

15. Ibid.

16. Nishitani, "The Personal and the Impersonal in Religion," in *Religion and Nothingness*, 55–56.

17. Noted in *The Self-Overcoming of Nihilism*, 196n. 25.

18. Nishitani, "The Standpoint of Śūnyatā," *Religion and Nothingness*, 131.

19. Ibid., 151.

20. Nishitani, *Religion and Nothingness*, 95 (modified), quoted from Langdon Gilkey, "Nishitani Keiji's Religion and Nothingness," in Unno, ed., *The Religious Philosophy of Nishitani Keiji*, 60.

21. Nishitani, "What is Religion?" *Religion and Nothingness*, 4–5.

22. Nishitani, *The Self-Overcoming of Nihilism*, 7.

23. Nishitani, "Śūnyatā and Time," *Religion and Nothingness*, 168.

24. Nishitani, *The Self-Overcoming of Nihilism*, 3.

25. Ibid., 5.

26. Ibid.

27. Nishitani, "Nihility and Śūnyatā," *Religion and Nothingness*, 110.

28. Nishitani, "The Standpoint of Śūnyatā," *Religion and Nothingness*, 139.

29. This is true even though Nishitani's Buddhism is "demythologized" and updated through his encounter with existential phenomenology and its theological correlates.

30. Nishitani, "Śūnyatā and Time," *Religion and Nothingness*, 201.

31. For example see Charles Taylor, *Sources of the Self: The Making of the Modern Identity* (Cambridge: Harvard University Press, 1989), 413.

Chapter Eleven

Critical Reflections on the Traditional Japanese View of Truth

MASAO ABE

In order to clarify the basic character of Japanese people and culture this essay tries to elucidate the Japanese view of truth based on the doctrines of life and nature in Shinto and Buddhism as well as several other key notions appearing in the intellectual history of Japan, including classical literature and modern philosophy. The traditional Japanese non-scientific view of truth based on an intuitive awareness of reality "as-it-is" is contrasted with the typical view in Western religion and philosophy based on rationalism that has given rise to modern science, now so important in Japanese society. The essay makes critical comments about both Japan and the West when each is seen in a comparative context, and it concludes with some suggestions for a continuing dialogue between Eastern and Western traditions in order to establish a harmonious world. According to my understanding, a postmodern vantage point at once clarifies and seeks to overcome the conventional distinctions between East and West, and the traditional and modern. It recognizes the cultural differences as differences without obfuscation or conflation, but at the same time constructively criticizes a problematic fixation with artificial distinctions held in polarization or binary opposition, thus pointing the way to a mutually critical dialogue between and potential synthesis of traditions.

The Relation between Shinto and Buddhism

It is necessary for an understanding of Japanese culture to have a sufficient understanding of Japanese religions, especially Shinto and Buddhism. This is somewhat similar to the case of Western culture, which can be understood well only in terms of a clear understanding of Hellenism and Judaeo-Christianity. Western culture has developed like a rope with two closely interwoven strands based on the Hellenistic and Judaeo-Christian traditions. Similarly, Japanese culture has developed in such a way that Shinto and Buddhism have been closely interwoven as the two main sources, although Confucianism has also played an important role and, after the Meiji Restoration (1868), the separation of Shinto and Buddhism for political reasons as well as the introduction of Western culture and civilization into Japan have been additional elements. While Shinto and Buddhism are the two main spiritual traditions out of which Japanese culture has been created, the origins of these two traditions are different. Shinto is the indigenous religion of Japan and is considered as old as the Japanese people. By contrast, Buddhism was originally a foreign religion to the Japanese. Born in India about the fifth century B.C.E. Buddhism was introduced to Japan by way of China and Korea early in the sixth century C.E. The term "Shinto" is retrospectively applied because at the time the tradition was not a formal "religion" in the modern sense, but the very way of life for ancient Japanese people, which included their views of the world and of life but which had no official scriptures, institutional organization, or a particular founder. This was a basic way of life in every sense, including spiritual and material aspects, that had been realized by Japanese people in their natural surroundings through the ages from remote antiquity.

The relationship of Shinto and the Japanese people may be said to be like the relationship of Judaism and the Hebrews and of Hinduism and the Indians. These three religions and three nations are respectively so closely related to one another that even a contemporary Japanese, Jew, or Indian who rejects his or her own religious tradition is not free from its ethos in the depths of his or her heart. These religions, however, are, by their nature, not widely applicable to a nation other than that of their birthplace. Scholars call this type of religion a "national religion," while they call Buddhism, Islam, and Christianity "world religions," because of their supernational, universal character. This being so, Shinto is a national religion which originated in Japan and is peculiar to the Japanese people. On the other hand, Buddhism is a religion which arose from ancient Hinduism and broke through its national framework in spreading to Central and East Asia. In this respect Christianity is not different from Buddhism. Originating in Judaism, Christianity broke through its national framework and obtained a supernational, universal nature.

How did Christianity and Buddhism become "world religions" by breaking through the national character of their predecessors? This was done by great religious personalities such as Jesus or Gautama Buddha, who were concerned, not necessarily with the nature and destiny of a particular nation, but rather with the very nature and universal suffering of human existence. Their teachings, which contain their universal understandings concerning the origin of human suffering and the way towards salvation, were later formalized into systematic and metaphysical doctrines. At the same time, their religions evolved religious orders and institutional organizations, with Jesus or Gautama Buddha as their founders.

Buddhism, which was introduced into Japan early in the sixth century, was an Indian-born religion with a universal character in the aforementioned sense, that is, a religion with a metaphysical doctrine of man and his salvation, many holy scriptures and commentaries, and refined forms of ritual and worship. Although Buddhism was entirely foreign to the Japanese people, there was only a little conflict among the political leaders of those days until Buddhism was officially accepted in Japan. Ever since then Buddhism has coexisted with Shinto, contributing deeply to Japanese culture and spiritual life.

When Christianity moved into the Germanic world early in the medieval age, it overwhelmed and absorbed the native religions of the Germanic peoples. Nowadays, in Europe and England, it is scarcely possible to find native religions or folklore beliefs in their living forms, as they originally existed among the Teutonic and Anglo-Saxon races, while Christianity is almost completely dominant in those areas. By contrast, in spite of its universal character and profound and systematic doctrine, Buddhism did not eliminate the native religions of the countries into which it was introduced. The different attitudes of Christianity and Buddhism toward other religions may be said to come from the very nature of their essential doctrines. Christianity is based on the only God who commands his people, "You shall have no other gods before me," (Exodus 20:3) and Jesus Christ who says, "I am the Way, and the Truth and the Life: no man comes unto the Father but by me." (John 14:6) This monotheistic character of Christianity promoted a somewhat exclusive attitude towards other faiths and entailed an elimination of native religions in the countries into which it moved.

On the other hand, Buddhism does not preach the idea of the only God who is the exclusive creator, ruler, and judge of the universe, but the principle of dependent co-origination (Skt. *pratītya-samutpāda, J. engi*), also referred to as relationality, relational origination, or dependent causation. The idea of dependent co-origination signifies that everything in and out of the universe, without exception, co-originates and co-ceases, and each is dependent on every other, for nothing whatsoever exists independently. This means that there is no God who is self-existing. Even the divine and the human, the holy and the secular, natural and supernatural, are completely mutually interdependent. This is one reason why Buddhism, with its universal and elaborate doctrine, did not eliminate Shinto after being introduced and accepted in Japan.

Another reason for the coexistence of Buddhism and Shinto may be said to come from the character of Shinto and of the Japanese people. Shinto, in its original form, had no doctrinal system and no theoretical structure by which it could respond to foreign religions and thoughts. At the same time, the essential nature of Shinto with its emphasis on natural harmony is not contradictory to that of Buddhism. The character of the Japanese people also was helpful in this respect. A Japanese appreciates synthesis rather than analysis, harmony more than logical consistency. This character of the Japanese people is also related to another main characteristic: Although the Japanese are always eager to introduce foreign cultures, they carefully maintain the traditional one and gradually create a new form of culture through synthesis. We should not, however, overlook that in the characteristics just enumerated there exists an underlying laxity in critical thinking and an easy obedience to authority.

After some conflict among the political leaders of those days, Buddhism was accepted by the Japanese people, and developed rapidly among the upper classes, and then gradually among ordinary people as well. As I mentioned before, however, in spite of its universal nature and systematic doctrine, Buddhism did not drive Shinto away but has always coexisted with it. The history of their coexistence, which has lasted for more than fourteen centuries, is, of course, not simple. In the course of this history, the syncretism of Shinto and Buddhism has been significant. There has been a deepening and dogmatization of Shinto as well as the Japanization of Buddhism through their mutual contact. There have also been counter-reactions to these developments, that is, attempts to purify Shinto's own essence from the influences of Buddhism and vice versa. In this process of mutual interaction, Confucianism has intermittently been a participant and, after the Meiji Restoration, Western culture as well. Consequently, the history of Shinto and Buddhism in Japan is indeed a complicated historical drama.

Nowadays there are more than eighty thousand Shinto shrines and many Shinto-oriented "new religions" with massive followings. Every New Year's Day, thousands and thousands of people visit shrines in urban and rural districts. At a ceremony for the commencement and the completion of an atomic nuclear study institute, Shinto priests are invited to perform a purification ritual. For instance, in front of a highly mechanized, massive nuclear-fusion reactor a Shinto priest, dressed in traditional clerical robes, waves a branch of a holy tree as part of a ritual of purification. A "progressive" critic may say that this is merely an anachronistic comedy, a mockery of religious ideals for the sake of sheer pragmatism. Before criticizing such phenomena cynically, however, we should try to understand the background of these social phenomena and the Japanese mentality which after all makes these practices possible. It may not be wrong to say that Japan is the only highly industrialized nation which still preserves the faith and rituals of its ancient native religion in their living forms. Maintaining such a pluralism or multi-value system is one of the main characteristics of Japanese society that is appropriate for postmodern thinking.

Shinto View of "Generation"

I said earlier that originally Shinto was the way of life for ancient Japanese people, and it included their views of the world and of life. To the ancient Japanese, nature was not seen as standing in opposition to people and therefore it was not considered something to be overcome. Nature in Japan is not understood as a bleak desert or severe, untameable landscape that must be controlled, but rather as a mild natural environment covered with green to be embraced. The ancient Japanese understood themselves as an intimate part of nature, realizing "life" as a common element of humans and nature. To the Japanese, animals and plants, and even stones and mountains, possessed the power of speech (*kotodama*). They felt a mystical power existing in the "life" or soul of humans and nature. The mystical power of life was that which made everything exist as such, and it was the most existentially real entity.

The term "Shinto," which was used to distinguish the ancient Japanese way of life from the newly introduced foreign religion, Buddhism, literally means "Way of *kami*." Although *kami* is often translated as "God," I think this translation is misleading for Western minds. By *kami*, ancient Japanese referred not to the creator or ruler of the universe in the Christian sense, but, according to the classic definition of Motoori Norinaga (1730–1801), to something unusual and superior in which they felt the remarkable mystical power of life. Thus, not only persons distinguished in their social status and abilities, but also large, majestic rocks, old high trees, special mountains such as Mt Fuji, rivers and oceans were called *kami* and reverenced as such. In this case, the quality of being "unusual and superior" includes something especially bad, awful, and harmful as well as something especially good, precious, and helpful. Therefore, thunder (*kami nari*), storms, dragons, wolves (*o kami* or *oh kami*) and so on were equally called *kami*. Accordingly, it has been said that there are *yao yorozu no kami* or eight million *kami*. According to this standpoint, it is not that we are surrounding the one and only *kami*, but that we are surrounded by a remarkable variety of *kami*.

The ancient Japanese who had engaged in agriculture from antiquity reverenced nature, praying to good entities for their beneficence and to bad entities to not harm their harvests. Among other things, water, wind, sun, storm and so on were the most familiar of the *kami*. Besides nature, distinguished and superior personages such as the emperor, a chief, or hero, were regarded as *kami*.

What the ancient Japanese felt surprise and joy about more than anything else was the mystery of something being born or appearing, whatever it might be. It is for this reason that *musubi no kami*, that is, the *kami* of generation, was regarded as the highest *kami*. Generation (the act or process of generating) is the most remarkable function of the mystical power of life. The theogony and cosmogony included in Japanese mythology show the story of *kami* bearing the world, countries, islands, in addition to other *kami*. The basic principle expressed in Japanese mythology is not creation but generation.

The Judaeo-Christian tradition, on the other hand, emphasizes creation rather than generation. God created the world by his word, which is the expression of his will. According to Genesis, among the creatures the *imago dei* was ascribed to humans alone by which they can respond to the Word of God. Thus, humans as rulers of all creatures have a personal relationship with God, the Creator. Based upon the divine-human relationship in terms of receiving the "word" or "will," all other doctrines such as original sin, incarnation, suffering, redemption, salvation, and last judgment are developed.

Shinto, which bases itself on the principle of generation, is quite different. First, in Christianity, when God's creation is emphasized, there is a clear distinction between creator and the created. The created cannot become creator. In the case of generation, however, that which was generated then becomes that which generates. There is no sharp contrast between them, but rather a continuity. Secondly, the fundamental factor of generation is not "will" but "life." The emphasis on will leads to a distinction between humans and nature and thereby promulgates human's anthropocentric attitude toward other creatures. In contrast, the emphasis on "life" opens up a common dimension for humans and nature, and it discourages anthropocentrism as well as any tension between creator and the created.

Western philosophy has two major philosophical currents: idealism and materialism. Idealism emphasizes idea, spirit, or human reason and intellect. Materialism reduces nature to lifeless matter and ultimately regards the human being as an impersonal mechanism. The conflict between the two "isms" is very serious, and when the respective views are considered diametrically opposed to each other this results in continual ideological conflict.

Shinto, though philosophically naive in the sense of only partially developing formal theological or ideological doctrines, offers neither idea nor matter as fundamental to reality, but rather a third principle—life, which is a vital force that can provide a synthesis of idea and matter. Ancient Shinto understood birth as the appearance of something from the invisible world into the visible world generated by the mystical power of life, while it regarded death as the disappearance or hiding of something from the visible world in the invisible world. Death is abominated and is regarded as something defiled that must be purified. There is no concept of death as "the wages of sin." Birth and this visible world are positive realities, while death and the other world are considered to be merely negative aspects of life. The standard for beings is this actual world, and this world is understood to be based on a mystical power of life which manifests the function of generation and development. Humankind is also understood to be rooted in this mystical power of life and to communicate with nature through the power of life.

Further, ancient Shinto understood evil and sin as defilement or pollution. Thus, evil and sin are not innate or original to humans but are something added to humans which should be and can be purified. So purification is an important ritual of Shinto, which does not have an idea of absolute evil and eternal punishment.

Neither good nor truth, but purity, is the highest value for Shinto, and neither evil nor falsity, but defilement, is the most remarkable anti-value. And the sense of purity and defilement is somewhat aesthetic rather than moralistic. Shinto's idea of purity, however, may be said to include good, truth, and beauty within itself. This can be seen in terms of Shinto's use of the mirror as a symbol for the value of purity, and its emphasis on the ideals of *seimei-shin* (pure and bright mind), and *shojiki* (honesty).

The song of Motoori Norinaga,[1] an outstanding scholar of "national learning" (*kokugaku*) during the Tokugawa era, well expressed the spirit of Shinto and the Japanese mind:

Shikishima no yamato gokoro o hitotowaba
Asahi ni niou yamazakurabana.

If one asks me what the Japanese mind is,
Let me answer,
"Cherry blossoms on mountains, fragrant in the rising sun."

The way of life realized in ancient Shinto is the fundamental driving force of the Japanese people, and has been consistently working at the basis of Japanese history. Today it still, consciously or unconsciously, exists in the depth of the Japanese mind.

Buddhist View of "Origination"

Buddhism understands that the fundamental problem of human existence is life-and-death, and it shows us a way to free ourselves from this problem. This way is to awaken to Buddhahood and to become a buddha. The term buddha, unlike the term God, does not mean something supernatural or transcendental, but one who awakens to the truth of the universe, that is, the truth of dependent co-origination. The historical Buddha is the first buddha who awakened to the truth, but he is not the only buddha. Anyone can become a buddha if he or she awakens to the truth of co-origination. There are no exceptions to this potential for awakening. Indeed, Buddhism ultimately teaches the necessity of awakening to our being originally enlightened. It also emphasizes that "All living beings without exception have Buddhahood." Thus, denying anthropocentrism, Buddhism opens up a common dimension for human beings and other living beings, that is, the dimension of "life." Buddhism furthermore says that "mountains, rivers, and the earth attain Buddhahood." This means not only the living beings but everything in nature, living or non-living, has Buddhahood. Thus it can be seen that both Shinto and Buddhism understand human beings as a part of nature, and, denying anthropocentrism, put human beings on a common basis with nature. For this reason I mentioned before that Shinto and Buddhism are not contradictory to one another.

There is, however, an important difference between Shinto and Buddhism. As I mentioned, Shinto finds "life" as the real entity in everything in nature, including mountains, rivers, and the earth, but Buddhism does not necessarily do so. The common basis of humans and nature for Shinto is "life," whereas for Buddhism it is "suchness" (Skt. *tathatā*, J. *nyo-nyo*) which is another term for Buddhahood. Suchness means that everything is realized as it is in its own particularity or in its original nature. Shinto understands life with a mystical power as the most real entity and death as something defiled that must be purified. Buddhism, however, takes death much more deeply and emphasizes that life and death are inseparable and that it is essential not to overcome death, but to be liberated from life-and-death itself. Are we moving from life to death? No! At any moment of our life we are living and at the same time we are dying. If we grasp our life not from without, but from within, we must say that without dying there is no living, and without living there is no dying. Living and dying are like the two sides of a sheet of paper which cannot be separated from each other. A rigid separation of life and death is an abstract and unreal conceptualization.

Then why does Buddhism ground human beings in a dimension common to humans and nature? In Buddhism, the life-death transmigration, as the fundamental problem of humans, is understood to be fully eliminated only when it is understood as a problem on a more universal dimension than that of human's life and death. In other words, human's life-death transmigration is fully eliminated only when it is understood as the more universal problem of generation and extinction common to all living beings or, more basically, as the most universal problem of being and nonbeing, which is common to all beings, including living and non-living. This means that in Buddhism the problem of life-death for human beings, though fundamental to them, is wrestled with and eliminated as the problem of being-nonbeing in a transhuman, universal dimension. Unless the impermanence or mutability which is common to all beings is overcome at the root of a person's existence, the problem of life and death cannot be properly and definitely resolved. In this way, Buddhism opens up a dimension common to human beings and nature.

But, how can the problem of being and nonbeing be eliminated? We usually are attached to life and try to avoid death; we appreciate being, and dread nonbeing. In doing so, however, we limit ourselves by adhering to an opposition and conflict between life and death, or between being and nonbeing. To resolve the problem of being and nonbeing it is necessary to go beyond the very opposition or conflict between being and nonbeing, and life and death. In the East Asian spiritual tradition, particularly in Buddhism, neither being nor nonbeing is given priority over one another. They are dependent upon each other and inseparable from each other. This realization is essential in order to overcome the seeming conflict between being and nonbeing and to awaken oneself to absolute Emptiness (śūnyatā) and real freedom. However, absolute Emptiness is not merely empty in the ordinary sense. Since it is beyond being and nonbeing, absolute Emptiness is at the same time absolute Fullness or suchness. In the realization of absolute Emptiness, both being and nonbeing coexist, and one can freely put being and nonbeing, life and death to practical use, without being involved in their conflicts. As an expression of the identity of absolute emptiness and absolute fullness, I will cite the following discourse by a Chinese Zen master of the T'ang dynasty:

> When I did not yet practice Zen Buddhism, to me a mountain was a mountain, and water was water; after I got insight into the truth of Zen, I thought that a mountain was not a mountain and water was not water; but now that I have really attained to the abode of final rest, to me a mountain is really a mountain and water is really water.[2]

Another way of understanding the Buddhist view of truth in relation to Shinto is to consider the symbol of the lotus flower. In spite of rising out of dirty mud, a lotus flower is pure and beautiful. Its purity is the purity realized through mud; likewise human passions can be regarded as "mud" in terms of attachment to life or being and dread of death or nonbeing. And yet, it is in and through human passions that Buddhahood can be awakened. The cherry blossom of Shinto and the lotus flower of Buddhism are equally pure. While cherry blossoms are most fragrant when they are in the rising sun, a lotus flower is especially beautiful because it rises out of mud.

Truth as "As-It-Isness"

In the *Manyōshū*, the ancient collection of Japanese poetry, Japan is called "a country where people, following implicitly the way of the gods, are not argumentative." Regarding this, the eminent modern Japanese philosopher, Nishida Kitarō (1870–1945), has made the following comment:

> This means only that argument is not indulged in for argument's sake and concepts are not bandied about for their own sake. As Motoori Norinaga explained in *Naobi no mitama*, "It [the way of the gods] is nothing but the way of going to things," which should be taken in the sense of going straight to the true facts of things. Going to the true facts, however, does not mean following tradition out of mere force of custom or acting in direct response to subjective emotions. Going to the true facts of things must also involve what we call a scientific spirit. It should mean following the true facts of things at the expense of self. "Not being argumentative" should be understood as not being self assertive, but bending one's head low before the true facts. It ought not to be a mere cessation of thinking or readiness to compromise: to penetrate to the very source of things is to exhaust one's own self.[3]

This passage well expresses the Japanese view of truth. Japanese have traditionally esteemed the individual fact rather than the universal principle, and have found reality in unification with things attained by "emptying" themselves. This involves a sharp contrast to the Western way of thinking.

From the time of ancient Greece the Western mind has been generally rationalistic. This bent is conspicuous in Greek philosophy, Roman law, and modern European natural science. It emphasizes idea, logos, ratio, reason, law, and so forth. The rational is always universal, essential, necessary, eternal, absolute, and is thus regarded as the prototype for phenomenal things because the latter are taken to be merely particular, nonessential, contingent, temporal, relative, and are thus regarded as copies of the former. However, the traditional Japanese view, rooted in "not being argumentative," does not regard phenomenal things merely as particular, nonessential, and contingent. They are something deeper than that; not copies of the universal, but rather in themselves prototypes for the universal. In other words, individual things or facts have a profound meaning which cannot be exhausted by rational thinking: it is the individual thing that makes the universal possible. The characteristic Japanese way of life sees in an individual fact something essential and absolute which cannot be measured by a universal law, and takes it as the norm for life and behavior.

This esteeming of the individual fact rather than the universal principle is not mere irrationalism or mysticism, for it does not altogether exclude the rational: it penetrates the depth of a fact by breaking through the rational framework. It is beyond both relative rationality and relative factualness, beyond both rationalism and irrationalism.

The ancient Japanese view of life regarded "facts" not as objects of intellectual cognition but as something realized through one's subjective activity. A fact is established inseparably by the active and not by the conscious self. That an individual fact is regarded as essential, eternal, and absolute is not therefore based on cognition or contemplation, but on action. One realizes truth by devoting oneself to practice in and through facts. Only in concentrative, egoless practice does the reality of a fact reveal itself.

In the West, cognition and action are clearly initially separated and are then subsequently to be connected. Cognition of an objective truth precedes an action that is carried out on its basis. For the ancient Japanese, action rather precedes cognition. For just as an individual fact does not follow a universal principle, action does not follow cognition. More strictly speaking, in the realization of truth, action and cognition as well as subject and object are not separated from one another, but go together as one.

This is why the Japanese term *makoto*, which means "truth," also indicates "sincerity" or "faithfulness." Literally, *ma* means "true" and *koto* means both "fact" and "word" (as noted in John Maraldo's essay in this volume). Therefore, *makoto* signifies "true fact" as distinguished from a fiction, and at the same time "true word," which in turn stands for "sincerity" or "faithfulness."

In other words, *makoto* may be said to denote a fact as it is without modification by human intellect, and at the same time a spirit to express it as it is, at the expense of ego-self. This is not unrelated to the fact that *makoto* has also been regarded historically as one of the fundamental ideas of Japanese aesthetics. In short, *makoto* involves cognitive, moral, and aesthetic truth because in *makoto* god and humans, humans and nature, humans (self) and humans (other) are understood to be completely fused.

Buddhism, which has nourished Japanese spirituality since the sixth century, deepened this original view of truth. Buddhism clearly denies the existence of something universal, rational, or transcendental behind or beyond facts. It realizes the "nothingness" as the basis of facts. This means an individual fact is completely and definitely realized *as it is*—irreducible to anything—through the realization of "no-thingness." This as-it-is-ness[4] supported by the realization of "no-thingness" stands for truth in the Buddhist sense. And as-it-is-ness is realized respectively in and through every individual fact. Accordingly, although all individual facts are different from each other in their individuality, they are equal in their as-it-is-ness. The Buddhist expression, "differentiation as it is is equality (*sabetsu-soku-byōdō*); equality as it is is differentiation,"[5] indicates this.

As-it-is-ness as truth is most clearly formulated in the fourfold worldview in Kegon (Ch. Hua-yen) doctrine. The first three stages are: (1) the world of phenomena, (2) the world of noumena, and (3) the world of unhindered mutual interpretation of noumena and phenomena as the higher unity of (1) and (2). Kegon philosophy, however, goes beyond (3) and takes as ultimate reality (4) the world of unhindered mutual interpenetration of phenomena and phenomena or of a single phenomenon with each and every other phenomenon (*jiji muge*). This is simply another way of expressing "as-it-is-ness" in which all individual facts, being different from each other in their individuality, while fundamentally different, are at the same time equal and undifferentiated in their as-it-is-ness. This is the basis for wisdom and compassion in Mahayana Buddhism which took deep root in the Japanese soil. The truth in this sense is not an object of contemplation, but the ground of existence and action. It should not be taken as a goal of cognition but as a point of departure for a life of truth.

"As-it-is-ness" is not contradictory to the modern scientific view of truth. In fact there is a striking similarity between them in the sense that both are realized at the expense of the subjective self. This is why, referring to the Japanese tendency to go to the true facts of things, Nishida stated that it "involves what we call a scientific spirit." However, we should not overlook the essential difference between Japanese truth and science.

Modern science presupposes nature as an objective entity and investigates the objective law functioning in natural phenomena through an emptying of subjectivity on the part of the scientist. In this case, the emptying of subjectivity means to objectify and rationalize natural phenomena. Therefore modern science accepts and follows phenomena as they are, and at the same time reconstructs them through a process of rationalization. Here the human intellect is the law-giver of nature. In modern science, human subjectivity is not altogether negated but rather strengthened through a partial self-negation. Contrary to this, the emptying of subjectivity in the case of "as-it-is-ness" indicates a return to and a realization of the ground prior to subject-object duality by an emptying of the corresponding objectivity as well. This is not an objectification or rationalization of nature but a total realization of the ground or the groundless ground (*Ungrund*) from which the very opposition of humans and nature, subject and object emerges. Realization of as-it-is-ness is nothing but the realization of this ground which is neither subjective nor objective and yet is really both subjective and objective.

This may be exemplified by the Japanese garden. Unlike the typical European garden which is designed by a geometrical arranging of flowers, trees, stones, and so forth, the Japanese garden looks somehow natural and nonartificial. Nevertheless, it is human-made, and in this sense it is not different from the European garden. But Japanese gardeners build a garden so that not the slightest trace of human artifice remains, thereby allowing nature to manifest itself in its essential form. They do not arrange rocks and plants merely from an artificial human point of view or try to copy wild nature. Theirs is an artificiality leaving no trace of itself, that is, in a form more "natural" than is found in wild nature. In Japanese gardens the highest reach of artificiality is rather the deepest reach of nature, with both being brought into oneness beyond their relativity.

This is true not only with Japanese gardens, but also with most traditional Japanese disciplines in which the view of truth realized in terms of "as-it-is-ness" is consistently found. However, this view of truth includes the danger of falling into mere antirationalism, shallow intuitionism, or sheer behaviorism. At least it must be acknowledged that the Japanese view does not intellectually analyze, synthesize, and reconstruct objects. This is the reason that rationalistic philosophy, experimental natural science and technology, by which humans can overcome nature, were not well developed in Japan until after they were introduced from the West beginning with the Meiji Restoration in 1868.

Postmodernism and Dialogue

In discussing Japanese thought, especially in religion, Western scholars often mention such distinctions as monotheism versus polytheism, personal God versus impersonal Dharma, or prophetic religion versus natural religion, presupposing that the former, that is, monotheism, personal God and prophetic religion, are higher than the latter, that is polytheism, impersonal Dharma and natural religion. What is the basis for this evaluation?

I do not begrudge an appreciation of the religious significance of monotheistic, prophetic religion and of a personal God. At the same time, however, I wonder whether it is the only basis for evaluating the religions of human beings. Is creation higher than generation in its religious significance? Is life-principle lower than will-principle in our religious life? Does not Christian personalism lead to anthropocentrism among creatures, and thereby promote human's estrangement from nature? Cannot the value of purity open up a significant value-dimension as a synthesis of good, truth, and beauty? Does not the idea of mountains and rivers attaining to Buddhahood suggest something inspirational to the Western mind?

However, Japan is changing, and the West is also changing. Now East and West have come together in a dialogue on a scale and depth never experienced before. Japan has eagerly studied Western culture for more than one hundred years. Recently, Japan has advanced economically and technologically to a degree well comparable with Western countries, but the Japanese people's understanding of Western religion and philosophy is still insufficient. On the other hand, in the West people have become somewhat acquainted with certain aspects of Japanese culture and literature, but their understanding of Japanese religion and thought is still quite limited. It is now urgently necessary to deepen our mutual understanding particularly in terms of the profound spiritual dimension of religious thought and truth without which a truly harmonious, unified world cannot be built.

For example, Japanese intuitionism excluding rationality may be insufficient and ineffective, whereas Western rationalism excluding intuition remains abstract and dichotomous. But in this dialogue it is not enough to recognize cultural differences; rather we must explore how critically and creatively to surpass them from a postmodern vantage point based on recognizing and yet at the same time overcoming distinctions. To overcome its inherent limitations and inherent dangers, the Japanese view of truth in terms of *makoto* and "as-it-is-ness" must be developed and deepened to include and encompass Western forms of rationalism, which have produced science, logic, law, technology, and the like. This is a future task for the Japanese people who through critical, creative dialogue must at once utilize the strengths of and go beyond their traditional conception of truth by incorporating Western ideals. If accomplished, such an integration will be a contribution to the advency of a postmodern world that is unified by virtue of acknowledging and embracing cultural differences as differences, as reflected in the traditional Japanese view of nothingness representing equality realized in and through differentiation. Thus, the Japanese view can serve as a basis for establishing the goal of a mutually critical synthesis of Eastern and Western views of truth.

Notes

1. Motoori Norinaga, in founding the *kokugaku* movement, was counteracting the exaggerated attention then given to Chinese literature. He studied ancient Japanese literature philologically and interpreted it from a purely Japanese point of view.

2. Masao Abe, *Zen and Western Thought*, ed. William R. LaFleur (London: Macmillan, and Honolulu: University of Hawaii Press, 1985), 4–18.

3. *Nihon bunka no mondai* (*The Problem of Japanese Culture*) in *Nishida Kitarō zenshū* (The Collected Works of Nishida Kitarō) (Tokyo: Iwanami, 1966), vol. XII, 279–80. See also *Sources of Japanese Tradition*, ed. Wm. Theodore de Bary et al. (New York: Columbia University Press, 1963), vol. II, 352.

4. Abe, *Zen and Western Thought*, 103, 208, 224.

5. Ibid., 177–78, 184, 209, 213.

Chapter Twelve

Japan, the Dubious, and Myself

KENZABURŌ ŌE

When Kawabata Yasunari was awarded the Nobel Prize—the first conferred on an author writing in Japanese—he gave, in Stockholm, a commemorative lecture titled "Japan, the Beautiful, and Myself". The lecture was indeed beautiful, yet its content was extremely vague. It was typically Japanese in its beauty, and likewise in its ambiguity. Perhaps I should say it was even *dubious*. *Vague, ambiguous, dubious.* These are but three translations for the Japanese adjective *aimai-na*. One large Japanese-English dictionary offers the following list of equivalents: *vague; ambiguous; obscure; equivocal; dubious; doubtful; questionable; shady; noncommittal; indefinite; hazy; double;* and *two-edged.* I have read this long list to show that the Japanese language has this one adjective—*aimai-na*—ready for use in diverse situations in life. And this, in my opinion, is evidence that Japanese are a people who speak a truly subtle and complex language. "Beware the Japanese. When they say 'yes,' they actually mean 'no.'" Or was it the other way around? The exact words elude me now, but President Clinton was reported to have scribbled something to this effect. Apparently he was giving President Yeltsin advice on how to deal with Japan. Such remarks by the president of the United States inevitably shattered the self-esteem of many Japanese who had high hopes for the newly-elected leader, and had welcomed his appointment. Uproar ensued, obviously. But had President Clinton said: "Beware the Japanese. They often make *aimai-na* promises"—had he used the Japanese adjective—I do not think he would have sparked the controversy he did. Although these would have been harsher words than the remarks made to Mr. Yeltsin, many Japanese would have admitted the aptness of such a description of their character.

Now, I do not, in any measure, mean to criticize the *aimai-na* quality of Kawabata's speech. His speech was not at all *doubtful*.

313

Nor was it either *questionable* or *shady*. but I must say that, in large measure, I felt it to be *vague, ambiguous,* and *obscure.*

From the beginning to the midpoint of his career, Kawabata was renowned not only for his lucid stories, but also for his crystal-clear criticism. What, then, led him to give that *obscure* lecture? Even the esoteric Faulkner, when standing on the same podium as did Kawabata, spoke in no unclear terms when he said: "I feel that this award was not made to me as a man, but to my work—a life's work in the agony and sweat of the human spirit, not for glory and least of all for profit, but to create out of the materials of the human spirit something which did not exist before." Thus did Faulkner convey to us his deep trust in our shared condition.

I can think of two reasons why Kawabata presented his lecture the way he did. One is that, with the passage of time, he arrived at a perception of beauty that had deepened to the point where it coalesced with Japanese mysticism, and then even transcended it to merge with Oriental mysticism. Kawabata began his speech by quoting two poems by the Zen masters Dōgen and Myōe. Dōgen lived from 1200 to 1253, and Myōe from 1173 to 1232. Let me read to you these poems, first in Japanese, then in English.

Dōgen's poem reads:

> Haru wa hana
> Natsu wa hototogisu
> Aki wa tsuki
> Fuyu yuki kiede
> Suzushi kari keri

And Myōe's poem goes like this:

> Kumo o idete
> Ware ni tomonaru
> Fuyu no tsuki
> Kaze ya mi ni shimu
> Yuki ya tsumetaki

If I were asked to translate these poems into English, I would bury my head in the sand. But fortunately, I have fine renditions by Edward Seidensticker, whose interpretative genius is evident throughout his English versions of Kawabata's works. Dōgen's poem reads this way in Seidensticker's English:

In the spring, cherry blossoms, in the summer the cuckoo.
In autumn the moon, and in winter the snow, clear, cold.

And for Myōe's verse, Seidensticker has given us this translation:

Winter moon, coming from the clouds to keep me company,
Is the wind piercing, the snow cold?

After reciting these poems, Kawabata said:

> When I am asked for specimens of my handwriting, it is these
> poems that I often choose. . . . I choose the first for its remarkable
> gentleness and compassion . . . the second, as a poem of warm,
> deep, delicate compassion, a poem that has in it the deep quiet of
> the Japanese spirit.

This statement is an unequivocal expression of what Kawabata
understood of the two poems. And there isn't a bit of ambiguity in
it. However, I doubt that Kawabata was able to fully express—in the
same simple and clear language in which he couched the statement—the profound meanings he had discovered in the Zen masters' poems. I say this because, in explaining Myōe's verse—the
second poem—he had to quote the long foreword, the lengthy ex-
planatory note, that the priest attached to it. Kawabata introduced
the note by observing that the second poem bore an unusually
detailed account of its origin, which served to explain the heart of its
meaning.

Though somewhat long, let me read to you Myōe's account, as
quoted by Kawabata. This translation, too, is Seidensticker's:

> On the night of the twelfth day of the twelfth month of the year
> 1224, the moon was behind clouds. I sat in Zen meditation in the
> Kakyu Hall. When the hour of the midnight vigil came, I ceased
> meditation and descended from the hall on the peak to the lower
> quarters, and as I did so the moon came from the clouds and set the
> snow to glowing. The moon was my companion, and not even the
> wolf howling in the valley brought fear. When, presently, I came
> out of the lower quarters again, the moon was again behind clouds.
> As the bell was signalling the late-night vigil, I climbed once more
> to the peak, and the moon saw me on the way. I entered the
> meditation hall, and the moon, chasing the clouds, was about to
> sink behind the far peak, and it seemed to me that it was keeping
> me secret company.

"There," continued Kawabata, "follows the poem I have quoted, and, with the explanation that it was composed as Myōe entered the meditation hall after watching the moon sink toward the mountain, there comes yet another poem:

> I shall go behind the mountain.
> Go there too, O moon.
> Night after night we shall keep each other company.

"Here," Kawabata said, "is the setting for another poem, after Myōe had spent the rest of the night in the meditation hall, or perhaps gone there again before dawn."

Kawabata first read out the introductory note to it:

> "Opening my eyes from my meditations," Myōe wrote, "I saw the moon in the dawn, lighting the window. In a dark place myself, I felt as if my own heart were glowing with light which seemed to be that of the moon."

Then he went on to reading the poem:

> My heart shines, a pure expanse of light;
> And no doubt the moon will think the light its own.

What we see in Kawabata's quotation of Myōe is the profound mystical experience of a Zen monk. Myōe first tells us that he had undergone a very singular experience which no prose—but only poetry—could express. And, it is after this observation that he presents his poetry, as if to say: "This poem is what it's all about!"

Kawabata went on to say that having arrived at a ripe old age, he was now able to fully understand the meaning of Myōe's poems—in particular the "winter moon" poem he had cited at the beginning of his speech. I believe the message he was trying to get across with those words was that his understanding of the poem—that understanding in itself—constituted his very own mystical experience. Moreover, he surmised that no amount of prose could communicate the depth, or should I say the interior, of his understanding of the poem. That is why he quoted it verbatim, and in Japanese, for that matter, knowing fully well that no one in the audience would understand it. That, however, was what he had to do.

Of course, the Japanese language has no monopoly over the literary phenomenon in which we witness the merger of mystical experience and poetry. We see this in English too. Take, for example, Yeats's well-known poem "Vacillation." In a letter to Mrs. Olivia Shakespear, Yeats divulged that the first stanza of the poem came to him as a mystical experience. He wrote:

> The night before letters came I went for a walk after dark and there among some great trees became absorbed in the most lofty philosophical conception I have found while writing "A Vision." I suddenly seemed to understand at last and then I smelt roses. . . . Yesterday I put my thoughts into a poem which I enclose, but it seems to me a poor shadow of the intensity of the experience.

The words Yeats penned of that experience are the awe-inspiring, opening lines of "Vacillation":

> Between extremities
> Man runs his course:
> A brand, or flaming breath,
> Comes to destroy
> All these antimonies
> Of day and night.

As Kawabata progressed in his years and deepened his understanding of the beauty of Japan, he, too, arrived at an experience for which its verbal description was but "a poor shadow." Yet, in Kawabata's speech, there was nothing of this "poor shadow," save the poems he quoted, that hinted at—even in part—the depth of his own mystical experience. The only way he could come close to expressing it was to profusely quote, from the archives, a plethora of classical songs that eulogized an experience he believed he shared with poets past. No wonder his speech was bedecked with such beautiful ambiguity.

I believe there was one more reason for the *aimai-na* nature of Kawabata's lecture. I don't think it occurred to him that he was addressing the peoples of Western Europe—despite the fact that his audience consisted mostly of Europeans and some Americans. His speech was clearly a grand panorama of the aestheticism that flowed in him—an aestheticism he drew from time-encrusted Japanese classics. Yet I wonder if Kawabata, even before he began, hadn't abandoned all desire to communicate this aestheticism to Europeans and Americans. I also seriously doubt if he wanted even Japanese people to understand him.

Who, then, was he addressing? The answer, I think, is reflected in the title of his speech: "Japan, the Beautiful, and Myself." Ironically, though, Kawabata himself knew that such a Japan did not exist; and, in any case, he knew that he himself was not part of that Japan. He was talking only to the fruit of his imagination, his apparition of beauty. And by so doing, he shut out the real world; he severed all ties with all living souls. It is only natural, therefore, that many people detected a nihilistic tone in Kawabata's delivery. Yet he ended his speech on the following enigmatic note. He said,

> Here we have the emptiness, the nothingness of the Orient. My own works have been described as works of emptiness, but it is not to be taken for the nihilism of the West. The spiritual foundation would seem to be quite different. Dōgen entitled his poem about the seasons "Innate Reality," and even as he sang of the beauty of the seasons he was deeply immersed in Zen.

What did Kawabata mean by all this? The audience—Europeans, Americans, and Japanese alike—must have found the purport of Kawabata's speech most ambiguous. The image that Kawabata projected was, and remains, undoubtedly that of a nihilist. But in Kawabata's mind—in his "Japan, the Beautiful, and Myself"—an "emptiness" or "nothingness" *did* exist as an embodiment of beauty: of beauty itself. And the message he was trying to convey in those closing lines was that there was no room, to begin with, for Western nihilism to weasel its way into the bond that united his very being to what he called "Japan, the Beautiful, and Myself." He was also saying that there was no room for Western Europe or the United States in his aesthetic world.

It happens that Kawabata was my senior by thirty some years. He was born in 1899 and he died in 1972. But heaven forbid were I to utter such words as "Japan, the Beautiful, and Myself." In the first place, I cannot bring myself to reckon with the aestheticisms of the classic Japanese poets and Zen priests. Secondly, I find nothing beautiful in contemporary Japan. I simply don't. At least not in the Japan I have seen and lived through. So if I were to emulate Kawabata in giving my speech a title, I would call it: "Japan, the Dubious, and Myself". Or perhaps you are thinking that the title ought to be: "Japan, the Dubious, and 'Oh no! Kenzaburō!' "

In any event, I think that in order to explain what I mean by the title I have given my speech, it is helpful to start with describing to you the characteristics I find distinctive about modern and contemporary Japanese literature. Japan embarked on modernization in the latter half of the nineteenth century, at a time that is called the Meiji Restoration. The country established itself as a modern state with Emperor Meiji as absolute sovereign at the center of authority; and it was with the call for modernization that Japan flung open its doors to Europe and the United States—doors which until then had been tightly closed to the outside world. In line with the modernization process—though actually there was a little time lag—came a large cultural revolution. It is important to note that this cultural revolution started with the introduction and assimilation of European lifestyles, first in Tokyo, a big city, which until the Restoration was called Edo. At the higher echelon, many of the rural samurai who had come to Tokyo to work or study, kissed their *chon-mage*, their feudal topknots, good-bye, and then set sail to Europe to pursue academic studies and other work in diverse fields.

The other cultural revolution was the fundamental reform of literature—a literary movement that encouraged writing in the vernacular. This movement sought to rectify the tremendous gap between the written language and what was spoken in the ebullient new-born city. Futabatei Shimei, a translator of Russian novels and a writer who wrote in the new, unprecedented style, spearheaded the reform. Futabatei, however, died rather young. Born in 1864, he died in 1909 at the age of forty-five. Yet the sudden and complete change in his literary style in the midpoint of his career is symbolic of the drastic change that was in progress. Natsume Sōseki, born in 1867, continued what Futabatei had started, and succeeded in giving the revolution its full expression. It was he who established a literary form in which style, theme, and character—all of which were truly revolutionary—merged harmoniously with each other. Prolific as he was, Sōseki, who died in 1916, penned all of his novels in the first ten years of the twentieth century. In one work after another of his earlier writings, we see a change in Sōseki's style—as drastic as that in Futabatei's. Each change Sōseki made in the first few years of his literary career is one that normally takes two or three generations. Sōseki's later works are penned in the vernacular, and have as their theme the life and thought of the citizens of Tokyo of the early twentieth century. His characters are portrayed so vividly that these works attract a wide readership even today, at the dawn of a new century. It is no exaggeration to say that Sōseki, and only Sōseki, represents twentieth-century Japanese literature. He and he alone stands out as revolutionary for his real-life literary style, his themes, and character creation. Sōseki depicted the lives of intellectuals who, in the throes of the rapid modernization process, were reduced to inactivity. Japan then was voraciously learning European ways, and aping them with a maddened fury. And in this climate, many intellectuals could not, in any way, envision a future Japan that stood on its own two feet. It was such an awareness—such hopelessness—on the part of the intellectuals that reduced them to listless inactivity. But with heart-rending compassion and empathy, Sōseki, though himself ridden with despair, wrote painfully about these broken men, and also women, who saw no light of self-liberation ahead. The situation in Japan today has not much changed since Sōseki's time, when he foresaw a Japan precarious in its relationship with Europe and the United States. Even today many Japanese are unable to resolve those very problems Sōseki foresaw. This, I believe, accounts for why his works still attract so many dedicated readers.

It is not without good reason that I, in talking to you about the distinctive characteristics of Japanese literature, stress the importance of Sōseki. I deem him important, not only because of his accomplishments, but because it is through him that I wish to reflect on the label I attach to myself, a label that reads: "Kenzaburō Ōe of Dubious Japan," or better, in Kawabata-fashion: "Japan, the Dubious, and Myself." There are many English translations of Sōseki available. And I wonder what impression those of you who have read him have of him. Sōseki wrote about confrontation and co-existence between Japan and the West. He wrote about it as a matter of Japan's fate, and made the intellectuals in his novels suffer the burden of the dilemma. However, he addressed only other Japanese, and did not attempt to communicate with Europeans and Americans. At least this is this impression I get, and I wonder if you don't feel the same way. As regards Kawabata, his literature is a monologue within a closed circuit that leads up to "Japan, the Beautiful, and Himself." But, in my opinion, Sōseki's literature is also a closed circuit. I find it to be a painful dialogue between himself and an entity of his creation, an entity that you might call "Japan, the Tormented, and Sōseki," an entity that laments the rapid modernization process by which Japan endeavored to catch up with Western Europe and the United States. And this entity foresees, not far in the offing, the dead-end of such modernization.

Sōseki, to be sure, was an authority on English literature. It was he that took over Lafcadio Hearn's post as lecturer of English literature at Tokyo Imperial University. This is why I wonder why a man such as Sōseki did not try to address Europeans and Americans, try to convey to them that entity of his creation which was himself—

that entity he could have called "Japan, the Tormented, and Himself"—and thus break the self-defeating closed circuit. Why he remained incommunicado with Europe and America is beyond me. Or was it perhaps his nature? Most likely so. Because, although Sōseki went to study in London in 1899, at the very end of the nineteenth century, and was there for some two years or more, all during those years, he hardly ever left his boarding-house room. He just immersed himself in reading, and kept his associations with the people of England to a bare minimum.

Which reminds me of a cultural anthropologist-cum-biologist, Minakata Kumagusu who was born in 1867, the same year Sōseki was born, and the year before the Meiji Restoration officially began. Like Sōseki, Minakata, or Kumagusu as he is more affectionately called, did research in London at the British Museum. He returned to Japan at the same time Sōseki set foot in London—a changing of the guards as it were. Kumagusu, though, differed from Sōseki in that he wrote profusely, in English, treatises on the diverse ethnic groups of Asia. Upon his return to Japan, he wrote a report to a Western European academy, again in English, about the research he had conducted on a new species of myxomycetes—a type of fungus he discovered thanks to the quality monocular microscope he had brought back from London. Kumagusu continued his life-long research in his hometown in Wakayama prefecture, and never made Tokyo the theater of his activities. And so although Kumagusu's circuit was open to the Western world, through the letters and reports he wrote in English, that circuit was closed to most intellectuals in Tokyo. In other words, Kumagusu never positively acted out the role of mediator between his contemporaries in Japan and those in Europe and America.

Neither Sōseki nor Kumagusu attempted to define clearly to the West what Japan and Japanese people were, which is due, in part, to their awareness of the apathy on the part of many contemporary Europeans and Americans. Okakura Tenshin and Uchimura Kanzō were expressive enough to win a limited audience among European and American intellectuals, but both were, in many ways, exceptions. On the whole, few Westerners were interested in reading about Japan or lending an ear to intellectual voices from Japan.

In any event, it is clear that Sōseki—the first and foremost representative of modern Japanese literature—made no attempt to communicate his thoughts to the outside world, or more specifically, to talk to Europeans and Americans about "Japan, the Dubious, and Himself." It is this same attitude of non-communication that is replicated in the lecture that Japan's first winner of the Nobel Prize for Literature gave in that commemorative speech he titled "Japan, the Beautiful, and Myself."

Now, I would like to talk about two of my own contemporary writers of the first order, Mishima Yukio and Abe Kōbō. Like Sōseki and Kumagusu, they were of the same age, in fact, born only a year apart from each other. The question I have regarding Mishima and Abe is: Did either of these two writers try to communicate seriously with the outside world on the theme "Japan, the Dubious, and Myself"?

Mishima had always placed great importance on European and American readers. He was very sensitive to their reaction and ardently wished to receive favorable responses from them. Moreover, he was confident that he would be well received if only his translators were good. But Mishima committed suicide, calling out to Japan's dubious Self Defense Forces to rise up in a coup d'état. Incidentally, dubious as their very existence is considering Japan's Constitution, which clearly renounces war and forbids the maintenance of armed forces, the Self Defense Forces are now in Cambodia under the pretext of engaging in peacekeeping operations there. It is the first time since World War II that a Japanese armed force is being deployed in a territory beyond Japan's borders. This is food for serious thought. But let us return to Mishima. Mishima killed himself, knowing fully well that his call for a coup would be a futile one. Indeed, he had thoroughly rehearsed his self-destruction. Intricate though his dying performance was, one thing is clear: his self-expression, too, was close-circuited. It was closed not only to the soldiers of the Self Defense Forces but to the Japanese people at large. And clear still, it was tightly shut off to the outside world. Mishima, who was so very conscious of Europeans and Americans who read his novels and his plays, in plotting his own histrionic death, had his back turned to such audiences; his back was especially turned away from other Asians. Sequestered within this grotesquely lonesome closed circuit, Mishima called out for a coup d'état that he knew would never be, and then underscored his appeal by committing *harakiri*.

Like Mishima, the late Abe Kōbō is a writer whose novels and plays are widely read in the United States and in Western Europe. He also has a considerable readership in the former Soviet Union, and in Eastern Europe. That Abe was very much conscious of his foreign audience is clear from the fact that he headed his own troupe of actors to stage one of his plays in Europe and in the United States.

Still, I doubt that he ever intended to communicate to Europeans and Americans what exactly he saw in Japan, and what he considered the realities of the people of Japan. His superb novel *The Woman in the Dunes* and his equally outstanding play *Friends* may well be excellent material for anyone doing research on Japan and its people. Yet I am inclined to think that Abe's basic approach toward writing was to portray not the people of present-day Japan, but human beings in their most universal condition—the Universal Man, so to speak. In one of his earlier novels, Abe wrote:

> You know that poem about a book that goes soaring through pitch-black space? I feel that you and I now are that very book. That poem was a prophesy. We're all books. And each of us is a star that confronts Earth. Look. If you do as I say, our plan will soon see results.

As we see in these lines, Abe's circuit was one that connected himself freely with the universe. I doubt, however, that Abe ever meant his circuit to serve as an intermediary between Japan and the peoples of Europe and America.

Throughout its entire spectrum, Japanese literature—from Sōseki to Mishima and Abe, that is, from modern to contemporary Japanese literature—has been greatly influenced by Europe and the United States. Yet no Japanese writer has, as yet, attempted to communicate Japan and its people, face to face, as it were, with the West. There are English and French translations of good novels and short stories by modern and contemporary Japanese writers. But these have been more like discoveries—made by a handful of Europeans and Americans—of writers found cloistered in a closet, running around a closed circuit with the same starting point and terminus: namely Japan! What's more, the manner in which these modern writers have been discovered is no different from the way Murasaki Shikibu and Bashō were discovered. All were unearthed under the dim light that reached Japan from European and American shores.

Some critics may argue that the introduction and acceptance of literature is most wholesome when it is discovered precisely in this fashion. But is that argument valid in light of today's international relations? After all, we're talking about literature—Japanese literature. And isn't Japanese literature the self-expression of the Japanese mind? Don't the Japanese people need to be responsible for expressing themselves? I strongly believe that they do. Primarily because there is too big a gap between our economic power and our self-expression. The gravity of Japan's economic presence in Europe and the United States far outweighs the words that Japanese people utter to those regions of the world. In Sōseki's time, Japanese people said almost nothing to the rest of the world. Granted, in those days, Japan's economy was, as Sōseki makes his protagonist in one of his novels lament, patheticially decrepit. But look how vocal the Japanese economy has become today! Right here in New York, for example! Who cannot hear it? But what about the people of Japan? The people who are making all this economic noise? Do you see them? And how? As fellow human entities? Or do they disappear before your eyes like the Invisible Man? Japanese poeple appear before you swarming into New York and elsewhere, but do they say anything? Indeed, their passports should read: "Japan, the Dubious, and Us." Worse yet, are not some Japanese beginning to impart grotesque impressions that make even the farcical Japanese in *Breakfast at Tiffany's* look rather decent? My heart would embrace a modicum of optimism if the image you have of a typical Japanese person were that of Truman Capote's character.

Confronted with a concrete, truer-than-life crisis such as this, I believe it is mandatory for Japanese to re-create the nature of the literature that we have been producing ever since our nation's modernization. Japanese literature must, with firm resolve, determine to communicate with the peoples of Europe and the United States; no, not just with Europe and the United States, but with the other peoples of Asia as well. Japanese writers need to tell the world what Japan is, who we really are. And once we make that resolve, we arrive at the stunning realization that we have more than a mouthful to say to the world, more than a mouthful that should not remain unsaid.

We should let the world know, for example, that no Japanese today can honestly rest complacent with such notions as "Japan, the Beautiful, and Myself." Moreover, we should admit that we are no longer in a position whereby we can turn our backs on the outside world, and sit twiddling our thumbs in the comfort of our stuffy closets. Like it or not, we can no longer remain self-isolated in that cozy place over which we like to believe we have a monopoly. Such being the situation, we must, with backbreaking resolve, determine to create a literature that is truly open to the world, a literature that earlier writers have proven unable to create. We must turn Japanese literature into a worldly medium that sizzles and overflows with diversity.

So far, almost all non-Japanese authors writing in Japanese have been Koreans born and raised in Japan. Recently, though, a young American writer has joined the ranks. I would like to think that the day is not far off when we will see writers emerge from among the ranks of the hundreds of thousands of foreign laborers in Japan. I expect that this new Japanese literature will reveal the very bowels of Japanese society. The indictments by the peoples of Asia with regard to Japan's war atrocities and damages are, from this writer's viewpoint, an encouragement, a springboard, for Japan to boldly cast off its old coat, and to evacuate its closets for a breath of fresh alpine air. As for their charges, the government should accept such indictments humbly as an opportunity for them, as human beings, to reflect on recent history and moral accountability.

Poor as my English is, I have come to this magnificent New York Public Library driven by an irrepressible urge to communicate with you. I would be most happy if, somewhere along the line, as this Oriental Division lecture series continues, you would remember me as a writer who has painfully wished to cast off his old coat—the old coat with the words "Japan, the Dubious, and Myself" embroidered on it. Yes, I would feel my efforts rewarded if you would remember me that way. You have been a most tolerant audience. Thank you.

Contributors

MASAO ABE, Professor Emeritus at Nara University, has taught at numerous American universities, including Princeton University, University of Chicago, Columbia University, and the University of Hawaii. Since the death of D. T. Suzuki, he has been the leading representative of Japanese Buddhism in the West. His publications include *Zen and Western Thought* (1985), *A Zen Life: D. T. Suzuki Remembered* (1987), *Kitaro Nishida: An Inquiry into the Good* (joint translation, 1990), and *A Study of Dōgen* (SUNY Press, 1992).

BERNARD FAURE is a French scholar who specializes in Chan/Zen Buddhism. He has taught Asian Religions at Cornell University and is currently Professor in the Department of Religious Studies at Stanford University. His recent publications include *The Rhetoric of Immediacy* (1991) and *Chan Insights and Oversights* (1993).

CHARLES WEI-HSUN FU is Professor of Buddhism and East Asian Thought in the Department of Religion of Temple University. He is the editor of several book series, including Resources in Asian Philosophy and Religion and the Asian Thought and Culture Series in addition to several series in Chinese. He has authored numerous books and articles on Eastern and Western thought, and has lectured extensively throughout Asia.

STEVEN HEINE, Associate Professor of Religious Studies at Penn State University, specializes in Japanese Buddhist thought in comparative philosophical perspectives. His publications include *Existential and Ontological Dimensions of Time in Heidegger and Dōgen* (SUNY Press, 1985), *A Blade of Grass* (1989), *A Dream Within a Dream* (1991), and *Dōgen and the Kōan Tradition* (SUNY Press, 1994).

S. YUMIKO HULVEY, Assistant Professor of Japanese Language and Literature at the University of Florida, specializes in premodern Japanese literature written by women and has translated several works by Enchi Fumiko. She has published in *Monumenta Nipponica* and contributed to *Japanese Women Writers: A Bio-Critical Source Book* (forthcoming) and *Dictionary of Literary Biography: Medieval Japanese Writers* (forthcoming).

JOHN C. MARALDO is Professor of Philosophy at the University of North Florida and was guest professor of Kyoto University in 1987–8 and guest scholar in 1984–5. A specialist in Japanese philosophy and the hermeneutics of Buddhist studies, he is the author of *Der hermeneutische Zirkel: Untersuchungen zu Schleiermacher Dilthey und Heidegger* (1974, reprinted 1984), co-author of *The Piety of Thinking* (1976), and co-editor of *Buddhism in the Modern World* (1976). He has published articles in *Philosophy East and West, Eastern Buddhist,* and other leading journals.

STEVE ODIN, Associate Professor of Philosophy at the University of Hawaii at Manoa, specializes in Japanese and comparative philosophy. The recent recipient of a Japan Foundation grant and a Fulbright grant, he is the author of *Process Metaphysics and Hua-yen Buddhism* (SUNY Press, 1982) in addition to numerous articles in journals including *Philosophy East and West, Journal of Chinese Philosophy, The Eastern Buddhist,* and *Buddhist-Christian Studies.*

KENZABURŌ ŌE, winner of the Nobel Prize for literature in 1994, is a postwar Japanese novelist and critic who has lectured extensively in the West. His works translated into English and other languages include *A Personal Matter, The Silent Cry* and *Hiroshima Years,* and additional novels are currently in the process of being translated. He recently completed the third part of a trilogy.

RICHARD B. PILGRIM is an Associate Professor in the Department of Religion at Syracuse University. He is the author of *Buddhism and the Arts of Japan* (2nd edition, 1993), and other works related to the intersection of religion and art, or of the religious and the aesthetic, in Japanese culture, including his co-authored book (with Robert Ellwood), *Japanese Religion: A Cultural Perspective.*

HARUO SHIRANE, Professor of Japanese Literature in the Department of East Asian Languages and Cultures, Columbia University, is a specialist in pre-modern Japanese poetry, prose, and literary criticism. He is the author of *The Bridge of Dreams: A Poetics of the Tale of Genji* (1987).

SANDRA A. WAWRYTKO is on the faculty of San Diego State University in the Department of Philosophy and the Asian Studies Program. Editor of *Hsin: Journal of the International Society for Philosophy and Psychotherapy*, her recent publications include *Buddhist Ethics and Modern Society* (1992), *Buddhist Behavioral Codes* (1994), and *Crystal: Spectrums of Chinese Culture through Poetry* (1994).

DALE S. WRIGHT is Professor of Religious Studies and Chair of the Program of Asian Studies at Occidental College in Los Angeles. His publications include essays on Buddhist thought in China and Japan and on hermeneutical issues in the cross-cultural study of religion in such journals as *Philosophy East and West, Journal of the American Academy of Religion,* and *History and Theory.*

Index

Abe Kōbō, 322–23
aimai-na, viii–x, 26, 313–25
Akutagawa Ryūnosuke, 15–16, 131–32, 134
Amaterasu, 62, 112
Amino Yoshihiko, 266
Arima, Tatsuo, 250–51
Aristotle, 230
Asada Akira, x, xiii, 3–4, 45
Ashihara Yoshinobu, 30–32

Barthes, Roland, x, xiii, 9–11, 19, 30–33, 51–52 n.27, 81–82, 90, 169; on Tokyo, 11, 30–32
Bashō, 55
Bellah, Robert, xi–xii, 98–99, 110
Berger, Peter, 98
Bergson, Henri, 255
Blacker, Carmen, 174–75
Bloom, Harold, 88–89
Bodhidharma, 269
Bourdieu, Pierre, 259
Burch, Noel, xiii, 9, 11
bushidō, 152, 239, 261

Campbell, Joseph, 30
Camus, Albert, 147, 151
Capote, Truman, 324
Cassirer, Ernst, 238
Chamberlain, Basil Hall, 177–79, 221 n.6
Chikamatsu, 152
Chi-tsang, 269
Chuang Tzu, 71
Cranny-Francis, Anne, 212–13

Dale, Peter, xiii, 38
Davidson, James, 131

de Man, Paul, 245, 262
dependent co-origination, 299–300, 304–6
Derrida, Jacques, x, 1–3, 5, 8, 12–13, 19, 76, 238, 239, 290
Diamond Sūtra, 255
Dillard, Annie, 76
Dilworth, David, 5, 247, 253, 255, 256, 258
Dōgen, vii, 2, 74–75, 236–37, 240, 252, 254, 259, 265, 269, 291–93, 314–15, 318
Doi Takeo, 33–34
Dore, Ronald, 40
Double Suicide, 123, 151–60
Durkheim, Emile, 255

Ebersole, Gary, 60, 70, 74
Eckhart, Meister, 249, 252, 255, 292
Eiga monogatari (*A Tale of Flowering Fortunes*), 170, 176, 180
Eisenstadt, S. N., 97, 101–2
Eliade, Mircea, 245, 262
Embree, John, 40
Empire of Signs. *See* Barthes
emptiness, 7–9, 263–65, 288–93, 306, 309
Enchi Fumiko, 169ff; and *Masks* (*Onnamen*), 172, 189, 190–95; and "The Old Woman Who Eats Flowers" ("Hana kui uba"), 172, 203–15; and *A Tale of False Oracles* (*Namamiko monogatari*), 175–81, 216; and *Waiting Years* (*Onnazaka*), 172, 182–84, 185, 187, 188; and *Wandering Spirit* (*Yūkon*), 172, 202, 211–12
Epic of Gilgamesh, 208–9